Culture-Centered Music Therapy

Brynjulf Stige

Barcelona PUBLISHERS

The publication of this book has been
financially supported by:

THE RESEARCH COUNCIL OF NORWAY

ISBN 1-891278-14-2

2 4 6 8 9 7 5 3 1

Distributed throughout the world by:
Barcelona Publishers
4 White Brook Road
Gilsum NH 03448
Tel: 603-357-0236 Fax: 603-357-2073
Website: www.barcelonapublishers.com
SAN 298-6299

Cover illustration and design:
© 2002 Frank McShane

Cover photograph: "Earthen Vessels"
© Beth Kingsley Hawkins

To the memory of my mother
KARI STIGE (1925 – 2001)
from whom I first learned how individual histories of suffering
may be linked to larger historical frameworks

he not busy being born
is busy dying.
(Bob Dylan)

others have done the work,
and you are sharing the fruits of their work.
(John 4:38)

BRIEF CONTENTS

DETAILED LIST OF CONTENTS

PREFACE

In this book I explore implications of a culture-centered perspective for music therapy practice, theory, and research.

Toward a culture-centered music therapy is a long way to go. The book is based on more than fifteen years of practice, research, and theoretical reflection. On the paths where I have been walking and in the communities where I have been working I have had the pleasure of meeting many people that have helped and inspired me. I want to thank Mette Kleive and Ingunn Byrkjedal, who were my first colleagues and with whom I did the first explorations of community music therapy in ecological and cultural perspectives. I want to thank Even Ruud and Kenneth Bruscia, who I consider my two main mentors in music therapy. The stimulating differences in their thinking have kindled my own work, and I highly appreciate the helpful feedback both of them have given over the years. I am also grateful to Clive Robbins, who through his lectures in Oslo in 1977 enthused me to study music therapy and who taught me how to wear a suit in New York twenty-two years later. Among many friends and good colleagues I also want to mention Carolyn Kenny, with whom I have the privilege of co-editing *Voices,* an online community and world forum for publication and cross-cultural dialogues in music therapy.

I want to thank Gary Ansdell for reading the second draft of the manuscript for this book and for advising me to write a third. I want to thank my previous and present colleagues at the music therapy education in Sogn og Fjordane University College, Sandane, especially Felicity Baker, Solgunn Knardal, Hanne Oftedal, and Randi Rolvsjord, who read drafts of the book and gave many valuable comments. Leif Edward Ottesen Kennair, evolutionary psychologist and adjunct faculty member, deserves warm thanks, for challenging my ideas in such an eloquent way. Also I want to thank all the students I have worked with over the years, and not least all the clients that generously have shared dreams and hopes through engaged acts of musicking. Thanks too to The Research Council of Norway, for financial support, and to the anonymous referee the research council used, who gave the most thorough and stimulating feedback. A special thanks goes to Barcelona Publishers and Kenneth Bruscia. In days as ours, when the latest developments of computer equipment make technologies of preparing and printing texts available at every second street corner, some ask why authors need publishing companies anymore. One possible answer is that they need the guidance and constructive confrontations that publishers can give. My experiences with Barcelona Publishers strongly support the relevance of this answer.

The chapters in this book are original, but the ideas communicated have been developed through several years of clinical practice, research, teaching, and writing. Earlier versions of sections of some of the chapters have been presented as papers at congresses or printed in proceedings or journals: Chapter 2 is partly a condensation, integration, and development of arguments presented in two previously published articles: "Perspectives on Meaning in Music Therapy," published in *British Journal of Music Therapy,* Vol. 12(1), 1998, and "Aesthetic Practices in Music Therapy," published in *Nordic Journal of Music Therapy,* 7(2), 1998. Chapter 4 is developed from my paper at the 7th World Congress of Music Therapy in Vittoria-Gasteiz, 1993. Chapter 5 is developed from my paper at the 8th World Congress of Music Therapy in Hamburg, 1996, and Chapter 6 is developed from my paper at the 9th World Congress of Music Therapy in Washington, 1999. Thanks to editors and publishers for permission to use the material.

Realities of my writing conditions have led me to do much of the writing of this book in other surroundings than my office in the university college in Western Norway where I work. Early mornings and late evenings of travels and visits to other countries and contexts have shaped many of the pages to follow. As author, this means that some of the pages have the flavor of the beautiful colors of Massachusetts autumn, others the rough edge of Northern Norway winter, still others the sweet taste of Italian spring. Coincidence made wet and windy Fiji in June the location of most of the final writing of the text. This gives me an opportunity to comment upon the concept of culture that will be developed in this book. I will not concentrate on culture only as a surrounding factor shaping music therapy practice. That might at times be important, but my main intention with this book is to explore how culture is integrated in biological, psychological, and social processes, and therefore how the individual and collective levels of human existence constitute each other. A culture-centered music therapy should therefore not exclude species-centered, client-centered, or music-centered perspectives.

While one may think that culture-centered music therapy should be especially relevant in multicultural contexts, or when working with members of certain subcultures, the main clinical examples in this book are developed in a culturally and socially homogenous community setting. The challenge of a culture-centered perspective is the paradox of taking local knowledge seriously in a global perspective. There is some sense in the paradoxical statement that humans are cultural by nature.

Brynjulf Stige
Sandane, July 2002

FOREWORD

The history of ideas in music therapy has been amazingly rich, despite its brevity. Like psychology, our work has evolved through various "forces" of thought, but in slightly different order. Our first force contributed discoveries about how music influences human behavior and the physical world. Our second force unearthed unconscious dimensions of music experience, and explored their implications for therapy. Our third and fourth forces explicated the role of music in self-actualization and spiritual development respectively.

This book heralds the coming of the fifth force in music therapy – culture-centeredness. This will be the force that reminds us that all of our work, whether it be theory, practice, or research, takes place within very specific and unique contexts – contexts that not only shape the work itself, but also predispose us to attach our own idiographic meanings to it. This will be the force that debunks many of our uncontextualized generalizations about the nature of music, therapy, and music therapy itself. This will be the force that reminds us that all interactions, musical and nonmusical, clinical and nonclinical, are situated within many larger, frequently overlooked frames of perception and communication. To be culture-centered is to be variously aware that there are frames of history, frames of environment, frames of ethnicity, frames of language, frames of belief and value, and the never-ending, shifting frames that evolve between individuals through moment-to-moment interaction.

Through concepts like "reflexivity" (identifying one's own frame of reference in relation to another), and "local versus general knowledge" (recognizing that one's understandings are delimited by the contexts and cultures in which they were derived), culture-centered thinking places considerable responsibility on the music therapist. Whether operating within the domains of practice, research, or theory – music therapists must continually act with a deep awareness of how culture and context "situate" each party in every interaction and the meaning that is created therein. We must do this not only by "locating" ourselves and those with whom we interact, but also by considering how our individual and collective histories particularize our frames of reference. To understand our ongoing interactions, we must disentangle and reweave our respective pasts and presents, for history and culture are the backdrops in which every story unfolds.

Once these admonitions of cultural awareness are embraced, it becomes obvious that all of our individual and collective ideas of and about music therapy have to be re-contextualized and situated, both culturally and historically. This means that each music therapist has to examine his or her own cultural embeddedness; in addition, the entire profession has to examine the cultural embeddedness of its various constituencies. All "forces" of thought that have arisen in the history of music therapy, whether consisting of individuals or groups, have to locate themselves within their respective cultural and contextual frames within the profession. And this goes for culture-centered thinkers as well! They too must be reflexive of their own cultural and contextual frames, as individuals, and soon as a viable group within the music therapy community. What will culture-centered thinkers learn from reflecting upon their own contextual and cultural frames (and limits thereof), and locating themselves within the history of ideas in music therapy? What does each preceding force of thought in music therapy learn from culture-centered thinkers, and what can culture-centered thinkers learn from each of its predecessors?

One of the lessons we are learning as a profession is that one new idea does not necessarily replace or surpass previous ideas; rather, each new idea enters into an already existing culture of ideas, where all ideas begin to interact. Thus, when a new idea is introduced, the entire culture is fertilized: existing ideas are influenced by the new idea, and the new idea is influenced by its integration into the existing culture. Thus, culture-centered thinking does not replace or surpass the behavioral, psychodynamic, humanistic, or transpersonal forces of thought; rather, it catalyzes them to be more culture-sensitive; in return, the established forces challenge culture-centered thinkers to somehow integrate existing values into their thinking. The developmental process is more holistic than linear, so that there is a place for every idea of continuing relevance.

For the profession to integrate the fifth force into its collective consciousness, all kinds of ideational negotiations will have to take place. Behaviorists will have to become more reflexive of their "received" view and the limits of their generalizations about the world of objects. In return, culture-centered thinkers will have to acknowledge that there are many real-world, cultural contexts in which objectivity and accountability are highly valued; they will also have to admit that there are many contexts in which behavioral or physical change trumps meaning, no matter how sensitively the meaning was derived.

The psychodynamic school will have to admit that their interpretations are one-sided and context-bound rather than universally true or even interpersonally valid; and like the behaviorists, they will also have to recognize that their way of thinking about clients leads to "othering." In return, culture-centered thinkers will have to take into account levels of consciousness, and how they influence cultural self-awareness. They will have to admit that, when the effects of the unconscious are considered, reflexivity is not as easy or as possible as they propose. One might even ask culture-centered thinkers whether their notions about the possibility of being reflexive are any less delusional than claims of objectivity by the behaviorists, or confessions of countertransference by the psychodynamic therapist. Perhaps, the goal of each force is not so different – we all have to find a way of utilizing and managing our subjectivity.

Humanists will have to look at their empathy, unconditional positive regard, and nondirectiveness, and ask whether such therapist attitudes are relevant in every context; they will also have to admit that these attitudes, like their psychodynamic counterparts, were pre-determined theoretically to be essential conditions for effective therapy. They are stances to be taken with all clients, irrespective of individual differences in need and culture, and regardless of moment-to-moment changes in situational context. Also, by their very nature, empathy, positive regard, and nondirectiveness leave the client alone in his or her quest for meaning; the therapist refrains from participation in the client's meaning-making process. Thus the meanings derived by the client in humanistic therapy are decidedly more individually constructed (client-centered) than interpersonally co-constructed (by client and therapist). Culture-centered thinkers will have to respond to the humanists by recognizing that client-centered change is as important as community-centered change, and that self-actualization is a pre-requisite to social change. They will also have to extricate the individual (and free will) from the ongoing influences of endless webs of context. Seeing the individual as embedded in culture can be just as deterministic as seeing the individual as determined by bodily functions, reinforcement schedules, or unconscious forces; only the agent of determination is different. How will culture-centered thinkers negotiate the balance between free will, cultural embeddedness, and social responsibility?

Transpersonalists will have to see that their very notions of spirituality are culture-bound; conceptions of consciousness, divinity, energy, and ultimate power differ not only from one individual to another, but also one community and culture to the next. Sometimes these conceptions are individually constructed, and sometimes they are co-constructed by like souls. Culture-centered thinkers have to somehow deal with the reality that most, if not all cultures recognize or construct a spirit as part of their belief system. Thus, no theory of culture-centeredness is complete if it has no place for spirituality.

The emergence of the fifth force at this time in history is a good indication that we are ready to integrate sensitivity to culture and context into our collective consciousness of music therapy. The challenge of doing so is to find ways of assimilating this new idea into existing structures, while also modifying existing structures to accommodate the new idea. No one force or school of thinking can remain viable if it has not been enriched by the other forces of thought operating within the community of ideas. And it is important to acknowledge, that even when so enriched, no one force can ever dominate our consciousness to the exclusion of another. There will be instances and contexts when culture-centeredness is the most appropriate frame of reference, and other instances and contexts when another frame must prevail.

Children play a simple game that teaches us all about the impossibility of ever imposing the same solution on every problem. Two children play at a time, and on the count of three, each child simultaneously makes a hand sign for either rock, paper, or scissor. To determine the winner of each round, children follow these rules: rock crushes scissor, scissor cuts paper, and paper covers rock. Thus, by nature, each object has its area of advantage and its area of disadvantage. To use only one, then, is to insure one's own defeat.

In music therapy, our developmental task is similar: to discover the specific areas of advantage and disadvantage of each force of thought, and to develop the flexibility needed to apply all of them when appropriate. This book issues the challenge. Can we open ourselves to accepting new ideas and using them to their best advantage?

Kenneth E. Bruscia
Professor of Music Therapy
Temple University

Culture-Centered Music Therapy

INTRODUCTION

we make culture and we are made by culture; there is agency
and there is structure. It is not enough to celebrate agency; nor
is it enough to detail the structure(s) of power, we must always
keep in mind the dialectical play between resistance
and incorporation.
(John Storey)

Lately there has been an increasing awareness about the relevance of culture for the understanding of music therapy. What exactly is this relevance, and how do we even understand culture? Such questions – related to music therapy practice, theory, and research – will be explored throughout the book, while the introduction will outline a context for this exploration.

HOW DEEP IS CULTURE?

It may be quite boring to talk about culture. If you sit with friends, and if you don't think twice, conversations about culture rapidly end up stereotyping instead of illuminating. Norwegians are shy and reserved, silent and non-communicative (no wonder, living among dark remote mountains as they are). Americans are different; they know how to smile and communicate (unfortunately, though, they are bragging and showing off all the time). Most of us hopefully get beyond phrases like these. To get beyond the basic assumptions about culture underlying and nurturing such stereotypes and prejudices may be more difficult. We tend to think of culture as fixed entities defined by ethnic or geographical borders: Maasai culture, Hispanic culture, Asian culture, etc. The alternative that will be explored in this book is to think of culture as something more flexible and elusive, not as an entity but as continuously developing ways of life and practices of meaning-making, ranging from the individual to the regional to the global level of social organization, and with communication, change, and interchange as basic prerequisites and characteristics.

Defined as a fixed entity, culture is a boring topic. The subtleties and complexities of individual life histories are much more interesting and appealing. This has led many music therapists to state that they go beyond culture, that they go deeper than culture. My argument is that to do so is hardly possible. Is culture an epiphenomenon or an integrated part of our biological, personal, and social life? Is culture a background variable, or a web integrating different qualities of human life? This book will be based on clinical examples, research, and theoretical arguments that suggest that we need to take the path proposed by the second part of these questions. Music therapy cannot be developed as a culture-free discipline. Contemporary urban multiculturalism and the renewed postcolonial awareness are important reminders of that. These are extremely important issues to deal with, but it would be limiting to stay with these issues only. Culture is not only about belonging to different groups, it is also about being different as individuals. Culture-centered music therapy is therefore about tolerance for diversity in the broadest meaning of the word.

We therefore need to go beyond "culturalism," the assumption that culture is an important factor. This assumption – as relevant as it sounds – usually is based upon the idea of culture as a coat that we may take off. I suggest that culture is deeper than that; it is ways of relating to the world, consciously and unconsciously, with and through others. This book is therefore more about humanity than ethnicity, important as ethnicity is. Without culture there would be an extremely limited social life and communication. There would be no art, no language, no music; in other words, no humanity as we usually think of this term. At the same time we must acknowledge that culture is not always something to celebrate. In many instances it is quite relevant to talk of the inhibiting effects of tradition, other times we even encounter cultural traditions that we judge to be oppressive. This could stimulate us to engage in inquiry and critique. It hardly makes it possible to go beyond culture, only – at best – to promote cultural change.

DIALOGIC AND ENACTIVE FACETS

One Monday afternoon in the early 1980s I had an experience that has guided much of my thinking as a music therapist, and that gradually led to the writing of this book. As a young and inexperienced music therapist I was about to lead the first session of music therapy with a group of adult clients with Down's syndrome. Together with my colleague Ingunn Byrkjedal I was welcoming the group members as they entered the music room. In many ways this room looked like any music therapy room at any institution, except that it belonged to the Community Music School and was located in the secondary school of the town where we were working. This difference turned out to make a difference. The same room was being used by the local brass band, of which there were several pictures on one of the walls. As the group members entered the room they did not head for the chairs that we had put out for them. Instead they went right over to that wall in order to be able to study the pictures more closely. A great enthusiasm spread among the group members: "The brass band!" "Look at that; the big drum, the blue uniforms!" When we finally gathered around the semicircle of chairs that we had arranged, Knut, one of the group members, asked: "May we too play in the brass band?"

The rest of this story is told in Chapter 4, and I will not divulge too much of it here. Instead, I want to dwell on how Knut's short and simple question got me thinking. It challenged so much of what I had learned as a music therapy student. I think it is fair to say that the culture of music therapy that I belonged to did not favor taking such a question very seriously. I had been told that music therapy was about creative improvisation or about the use of music carefully composed or arranged to meet the specific needs of each client. It was not about leaving the music therapy room to play with a local brass band! Still, my colleague and I felt that Knut's question was important, and that it called for a serious rethinking of our approach. One of the health threats experienced by the group members was isolation in the local community, and when these people demonstrated such a vivid interest for participation in their local culture, how could that not be significant?

By talking about culture in relation to local community *and* a brass band, I have – in one sentence – used the term in two different ways, and I am already saying something about the concept of culture; it is multifaceted and used in several ways. It is about community and custom, it is about art and meaning. It is at this stage legitimate to use several metaphors and descriptors in an attempt to approach the question of defining the term. The illumination and discussion of this will be the main topic of Chapter 1. Here it suffices to say that the *local* aspect challenges some traditional notions that tend to connect culture mainly to nations or ethnic groups. Consider for instance this statement made by one of the pioneers of music therapy:

> Now I have met one or two music therapists who have strongly the idea that children should only be given the folk music – or music similar to the folk music – of the country in which they were born ... I think this is so terribly narrow, that you give a child born in Russia only Russian folk music – or that kind of music – as therapy (Paul Nordoff, in Robbins & Robbins, 1998, p. 136).

It is not difficult to subscribe to the suggestion that it could be limiting to use only Russian music with a Russian child. As a music therapist in Norway I have more than once worked with clients who can relate to almost any kind of music except Norwegian folk music. Nordoff's argument is based on some premises I do not share however. I do not think culture follows race or national borders or that it functions as discrete entities. Culture develops as ways of life shared by groups (small or large), and is thus in constant change *and* exchange. Culture is interactive and historical, and cultural elements and artifacts – such as musics – are (partly subconsciously) internalized, identified with, or rejected by the individual. Thinking about music as private expressions or as a universal "language" constituted of archetypes going deeper than culture would not sensitize a music therapist to the significance of Knut's question. (This is not to say that there are not personal aspects of and biological foundations to human music making.)

I suggest then that we take a different perspective to culture than what I find implied in Nordoff's statement. This is not to say that one cannot learn from his clinical work! In fact I consider it to be one of the more important exemplars in the history of modern music therapy, and an improvisational approach inspired by Nordoff and Robbins's (1977) model, Creative Music Therapy, turned out to be vital in trying to give Knut a decent answer to his question. He wanted to play in the local brass band but was hardly able to hold a basic beat. Given the values of the local brass band he would have been rejected if we immediately had left the music therapy room heading for an appointment with the conductor of this band. Instead, more than two years of dialogical improvisations in music therapy sessions combined with active engagement in the public life of the town in order to stimulate more inclusive values and practices of music making preceded Knut's first meeting with the brass band.

This vignette and the brief detour to Nordoff's statement could illustrate several points. First, this text stands in a close relation to existing traditions of music therapy. While I at times find it necessary to voice alternative views and criticize theoretical statements made by other music therapists, I acknowledge the value of their work and the fact that I often stand on their shoulders. Second, I value the interplay between clinical experiences and theoretical reflections. Supported by research and philosophical critique I consider this interplay a major impetus for the development of the discipline. Third, a culture-centered perspective should not be totalized. I am not advocating culture as an answer to all questions, with a concurrent neglect of, say, biological processes. I consider human personal life to be interplay of biological, psychological, social, and cultural processes, and it is especially important for me to overcome the dichotomies sometimes constructed between biological and cultural perspectives. The basic ABC of this text could therefore be said to be "Acknowledgement of Biology and Culture." There is a DEF too. If we want to go beyond a conception of culture as static entities we need to take the "Dialogic and Enactive Facets" of culture seriously. Cultural determinism, the individual as a product of his culture, is not a necessary corollary to a culture-centered perspective; rather one could study how individual identities are negotiated in social and cultural contexts.

If the book is read, understood, and appreciated – none of which an author can take for granted – what I hope to achieve is therefore *not* that some music therapists start labeling their work as CCMT. The ambition is both less and more than that. It is less, as the text is not formed as a description of procedures and techniques that would warrant the idea of proposing a new model of music therapy. It is more, as what I hope to achieve is to contribute with one voice in a development that will make all music therapists more culture-centered in their work and thinking, not by labeling their work as such but by integrating cultural perspectives in their thinking.

Knut's question therefore may be converted to a more general one, addressed to all music therapists: What is the relationship between the music therapy session and the context it belongs to?

CULTURE-CENTERED VERSUS ECOLOGICAL MUSIC THERAPY

Throughout the 1990s there has been a growing awareness about and acceptance of ecological perspectives in music therapy, as illuminated by Bruscia's (1998a) inclusion of *Ecological Music Therapy* in the second edition of *Defining Music Therapy*. A question then arises, what are the relations between culture-centered music therapy and ecological music therapy? A preliminary answer is that while ecological music therapy may be defined as an area of music therapy *practice* (Bruscia, 1998a), culture-centered music therapy – as presented in this book – is a *theoretical perspective* on music therapy. This perspective may work as a basis for community work and ecological interventions, but is not restricted to that. It is also relevant for individual music therapy in more traditional formats and contexts. The proposals given in this book are therefore addressed to all music therapists, not just to those who see themselves in ecological practices. The goal I have in writing this book is not as much to promote specific new forms of practice as to develop fresh ways of understanding both new and established practices of music therapy.

My own process of learning may illuminate how culture-centered perspectives are relevant for ecological practices, but not limited to that. As illuminated through the vignette about Knut's question, the first germs of this book stem from my experiences of community music therapy in Sandane, Western Norway. That work culminated in a book about community music therapy as cultural engagement (Kleive & Stige, 1988). One of the main references in that book was a publication I had encountered fifteen years earlier. It was a book about culture, variation, and continuity (Klausen, 1970) that I had been looking through as a teenager, when my family lived in Eastern Africa for a couple of years. My father worked there as a teacher, and he had bought the book in order to prepare himself for the cultural diversity we would meet. Tanzania, where we lived, was a country of enormous cultural variation, with 120 tribes and local languages combined with strong Arabian, Indian, and European influences. So, I felt there were reasons to take Klausen's book down from the shelf now and then. Ten years later, as a young music therapist, I discovered that the same book also was helpful for my understanding of community music therapy in a culturally very homogenous region of Western Norway. The two places in which I read Klausen's book could not have been more different, and I was driven to search for answers about how the cultural specificity of human life articulates something universal about humanity.

In searching for new understanding I have learned much from cultural psychology, with Russian pioneers such as Lev Vygotsky and contemporary American advocates such as Jerome Bruner and Michael Cole. My search has also included readings from several other disciplines, such as philosophy, sociology, anthropology, and new musicology. The ideas that I will discuss may grow complex in theoretical context, but they are all based upon rather basic clinical experiences. Knut's question has already been mentioned. Later clinical experiences stimulated me to elaborate further the ecological perspectives on music therapy, such as when I in the early 1990s worked with children and observed how their skills and ways of being changed from context situation to situation. When I more recently worked as a music therapist in a psychiatric clinic, I was struck by the strength of my clients' relationship to music as a cultural and social phenomenon. These clinical experiences have challenged me to study culture and practices of meaning-making in context.

Modern music therapy is still in a state of becoming. I am sure there are several areas and subareas of practice not yet developed and also important theoretical concepts that need to be coined and enlarged upon. I hope that the culture-centered perspectives advocated in this book may fuel such a process, while the perspectives themselves should be objects for revision and critique. They are to be considered as steps and drafts toward a culture-centered music therapy, not final conclusions. To name them steps and drafts does of course not mean that there was nothing before them. Although I assert that social, cultural, and ecological perspectives do not have the place they deserve in music therapy discourse, several important inputs on their relevance have been made, by Trygve Aasgaard, David Aldridge, Gary Ansdell, Ruth Bright, Julie Brown, Leslie Bunt, Mariagnese Cattaneo, Karen

Estrella, Lucy Forrest, Isabelle Frohne-Hagemann, Carolyn Kenny, Joseph Moreno, Mercédès Pavlicevic, Michael Rohrbacher, Even Ruud, Christoph Schwabe, Chava Sekeles, Manal Troppozada, and others. While I with this book in no way attempt to give a comprehensive presentation of these authors' contributions, and while I may agree or disagree with their perspectives, I want to acknowledge here the value of their work.[1]

METHOD OF WRITING

With this text I hope to contribute to theory development in music therapy, including metatheoretical aspects. Metatheory sometimes designates theory about theory (or about theorizing). This is often understood in a hierarchic way; metatheory is "higher" (more philosophical or more abstract) than theory. I take a more horizontal approach and use the term metatheory to denote any theory that is helpful in critically reviewing the viability and validity of the theoretical proposals that are emerging. What is considered theory in one context could then be metatheory in another. For instance, cultural psychology, when used in a music therapy context, could have a metatheoretical function, by generating new ideas and by guiding the interpretations made in, say, a cultural perspective.

Taking the interplay of metatheory, research, theory, and practice into consideration, my aim when writing this text has been to develop theoretical statements of clinical relevance, but not always as specific guidelines for clinical practice. Often my aim has been to do groundwork for further theoretical development of the discipline of music therapy. This is reflected in the ways I have been going about producing the theoretical proposals made in this book. These proposals are based upon *explication* of clinical experience, *interpretation* of qualitative empirical data from my own clinical work, as well as *assimilation* and *evaluation* of relevant concepts developed in neighboring disciplines. They have then been modified and refined through argumentative *critique*.

The aim stated here, and the premises outlined, demand some brief comments on my method of writing. My approach is based in the humanities, but not in a "freewheeling" version. I think that there are issues of mutual interest for science and the humanities, and that there are reasons for being both optimistic and skeptical about the increasing interest for convergence of science and the humanities. If the envisioned result of this process is a merging of perspectives we might be disappointed. If we work for possibilities of dialogue, for the crossing of cultures, I think there is much more to hope for. A dialogic enterprise can acknowledge differences as well as the need for sharing codes to make communication possible. Polyphony and dialogue is thus, in my view, promising metaphors for the process of developing theory. In order to have a dialogue there must be differences, not only in answers but also in questions. To think that we could have the questions traditionally asked by the humanities "finally answered" by the more reliable methods of natural science is therefore futile. Similarly I will suggest that it may be a mistake to ask questions within the humanities without paying attention to the knowledge developed in the natural sciences.

To follow up such suggestions means to include multidisciplinary as well as philosophical discussions in the arguments. I have tried to do so, which probably made the text more difficult to write and to read. A natural question then is: Why not choose a more easy way out and concentrate on the literature of music therapy only? I want to answer through use of one of the stories told in Norse mythology about Thor, the son of Odin: Thor was the god of thunder and the defender of the superior gods living in Åsgard. We remember Thor weekly since he gave name to the day Thursday, but the story to remember here is his journey to the court of Útgardaloki, in the area inhabited by giants and trolls. Here Thor was put to a series of tests. In one of them he was to prove his drinking prowess. He was given a horn "not all that big, but rather long," as Snorre Sturlason – the Icelandic author that in the thirteenth century wrote down much of Norse mythology and history – put it. Thor was then told that it was considered well drunk from this horn if it was drained in a single draught. Some would drain it in two, while no one was so poor a drinker that he could not manage to drain it in three. Thor – after three hefty pulls – only made a moderate impact on the level of liquid in the horn. He was of course utterly humiliated. Only the day after was he told that his performance in fact had shocked the giants. The horn had been connected to the ocean, which had ebbed visibly during his drinking. From that time the tides did commemorate his feat (Orchard, 1997).

We can hardly aspire for comparable drinking capacities. To think that we can even try to drain the ocean of human knowledge is of course hubris. There is an almost infinite pool of topics, questions, and theories "out there." On the other hand; to imagine that our horn is not connected to the ocean is naïveté. It is not possible to isolate discussions in the discipline of music therapy from discussions within other disciplines and within science and philosophy. Sometimes we may think we can, but basically, I propose, that is a false impression. I can illustrate this by using another analogue, taken this time from my own geographical context: The town of Sandane, where I live, is located at the end of an arm of a fjord. Surrounding this fjord-arm are mountains in all directions, so, if you did not know, you would think it was a lake. Usually the fjord is quite calm and the waters are just nice and easy. You could launch your tiny rowboat, find pleasure in the harmony, and enjoy the mountains reflected by the calm water. It is a rather contained experience. But there are reminders; changing tides show that the fjord is part of a larger ocean, and there are days with tricky waves reflecting the swells of the sea. You realize that you do not know the fjord before you have seen the ocean.

If music therapy is a discipline, it is not a lake, but a fjord. It is connected to other fjords, other disciplines, and it is connected to an ocean of shared concerns and metatheoretical problems. In sum I therefore think music therapists must work and think in a multi-disciplinary field. In this I agree with for instance E. Thayer Gaston (1968/1995). While Gaston refers to Leonardo da Vinci as a possible role model I am not so sure. I think most of us will have to accept that that would be a rather tall order. Not only was da Vinci a very special man; the times are also very different. Just as little as we can aspire for Thor's drinking capacities can we imagine ourselves in the role of a Renaissance man. Multidisciplinary thinking cannot mean to cover it all, but rather to cross a fjord or two and to invite others to do the same. As individual scholars our capacities are quite limited. As a community of scholars more could be achieved. This book could therefore be seen as an invitation to critique and continuing dialogue, as well as an acknowledgment of the shoulders I have been standing upon in order to try to catch a glimpse of the ocean.

HOW TO READ THIS BOOK

You think differently in different languages, at least to some degree. Writing in a foreign language is a challenge and a special opportunity to reflect upon the possibilities and limitations language brings to our thinking. The main input I want to give on language in this context is not about belonging to different nationalities though, but about belonging to different theoretical traditions. It is common to find the same word used by several traditions, with rather different meanings implied. I know for instance that I in this book will use some words – such as "action," "activity," "learning," and "reflection" – in ways that may be different from how many American music therapists use these words. Even with our best intentions there is no possibility for streamlining language to a point where such things will not happen. Words that belong to our vernacular language have been inscribed in several, rather different, theoretical traditions. Even words that mainly have grown out of scholarly discourse, such as "hermeneutics" and "phenomenology," take on quite different meanings due to the existence of several traditions of use. I therefore invite the reader to beware my clarifications of concepts, and to try to understand them in the theoretical context where they have been developed. In order to support the reading, I have constructed a glossary of some of the major concepts used in the text.

The book consists of four parts – Premises, Practices, Implications, and Investigations – each with three chapters. In *Premises* I outline a definition of culture with relevance for the understanding of humankind, music, meaning-making, and aesthetics. The assumption that a cultural perspective has implication for practice, theory, and research in music therapy then is the foundation for Part II, III, and IV respectively. In *Practices* three culture-centered case examples presented in the context of relevant theory will be examined. In *Implications* I discuss general implications for music therapy theory; first I discuss implications for definitions of music therapy as discipline, profession, and practice, then I discuss a model of the music therapy process in context, before I consider implications for music therapy's relationship to society and other disciplines. In the last part, *Investigations*, ideas about research approaches that may strengthen the development of culture-centered music therapy will be explored.

The structure of the book partly reflects my way of thinking about the discipline, partly the limitations of a written text. It reflects my way of thinking in that the Premises describe some metatheoretical assumptions that inform the discussions of practice, theory, and research in the three parts to follow. Practice, theory, and research sometimes are considered the three main "legs" of a discipline. E. Thayer Gaston (1968), for instance, in his seminal book about music in therapy, suggested that theory, practice, and research form a tripod, each necessary for the two others to stand. This proposal has to a large degree been accepted within the discipline, see for instance Wheeler (1995b, pp. 4-5). While I agree with Gaston and Wheeler in that practice, theory, and research are all necessary and support each other, I insist on the importance of a fourth leg: metatheoretical critique.[2]

I do this not only through a cheap use of the allegory (four legs usually give smoother walking than three, and a discipline needs to be on the move), but because I consider the relationships between practice, theory, and research to be *reciprocal*. I do not think for instance that it is possible or desirable to establish a unidirectional flow of information from research to theory to practice. This would have suggested a prescriptive use of music therapy theory that I consider incompatible with a culture-centered perspective, at least if dialogic and enactive aspects are included. Reciprocal relationships between practice, theory, and research may be fruitful then, but certainly also confusing. There will be aspects of practice that are not covered by theory, or that will be difficult to explore in research, and there may be contradictions between practice and theory, etc. Metatheoretical critique is necessary in order to guide the scholar in dealing with such dissonance. Metatheory and the practice of reflexivity is therefore stressed throughout this book, and the Premises will outline some of the basic assumptions guiding the subsequent discussions of practice, theory, and research.

By underlining the metatheoretical aspect, I also want to make very clear that the theoretical propositions made in the text are based on some general premises concerning culture's rank in conceptions of humankind, music, health, and therapy. These premises, which for the most part are outlined in Part I, could of course be challenged as much as the theoretical and clinical implications could. One of the best tools we have for this is research (quantitative and qualitative) combined with critical reflection. The relationships involved could be illustrated in the following figure:

Figure 1: Reciprocal relationships between practice, metatheory, research, and theory. The figure suggests that research may inform and challenge metatheoretical and theoretical assumptions, which both inform practice.

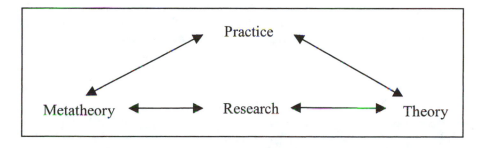

The reciprocal two-way arrows of the figure imply that research methodology, theory, and practice may be given a metatheoretical critique, or that metatheory, practice, and theory may be challenged by research, etc. In the middle of the figure I have placed practice and research, which may illuminate the central role of these domains of the discipline. Some readers may suggest that an arrow is missing in the figure, between research and practice. This objection may be valid. There are probably occasions when research informs practice directly, but generally this happens in interplay with theoretical and metatheoretical assumptions.

Given the argument about *reciprocal* relationships it must be argued that the specific sequence of sections that I have chosen for this book is arbitrary, at least to some degree. This is where the limitations of a written text come in. Reciprocal relationships are not easy to communicate in a one-word-at-a-time system. A hypertext presentation would have helped, giving the reader increased possibilities for choosing several and varying paths in the process of reading. The format of a book gives clear limitations in this respect, although I have tried to use the hypertext possibilities that *do* exist in this technology: a detailed list of contents, notes, a glossary, a rich list of references, and an index of authors. I hope the reader may use these hypertext possibilities actively, and that he or she will feel free to read the chapters of the book in a sequence that suits his or her interest. Some readers will for instance find that they will enjoy the metatheoretical discussions of Part I more after having read the practical cases described in Part II. I have also tried to write in a way that will make it possible for a reader to search out information on specific topics. It should, for instance, be possible to read Chapter 11 on Participatory Action Research with some benefit without reading all the other chapters.

I therefore grant the reader considerable freedom in reading this text, which is altogether a suspiciously unnecessary thing to say, as most readers take whatever freedoms they want without asking the author. At another level therefore, there must be something more I want to say, which I think is: The text is written as a continuous argument, and as such the different chapters link and should be seen in connection to each other. If the book is read as a whole, the depths and relationships of the arguments will be better understood.

NOTES

[1] Recently, several essays, reports, and columns in *Voices: A World Forum for Music Therapy* have focused upon cultural aspects of music therapy, see Kenny and Stige (2002).

[2] Finding a metaphor to cover all functions of metatheory is less than easy. By talking about a "fourth leg" I advocate a view that underlines the interplay of metatheory with research, theory, and practice, and which takes metatheory down from an "unassailable abstractness," or alternatively, challenges the assumption that metatheory is a firm foundation. As Kenneth Bruscia notes in a comment to the manuscript, though, there are aspects that are not so well covered by the leg-metaphor; a metatheory may function as container or space for research, theory, and practice, and as a perspective be a way of viewing rather than thing viewed.

Part I:

PREMISES

Even the experience of the materially and sensually given
world depends upon my being in contact with other men, upon
our common sense which regulates and controls all other senses
and without which each of us would be enclosed in his own
particularity of sense data which in themselves are unreliable
and treacherous.
(Hanna Arendt)

Part I focuses on the premises for the perspective developed in this text. Chapter 1 elaborates upon a notion of humankind in relation to a concept of *culture*, and an argument about the relevance of *cultural psychology* for music therapy is developed. In Chapter 2 the issues of *meaning, narrative,* and *aesthetics* are discussed and related to the notion of culture proposed in the first chapter. Chapter 3 explores the ontology of *music* from the three perspectives of *protomusicality* (music as a shared human capacity), *musics* (music as a plurality of cultural traditions), and *musicking* (music as situated activity).

Chapter 1:

WHY CULTURE?

*The single adequate form for verbally expressing authentic human
life is the open-ended dialogue. Life by its very nature is dialogic.
To live means to participate in dialogue: to ask questions, to
heed, to respond, to agree, and so forth. In this dialogue a
person participates wholly and throughout his whole life:
with his eyes, lips, hands, soul, spirit, with his whole body
and deeds. He invests his entire self in discourse, and this
discourse enters into the dialogic fabric of human life,
into the world symposium.*
(Mikhail M. Bakhtin)

At the dawn of the twenty-first century the human genome has been decoded and implications and medical possibilities are about to be explored. There are prospects for the development of a technology of life and health. In this situation some may think it is an anachronism to speak of humankind and culture. Biology seems to be the future. Thinking it over, we soon realize that it is not even possible to speak of human existence without a notion of culture. This chapter defines and clarifies a concept of culture and its relevance for music therapy. The argument is based on an integrative conception of the human being. The details of the argument may soon be considered out-of-date; the paleoanthropologists are persistently presenting new findings about humankind's cradle in Africa and cultural and evolutionary theory is continuously developing. The main story line, centered around the integration of biology, history, and culture, is not so likely to be questioned next week, and the story told may challenge some traditional conceptual oppositions, such as those between nature and nurture and between the individual and the collective.

A VERY BRIEF HISTORY OF THE CONCEPT OF CULTURE

"Culture" is a word of which there is a profusion of connotations both in scholarly texts and in everyday language. The word originates from the Latin verb "colere" and the corresponding noun "cultura," with its meaning related to tillage of the earth. Already the ancient Romans had a metaphorical usage of the word. They spoke of "cultura animi", cultivation of the soul. Since the seventeenth century this metaphorical meaning has gained increasing importance in Western thinking. European colonialism and the concurrent need to understand the natives and their forms of life probably fueled this modern usage (Fornäs, 1995). Today it may be common to underline that to understand other people is indispensable in any attempt to understand oneself, but it is obvious that the early pioneers of cultural description often had less noble goals in mind. The words "colony" and "culture" have their origin in the same Latin word, which reminds us about the fact that the problem of ethnocentric description is at the heart of any account of culture. It is not possible to step out of your own culture in an attempt to understand another. In other words, a completely objective account of culture, with a precise balance of outsider and insider perspectives, is not attainable. This is sometimes called the etic-emic dilemma. As will be illuminated from different angles throughout the book, some kind of *pluralistic dialogue* is probably one of not too many ways of dealing with this dilemma.

Broadly speaking there are two main streams of the modern use of the word culture. There is a normative use, to denote what is considered first-rate in arts, manners and scholarly pursuits. One may for instance speak of the cultural life of a city and think of the high arts. Then there is a more descriptive use of the word, typically found in the social sciences, to denote a way of life built up by a group of humans and usually transmitted from one generation to the next. Both streams of usage have a history that shows us that a term like culture cannot be "innocent." There is for instance a history of instrumental use of the term, as part of a project of differentiation. The term culture has been used as a tool to create and preserve social hierarchies within and between societies. "A man of culture" would usually mean a cultivated man of the upper social classes, to be distinguished from "the people" not only because of his money and his social status, but also because of his cultivation. Hierarchies have also been created concerning "ways of life." In the Western world the word "culture" – and its relative; "civilization" – have been used for centuries as tools to distinguish between higher (read Occidental) and lower (read Oriental, etc.) forms.

While the word "culture" is much used and misused, culture may also be considered as something we do not easily speak of. We might even forget about it, because it is surrounding us all the time. As several authors have noted, when it comes to culture, we are fish in the water. We are not able to leave the river in order to take a distanced look at it. Given this – and the complexity and diversity of the cultures of the world – one might be tempted to do like Wittgenstein (1953/1967) when discussing language: refuse to make any clear-cut definition. Wittgenstein considered language to be such a complex and multifaceted phenomenon that he proposed that any definition would run short of capturing this complexity. He also resisted the idea that there was any *one* characteristic we could use in describing language. Instead he preferred to speak about language as groups of *language games* with certain *family resemblances;* there are some common features with one group of games, other common features with another group of games, but no shared essence.[1] As language must be regarded an important part of what we think of as culture, Wittgenstein's objections to defining language should be given serious consideration. One consequence may be to think of "culture" as a *sensitizing concept* instead of an exact concept; it may be helpful by pointing out a direction in which we can search without attempting to give any specific description of a phenomenon.

When trying to work out a viable concept for use in a scholarly discourse, the task may be considered somewhat different from the philosophical discussion developed by Wittgenstein. A professional practice requires a disciplined discourse (Ansdell, 1999), and we need to take a closer look at scholarly definitions of culture in order to be able to develop one that is relevant for music therapy. The strongest tradition of using culture as a scholarly concept is probably to be found within anthropology and ethnography. Researchers in these fields usually relate their writings to the descriptive use of the word culture, roughly defined as *ways of life and practices of meaning-making built up in communities*. This descriptive use is also dominating in this book, but value judgments are part of any practice of meaning-making, so this usage does not exclude the normative perspective. One of the pioneers of modern anthropology, Edward B. Tylor, gave in 1871 a definition of culture that was very influential for decades, and which in many ways still is. As an anthropologist he searched for a descriptive definition, culture as something ordinary in everyday life, not as "the best which has been thought and said" as the British poet Matthew Arnold had expressed it. The definition Tylor gave was:

> Culture or Civilization, taken in its wide ethnographic sense, is that complex whole which includes knowledge, belief, art, morals, law, custom, and any other capabilities and habits acquired by man as a member of society (Tylor, 1871/1958, p. 1).

This definition indicates how multifaceted the phenomenon of culture is, and also reveals very clearly that clarity is not necessarily achieved through definition (which in this case says as much about the phenomenon in question as about the definition). Tylor's definition has been very influential, though, and its characteristic phrase "complex whole" points toward the focus upon *systems* that became so prominent in twentieth-century social theory. Another phrase of his definition, "capabilities and habits acquired by man as a member of society," also points at a characteristic of culture that most scholars agree upon. Culture is related to learning, and as such with the intersection of individual and social life. Apart from this there has been plenty of disagreement on how one exactly should understand the term culture, and attempts to define culture surely did not stop with Tylor. A plethora of definitions have been produced, with differences in focus upon behavior versus meaning, processes versus products, change versus stability, and so forth. In 1952 Kluckhohn and Kroeber in a critical review of the American literature listed more than 160 definitions of culture (Eriksen, 1995, p. 9). What the number of definitions worldwide would be today, nobody knows. This plethora of definitions, which relates to the fact that the concept has and must have a history of use, makes it necessary for any scholar to clarify how one uses the term. How, for instance, could culture's relationship to biological, psychological, and social aspects of human life be conceived?

Despite the conceptual difficulties outlined above, I consider culture an indispensable term in research, theory, and practice on human interaction, since such interaction seems to be embedded in culture, whatever biological, psychological, and social processes involved. This contention is hardly controversial, and to define culture has therefore been considered a challenge not only for cultural anthropologists, but for biologists, psychologists, and sociologists as well. Not only are there many existing definitions, but they also differ to a considerable degree in scope and focus. Broadly speaking one may say that on one end of the spectrum there are definitions stressing human diversity, that is, cultures (in plural) as something that distinguish groups of people. On the other end of the spectrum there are definitions underlining human unity, that is, culture (in singular) as shaped by universally shared capacities developed in the evolution of the species.

Culture, consequently, could be said to be something that we do not know exactly how to define, but which we still consider very important. How then could the problem of definition be approached? I propose that two strategies will be fruitful. First, music therapists could learn from scholars in the humanities and social sciences who, walking in Wittgenstein's footsteps, have acknowledged the value of vagueness and of sensitizing concepts. Other times more precision is required, and the second strategy for defining a term like culture could be to provide more concise definitions when relevant for use in specific contexts. Later in this chapter I will attempt to develop a definition of culture that may be relevant for contemporary music therapy, but first I will relate the question "What is culture?" to the basic question "What is humankind?" While this last question, even more than the first, presents a rather tall order for this chapter, I find it necessary to deal with it, if only briefly, in order to contextualize my understanding of culture.

TOWARD AN INTEGRATED CONCEPTION OF HUMANKIND?

It is probably not correct, as some have advocated, that humans differ from all other animals by having culture, but it is certainly correct that humans differ from animals in their richness in culture and in the importance it is given. Any notion of culture then makes it necessary to clarify a notion of humankind, and this contention becomes no less relevant when the context of discussion is therapy. It is obvious for most people that therapeutic practices based upon a notion of the individual as an *organism* with no personal or social life are narrow and restricted, as are practices focusing upon the *psychological* with neglect of the biological and the social. It is therefore no surprise that the last few decades have seen an increasing interest for so-called biopsychosocial approaches. Two questions then become crucial: How are these levels of analysis possible to integrate? and: What is the role of culture? By posing these questions I want to indicate that the challenge may be something more or different than the search for more inclusive conceptions of humankind; we may need a more *integrative* conception. The route I will follow is to see how a focus upon culture can contribute in our search for such an integrated conception.

One of the scholars who first addressed this is the anthropologist Clifford Geertz (1973/1993), and I will present his argument in some detail. To anticipate Geertz's conclusion, what he suggests is something different from thinking about culture as a fourth factor in addition to the biological, psychological, and social aspects of human life. Geertz suggests that humans are in effect cultural, and in order to understand human biology and the personal and social life of humans we need to understand culture. In his discussion of the impact of the concept of culture on the concept of humankind, Geertz suggests that most culture-inclusive theories have been based on a "stratigraphic" conception of the relation between biological, psychological, social, and cultural factors in human life, a conception he finds reasons to challenge:

> In this conception, man is a composite of "levels," each superimposed upon those beneath it and underpinning those above it. As one analyzes man, one peels off layer after layer, each such layer being complete and irreducible in itself, revealing another, quite different sort of layer underneath. Strip off the motley forms of culture and one finds the structural and functional regularities of social organization. Peel off these in turn and one finds the underlying psychological factors – "basic needs" or what-have-you – that support and make them possible. Peel off psychological factors and one is left with the

biological foundations – anatomical, physiological, neurological – of the whole edifice of human life (Geertz, 1973/1993, p. 37).

The problem Geertz sees here is that the stratigraphic conception is based upon a dualism between universal aspects of culture – based on subcultural (such as biological and social) realities – and local and arbitrary aspects of culture. According to Geertz it is difficult and not very helpful to try to draw a line between what is natural, universal, and constant in humankind versus what is cultural, local and variable. What are typically considered universals in culture Geertz often regards as bloodless or fake universals. He uses religion, one of the suggested universals, as an example. If one for instance defines religion as humankind's most fundamental orientation to reality, then one cannot at the same time assign to that orientation a highly circumstantial content: "The obsessive ritualism and unbuttoned polytheism of the Hindus express a rather different view of what the 'really real' is really like from the uncompromising monotheism and austere legalism of Sunni Islam" (Geertz, 1973/1993, p. 40). A universal definition of religion thus, according to Geertz, becomes too abstract to be of real value for the understanding of humankind.

Instead of searching for lower common-denominator universals in culture, based upon a stratigraphic conception, Geertz proposes that we should take interest in cultural particularities and search for a *synthetic* conception of humankind, where cultural factors are treated within unitary systems of analysis. To take interest in cultural particularities might be seen as recourse to total relativism, but Geertz argues convincingly that this does not need to be the case. The concept of generalization that he utilizes is based on a search for *systematic relationships* among diverse phenomena and not on substantive identities among similar ones. The synthetic – or integrative – conception of humankind that he then launches is based upon two ideas. The first idea goes back to the issue of defining culture. He sees culture not as concrete complexes of behavior patterns, but rather as the "control mechanisms" governing these behaviors. The second idea is that individuals and groups of the human species most desperately depend upon such extra-genetic control mechanisms for the ordering of their behavior (Geertz, 1973/1993, p. 44).

These proposals are controversial on certain levels. Some scholars suggest that Geertz's definition of culture is too narrow and too focused upon *meaning*. Others suggest that he underestimates the specificity of the psychological mechanisms evolved in human phylogeny (see for instance Tooby & Cosmides, 1992). Whatever position one takes in these debates, it is obvious that a more careful examination of biological evolution, cultural history, and individual development – and the systematic relationships between these processes – is necessary in order to evaluate the idea of an integrated or synthetic conception of humankind. To these issues I will now turn.

CULTURE AND THE EVOLUTION OF THE HUMAN SPECIES (PHYLOGENY)

There is – almost per definition – scarcity in evidence for the details of the stories told on the evolution of the human species, constructed out of a few bones and stones as these stories are. With the help of refined research tools such as modern genetics, and with the guidance of evolutionary theory and comparative studies of primates and other animals, much can be understood from bones and stones, however. To study cultural aspects such as music and language use of forefathers that lived several tens and hundreds of thousands of years ago remains rather difficult, although a few rough measures do exist. Did, for instance, these forefathers have the anatomic equipment necessary for speech (Frayer & Nicolay, 2000)? With the forefathers and mothers that *did* have this anatomic equipment, how should we be able to know anything about the language they used? It is not easy to find a direct trajectory for answering such a question. Indirectly of course one can guess and assess guesses, for instance by assuming which level of linguistic practice would be necessary to support the social organization and the practices of tool making that archeological findings suggest existed (Cavalli-Sforza, 2001).

Like language, neither songs nor musics fossilize. A few prehistoric musical artifacts, such as bone flutes, have been found (Kunej & Turk, 2000), but it is difficult to theorize the course of development of the human species' musical capacities, and the evolutionary mechanisms that made this development possible. Generally music has also been neglected in the study of human evolution, although Darwin (1871/1998) in *The Descent of Man* included passages of reflection about the role of sound, voice, and music. A common view in contemporary evolutionary theory has been that music is not a human adaptation (Pinker, 1997), that is, music has not been considered a biological trait that in the phylogeny of the human species promoted survival or reproduction. This view has been challenged lately though; an evolutionary musicology has been advocated (Wallin, Merker & Brown, 2000), and several authors have proposed that music *is* an adaptation of major importance for the evolution of the species (Dissanayake, 1992/1995, 2000a, 2000b, 2001; Miller, 2000, 2001).[2] It may be time for reassessing the place of music in evolutionary theory, and of evolutionary theory in music therapy for that matter.

One version of the story of human phylogeny[3] goes: About 5 or 6 million years ago a population of apes somewhere in Africa became reproductively isolated from other apes. This group evolved and split into new groups, leading to several different species of bipedal ape of genus *Australopithecus,* creatures made famous by Louis and Mary Leakey's discovery of the "Nutcracker man" in Olduvai Gorge (Tanzania) in 1959. These creatures walked upright and had developed a more complex social structure than their forerunners, but it is only in the later period of their existence – around 2.5 to 1.5 million years ago – that there is evidence for tool use. Simple stone tools have been found in sites they inhabited. It is of course possible, even plausible, that *Australopithecus* before that used even simpler tools, such as wooden sticks, but it is naturally very hard to find evidence for the use of such tools dating back millions of years. *Australopithecus's* successors had evolved so much that a new genus designation has been used, namely *Homo. Homo habilis* are usually given credit as the earliest tool makers, while *Homo erectus* – emerging approximately 1,5 million years ago and surviving for more than a million years – developed sharp-edged stone tools and control over fire. Then – some 200,000 to 250,000 years ago, still somewhere in Africa – one population of *Homo* began on a new course of development. This group out-competed all other populations of Homo, and their descendants are known as *Homo sapiens* and later *Homo sapiens sapiens.* This new species had some new physical characteristics, such as larger brains. Even more striking, though, were the new cognitive skills and products they created. They started to produce a plethora of new tools, they began to use symbols to communicate (including artistic and other non-linguistic symbols), and they engaged in new and more developed social practices and organizations (such as burying of the dead and domestication of plants and animals).

Such practices are often considered species-specific for human beings, and before proceeding it could be helpful to comment upon the idea of species-specific skills and abilities in humans. According to the Genesis of the Bible humans differ from animals in most important ways. This account became integrated into European culture, and for a very long time was the "official story," in fact until the nineteenth century, when theories on evolution began to develop with pioneers such as Lamarck, Darwin, and Wallace. Charles Darwin was not alone in suggesting an evolutionary perspective, but his *Origins of Species* (1859/1962) and *The Descent of Man* (1871/1998) have been most influential because he produced a more convincing argument for the mechanisms involved than what Lamarck did, and because he in contrast to Wallace suggested that the difference between humans and the higher animals is one of degree and not of kind. This "difference in degree" created a storm of reactions, due to the breach it represented with traditional

Christian theology. Today – in most cultures – this issue may be discussed in a calmer atmosphere, and we may ask; what is degree and what is kind? When does a quantitative difference turn into a qualitative difference? Scholars that want to propose defining differences between animals and humans need to specify their claims in order to be taken seriously. This has not brought the production of such suggestions to a standstill, however. Three of the more common are: humans are different from animals in that they have *language*, they are different in that they have *tool use*, and they are different in that they have *culture* (a proposal that subsumes the two others).

Counterarguments against these suggested defining differences have been produced. Apes have been taught to use simple signs and language, they are observed using simple tools, and they may also show some indications of culture understood as patterned conduct or styles of behavior. Interpretations of such findings are disputed, though. Chimpanzees may learn some language, but only with a limited number of topics, while a hallmark of human language is the infinite number of topics. The tool use of primates other than humans is mostly fragmented and rudimentary, and hardly developed over generations. Similarly the cultural behavioral patterns among apes do not show much sign of development over time. Such information may contextualize the contemporary claims that are made as to continuity or discontinuity of species. To propose continuity advocates the relevance and importance of biology in the study of humankind, and to stress discontinuity suggests that the humanities and social sciences may operate with little consideration of biological knowledge. A middle ground position is taken by cultural psychologists who suggest that there is both continuity and discontinuity. They accept Darwin's general theory of descent, but advocate that Homo sapiens differ from other species in both degree and kind; new levels of organization – cumulative culture – have resulted in new principles of psychological functioning. In order to understand the human species it then is important to understand humans' specific capacity for cultural learning, and to understand what makes it possible (Cole, 1996).

It took humans just a few thousand years of cultural development to change from caveman to spaceman, which indeed indicates the power of the capacity for cultural learning. Cultural psychologists have often opposed the sociobiology of Edward O. Wilson and his followers, by criticizing this perspective for neglecting the importance of cultural history. Much of this criticism is relevant, but not all aspects of sociobiology are incompatible with cultural perspectives though, at least it is possible to state that sociobiology (and more recent developments such as evolutionary psychology[4]) acknowledge the specific cultural character of human social life. Wilson (1975/2000) suggests that there are four pinnacles of social evolution: the colonial invertebrates, the social insects, the nonhuman mammals, and humans. The sequence given here proceeds from primitive to more advanced – biologically speaking – while Wilson suggests that the key properties of social existence – including cohesiveness, altruism, and cooperativeness – decline. "It seems as though social evolution has slowed as the body plan of the individual became more elaborate" (Wilson, 1975/2000, p. 379). While the colonial invertebrates have come close to producing what Wilson calls perfect societies, there are already more conflicts between the social insects and there is definitively less cooperation and more aggression among the nonhuman mammals. Aggressiveness and discord is of course not especially foreign to human societies, but humans have reversed this tendency in some important ways. "Human societies approach the insect societies in cooperativeness and far exceed them in powers of communication" (Wilson, 1975/2000, p. 380).

While humans are social animals, and not unique in that regard, there is something specific with the human way of being social that we need to comprehend. Some characteristics of human societies and communities are: enriched communication, formation of bonds and cliques, development of traditions and customs, a greater role for learning, and more precise recognition of individuality and idiosyncratic behaviors. As cultural psychologist Michael Tomasello advocates; this special human way of being social is linked to humans' *capacity for culture*. In human societies domains of social activity have been transformed to domains of *cultural activity*. Object manipulation, enhanced among some primates through the use of simple tools, has in human societies been developed through the creation of artifacts. Communication, possible for many animals through the use of signals, has been developed among humans through cultural symbols such as music and language (Tomasello, 1999, p. 210). What has made this cultural development attainable? Higher mental capacities for problem solving seems to be an obvious answer, but this is probably only a necessary, not a sufficient, condition. One answer proposed by Tomasello is that the complex human cognitive skills did not evolve one by one, but have a single biological root: the capacity of humans to pool their cognitive resources with others in their social group. This capacity, he argues, is unique to humans, and can thus be defined as a species-unique skill of *cultural learning*, based on the ability to understand conspecifics as *intentional and mental agents*. This skill is then to a high degree responsible for the evolution of language and other cultural artifacts (Tomasello, 1999).

Tomasello's arguments differ from some influential hypotheses in evolutionary psychology. During the 1980s and 1990s several influential evolutionary theorists have hypothesized that in phylogeny there was a genetic event (or several such events) that led to the development of, say, language (Pinker, 1997), and that this event in principle was unrelated to genetic events responsible for other human cognitive capacities. This events responsible for other human cognitive capacities. This hypothesis suggests that humans have a *modular mind;* we are equipped with innate modules as the basis for specific cognitive functions. It is beyond the scope of this book, and of my study in human evolution, to go deep into the ongoing debates on the nature of genetic events, in order to resolve the differences between Tomasello and Pinker. The issues at stake are both the nature of the genetic events in the process of human evolution and the relative importance of genetic events versus cultural history. At this point I find it sufficient to underline the fact that humans have a capacity for understanding conspecifics that seems to be very special. Many aspects of human cognition are shared by other primates, such as perception, memory, attention, and capacity for categorization. During phylogeny modern human beings in addition to this evolved the ability to *identify with conspecifics* and to develop a *theory of mind,*[5] that is, to understand the other as an intentional and mental being similar to oneself. This enabled new forms of cultural learning through imitation, teaching and collaborative endeavors, which led to the development of cultural artifacts and traditions of conduct that accumulate and change over time.

CULTURAL HISTORY

An increasing number of researchers now agree upon the basic assumption that phylogeny and cultural history cannot be separated. The human species did not develop biologically without any contribution of culture and then, when biological evolution had done its work, start cultural history. Such a story line would support a stratigraphic conception of humankind. This notion has had its supporters and it preserves the idea that researchers in the natural sciences, the social sciences, and the humanities do not need to talk together. There is an alternative story that is more plausible though, which may be called the gene-culture co-evolution hypothesis. The zoologist Theodosius Dobzhansky was concerned about this at least as early as in the 1950s and 1960s. In the 1970s, from a sociobiological perspective, a gene-culture co-evolution hypothesis was advocated by Edward O. Wilson and others. In an account of cultural psychology, Jerome Bruner (1990) refers to Gerald Edelman's neuroanatomy, Vernon Reynold's physical anthropology, and Roger Lewin and Nicholas Humphrey's primate evolutionary data as scholarly works produced between 1980 and 1990 in support of this hypothesis. The co-evolution hypothesis has therefore gained increasing support, from quite diverse perspectives. Some of the most important disagreements relate to the degree of difference between the processes involved, and I will briefly elaborate on that.

Co-evolution does not necessarily mean shared temporality. The first part of cultural history started at some, possible rather early, point in phylogeny, and then gained pace after the biological evolution slowed down. Before the first homonids evolved 1.5 to 2 million years ago the speed of the biological evolution of our species seems to have been rather moderate. The evolution toward Homo sapiens and then Homo sapiens sapiens accelerated, possibly due to phylogeny-culture relations and probably with a "final spurt" around the evolution of Homo sapiens sapiens about 40,000 years ago. After that not much happened with human biology, while human culture developed rather radically, gradually at first and with an "explosion" – at least in some parts of the world – the last few hundred years.

This timeline illuminates what all serious biologists now assert: Humans comprise *one* species only. We are sons and daughters of a diaspora of Africans, and thus share a common genetic heritage. The differences between races are minimal to the degree of making the concept of race meaningless, and are for most part limited to skin color, body size, and other adaptations to climate (Cavalli-Sforza, 2001). What is striking then is the biological unity and the cultural diversity that characterizes the human species. All humans share a human nature, but not all share a common cultural history, except – probably – for the very first part of it. For this, and other reasons, it is important to consider similarities and differences between biological and cultural evolution. In everyday language we use evolution as a generic term, connected to any process of growth and development. But does biological and cultural co-evolution mean that these processes share characteristics? Some of the proposals made would suggest that,[6] but I find it relevant to clarify possible differences also. In fact, I consider these differences to be so crucial that the term "cultural evolution" in fact becomes problematic, since it may be interpreted as suggesting a close analogy between biological and cultural development.

A closer look at cultural development reveals that in many ways it may be different from biological evolution, and some of these differences are indicated by the term *history,* as the term is understood in the humanities. To talk about cultural development as history means of course that things change over time, but so they do in biological evolution. One important characteristic of cultural history is that there is a *transmission of acquired skills and abilities.* This form of heritage – often called Lamarckian – does not occur in biological evolution. Cheetahs do not run faster than lions because their forefathers and mothers practiced running intensively. Lamarckian heritage is often used as a metaphor for *cultural heritage,* however. Learned skills may be passed on to a new generation of learners. The usage of this concept must then be restricted to this level of analysis. There is no biological heritage of the skills that have been learned. Lamarckian transmission in cultural history is due to processes of learning from conspecifics, through spontaneous imitation or through practices of teaching and instruction (Cole, 1996). Another difference to biological evolution is that cultural and social history allows for *agency*.[7] While biological mutations are arbitrary, cultural variations may be intended and directed by human agents. This does not mean that human agency is without constraints. It is in operation within biological, ecological, and social limits, though quite often aimed at transcending or transforming them. A third difference, one that I have already touched upon, is the time-scale or temporality involved. Cultural history sometimes changes at a very high pace, and the agents involved *relate* to the changes as they happen. People live in the present, but with memories of a past and expectations of a future.

We need a notion of cultural history that may include the *cumulative* quality that is typical for human culture, while avoiding ideas of unilinear development based on an ungrounded analogy with biological evolution. As we have seen, chimpanzees and other primates may create and maintain cultural traditions if broadly defined. What is typical for *human* culture is the capacity for *powerful cumulative cultural development*. Each generation may stand upon their predecessors' shoulders and build upon prior culture. As ideas, skills, tools, and artifacts produced in human culture are passed down from generation to generation[8] they tend to have novel enhancements made to them. Modifications are made – individually or collaboratively – and over time artifacts evolve in complexity, form and/or functionality. This has been called the *ratchet effect*. The argument is that cumulative cultural evolution depends on two processes – innovation and imitation – and that these must take place in a dialectical process over time such that one step in the process enables the next (Tomasello, 1999, p. 39). Social communication and collaboration is therefore essential for human culture.

It seems obvious – and also well documented – that even basic tools like hammers have been modified over generations: from simple stones, to composite tools with a stone tied to a stick, to various types of modern metal hammers (not to speak of the electric nailing pistols used by contemporary carpenters). The possible *power* of the ratchet effect may be illustrated by the juxtaposition of two periods in cultural history: the rapid emergence of new human skills and practices 40,000 years ago and the technological revolution of the twentieth century. Many unique human abilities, such as the invention of sophisticated composite tools and tailored clothes, seem to have emerged quite rapidly around 40,000 years ago. The speed of the process has puzzled many researchers, and it is often suggested that some biological evolution of the brain must have taken place at the same time, although the homonid brain already reached its present size 200,000 years ago. Consider then a future archeologist who discovers the sudden technological development in the twentieth century, when humans visited the moon for the first time, just a few decades after they were able to make an airplane work for the first time. Might not the future archeologist speculate that some biological evolution must have supported this extremely rapid development? Certainly he might, but while biological evolution *may* be part of the picture 40,000 years ago we *know* that that is not the case concerning the more recent technological revolution. Cultural history, or the ratchet effect, is responsible for this change alone.

What I have suggested so far is that there is a shared human nature that needs culture in order to operate fully, and that human culture may be cumulative. Artifacts tend to develop over time. Much of this development may be interpreted as *improvement*. A modern metal hammer is usually considered a better tool than a stone tied to a stick. To identify cultural development with improvement is problematic, however. What counts as improvement is only possible to decide in context and relates to a set of values. Consider, for instance, the different opinions on modern technology's ability to preserve or destroy our earth. There is more to cultural history than improvement. Cultural history is characterized by *diversity*. One way of relating to diversity is total relativism: any cultural variant is just as good as any other. An alternative is ethnocentrism: certain cultures – the culture one belongs to oneself usually being a good candidate – are more developed and therefore of higher value than other cultures. Both ways may be problematic.

The problems of ethnocentrism have been discussed quite widely, as the increasing interest for *postcolonial theory* illustrates, fueled by Edward Said's (1978/1995) seminal book *Orientalism*. That persons and groups to a large degree identify with the values and worldviews of their own upbringing and cultural context is of course inevitable and in itself not problematic. Problems arise when such taken-for-granted views are integrated in oppressive practices. Indirectly this is a problem also for contemporary scholarly disciplines, to the degree that knowledge produced becomes linked to power. One field of inquiry that has struggled with this issue is psychology, a modern science growing strong in the twentieth century, mainly through the contributions of European and North American scholars. An illuminative example is the huge problems met when psychologists have tried to develop culture-fair tests of memory and cognition. Michael Cole (1996) discusses this issue in detail, and suggests that it is hardly possible to develop such tests at all. How people organize and remember what they perceive is embedded in culture, and these cultures are much more specific than conventional broad labels such as literate versus illiterate. General proposals on skills and abilities of illiterate people as compared to people from more "developed" cultures are therefore highly problematic. Cole's conclusion is that to categorize groups of people as more or less cultured is misconceived. In a way, human societies are equally cultured. They are cultured and sensitized to different tasks and contexts, however, depending upon their forms of life. In each community much social work goes into the construction of cultural artifacts that built up in complexity over generations and centuries. These provide cultural niches for ontological development.[9] In evaluating these institutions and artifacts one must take *context* and form of life into consideration, which leads Cole (1996, pp. 175-177) to propose a *conditional relativism*. No notion of "level of thinking" as a single, general, psychological trait is universally appropriate.

Skills of the city are not higher than skills of the jungle then, except if one lives in the city. Cultural groups interact, however, and this interaction generally takes the form of competition for resources. In this competition certain cultural artifacts and traditions have given certain groups advantages. This is a social reality of the world; sometimes called development, sometimes violence and imperialism. The continents of the world also have constituted quite different biogeographic conditions for cultural development (Diamond, 1997/1998). While cultural differences earlier were interpreted as consequences of racial differences, this interpretation is *not* based in current biological knowledge. The explanation of cultural differences is historical, and related to a variability of ecological conditions in each continent. It is therefore not possible to treat cultural history as if it was *one* history. We need to take interest in specific – although quite often interacting – cultural *histories*.

CULTURE AND INDIVIDUAL DEVELOPMENT (ONTOGENY)

The discussion above illuminates that human beings must be understood in a context of historicity. The consequence for a discussion of individual development, ontogeny, is that both genetic and cultural heritage must be considered. The perspectives outlined in this text suggest that the human mind to some degree is a biologically adapted mind; it is not a tabula rasa at birth. A child's development may still be understood as *enculturation*. A child grows up in the midst of culturally constituted artifacts and traditions. Children benefit from the accumulated knowledge of the group, and through the learning of linguistic symbols they develop abilities to represent their world and to engage in metacognition and dialogic thinking. Human development must then be understood as a process situated in an evolving social context. It is not only a question of how environments influence individuals in the course of development. It is also necessary to consider how individuals and groups select and shape the environments that influence their development. The child is not a passive recipient of stimuli, but may in various ways influence the course of development, through activity and creativity. The process is not a one-way influence from the environment but takes the form of a reciprocal process of interaction, for which the word *transaction* sometimes is used (Cole, Engeström & Vasquez, 1997).

Individual development includes the development of *self* and *identity*. The integration of perspectives argued for above suggests that the self is not a static core biologically determined; rather the self evolves through social activity and experience as internalization of culture with the tools given us by phylogeny. Each individual develops differently as a result of his specific biological and cultural heritage, and of his particular *relations* to the individuals and communities that he interacts with (Bruner, 1990). These statements may serve as an outline of the ontogenetic process in general. From birth the child is biologically programmed to be directed to other humans, and through affiliate interaction with adults the baby starts on a trajectory of cultural learning (Dissanayake, 2000a). While Vygotsky and the early Russian cultural psychologists thought of cultural influence as something which became strong with language acquisition, contemporary cultural psychologists underline that cultural influence is part of the mother-infant interaction from the very beginning (Cole, 1996). This view has found support in recent research on mother-infant interaction (Dissanayake, 2000a) (Trevarthen & Malloch, 2000), and this research also underlines what most cultural psychologists have advocated: that the child plays an active role in constituting his own world.

The reciprocal character of the communication involved does *not* mean that the child and the adult have exchangeable roles. Vygotsky's term of *Zone of Proximal Development* (ZPD) is illustrative to this point. Vygotsky distinguished between the child's actual developmental level (mental functions established as a result of already completed developmental cycles), and the child's potential developmental level (his ability to perform under the guidance of an adult). He then defined ZPD in this way:

> [ZPD] is the distance between the actual development level as determined by independent problem solving and the level of potential development as determined through problem solving under adult guidance or in collaboration with more capable peers (Vygotsky, 1978, p. 88).

According to Vygotsky, and most cultural psychologists after him, learning leads development, which should not be interpreted as being in opposition to the contention that biological maturation is important. In a child's learning process more experienced learners, such as adults and capable peers, play an essential role. A child learns in interaction with more mature learners, especially if they are sensitive to the level of development of the child and adjust their interaction to that. Vygotsky advocated that the term ZPD furnishes psychologists and educators (and I would add therapists) with a new tool for understanding the course of development: "By using this method we can take account of not only the cycles and maturation processes that have already been completed but also those processes that are currently in a state of formation" (Vygotsky, 1978, p. 87). The term ZPD reminds us about the role of learning in social interaction, about the importance of the sensitivity of the adult, and about the importance of taking a developmental perspective to education and therapy.

While Vygotsky's term was based on experiences with older children, recent research on mother-infant interaction has given us new knowledge about how adults adjust to children from birth (Dissanayake, 2000a; Trevarthen & Malloch, 2000). One of the terms developed for the description of this adjustment is *affect attunement* (Stern, 1985/1998), and we are reminded about the fact that both a cognitive and an emotional adjustment to the child are necessary. Research on early interaction has also given much information on the child's (biological) preparedness for reciprocal communication. Already from birth the child is prepared for this and capable of engaging in neonatal mimicking and "proto-conversations." With time the child understands "that others make choices in perception and action and that these choices are guided by a mental representation of some desired outcome, that is, a goal" (Tomasello, 1999, p. 205). A foundation for this learning, then, is the human capacity for understanding other humans as like themselves, not only as animate beings but also as intentional and mental agents, with goals and plans. From the age of about nine months the child develops a beginning theory of mind, in the broad conception of this. The child discovers the intentionality in the other. This "nine month revolution" is by Stern (1985/1998) conceptualized as the development of the *subjective self*, by Trevarthen (1988, 1995) as the development of *secondary intersubjectivity*.

The relevance of mother-infant interaction for the understanding of music therapy has been advocated by numerous music therapists; see for instance Pavlicevic (1997). It seems reasonable to advocate that music therapists can learn from the study of cultural learning in infancy. To concentrate on cultural learning through language, as the early cultural psychologists did, would not be reasonable for a discipline concerned with the use of musical and non-verbal interaction. To go to the other extreme and solely base music therapy theory upon theories of say mother-infant interaction would be inadequate, however. We do well in considering language acquisition and other later forms of cultural learning. These forms of learning in ontogeny transform the child's development and experience of himself and the world, a process often described as identity building. A cultural perspective on development suggests interest for cultural learning throughout a life span, not just in the first year or two of life.

Two forms of cultural learning of great importance in ontogeny are *learning through play* and *internalization of narratives*. The importance of internalization of narratives to live by is covered nicely by Jerome Bruner (1990). Here I will briefly exemplify the importance of play. One illuminating example of play as "mediated activity" – activity where shared social meaning is internalized and used by the child – is given by Michael Cole:

> From about 12 to 18 months, babies use objects in play much as adults would use them in earnest; that is, they put spoons in their mouths and bang with hammers. But as they near their second birthdays, babies begin to treat one thing as if it was another. They "stir their coffee" with a twig and "comb the doll's hair" with a toy rake or pretend that the edge of a sandbox is a roadway. This kind of behavior is called symbolic play – play in which one object *represents* another, as the rake stands for a comb. For the next several years, play will be an important cultural context within which children can simulate the cultural practices they observe and participate in, including the roles they will be expected subsequently to carry out in earnest. Play is proleptic (Cole, 1996, p. 197).

With the term "proleptic" Cole underlines that children live in a world of adult scripts, or more precisely, a world of adult scripts as interpreted by the child. The quote above illuminates well both the role of imitation in ontogeny and the role of symbols as a tool for relating in cultural yet individual ways. Humans have a very long ontogeny compared to other primates. There is a large amount of individual learning necessary to be able to function in a human society. This process enables social and cultural adaptation *and* individualization. Young children have a very strong tendency to imitate what others are doing, and can use cultural artifacts as tools in their development. One of the reasons why humans develop cumulative culture is that they ape much better than apes do, *and* it must be added, understand the intention of the act they ape. The early childhood period is to a large degree concerned with the child's entry into the world of culture through mastery of artifacts and conventions that were there already at their arrival on the scene. These artifacts and conventions they then may adapt for creative use as their mastery progresses. This creative use is what is usually recognized as individuality (Tomasello, 1999, p. 160).

THE RELEVANCE OF CULTURAL PSYCHOLOGY FOR MUSIC THERAPY

The notion of humankind outlined in this chapter may be summarized as a perspective focusing upon humans' capacity for *community and reflexivity*. Humans are born with a strong need for experience of community, with motives for cultural learning and with communicative skills that enable them to engage in the interactive learning processes necessary to achieve this. The path to individualization thus goes through the experience of *community* and intersubjectivity, through social and cultural learning, and through internalization of cultural values, knowledge, and skills. An indispensable element in this process is *reflexivity*, the ability to think of oneself in relation to others. While the experience of community is framed by social organization, reflexivity is made possible by the operation of signs belonging to cultural systems. This suggests that "the cultured animal" is a good description of the human species. The necessity of and ability for culture is something universally shared among human beings. Humans are born cultural, so to say, with a capacity and need for cultural learning.

A stratigraphic conception of humankind may suggest that biology is the cake and culture the icing, an image that may be misleading. In search for a more integrated concept it is helpful to study phylogeny, cultural history, and ontogeny in relation to each other. Phylogenetic capacity for culture has produced humans as beings in need of a cultural history (shoulders to stand on) and in need of a long ontogeny for internalization of cultural artifacts. It seems necessary therefore to supersede the oppositions traditionally suggested between biological evolution and sociocultural history. The brain, speech, music, tools, and complex social life evolved together to produce Homo sapiens sapiens. My argument is neither that culture is something good nor that it is something important. It is more than that; it is unavoidable. A biopsychosocial perspective is not completely satisfactory in the study of humans then. One proposal could be a biopsychosociocultural perspective. Apart from the obvious awkwardness of the name, we have also seen that culture is part of human biology, psychology, and social organization, so that an alternative formulation might be that we could study the biopsychosocial in a cultural perspective.

One of the things we can learn from the discussion above is that the traditional nature versus nurture divide is not very constructive. A child who is not dynamically interacted with on a regular basis will not develop cognitively as he should and will not be healthy from a mental or emotional perspective. To say this is not to take the nurture side of the nature-nurture divide. Rather, the discussion so far suggests that this divide is not helpful at all. What I have tried to clarify is that social nurture enables cultural learning and that this must be seen in relation both to phylogeny and cultural history. Cultural learning may in some respects be called a product of evolution or one of the "strategies" of evolution. In that way we may say that nurture is one of the forms that nature may take. But this process is not possible without a cultural history that provides the tools and artifacts necessary for the child's process of cultural learning. At birth the child is provided with the genes he needs for building structures, and a culture is prepared for him to use. Then there is work to be done, in interaction with adults and more mature learners sensitive to the child's Zone of Proximal Development.

Human nature, then, demands social nurture mediated by cultural artifacts in order to develop. There are – as we have seen – different perspectives on the details of human phylogeny and ontogeny, but we know already enough to suggest that scholarly isolationism is counterproductive. The disciplines of biology, psychology, sociology, and anthropology will have to communicate and collaborate in order for us to have a more complete and differentiated notion of humankind. Such communication and collaboration will not be without academic conflicts and disagreement. One well-established frontline has only been briefly touched upon, and a full treatment of it is beyond the scope of this book: the disagreements between scholars who want to build a science of culture on the basis of biology and scholars who think that this is a futile ambition. In the first group one will find sociobiologists and evolutionary psychologists, in the last group one will find many anthropologists and scholars of the humanities.

In my judgment the relevance of biology for an understanding of humankind is beyond doubt. There may be disagreement as to how specific cognitive modules are, but this hardly allows us to neglect the possibility that these modules, as evolved in phylogeny, to some degree impose structure on human perception, cognition, and culture (Tooby & Cosmides, 1992). I find evolutionary theories problematic though to the degree they neglect the relevance of cultural history and advocate the possibility of a *science* of culture based upon an analogy with biological processes. While this last analogy deserves merit for linking biology and culture, the link suggested is not unproblematic. Voestermans & Baerveldt (2000) argue that: "evolutionary psychologists tend to forget that the brain is not a mere controlling system, but exist in an embodied form and is not singular but plural. For a good understanding of culture, not just one single brain is crucial; crucial are the mutually attuned and coordinated bodies of which the brain is a part." Exactly how evolutionary biology may be integrated into psychological and cultural theory is still controversial then, but it is important to note that cultural psychology, which is the tradition Voestermans & Baerveldt work within, needs to be – and already is – aware of the developments within evolutionary theory.

This is a relevant backdrop for the discussion of interdisciplinary thinking in music therapy, of which the relation to psychology shall be the focus in the following paragraphs. For some music therapists the need for psychological thinking is very obvious. They see music therapy as an intra- and interpersonal process that should be guided and supervised through the use of psychological and psychotherapeutic theory. Others stress the uniqueness of music therapy and advocate music-centered perspectives, indigenous theories, etc.[10] The cross-disciplinary perspectives that have been outlined in this chapter suggest that we move beyond "for or against" the use of psychological theory in music therapy and start asking questions such as "which theory?," "for whom, when, and for what?", and "how could we best use theory from other disciplines?"

While music therapists traditionally have taken interest in the established four forces of psychoanalytic, behavioral, humanistic, and transpersonal psychology, I propose that it is about time that we take more interest in *cultural psychology*. There are of course also other developments within contemporary psychology that may be of interest for music therapists, such as the aforementioned growing interest in evolutionary psychology or the achievements within cognitive research, or the efforts to establish health psychology as a field of study for that matter. When I here choose to see music therapy in relation to cultural psychology it is because this tradition of research directly links to the notion of humankind outlined in this chapter, with a clear awareness about the interplay of phylogeny, cultural history, and ontogeny. I will start by situating cultural psychology within the context of contemporary psychology.

With Michael Cole (1996), one of the advocates of contemporary American cultural psychology, we may ask why culture has had such a minor role within the discipline of psychology. In mainstream psychology culture usually has been reduced to a "stimuli" or an independent variable in cross-cultural research. In contrast to this, cultural psychologists advocate that human processes do not stand apart from their activities but are constituted by them, which implies that human agency is created through internalization and creative use of cultural artifacts in social contexts. Vygotsky and the other Russian cultural psychologists were, as already stated, the pioneers of this line of thinking. In the last few decades there has been a renewed interest for culture among psychologists, some of the influential theoreticians being Jerome Bruner, Michael Cole, Richard A. Shweder, and Michael

Tomasello. The contemporary field of cultural psychology is concerned with the biological and psychological foundations of cultural communities *and* with the cultural foundations of mind. Cultural psychology thus can be said to be concerned with how culture and mind affect each other, over the history of the community and over the life course of the individual.

The previous discussion of humankind and culture suggests that cultural psychology is an important corrective and supplement to contemporary mainstream psychology. While some traditions of psychology, such as behavioral psychology, have been eager in adopting the research methods of the natural sciences they have often been quite reluctant in accepting the knowledge developed by, for instance, evolutionary biology. Cultural psychologists have often balanced this in a different way: with more willingness to accept biological knowledge and with less enthusiasm for the idea of restricting the study of humans to quantitative and natural science-inspired research methods. For music therapy this addendum and critique should be of especially high relevance, since the act of musicking so convincingly is interplay of biological, psychological, social, and cultural processes, as we will see in the next chapter. To learn from, and reciprocate with, cultural psychology may then be a promising strategy in developing theoretical conceptions of processes of music therapy. This school of psychology[11] provides music therapists with tools for superseding oppositions in our thinking that have been shown to be rather unproductive, such as the aforementioned "nature versus nurture" and "individual versus collective." Cultural psychologists have developed theories of human development and learning that illuminate how these levels interact and reciprocate.

So far there is, to my knowledge, not much material available on the direct relevance of cultural psychology for clinical thinking. I agree with McLeod (1997), though, who suggests that narrative therapy, with pioneers such as Spence (1982), Schafer (1980), and White and Epston (1990), is a possible link between cultural psychology and clinical therapy theory. Other links also exist, such as "mediation-oriented" interventions with children at risk (Klein, 2001) and the therapeutic use of reminiscence working with elderly people (Bender, Bauckham & Norris, 1997), to take two examples from each end of the human life span. There is still a relative lack of concrete connections between cultural psychology and clinical theory, but I do not consider this to be a major argument against the significance of cultural psychology for music therapy. I do not propose cultural psychology as a clinical theory for music therapy practice, rather I propose that cultural psychology – based upon an integrated notion of humankind – may be a *metatheory* guiding the use and development of relevant clinical theory in specific contexts of music therapy. Such a metatheory will not regulate the details of clinical theory and practice, but may provide some direction and also some conceptual tools for clarifying constructive and less constructive directions in research. Using cultural psychology as a metatheory is then very different from two polarized positions all too common in contemporary music therapy, where psychological theory is either neglected or adopted with little creative adjustments and modifications to the specific contexts of music therapy. My proposal is that cultural psychology could function as a platform or container for the development of more specific clinical theories in music therapy.

The fact that clinical theories based upon cultural psychology are rare may at first be a difficult starting point. On the other hand, some metatheoretical guidance is provided while freedom in the development of specific theories is also given. Freedom goes with responsibility, and part of the responsibility in this case is to explore the possibility of rethinking what we mean by clinical theory and practice. Cultural psychology may, for instance, give the discipline conceptual tools for dealing with the fact that only some music therapists seem to be doing therapy in the common meaning of that word in the modern world: curative work. Many music therapists are doing some other – though related – things, like habilitation and rehabilitation, prevention and promotion, palliative care, etc. Many also work in untraditional settings, not only in therapy rooms in clinics, but sometimes in the hall of a hospital, in a music school classroom, or in the playground of a kindergarten. Some may interpret this as a deficit and as a lack of recognition of the profession: "Not all music therapists are allowed to do proper therapy yet, and they do not have proper therapy rooms either." I think it is more promising to look at this from another perspective: What possibilities and limitations do these different types of interventions and these different contexts offer? What kind of theoretical concepts can guide the music therapists facing this diversity?

The answer to this last question is hardly "look to cultural psychology" only, and the proposals of this book could not be reduced to "music therapy in the perspective of cultural psychology." I suggest that music therapy relate to a broader interdisciplinary field, including disciplines such as evolutionary biology, anthropology, and musicology. In such a broad field it is necessary to focus, though, and I suggest that cultural psychology may provide music therapists with tools for developing integrative concepts within diverse contexts. Throughout this book this suggestion will be elaborated. I will do this not by restricting theoretical discussions to concepts from cultural psychology, but by using such concepts whenever relevant and by supplementing with theoretical contributions that are compatible in ways that support and challenge the perspective.

CULTURE DEFINED FOR MUSIC THERAPY

With some knowledge of the history of the concept of culture, and after a discussion of an *integrated notion of humankind* as well as of the relevance of cultural psychology, I think we now should be ready to approach the question of how to define culture in a way that is pertinent for music therapy. We have seen that in the case of the human species, nature has chosen culture. Culture is therefore part of what makes us human. At the same time we often speak of culture as something *not* universally shared; culture as something belonging to a distinctive group of people. In this way we speak of *different* cultures, culture in plural, related to ethnicity and identity, disparity and diversity. These differences in use, together with the "narrow" (normative) and "broad" (descriptive) uses outlined in the beginning of this chapter, make culture a rather open term. I proposed earlier in the chapter that this situation could be approached with two strategies: to acknowledge the value of vagueness and sensitizing concepts, and to develop more specific definitions when required for development of scholarly discourse. For a large part the first strategy has sufficed for the discussion so far in this chapter. I will now try to develop a specific definition, to see if it may help in clarifying the relevance of culture for an understanding of music therapy.

The definition proposed below must be understood in the context of this intention. While it may be broad enough to connect to fields other than music therapy, the main intention is not to propose a comprehensive definition covering all aspects of culture, but rather to develop a tool for the discussion of music therapy and culture:

> Culture is the accumulation of customs and technologies enabling and regulating human coexistence.

In other words, culture is what happens when people spend time together; they act and they interact, they produce artifacts and they use artifacts, and they do this as they make rules and break rules, if only to make new rules. Culture then is shaping people and shaped by people, in conscious and nonconscious ways, some of the latter being related to human nature as evolved in phylogeny.

In an attempt to make this definition a viable tool for discussion and critique, and for the development of music therapy theory, I will clarify some of the major concepts used in it. The main arguments and references have been given earlier in the chapter, so descriptions will be brief:

Accumulation, as used in this definition, may have two meanings that both are of relevance: growth by continuous addition, and state of being accumulated. As underlined in the discussion of cultural history, culture is always change and exchange, sometimes at a slow pace, other times at a very fast pace. As experienced at a given point in time, culture may also be seen as a state of what has been accumulated over history. Accumulation is different from addition; a process of selection is involved. Ways of doing and expressing that work especially well or are especially beautiful may have more chances of being accumulated than other innovations. A general and rational description of this is not possible, though, since selection in this connection also is related to power relationships in a community.

Customs is a term that covers behaviors and beliefs, and these often develop jointly over time. Behaviors include rituals, practices of tool making, and routines of daily life. Some behaviors are conscious, others automatic and nonconscious. Beliefs include values, norms, and religious and scientific systems. Again conscious and non-conscious elements coexist. Sometimes the term *life-world* is used to denote those aspects of culture that are taken for granted by an enculturated individual, and which therefore are not easily made explicit.

Technologies are developed over time by groups of people, in relation to the shared biological makeup and to the environmental pressures and the possibilities experienced. As used in this definition, and by some cultural psychologists and sociologists, technologies include both physical and symbolic tools. One type of technology is then the sum of ways in which a group provides themselves with material objects. Another type of technology is the sign systems developed, such as language and music, as tools for communication, self-understanding, and self-construction.

Human coexistence may be considered the main mode of human existence, as indicated by the epigraph used for this chapter. Human existence may be understood as basically dialogic and communicative, even when a person is isolated. This should not be interpreted as collectivism. The idea is rather to underline the co-constructed character of human cognition and experience, that is, human existence is constituted as coexistence through the species' enhanced capacity for community and through the reflective use of cultural artifacts. Coexistence may be experienced as face-to-face communication, or as virtual community (in thinking and dreaming, or – of course – through use of physical technology such as computers).

Culture is *enabling* human coexistence, which means that the ways humans relate to each other and to themselves are culturally constituted, even though they are based upon shared biological capacities. On a general level, the enabling aspects of culture may be expressed as Tomasello (1999) did: in human societies domains of social activity have been transformed to domains of cultural activity. Object manipulation and communication have been enhanced through the development of physical artifacts and cultural symbols. While "proto-conversations" to a large degree have biological roots, conversations are enabled by cultural artifacts such as language,[12] a contention which of course does not exclude the possibility that the capacity for language acquisition has a biological origin.

Culture is also *regulating* human life, for instance by limiting possibilities for expression and action. This may be helpful and necessary, by reducing chaos and confusion, but may also function as repressive and cruel restrictions of human agency. The regulating aspects of culture are not always obvious or easily discerned. Values and norms may be internalized and taken for granted. Cultural awareness therefore should, in my view, include concern for cultural critique and empowerment.

The aspects of culture focused upon in this definition may be studied at several levels: individual, group, community, society, and groups of societies. One way of dealing with this complexity is to take a systems perspective, which suggests a focus upon interdependent variables existing in dynamic integration rather than upon a sum total of certain characteristics. As any system is part of a wider system (which again is part of a wider system, etc.), the ecology of systems of culture could then be a major focus of interest. A cultural phenomenon exists in relation to and interaction with other cultural phenomena, and receives input from and sends output to an environment. Another way of saying this is that if we speak of culture as systems we must focus upon *open* systems.

This may be a helpful perspective, as it gives conceptual tools for dealing with interaction of cultures; for instance between a subculture and a dominating culture. It is also relevant for the development of ecological perspectives on music therapy, as will be discussed in Chapter 5. Many anthropologists, such as Clifford Geertz (1973/1993), have incorporated the concept of system in their writings. The problem with a systems perspective may be that it does not give very good conceptual tools for description of individual agency, and Geertz has been criticized for underestimating the individual differences in values and perceptions between people belonging to a community. A systems perspective easily leads to too much focus upon the idea of unified cultural systems, while contemporary anthropologists increasingly argue that the cultures of modern and postmodern societies are fragmented and diversified. They therefore often prefer to speak of a plurality of life-worlds. This is an important reminder, but these life-worlds do not exist in vacuums, but are related in systematic ways.[13] Instead of focusing upon unified harmonic cultural wholes, a systems perspective to a contemporary understanding of culture then may take the reality of conflicting subcultures into consideration.

CULTURE-CENTERED MUSIC THERAPY

By means of this definition it should be possible to clarify the term *culture-centered music therapy*. Hopefully it is by now clear that what is meant is not an anti-biological or anti-psychological approach. If it is true that cultural aspects too often have been neglected by music therapists, little would be won by reducing everything to culture. At the same time, the argument developed above hardly suggests that culture is something that could be neglected. I find it helpful to distinguish between two ways music therapists may choose to relate to culture: we could speak of *culture-specific* and *culture-centered* music therapy.

Culture-specific music therapy acknowledges the fact that a client comes to music therapy with a cultural identity, as does the therapist, and that music therapy therefore may not be considered a "culture-free" enterprise. One implication could be that therapists, in showing respect for clients and their culture, adjust their way of working to each client, for instance by choice of musical styles. This is already an important implication, but it must be noted that cultural differences may be reflected in many aspects relevant to therapy, such as notions of health and of relationships, ways of expressing emotion, etc. Openness for reflexive dialogues on these matters may be required in order to provide qualified and ethical defensible therapy.

It is not always possible to adjust completely to a client's culture, enculturation and acculturation are usually long and complex processes. In such cases the *interest* and *respect* communicated may be more important than the degree of success of adjusting to the specific cultural codes. This argument is exemplified by Michele Forinash, who in an interview talks about her experience of working with elderly Jewish people in an American city:

> coming from a non-Jewish background and needing to learn the music of my clients, which I think is applying to any ethnic population that you work with. But not only learning, but learning to live in the music that I really was not born with, did not grow up [with], did not begin to listen to until I was in my early 30s ... really needing to develop appreciation for a whole type of music that I did not appreciate or know anything about. ... I can't perform Klezmer music at all. But the music I did with them – the Hebrew folk songs [and] things like that – I played [them] with the clients, because they really liked them. And so I could play them well enough to play with the clients, you know; sing with them and improvise a little bit around some of those songs. But no, in terms of actually performing Klezmer music, or performing in that tradition, no – I would never do that. I am not

that good, but I certainly have learned to love it enough to make that kind of music with my clients … and it actually ended up with being a good thing therapeutically, because I never pretended to be Jewish, I never pretended that I grew up with this music. And I really allowed them to teach it to me, and I allowed them to give me feedback on "How fast does this go?," "How do we do this?," you know. And I really put them in the role of sort of mentoring me, because they had grown up with it, and they really had the feeling for the music. So, it ended up being a good therapeutic tool to use. I did not know [the music], and it was fine to go to them and say, "OK, of these 10 songs, which are the 5 that are the most important to you?" And they could really fill me in on the story behind them. Because some Jewish songs that I thought were traditional Jewish songs were actually written by Americans – and were popular in America –, but they were not really, really the songs that were most meaningful (Forinash, 2000, p. 81).

Culture-specific music therapy is becoming increasingly important, as most modern societies progressively become multicultural, especially in urbanized contexts, and as the value of cultural identity is acknowledged more than before. Some recent and fine discussions of multicultural issues in music therapy are provided by Brown (2001), Estrella (2001), and Forrest (2000/2001).

While culture-specific music therapy may be described as awareness about music therapy *in* culture, *culture-centered music therapy* may be understood as awareness about music therapy *as* culture. These should not be interpreted as polarities, however, as culture-centered music therapy necessarily also is culture-specific. What comes in addition is the willingness to rethink music therapy at a more basic level, taking an integrative notion of culture, such as the one outlined above, into serious consideration. Culture-centered music therapy may go beyond the adjustment of existing models of music therapy to individuals and local context, and may result in completely new ways of practice and in new music therapy theories. Culture-centered music therapy therefore suggests the possibility of a more radical reevaluation of what music therapy is and can be.

This perspective represents a challenge to the standard conceptions of what music therapy is, by a willingness to consider far-reaching implications of the cultural character of human life. This may be exemplified if we reflect upon the standard format of most therapies: individual sessions on a weekly basis. There are of course numerous exceptions to this format; some therapies are conducted more often or more seldom than this, the group format is also well-established, etc. Still, there may be reasons to ask why this "standard format" is so well-established. Is it because we *know* that this is the most helpful way of working, or is it because this format has been established as a cultural model that has been reproduced over generations of therapists and across various types and traditions of therapy? If the latter is the case, one may need to examine why this model has been reproduced. Rye (1993), McLeod (1997), and other authors have suggested that the traditional individual session format is a heritage from the medical model, brought into psychotherapy and other therapeutic approaches via Freud's psychoanalysis. While there has never been any lack of critique of the theories that Freud proposed, the individual session format has been questioned to a much lesser degree, perhaps because the format represents a model of prestige and because it provides the therapist with a safe and clear role to play in relation to the client. Culture-centered music therapists sometimes take music therapy out of the music therapy room and out of the context of a session with a defined start and end. My argument is not that the individual session format is bad; often I believe it to be the best format available. Chapter 6, for instance, presents a therapy case where this format has been used. Culture-centered perspectives in this case are represented through the search for more culture-sensitive theories for understanding the music therapy process. In many cases, therefore, traditional formats of therapy may work well. The point is that we should not take them for granted but examine rather carefully when and how other formats could do better, as will be exemplified in Chapters 4 and 5, where a community-based and ecological approach is discussed.

Format is just one example of issues that may need rethinking. The definition of culture given above presents some key issues that could be considered. From thinking of music therapy as culture it follows that cultural learning comes into focus. Therapy as *learning in relationship*, that is, as enculturation and *accumulation* of cultural knowledge about oneself and the world will be an important issue to examine in the study of music therapy processes. Similarly, music therapy may relate actively to the *customs* and *technologies* of clients and contexts, for instance to *rituals* of the local community, to computer technology, etc. To use cultural artifacts in attempts of *enabling* the client for participation in a community and for the experience of *human coexistence* may be important, as well as the confrontation of *regulating aspects* (in a community or society) in the cases that these have negative consequences for the client. In Chapter 4 we will for instance see how both of these two last aspects were approached with a group of mentally retarded clients, a group of people who often encounter that possibilities of participation are closed due to their own lack of experience and skills and due to noninclusive attitudes and cultural norms in the music life of a local community.

The overview given in the above paragraph summarizes topics that will be discussed throughout this book. It is perhaps necessary to reiterate that culture-centered music therapy necessarily is culture-specific. The practical examples given in Part II must be read with this in mind. I see no other way of communicating experiences of working in a culture-centered way than to give culture-specific examples, but the idea is *not* that the forms of practice exemplified in Chapters 4 to 6 should be models to transplant to all other contexts. Maybe *some* therapists will see that they can do similar things in their own contexts, while others will practice culture-centered perspectives in completely different ways, related to the qualities and possibilities of the contexts they work in.

These culture-specific elements must be acknowledged, and while such specific elements are inevitable in any practice of a culture-centered perspective, the specific elements of any one context of music therapy should hardly be reified as the basic elements of a culture-centered approach. In Chapters 7 to 9 I therefore will try to discuss some general implications of a culture-centered perspective, to be tried out and challenged in specific contexts. Issues covered in these chapters will include definitions of music therapy, a culture-inclusive model of the music therapy process, and possible new arenas and agendas for music therapy. In Chapters 10 to 12 approaches to research that can give context- and culture-sensitive knowledge about music therapy will be examined. Before we move on to Parts II, III, and IV of the book, however, I find it helpful to clarify premises concerning the understanding of notions such as "meaning" and "music," which will be the topics of the next two chapters.

NOTES

[1] Wittgenstein's notions will be elaborated in more detail in the next chapter.

[2] Miller and Dissanayake represent quite different perspectives upon music as an adaptation, the first stressing male competitive sexual display and the other communal instances such as mother-infant interaction.

[3] Darwin's (1871/1998) *The Descent of Man* is still a major source of inspiration for researchers on this topic. The presentation to follow is informed by paleoanthropology (Leakey & Lewin, 1993; Leakey, 1994), evolutionary psychology (Barkow, Cosmides & Tooby, 1992; Pinker, 1997; Kennair, 1998; Clamp, 2001; Miller, 2001), and by cultural psychology (Cole, 1996; Tomasello, 1999).

[4] Evolutionary psychology is sometimes framed as "sociobiology in disguise," but this is an inaccurate description, as evolutionary psychologists have incorporated criticisms of sociobiology, for instance by paying more attention to context

(Kennair, 1998).

[5] A valuable discussion of the evolution of "mindreading" is given in Simon Baron-Cohen's book *Mindblindness. An Essay on Autism and Theory of Mind* (1995).

[6] Consider for instance Richard Dawkins's (1976) concept of memes, based on an analogue between genes and cultural units.

[7] This is of course a controversial issue. There are notions of history – some times called historicism – that stress history as processes determined by ecological conditions, processes of production, etc., without accounting for human agency as a dynamic element in the process. I do not subscribe to such notions.

[8] The term generation is here not linked to biological parenthood, it is used more broadly to denote "generations of learners." Inexperienced learners learn from previous generations of learners, that is, more advanced learners.

[9] This discussion is highly complex. Cole's discussion challenges traditional perspectives in Western psychology, but could themselves be challenged. It is, for instance, probably relevant to speak of contexts which are "less cultured" in that they represent deprived niches for ontogenetic development. War and poverty may be among the social conditions leading to the development of deprived contexts.

[10] This debate has maybe been especially strong in Britain, see for instance Streeter (1999), but could be seen in many countries.

[11] For a general introduction to this approach to psychology, see for instance Cole (1996). For specialized treatment of specific themes, see for instance Bruner (1990) on meaning and Tomasello (1999) on the cultural origins of human cognition. Cultural psychology has also contributed to a rethinking of the concept of learning in education, see for instance Lave and Wenger (1991).

[12] One aspect of this is clarified in Wittgenstein's (1953/1967) so-called *private language argument*, where he convincingly shows that meaning systems cannot be private. This is not to say that there is nothing like personal meaning, but that this consists of a mosaic of negotiated meanings stemming from situations of interaction with other people. In the private language argument Wittgenstein illuminates the idea that our grasp of our inner life is dependent on the existence of outer criteria, which is compatible with Bakhtin's notion of a dialogical psychological reality.

[13] One attempt at integrating systems perspectives and life-world perspectives has been developed by Jürgen Habermas (1981/1987).

Chapter 2:

MEANINGS

*the central concept of a human psychology is meaning
and the processes and transactions involved in the
construction of meanings. This conviction is based upon
two connected arguments. The first is that to understand man
you must understand how his experiences and his acts are
shaped by his intentional states, and the second is that the
form of these intentional states is realized only through
participation in the symbolic systems of the culture.*
(Jerome Bruner)

In the case of humankind nature chose culture. This has implications for the disciplines working with and studying humans. For everyday purposes as well as for celebrations and special occasions humans engage in the production and interpretation of *meanings*. These meanings are situated in cultural contexts; they are located in time and space and have a *history* that cannot be accounted for by reduction to any laws of nature. A natural science perspective on the study of human beings will therefore not suffice and must be supplemented by contributions from the humanities. Perspectives on meaning, narrative, and aesthetics may sensitize music therapists to the situated character of meaning-making and aesthetic judgments and will add to the discourse on how to define and develop the discipline of music therapy.

MEANINGS OF MEANING IN MUSIC THERAPY

Several forms of psychotherapy – such as psychoanalysis and client-centered humanistic therapy – are concerned with either the revealing of *hidden meaning* or with the construction of *new meaning*. In contrast there are also forms of therapy that apparently do *not* put the issue of meaning in the center of interest, such as behavioral therapy or physical therapy. If we then turn to music therapy, is it reasonable to suggest that some music therapy practices should be concerned with meaning and some not? Humankind's reliance on culture suggests that this would be an oversimplification and that issues of

47

meaning and interpretation of an individual's life-world are central for most forms of music therapy.

In the literature of music therapy the concept of meaning is not among the most elaborated and discussed, however. Frequently other terms have been chosen for description of process and outcome. In many improvisational models of music therapy, related terms such as spontaneous expression, personal experience, and symbolic association have been used (Bruscia, 1987). In models closer to the behavioral and medical traditions, music's effect on skills and behaviors, or on the physical, mental, or social *function* of the client may be discussed (Davis, Gfeller & Thaut, 1999). A closer look at the practices and discourses referred to above would reveal that the issue of meaning is still relevant. Music therapists working with the *function* of a patient need to ask questions about what loss and gain of functions *means* for the individual in his life situation. Therapists that work with improvisation and self-expression will have to consider the suggestion that every expression is already inscribed in a *meaningful life-world*. Meaning or not meaning is therefore not the question, but rather what kinds of meanings are central for music therapy, when and in which ways, and how they are constituted.

Even though the literature on meaning in music therapy is rather sparse in quantity, there is already plenty of diversity in the theoretical assumptions that have been made. To give just a few examples: Even Ruud (1987/1990, 1998) suggests that meaning in music is constructed and *relative* to context, while Kenneth Bruscia (1998a, 2000) suggests that there is an *objective* and universal level involved. Dorit Amir (1992, 2001) focuses upon the *experience* of the client and the therapist, and introduces the notion of *meaningful moments*, while Colin Lee (2000) suggests that *the music itself* must be analyzed. Mercédès Pavlicevic (1997) links meaning in music therapy to *interpersonal processes*, understood both in traditional psychodynamic terms and in terms of more recent theories on mother-child interaction. Henk Smeijsters (1998) has developed a theory about music as *analogy:* he proposes that there is a correspondence between clients' life and personality and their musical expressions in therapy. Lars Ole Bonde (1999) and Jungaberle, Verres and DuBois (2001) have proposed that personal meaning generation through *metaphors* is essential in music therapy. From an ethological perspective Dissanayake (2000b) argues that music must be considered an evolved behavior and that mutual and ceremonial participation in music is a human "need" related to the experience of meaning in life.

The list of examples above suggests that it is futile to propose one general theory on meaning in music therapy. While these differences in perspectives would be important to discuss and evaluate, there are good reasons for believing that the theoretical diversity also is related to the complexity of the phenomenon. Music is incredibly multifaceted; it is an acoustic phenomenon, it is a mode of expression with its own syntactic rules, it is a symbolic medium, and it is a tool for action and interaction in social contexts. Music may trigger physical reactions, emotions, association, and memories; and it may function as a personal, social, or transpersonal space. When discussing meaning in music therapy, music therapists therefore are concerned with issues such as music as product versus music as process, or, music as "text" versus music as context. In addition, they must take into consideration that issues of meaning in music therapy do not only relate to music; they relate to the biography of the client, to the clinical understanding of the therapist, to the immediate communicational context, and to the cultural context of the therapy session. "What meaning?" is then not the only issue, "whose meaning?" is also a major question. Then there is the perennial theme as to whether meanings related to music are expressible in language or not, whether music is absolute or referential, etc.

Given the complexity described above, it is clear that any comprehensive answer as to what kind of meanings are central for music therapy, and how and when they are central, is far beyond the scope of this chapter. There are several legitimate foci in the study of meaning. My main agenda in the following will be to examine the thesis that meanings are always situated in cultural contexts. This is not to say that cultural context is all there is and all that constitutes meaning, but that cultural context is always there, and that this matters. It is not adequate to study meanings as if they were ahistorical or immanent to musical structures, for instance. I will take as point of departure that meanings may have universal, local, and personal sources, and especially the two first levels obviously provide possibilities for stability in meaning. The universal level relates to the capacity for meaning evolved in the phylogeny of the human species, while the local level relates to the cultural history of the groups the individual belongs to (and therefore also the history of other groups, communities, and societies). The personal level relates to biography or individual history, that is, the previous learning and experience of the individual. I also take as point of departure that these levels may be separated only for theoretical and analytical purposes. In real-life situations they merge and interact.

The thesis outlined here suggests that the *pragmatic* level of analysis of meaning-making should be given significance. While sounds in music are organized according to *syntactic rules*, neither these rules nor the *semantic level* escape the situations they are part of. All aspects of music are linked to situations of use, where human agents act and interact.[1] The theoretical explorations that follow are based on these assumptions, and I will concentrate on the co-constructed character of meanings, and also expand the discussion to related issues such as narrative and aesthetics. The issue of co-constructed meanings is related to the assumption that humans are "born cultural." They have a biological disposition for taking interest in sounds, movements, and signs in relation to social interaction, that is, in shared meaning-making (Trevarthen, 1995). The elaboration to follow is therefore based upon theoretical contributions that go beyond constructing oppositions between biology and culture and the individual and the collective level. When we approach an individual we approach the issue of meaning, and when we approach the issue of meaning we approach the social and the cultural, including narratives and aesthetic dimensions.

While the proposals to come may challenge some conventional conceptions of meaning, framed by ideas about the unitary, bounded, and self-sufficient self, the alternative proposed is not equivalent with a neglect of individual and personal aspects. *Relational aspects* of human life will be stressed, and what I hope to achieve is to suggest ways of thinking about meanings that do not construct unbridgeable schisms between universal and local, collective and individual, or verbal and nonverbal. Instead of choosing positions in such constructed dichotomies, music therapists could take interest in the relationships involved *between* these elements, processes, and levels of analysis. The situated character of meaning production that will be highlighted should not totalize a social or collective level. The idea is rather that we need to study the individual within collective contexts and the collective within individual contexts. It is in the interaction of these two levels that individuality and community is born.

FROM NAMES TO MOVES IN LANGUAGE GAMES

In order to develop a notion of meaning viable for music therapy practice I will make a brief excursion to the later philosophy of Ludwig Wittgenstein, who developed a pertinent perspective on meaning in relation to social human life. Wittgenstein has given inspiration to very different schools of philosophy. His early work was used, some would say misused, by the logical positivists, while his later work inspired British analytic philosophy. Some of his later writings are also compatible with radical hermeneutics and aspects of postmodern thinking. This astonishing breadth in influence is partly due to the span and development in Wittgenstein's philosophical contribution. It may also be due to the fact that his style was idiosyncratic and poetic, thus open for various interpretations.

One of Wittgenstein's main foci was meaning in language, and his perspective changed quite markedly throughout his life; from seeing words as names to seeing them as moves in games, to put it crudely. The difference between his first major work, *Tractatus Logico-Philosophicus* (originally published in 1921), and his most influential text, *Philosophical Investigations* (published posthumously in 1953), is amazing. In fact, in *Philosophical Investigations* he argues that the author of *Tractatus* was wrong in most of his ideas on how language works. Nevertheless, there are some common features in the two works, such as the suggestion that the philosophy of language is essential for our understanding of all philosophical problems and a vision of philosophy as a practice not aimed at solving problems but at re-solving them through a better understanding of language.

In *Tractatus* Wittgenstein suggests that the most important function of language is *referential:* the meaning of a sentence is its correspondence with the facts of the world. A sentence, to be meaningful, has a logical structure that is in *correspondence* with the logical structure of the actual state of affairs in the world. We could call this a *picture theory* of meaning. Mathematics and logic is then the model of true language, and in this sense there is only one meaningful language. Thus, ordinary everyday language is imperfect; it needs to be clarified by logic. This picture theory of language was influential on the development of logical positivism, and it is compatible with the idea of "unified science": the belief that there is *one* scientific method that guarantees for logical, universal, and true statements. Although in a watered down version, we often operate from a picture theory of language when we ask for precise definitions of phenomena.

There are some logical problems connected to a definition of language as a logical picture of the world. A metaphorical expression of this insight was possibly given by Wittgenstein already in *Tractatus*. In 6.54, the penultimate note of that book, he states: "My propositions serve as elucidations in the following way: anyone who understands me eventually recognizes them as nonsensical, when he has used them – as steps – to climb up beyond them. (He must, so to speak, throw away the ladder after he has climbed up it)." The correspondence theory of meaning in language does in itself not correspond to any given reality. There is an inbuilt problem of self-referential incoherence in the picture theory of language. Wittgenstein himself changed perspective in his later works, and argued that a plurality of language functions must be acknowledged, and that these develop as elements in social communication. Thus he gradually sought for new perspectives on the issue of meaning, and by the early 1930s he stated:

> But if we had to name anything which is the life of the sign, we should have to say that it was its *use* (Wittgenstein, 1958/1969, p. 5).

In this new perspective, everyday language is seen no longer as an imperfect and messy mass that ought to be cleaned up by logic and the language of science. Now ordinary communicative language is seen as something to study in order to learn more about what language actually is and how "dead" signs become meaningful. Local contexts are then not arbitrary sources of variation and distortion, but environments that keep signs alive, so to say. One term developed by Wittgenstein to demonstrate this is *language games*. He suggested that language operates as part of social practices embedded in forms of life. Words then are moves in social "games" that include both verbal and nonverbal activities. In the first part of *Philosophical Investigations* (§§ 2-21) he gives a well-known example of this: a situation where some builders are working together and using words such as "block," "pillar," "slab," and "beam." Traditionally, one would think that the word "slab" acquires its meaning as representation of a thing in the physical world. When two people are working together, "slab" instead might be an order, not a description. The meaning, in this case, is not understood before someone complies, or refuses to do so. Wittgenstein shows how words actually get their meaning as moves in a social world, that is, in language games.

Meanings, in this case in language, therefore are constructed by actions and interactions of participants in "games." Social agents are following or not following certain sociocultural and linguistic rules. Going back to Wittgenstein's example one could of course argue that "slab" is also a name, or even that it is usually a name. Then one has already transgressed the limits of the particular game, though, and this is probably one of Wittgenstein's major points: to understand, you must understand the particular game and the form of life of which it is a part. This notion suggests that meaning is linked to local context and integrated in human activities. *Vagueness* may then be a necessary condition of language in many contexts; precise definitions are not always achievable. To define is not necessarily to clarify. Actually it could bewitch our understanding, making us blind because we think we see. If you do not know what a slab is, to use a dictionary will tell you how the word often has been used, but this will not help much if you do not understand the particular language game the word is part of. Operational and other specific criteria for the definition of a slab as opposed to other building components would not add to your understanding, while sensitizing yourself to the context would. Meaning and context can then not be separated.

The later Wittgenstein refused to define language, although his whole life in philosophy was devoted to the issue. Concepts like language bear more comparison with family names than with personal names, he proposed. Wittgenstein discussed this in *Philosophical Investigations:*

> some might object against me: "You take the easy way out! You talk about all sorts of language-games, but have nowhere said what the essence of a language-game, and hence of language, is: what is

common to all these activities, and what makes them into language or parts of language" ... And it is true. – Instead of producing something in common to all we call language, I am saying that these phenomena have no one thing in common (Wittgenstein, 1953/1967, § 65).

Wittgenstein continues by comparing the proceedings that we call *games*, arguing that there are common features between groups of games, but no common features of all games. He then states:

I can think of no better expression to characterize these similarities than "family resemblances," for the various resemblances between members of a family ... overlap and criss-cross in the same way, – And I shall say: "games" form a family (Wittgenstein, 1953/1967, § 67).

To summarize; Wittgenstein suggested that the meaning of a word or sentence is its *use* in a *language game,* and that language games are too various to have a common structure that can be captured in a theory of meaning. Rather, games are characterized by *family resemblances:* a particular language game will have some common features with one group of games, other common features with another group of games, and so on. This argument suggests that general and abstract theories on meaning at best are insufficient, and the relevance of *local knowledge* is implied (although Wittgenstein himself did not use this particular term).

MEANING GAMES

Wittgenstein's later philosophy has been a major influence on the so-called linguistic turn in the philosophy of the twentieth century, and also in what has been termed the anthropological and interpretive turn in several of the social sciences. What is proposed is a new awareness for cultural context, and for the historically situated character of knowledge and meaning. It is disputed to what degree Wittgenstein's perspectives are compatible with social constructionism or radical relativism, however. Probably they may be identified with such positions only through oversimplification, and it may be more relevant to use his philosophy in attempts at getting beyond objectivism and relativism, as proposed by Richard J. Bernstein (1983). For instance, the suggestion that actions and language must be seen in relation to each other calls on explorations of human nature, of cultural history, as well as of each particular situation.

Wittgenstein's importance in disciplines as diverse as linguistics, aesthetics, anthropology, and cultural psychology is in itself an invitation to examine his relevance for music therapy, and his discussion of the *mutuality of agents* interacting in *specific settings* could hardly be neglected by any discipline focusing upon human dialogue and interaction. As Wittgenstein's discussion first and foremost is related to language, a note about meaning in music must be added (see also the next chapter). It is obvious that music and language are different media of meaning. Language is almost entirely consti-tuted by arbitrary (conventional) signs. This is not necessarily so with music; indices and iconic signs seems to play a greater part, in interaction with con-ventions, of course. Words often have designative meaning, while musical elements only rarely have this function. These differences should not be exaggerated to the degree of constituting music and language as dichoto-mies, though. In any human communicative act verbal and nonverbal ele-ments interact and give meaning to each other.

Partly in continuation of the Romantic philosophy of the nineteenth cen-tury, which cultivated music's ineffable character, the *differences* between music and language have been stressed in many music therapy milieus. Some music therapists may for instance contend that "language is about emotion, but music *is* emotion." Language is then reduced to the function of *naming things*. Such comments are often connected to suggestions about music's ability to express what cannot be expressed in words. In support of this view, Susanne Langer's (1948, 1953) philosophy of art and music has been used. Peregrine Horden, who has edited a book on the history of music therapy, comments upon Langer's position in contemporary music therapy theory:

> the aesthetics of Susanne Langer, for whom music was *par excel-lence* a symbolic analogue of the inner life, survive in the writings of music therapists when they have been rejected by most philosophers of art (for their Cartesian separation of inner world from outward be-haviour, their unanalysable concept of an emotion's logical structure, and the circularity implied in asserting that emotions can be de-scribed in musical terms) (Horden, 2000, p. 15).

While Langer's arguments in fact partly are based on the early picture theory of Wittgenstein, the later works of the same philosopher offer a way out of the problems indicated by Horden's criticism. It is possible to get beyond the limitation of thinking of music in the abstract and general; instead, we may consider meaning-making as situated processes in which sounds, movements, and linguistic signs interact and affect each other. The idea is not that music and language are the same, rather that differences may not be constituted as static and independent of context.

One of the more important contemporary philosophers and theorists on communication, Jürgen Habermas, comments upon Wittgenstein's notion of language game in this way: "Language and action interpret each other reciprocally" (Habermas (1968/1971, p. 168). This description may be extended to include music. Language, action, and music interpret each other reciprocally. It may be helpful then for music therapists to think of meaning as constituted in situated *meaning games*. In these games the clients use their bodies and voices, as well as artifacts such as words, songs, and instruments. The games are played by rules that may be constituted at several levels, and which may be followed or not, depending on the moods and intentions of the agents involved. An example relevant for music therapy may be the use and choice of musical intervals. Inclinations for choosing specific intervals may partly be biologically determined; it is at least established that the fifth and the octave seem to be used in all cultures (Nettl, 2000). Preferences obviously also have a cultural history; they vary from subculture to subculture. These biologically and culturally determined meanings may be experienced by the client and therapist as "natural" or inevitable; some intervals are pleasant, some are interesting, and others may be strange or anxiety-provoking. Part of the music therapy process may in fact be that such preferences and ideas change and develop over time. There is hardly then a free space given for construction of meaning, but the agents are free to use the meaning game to reconstruct meanings. In this reconstruction words, movements, and sounds are more than likely to interact and interpret each other.

In order to understand meaning games it is therefore important to include the *time* aspect; a game develops in time and is linked to other games and other times. A narrative perspective is warranted.

THE NARRATIVE TURN

Meanings, understood as relationships constituted by social agents interacting in cultural contexts, are closely related to *narratives,* that is, to human time organized in "stories." The notion of narrative that then is of relevance is not only the clear-cut story written or told by an individual author, but also open-ended "inhabited and enacted stories." The perspective taken is that human life is participation in an endless human conversation involving the constant reworking of stories and dramas. Cultural psychologist Jerome

Bruner formulates the social, enacted and performative character of narrative in this way:

> when we enter human life, it is as if we walk on stage into a play whose enactment is already in progress – a play whose somewhat open plot determines what parts we may play and toward what denouements we may be heading (Bruner, 1990, p. 34).

This statement, taken from Bruner's book *Acts of Meaning*, is part of a general argument on the crucial role of narrative in human development. As McLeod (1997) argues, one may speak of an interdisciplinary narrative turn since the 1960s and 1970s, and especially since the 1980s. Scholars in disciplines such as philosophy, linguistics, psychology, and other social sciences, have challenged the decline of narrative knowing that has followed the scientific revolution of modern societies. While the value of science is not necessarily at stake, its inclinations to invade increasingly broader areas of life and to devaluate other forms of knowledge may be. The advocates of the narrative turn suggest that communication through telling stories is not just a task for parents, actors, and indigenous people of illiterate societies, but is a basic human activity. An argument in line with such a contention has been developed by the French philosopher Paul Ricoeur (1983/1984, 1984/1985, 1985/1988), who in his seminal work *Time and Narrative* has promoted that human existence – linked as it is to time conceived as past, present, and future – best is understood in a narrative perspective.

The narrative turn may clearly contribute to a culture-centered understanding of music therapy. It provides us with one approach to the study of how the individual and the collective levels of culture link:

> It begins to be clear why narrative is such a natural vehicle for folk psychology. It deals ... with the stuff of human action and human intentionality. It mediates between the canonical world of culture and the more idiosyncratic world of beliefs, desires, and hopes (Bruner, 1990, p. 52).

With good reason then there has been a heightened awareness and application of narrative perspectives in therapy. This has happened in psychotherapy, and even more so in family therapy. The basic idea in narrative therapy is that peoples' problems are constructed as performances of oppressive and dominant stories of knowledge. Therapy is then based upon a text analogy, in contrast to therapies based on analogies from, say, physical science, where problems are constructed as breakdowns or damage and solutions as correction and "reconditioning of the mechanism." Solutions to problems understood in a narrative perspective are constructed in terms of opening a space where the client, in interaction with the therapist, may be able to co-author and perform new and liberating stories (White & Epston, 1990). The term *co-authoring* is used to underline the *social* aspects of the therapy process and the co-constructed character of narration and meaning-making. The traditional concept of author may imply a self-sufficient self, while narrative therapy is linked to co-authoring as reciprocal sensitizing to changes in text-context relationships. A person will use many voices, depending on what situation he is in (McLeod, 1997).

The narrative perspective has not established itself with a very firm foothold in music therapy yet, perhaps because it has been interpreted narrowly as focused upon stories in language. It is worth noting though that some music therapists have been touching upon the issue through the discussion of music autobiography, music and metaphor, music and discourse, and music and identity, so some steps toward a narrative understanding of music therapy have been taken.[2] Chapter 6 in this book presents an individual case where I try to demonstrate that music therapists may do well in being informed by narrative therapies while also developing their own ways of working with meaning, narrative, and aesthetics; ways that take advantage of the polysemic and multimedia characteristics of processes of music therapy. The idea is not that music may tell a story in ways similar to what can be done with words, rather that what music *shows* may be understood in a narrative or proto-narrative context. We are talking about enacted open-ended and inhabited stories with aesthetic qualities.

THE AESTHETIC DIMENSION

Conventional aesthetic judgments do not necessarily come into practice in therapy, which indicates that such judgments are not objective or universal in the first place, but are positioned and situated. While music therapists are ready to except non-conventional music and to work with clients with minimal musical skills and competency, this is not to say that aesthetic judgments do not count in the therapy process. Rather I contend that the aesthetic constitutes an important dimension in the meaning-making and narratives of music therapy practice. My experience as a clinician and music therapy researcher is that it is more the rule than the exception that clients make comments on topics related to taste and value. The comments made may vary in many ways. Some of them are straightforward and simple comments on the music as heard: "This was nice." "That was kind of strange." Other comments are more elaborated, and may focus more directly upon the client's experience: "When I played freely on the bass, and you read that poem, then I found that feeling of freedom, that feeling I'm searching for but never know where I'll find." "When I listen to that kind of music, with this interplay of tones high up on the piano, something inside me grows effervescent. It's like when I went to high school and knew I had done well on a test." Such comments are often conveyed with sincerity and intensity, suggesting that the issue of aesthetics deserves serious attention in music therapy theory.

The words "aesthetic" and "aesthetics" tend to take on several meanings. "Aesthetic" as an adjective is used in the vernacular, by more and more people since questions of taste and value have become an increasingly important part of late modern societies (Nielsen, 1996). The noun "aesthetics" usually belongs to the discourse of art and philosophy. In this discourse aesthetics may refer to questions and theories on a) the nature and meaning of art, b) beauty and the sublime, c) taste and value, and d) sensory experience coupled with feeling. The last meaning seems to be derived from the meaning of the ancient Greek word *aisthetikos* (of sense perception).

Since music in various ways is linked to art, beauty, taste, and sensation, one should expect aesthetics to be an important part of the music therapy discourse. That is hardly the case. One could read textbooks on music therapy and hardly come across the word aesthetics. Frequency of the use of a word is of course a bad measure for reflexivity, but it is nonetheless striking that aesthetics has been so little discussed within the discipline.[3] Ken Aigen (1995a) suggests that in the United States aesthetics has been neglected within music therapy because the music therapists have tried to achieve recognition through quantitative research informed by a positivistic theory of knowledge. Within this framework music therapy has been described as an objective science, and music as a sound stimulus. Aesthetic aspects of the music therapy process have then been regarded subjective and therefore not of any major value to this perspective on music therapy. This explanation is probably less valid for some European music therapy traditions, where positivism has not been as dominating. A possible hypothesis, which I will elaborate on later in the chapter, is that some music therapy communities have defined themselves as countercultures with anti-elitist values, and that this has fueled a refusal of aesthetic theories, which have been conceived of as carriers of exclusive values.

Whatever the reason for lack of discussion of the aesthetic dimension, I propose that aesthetic aspects are never nonexistent or nonrelevant in music therapy. To think of *some* music therapy practices as aesthetic and *others* as not is, in my opinion, confused and confusing. I propose that the issue is rather *in which ways* a music therapy process is aesthetic, and how this is *experienced and framed* by the client and therapist. I will briefly illustrate this by giving some concrete examples, focusing upon the activities of a) *preparing the arena*, b) *playing the game*, and c) *framing the game.*

Preparing the arena: Already when preparing the physical environment the music therapist makes many choices that may be understood as aesthetic. The physical environment is an important context for the moods and communications developed in therapy, and provides conditions for the activities, roles, and relationships of the music therapy process. Is the therapist preparing for contemplation by providing chairs or mats as the focal point in the room? Is the room packed with instruments, or is there space for dance and movement? What kind of musical genres and activities do the choice and arrangement of instruments suggest? How well suited is the room for making changes in activities and roles? These choices are clinical, but they have aesthetic dimensions to them. Activities made possible by the arrangement of the room are linked to traditions of value and aesthetic judgment. This is also obvious when other aspects of preparing the arena is mentioned, such as choice of colors and lighting, choice of furniture and room decor, etc. For the client it may make a difference whether the arena reflects the culture of an institution, or also the therapist's personal preferences. How the arena is prepared then may be important, but before that there is of course the issue of *which arena.* Culture-centered approaches, in paying attention to the client's relationships to local context, may at times depart from what has been considered typical and conventional choices within modern therapy practices. Preparing the arena may mean to choose *another* arena than the typical music therapy room in a clinic. Arenas such as a community music school, a school-yard, or a local club may have different possibilities to offer, and could be considered.

Playing the game: The discussion of meaning games above suggest that music interaction should be seen in relation to words and language, movements and other activities, through which there is a continuous negotiation on values and meanings. While for instance *improvising* with the client the therapist may use *clinical techniques*, such as those described by Bruscia (1987). Since such techniques do not exist in a cultural vacuum, the music-making coming out of this will also be linked to traditions of music-making in the society at large. What grooves, chords, scales, and registers do the therapist tend to use? Are styles of phrasing and the sound (timbre) linked to certain musical genres? What may different instruments signify as to cultural and aesthetic values; how does a client relate to, for instance, a grand piano versus an electric guitar, or an African drum versus a European recorder? It is implausible to assume that instruments and ways of playing are culture-free. Rather, they are carriers of certain cultural values, even when free improvisation and spontaneous expression is stressed.[4]

Framing the game: While music and other modes of expression interact and are therefore not separated clearly in the description above, it is still helpful to distinguish between "playing the meaning game" and "framing the game." There is usually a meta-level involved in human communication, as when gestures and body-language modify the meaning of a word. When this meta-level of communication in a music therapy session involves a *time-shift*, reflecting back on what just happened, I suggest we may use the term "framing the game." This is an important aspect of a therapy session. The music made in therapy is always framed in some way or another, through use of body-language (smiles, grimaces, posture, etc.), through verbal discussions, and sometimes through use of other media.[5] What happens when an experience, a phenomenon, or an object is framed or reframed is that new aspects and values may be discovered. Provided one is open for it, a process of reflection upon and redefinition of one's own values and perspectives may start. In music therapy one could say that psychological processing and aesthetic framing become reciprocal and dependent upon each other.

The three types of activities that I have described above interact in different ways. For instance, it is easy to see that preparing the arena is related to both playing and framing; it provides conditions for both. What I hope to have demonstrated is that the aesthetic dimension is not something that a music therapist easily can get beyond. Meaning, narrative, and issues of taste and value are closely linked together. While the general ethics of therapy implies that therapists should respect clients and their world, it is not my point that aesthetic preferences necessarily should be congruent. Such an ideal would be unattainable, and it may well be that a clash in values at times may *open* a space for communication instead of closing it. This depends upon the needs and problems of the client and upon the relationship between the client and therapist. What is asked for here, I think, is not a total match of values, but rather an ability to communicate about them.

The arguments above are based on the theoretical premise that it is meaningful to talk about the aesthetic dimension as something *universal and local* at the same time. The universal aspects are linked to human phylogeny; humans are biologically prepared for aesthetic sensitivity (Dissanayake, 1992/1995, 2000a, 2000b, 2001), and it is not possible to establish a music therapy practice and imagine that clients do not care about the qualities and values expressed in the sounds produced. The local aspects are linked to the inevitable condition that judgments are situated and linked to specified cultural histories (Geertz, 1973/1993, 1983). What is strong and beautiful for one person is noisy and intolerable for another. Judgments as these depend on personal histories, but also relate to broader contexts and discourses about music and art. Some discourses are privileged and dominating in each historical epoch, and in examining the role of aesthetics in contemporary music therapy a brief excursion to the history of the philosophical discourse on aesthetics therefore may be illuminating.

ART AND VALUES

Although many of the questions that we today relate to aesthetics were discussed in ancient Greece and before that, the word "aesthetics" was not used in philosophy before being introduced by Alexander G. Baumgarten in the eighteenth century. In *Aesthetica,* published in 1750, Baumgarten used this concept in his theory on beauty and sensory perception. As a rationalist philosopher Baumgarten argued that aesthetics should be able to explain beauty as a product of perfection (Hammer, 1995, p. 21). Baumgarten may thus be said to have introduced aesthetics as a discipline, but Immanuel Kant was probably the philosopher who contributed most to the European understanding of the concept, through his "third critique": *The Critique of the Judgment of Taste* (1790/1951).

Kant searched for a third approach in between a dogmatic rationalism and a skeptical empiricism, and was therefore explicitly critical of Baumgarten, who he thought made a fallacy of reduction by trying to explain aesthetics as qualities in the object. This criticism was related to the insights Kant had developed in his two previous critiques, where he had stressed the subject's active participation in the creation of all knowledge, including perception. The reality as such, "Das Ding an Sich," will never be known. We know the world only through our senses and through a priori knowledge used by the subject when making sense out of the sense data. This, Kant argued, is so for aesthetic experiences also. As can be seen, Kant stressed the role of the *subject* when discussing aesthetics. Aesthetics cannot be based on a rationalistic theory on qualities in the object. Kant was not arguing for a solipsistic theory of aesthetics, however. People *communicate* on aesthetic judgments. The fact that such communication is even possible Kant took as an argument for the view that judgments on taste have a general validity, provided they are based upon a culture that has developed some kind of harmony in the practice of making judgments of taste (Hammer, 1995, p. 26). Kant therefore stressed inter-subjectivity and what we could call "a democracy of taste" in a way that would be completely unthinkable for a rationalist like Baumgarten.

This brief, and indeed very incomplete, presentation of Kant's ideas helps us to see that since the beginning of a philosophical discourse on aesthetics, the discussions have been related to some of the most complex and important questions in philosophy. The way I have presented Kant may make him sound quite "contemporary," or at least compatible, with many current thinkers in aesthetics. This may reveal the degree of influence of Kant's ideas. It is worth noting though that some of his ideas have also been among the most controversial in twentieth-century aesthetics, one of them being his notion of *aesthetic disinterestedness:* the idea that a degree of detachment from or non-identification with the art object or performance is necessary in order to secure judgments made on aesthetic criteria. Also, Kant's influence on German idealism in the nineteenth century, with romanticism as the main aesthetic theory, has been under much debate. The focus upon the *genius* that grew out of romanticism, and which to some degree still colors the discourse of aesthetics, found support in Kant's third critique (1790/1951, §§ 46-50), and has been challenged more than once.

The development of aesthetics as a discipline in the nineteenth century may also be seen in relation to the development of capitalism, which enabled *art* to establish itself as an autonomous institution in the society. Aesthetic theory often then dealt with the so-called high arts only, and in the 1830s Gautier introduced the expression "l'art pour l'art" suggesting that art does not need to serve social or other interests but could be valued as a value in itself, and that this is the main value of art. It may be said that this "high-art" conception represents elitist and essentialist values and legitimates a practice of expulsion, as is evident also in the way these values have been part of the twentieth century discourse on aesthetics. Arnold Schönberg once expressed:

> If it is art it is not for all, and if it is for all, it is not art (Schönberg, in Scott, 2000, p. 3).

Some, especially late twentieth century scholars within popular music and ethnomusicology, would advocate that this phrase is a very illuminating example showing that arts and the aesthetic theories in Western societies have become too linked to elitist and exclusive values to be of any value for the understanding of everyday practices. Many scholars and lay commentators have come to the conclusion that the discourse of aesthetics is a discourse of power; good taste is a privilege of the privileged classes. Some propose then that it is not even relevant to use aesthetic theory when discussing music used in everyday life situations, such as in therapy and in community rites. There seems to be a split in values between high-art traditions and some alternative traditions of art and music-making. Are the arts for the happy few or for everybody? Is art something anybody can produce and use, or is production reserved for geniuses and real understanding for a cultivated minority? Is art about individuality or about community? Table 1 gives an overview of some differences in perspective.

Table 1: Exemplification of polarization of values in aesthetic discourse.

"High-art" values:	"Alternative" values:
Art is autonomous; it belongs to another "sphere" than everyday life.	Art is heteronomous; it is closely related to our everyday experiences.
Art has a perfect or at least balanced form.	Spontaneous elements, even if rudimentary in form, are most valuable.
Art is technically advanced, which necessitates high levels of competency in the creator, the performer, and the receiver.	Personal expression is more important than technical proficiency. Expectations to levels of competency should be adjusted to the resources and qualifications of each person.
Art is connected to individuality; it is created by individuals and to be received by individuals in a state of contemplation.	Art is a social phenomenon; it is interaction, communication, and community.
Art is for the happy few.	Art is for everybody.

As will be evident from the continuation of my argument, I find it important to transcend this polarization of aesthetic discourse. Also, it is important to distinguish between the issue of "high art" as a social institution and the issue of art genres. Music that traditionally has been linked to high art has been used and may be used in a multitude of ways.

I will not go into a specification of milieus in which the alternative values listed above have been influential, but there are several such milieus. As far as I can see, these alternative values have been central also in much of the music therapy discourse. I will therefore dwell a little with the situation in my own country, as an example of how such an intra-disciplinary discourse is linked to society and history:

To some degree Norwegian music therapy, especially in the founding years, constituted itself as a counterculture to high art. In the 1970s, the dawn of modern music therapy in Norway, this became part of the legitimization of the new discipline and was linked to changes in the national politics of culture. Up to this point in Norwegian history, the government support of arts mainly had been related to the high arts of elitist institutions in the main cities, such as the major theaters and the symphony orchestras. In the seventies there was a shift in the political climate, and an effervescent debate on cultural politics developed. The result of this debate was that the government politics changed, giving more support to popular and folk-arts activities. It was argued that the value of arts was not only related to the quality of products produced by professionals, but also to people's possibility of *activity and participation*. This should be accessible to everybody. Gender, ethnicity, social class, age, or personal resources should not intervene on a person's right to participate, and neither should geographical location. Rights to arts and aesthetic experiences should be given to everybody, whether they lived in a city or in a remote valley. When music therapy in this country got a foothold in the same decade, the pioneers focused upon the cultural rights of handicapped people (Ruud, 1987/1990). I will argue then that music therapy in this epoch in this country could be described as a more or less politically correct *anti-elitist counterculture*.

Whether or not one identifies oneself with the counterculture values described above, I think it is beyond doubt that these values helped establishing music therapy in Norway, and also that they to a large degree helped music therapists to work actively for the development of more inclusive values in the Norwegian society, for instance in music education (Stige, 1995). I myself have identified with counterculture values, and I find it relevant to argue that to some degree music therapists have an obligation to do so, at least in the general sense of being critical to power and privilege. This is different, though, from giving a single set of countercultural values essential and ahistoric status. In relation to the issue of aesthetics, such a self-conception as counterculture in the long run will corroborate instead of challenge the split between high arts and the so-called "low" arts. Counterculture alternative values are then alternative by defining themselves in relation to the tradition of high art. This may in fact *contribute* to the construction of Western high art as fundamental, while this is of course only one very specific tradition of art, quite dissimilar from traditions in other cultures and other times. A different and probably more fruitful approach then would be to sensitize oneself to other traditions of art, and to try and *develop* aesthetic theory in *inclusive* directions instead of just to drop the term because of high-art connotations.

Such supplementary traditions of art exist not only in history and in pre-literate cultures, they exist in the middle of any late modern society, as folk arts and popular culture. While high art has its own separate institutions, folk art is everywhere, in small rural communities and in big cities, in backyards and in the streets. Folk art is integrated into almost every aspect of daily life. It is made by ordinary people for other ordinary people, often in the service of making an occasion less ordinary. Folk art is and has been used to amuse children, court lovers, and honor ancestors, and as such it is a manifestation of the dreams and fears people have, a device for relating to the physical, social, and spiritual worlds (Dissanayake, 1992/1995). Sociologists of culture have shown that popular music often is used in much the same way (DeNora, 2000), and that high-art music is more than art for art's sake; it is for the sake of distinction, for the sake of contemplation, or, for instance, for the sake of contributing to the intensity of a scene in a movie. As all art is related to human activities, all art to some degree is applied art. Meaning, function, and value are related to context.

SCHIZOPHONIA AND THE THERAPY MUSIC MARKET

With a deconstruction of the dichotomy between high art and other forms of art, one may ask if music therapy itself is an art form. Clive Robbins – a major pioneer of modern improvisational music therapy – suggests this:

> When Paul Nordoff and I published *Creative Music Therapy* [1977] … we were quite clear as to our intentions in making excerpted recordings of clinical sessions publicly available. We knew without doubt that the studies of Edward, Anna, and Logan would, in the context of the book, demonstrate musical and clinical techniques and processes intrinsic to an essentially creative approach to music therapy. But we also had broader cultural purposes in mind. We wanted to make the depth of the connection between the human self and music more livingly evident. We wanted to highlight the inherent significance of music itself, and music's intimate bearing on the drama of the human condition, in bold chiaroscuro. We felt the need to offset as much as possible the rather myopic and passive perception of music then prevalent in music therapy academia, where music was seen merely as some kind of commodity having behavioral/psychological effects. For us, it was important to perceive music therapy as a new and historically significant creative art, and for music therapists to recognize themselves as artists with the potential of mediating the art of spontaneous musical creation to incept and support creative healing processes in their clients (Robbins, 1998).

Nordoff and Robbins's ambition is probably best understood in the context of the prevailing music therapy traditions of that time. The behaviorist tradition of music therapy neglected the aesthetic aspects of music, focusing on music as a sound stimulus. Also, Nordoff and Robbins disagreed with the advocates of anthroposophy who suggested that only high-art composers like Mozart had created music with any value for therapy. In contrast, Nordoff and Robbins took the child's own sounds and expressions as the departure point for an interactive and improvisational approach to music therapy.

This century has seen the birth of many new art forms: photography, film, video and computer art. The number of art forms then, hardly is fixed;

new forms will be born and others will die, and why not music therapy as a new art form? Listening to the recordings of Nordoff and Robbins's work, and to the intriguing intensity of the improvisations, one may often feel that the best description is: "This is art." There would undeniably also be some problems connected to such a suggestion, however. The idea of music therapy as art could, for instance, restrict the therapists' use of music, if they are led to feel that they have artistic obligations to create *new and interesting* music. Such music is sometimes helpful for the music therapy process, but not always. Alan Turry, codirector of the Nordoff-Robbins Center at New York University, touches upon this from another perspective:

> There is also the danger that the therapist will make music "sound good" for either the client or an outside observer, whether that be a supervisor, colleague, or student. There is a part of the improvising therapist similar to that of a performer that wants to be heard and acknowledged. These needs are natural but must be brought to awareness in order for the therapist not to be unconsciously influenced by them, as they can detract from one's focus on the client (Turry, 1998, p. 181).

There is a difference between the creative process and its products, and this difference is paramount in music therapy.[6] If we define music therapy as an art form we could of course try to advocate the value of process above product. I believe, though, that a focus upon music therapy as art would increase the pressure to "sound good," also because art in modern capitalistic societies usually is related to competition in a market. I will explicate this, using the concept of *schizophonia*, a term coined by Canadian composer Murray Schafer in 1969 and later used by Steven Feld (1994b, 1996) in the discussion of *World Music*.

World Music was a concept originally used by scholars, especially by American ethnomusicologist, to describe music traditions in the (usually non-Western) cultures that they studied. From 1986-87 the music industry started to use "World Music" as a label to stimulate the promotion of music from non-Western cultures, which had become increasingly popular among music record buyers both in "authentic" versions of traditional music and as fused versions of traditional music and modern Western popular music. The music industry took advantage of this, and traditional music – much of it originally an inseparable part of indigenous rituals – has been promoted as artistic products under the new label of World Music. Using the term coined by Schafer, the ethnomusicologist Steven Feld (1994b, 1996) describes this situation as "schizophonia": musics have been de-connected from their original contexts of use and produced for consumption in other contexts.

Could the idea of music therapy as an art form stimulate a similar development within music therapy? Could we expect that music originally created in the context of therapy be produced on records, to be listened to "for its own value"? In other words, could we in some years expect to find *Therapy Music* as well as *World Music* as a label in the music stores? This idea might seem a bit farfetched at the moment, but several music therapists, many of them working in the Nordoff-Robbins tradition, have started to argue that the music created in therapy has an "aesthetic value in itself," see for instance Gary Ansdell (1995) and Colin Lee (1996). Both Ansdell and Lee have produced (very interesting) books with accompanying CDs, and suggest that the music on these CDs has value, not only as documentation of therapy, but also as "music in itself." I am not trying to argue that this music does not have value in itself, but would like to elaborate a little on what consequences might be the result of schizophonia in music therapy. If music therapists start to detach music from its context, stressing the value of it as works of art to be listened to, *Therapy Music* in the music stores is just the next step. This is, as far as I know, not Ansdell and Lee's vision. But I want to stress this aspect to illuminate that it is not unproblematic to argue for music therapy as an art form, or for the value of the music-therapy music in itself. One aspect of this is the fact that capitalistic societies tend to transform all values into economical value.

When Steven Feld (1994b, 1996) uses the word *schizophonia* for music detached from its social and cultural context and produced for consumption in other contexts, he also stresses the fact that this process usually is more beneficial for the music industry than for the subjects in the original context. If this is so, similar problems might be expected related to the "forthcoming" label Therapy Music. The listener will probably not be the loser. He can choose for himself whether he wants to listen with heartfelt sincerity or with ironic distance to authentic autistic music or to the schizophonia of schizophrenia. The problem is, rather, connected to the possibility that music therapists start to choose clients that are musically interesting, to strengthen their chances in the Therapy Music market. The clients, maybe both those that will be chosen and those that will not be, are more likely to lose freedom and possibilities.

Therapy Music, as a possible scenario for the future of interactive improvisational music therapy, is already a fact within several traditions of *receptive* music therapy. In any music store you might find New Age records with suggested effect on almost any condition. Agnus Dei is promoted as music to soothe your soul, not as music to praise the Lord, and under the label "Musik Rezept" you might find "Musik zum Helfen & Heilen"; classical music selected after "music therapy principles" by Prof. Dr. Herman Rauhe. What is next? Could we in the future expect to find electronic catalogues presenting the "hottest" music therapists available, with music examples to stimulate the interest, in similar veins as we today may buy "The Rough Guide" to "The Music of Kenya and Tanzania"?

These comments are not written in the belief that music therapy could or should be completely deconnected from the market. While my own background is a national culture where welfare services so far mostly have been decommodified, that is, provided by the authorities to everybody for free, I realize that in most countries this is not the situation. I acknowledge of course that music therapy services in many countries are operating on a market. The question is, what does the music therapist sell: the health benefits or the musical products? In both cases the practice of music therapy and therapeutic process will be affected. A focus upon therapeutic outcome tends to drive therapy in the direction of short-term contracts and structured procedures. A focus upon the aesthetic qualities of music therapy as outcome may affect the therapeutic processes in some other ways. We probably do not know exactly *how* yet, but this issue is ethically important and relates to the future identity of the profession.

- THESE PEOPLE JUST CANNOT SING TOGETHER

Earlier in the chapter I argued that the notion of art may be detached from a Western high-art connotation, that is, it may be linked to several traditions, which then constitutes a new challenge for aesthetic theory. Several art forms and traditions exist, and some of these connect the arts much more directly to *everyday experience*. The relevance of everyday experience for a theory of aesthetics has been advocated by Ken Aigen (1995a), who presents an interesting discussion of aesthetics in music therapy based upon John Dewey's work. In *Art as Experience* (1934/1980) John Dewey argued that aesthetics is closely related to everyday experiences. Dewey's argument was based upon a criticism of the modern society and its splitting of means and ends. An example might be people's relationship to their jobs; many jobs have such a character that people do not find meaning in the job itself, it is just a means to earn the needed amount of money to be able to survive and live. For Dewey the importance of the aesthetic experience was related to this criticism, since he considered one of the main characteristics of the aesthetic experience to be that means and ends merge. A means that is its own end he named a *medium*. A simple example could be given:

> Dewey observes that there are two kinds of means: those that are external to what is accomplished and those that are incorporated in the

outcome. When we travel just to get to a desired location our trip is a mere means that we could just as well do without; alternatively, when we travel for the pleasure inherent in the experience, our trip becomes a *medium* for aesthetic enjoyment. In this latter example, it does not make sense to say that we would just as well do without the trip in accomplishing our goal because our goal *is* the trip. When we characterize something as a medium it is because we observe a certain identity or unity of means with ends and this, to Dewey is a defining characteristic of aesthetic value (Aigen, 1995a, pp. 238-239).

This distinction Aigen finds relevant for music therapy, and he argues that music in music therapy never should be reduced to a means, but should be a *medium* for interpersonal, emotional and aesthetic experiences. This argument I find plausible, and the suggestion that aesthetics is connected to everyday experience as well as to art seems relevant for music therapy. A closer look, however, reveals that Aigen (with Dewey) has not given a very radical critique of the nineteenth century's essentialist aesthetics. Some of the aesthetic ideals and norms – such as unity, wholeness, and completion – have not changed, and are presented as essential and universal. An example from Aigen's text should illustrate:

> For Dewey, the aesthetic is that quality of existence that provides unity, completion and wholeness to our experience. … Some of our experience is fractured, not integrated into meaningful units, and begins and ends in arbitrary places: this is an unaesthetic experience (Aigen, 1995a, pp. 239-240).

It may be advocated that the interest in *forming* may be part of humankind's biological preparedness for aesthetic practices (Dissanayake, 1992/1995). It is even possible that there are "naturalistic criteria" for aesthetic quality, and that these include elements of form, such as accessibility coupled with strikingness (Dissanayake, 2000b, p. 209). Nevertheless I consider it problematic to develop general criteria linked to *form* as tools for distinction between aesthetic and unaesthetic experiences. What is forming for one person is deforming for another. What is unity, completion, and wholeness and what is fractured or arbitrary are to a large degree situated judgments. Many early critiques of Dostoevsky's novels, for instance, suggested that they were disorganized since they did not conform to well-established European standards of unity and completion in writing. Later critics, many of then fueled by Bakhtin's (1929/1984) groundbreaking study of Dostoevsky's poetics, have suggested that this deviation from the established standards was a major contribution and that the earlier critics had been blinded by a "monologic"

European tradition that had made them unable to see the value of the dialogic diversity inherent in Dostoevsky's form. A few other examples should
illuminate the situated character of aesthetic judgment:

Many artists in the twentieth century have specifically rebelled against
the well-established values stressing unity, wholeness, and completion in
Western art; values they have felt would inhibit their creativity. Instead some
of these artists cultivated fragmentation, as Picasso did in some of his works.
In many of his pictures fragmentation is a major style element; bodies and
bodyparts are spread out on the canvas. While Picasso today certainly is part
of the canon of painters, many contemporaries struggled with his art and
criticized it because of its fragmentation and "unnatural forms." Carl Jung
for instance, a psychoanalyst taking great interest in the arts, thought that
these pictures showed that Picasso had a psychotic disposition in his personality (Mørstad, 1998).

Picasso's art is an example among several others from the same period
of time, and could hardly be understood through diagnostic concepts. The
diverse arts of the twentieth century have made it extremely clear that art
might be related to many and very different sets of values. Wholeness and
completion could hardly be said to be universal or general values. Many
works of arts cultivate fragmentation; they are open-ended and post-
conventional. This might also be true for modern reinterpretations of classical works in music. A famous example is Glenn Gould's 1965 recording of
Mozart's Sonata No. 11 in A-major (K 331), where he plays some of the
variations of the first movement in an extremely slow tempo. The elements
of the melody are isolated and the continuity of the theme deliberately un-
dermined so that the whole piece almost falls apart, which of course frus-
trates some listeners and delights others.

Another clear example illuminating the problems with defining general
or universal criteria of form is given by Steven Feld (1994a) in his discussion of the Kaluli people of New Guinea and their "Lift-up-over-Sounding,"
which could be described as free and – by Western standards – wry polyphony. Kaluli standards on song, music and conversation are quite different
from those valued in the Western world. Unison forms and turn-taking are
usually avoided, while their "Lift-up-over-Sounding" creates a complex *web*
of sounds; there are layers on layers of patterns each starting at what for an
outside observer may seem to be random points. Feld thinks these aesthetic
preferences reflect both the natural context the Kaluli people live in (the
rainforest and its complex web of sounds) and the social structure of the
Kaluli communities (stressing spontaneity and participation more than hierarchic structures). Feld continues by reflecting upon the fact that in Western
ears "Lift-up-over-Sounding" very often is interpreted as some kind of defi-

cit, that is, as lack of structure and unity. He illustrates this by quoting one of the missionaries in the area:

> Well, I'll tell you one thing we've noticed over the years; these peo-
> ple just cannot sing together. Even when we count before singing a
> hymn, they are all off in their own direction after a few words ...
> They just can't sing together, even brothers and sisters can't ... I
> reckon they'll keep the tune jolly well, [but] never in the same place
> at the right time (Feld, 1994a, pp. 133-134)!

Aigen's (1995a) attempt of freeing the aesthetic discourse in music therapy from that of high art, by relating aesthetics to everyday experiences, may lose some of its "emancipatory potential" by not clarifying that descriptions of aesthetic qualities are always related to a specific set of values that will not be shared by every person in every context. I am of course not suggest-ing that beauty and form are irrelevant in music therapy, but if one neglects the *situated character* of any discourse on aesthetics, statements about form may close the door for other perspectives and thus have repressive functions, even when the intentions are the best. To develop a general aesthetics of music therapy seems not to be a good idea, be it elitist aesthetics, countercul-ture aesthetics, everyday aesthetics, or whatever. Any general aesthetics will reproduce some values and repress others. A more fruitful strategy could be to acknowledge a diversity of situated aesthetics and to examine music ther-apy as a set of aesthetic practices in relation to other aesthetic practices in a society.

A PLURALITY OF POLYPHONIC PRACTICES

"Anything goes" or "laissez faire aesthetics" is no alternative to "aesthetic essentialism" based upon abstract and general statements about music, art, and aesthetic value. If we do not take music and musicking seriously we do not take the client seriously either. The aesthetic aspects of the music ther-apy process *are* important, and one of the major challenges for a music therapist is to find his way between the Scylla of aesthetic essentialism and the Charybdis of total relativism.[7] Some of the prevailing music therapy literature is probably closer to the essentialist position, for instance in mak-ing general statements on the value of form, wholeness, and unity. The brief look taken above at the diversity of art forms in the world suggests that such positions are hard to defend as viable perspectives on the aesthetics of art. As statements on aesthetics in music therapy a defense in fact *could* be put up, since it may be argued that many clients – compared to other people of their culture – struggle with the experience of form, wholeness, and unity. Quite often these issues then serve as relevant clinical goals. Quite often is not the same as always, though, and this difference makes a difference for the theory and practice of music therapy. Sometimes the therapist needs to establish value in fragmentation, in "ugly" but expressive sounds, and in fuzzy sounds of silence. To promote an essentialist defense for alternative values would of course not help much, however.

The development in contemporary society suggests that the difference between high art and other forms of art is reduced; at least the line between them is less clear than it used to be. Both within cultural anthropology and within popular and folk music studies, established aesthetic conceptions have been challenged for quite a long time now. One has realized that to give general statements on aesthetic qualities in music is a doubtful case and that such statements are connected to cultural values and life forms. The concept of *meaning games,* outlined in the beginning of this chapter, suggests that description of form and syntax is one thing, meaning and aesthetic value another. The value and meaning of music is not a reflection of the structure of the object. Rather, meanings (several are usually possible) are relationships between objects ("texts") and contexts. One could then go beyond the conundrum of immanent meaning versus attributed meaning. To realize that meaning may not transcend or escape cultural and contextual mediation is not the same as suggesting that the actual musical components and qualities of the improvisation are insignificant. They are significant in context.

Meaning and value does not belong to the level of syntax alone but involves the level of pragmatics. It would still be wrong to adopt the position that the level of syntax is unimportant or irrelevant. Not all is left for free construction; meanings may be conditioned both by human nature and cultural history. Colwyn Trevarthen suggests, for instance, that based in the biology of the human being there is some kind of universal experience of tempo and phrasing, and that this is related to mood (Trevarthen, 1997, p. 65). In the cultural vein, Linda Phyllis Austern (2000) argues that expressions of melancholy in music have shown a remarkable degree of consistency through history from the songs of the seventeenth century composer Monteverdi to the rock ballads of The Smashing Pumpkins. As Penelope Gouk summarizes the argument: "Certain kinds of melodic and rhythmic structure are used to express emotional states which are recognized and shared by the audience as well as composers themselves. Although this musical language seems inherently 'natural' in the way it mirrors our innermost feelings, it is nevertheless a highly sophisticated cultural artefact which has been developed and refined over centuries. ... Both the music itself and the emotions it arouses are culturally negotiated as well as being mutually inter-dependent on each other"(Gouk, 2000, p. 13).

This suggests a *relative relativism* in the study of meaning and aesthetic value. Concrete contexts must be explored, but the *comparison* of contexts is also of interest. To clarify and to relate this discussion more specifically to the aesthetic aspects, I will explicate the notion of *aesthetic practice*, which has been used with inspiration from Wittgenstein's philosophy.[8] Wittgenstein himself did not use the word "practice" much; he would rather speak of activities, language games and forms of life. "Aesthetic practice" has been used as a concept by Kjell S. Johannesen (1994) and other interpreters of Wittgenstein's work, however, and the term will be used here in order to illuminate how aesthetics is situated as practices in historic and cultural contexts. Again Wittgenstein's concept of *language games,* as outlined earlier in this chapter, is a departing point. Within aesthetics Wittgenstein's theory on meaning has been a foundation for several scholars. Johannesen suggests that Wittgenstein's influence on modern philosophical aesthetics could be subsumed in the following statements: 1) There is a radical indeterminacy of aesthetic concepts; 2) There is a logical plurality of critical discourse (and this may be noticed at two levels: recognition of the logical variety of critical *statements* and recognition of the plurality of critical *frameworks*); 3) There is an indispensable cultural historicity of all art and art appreciation (Johannesen, 1994, p. 218).

To use Wittgenstein as a foundation for a systematic theory on aesthetics is probably to misinterpret his intentions. In *Philosophical Investigations* Wittgenstein repeatedly insists that he is not developing a theory. Instead he gives examples and case studies, and in this way reminds us that everything could be different.[9] The notion of aesthetic practice, which is a sensitizing term more than an exact one, suggests that aesthetic judgments are made in communities, real or virtual, where discourses on meaning and values are in reciprocal relationships with the aesthetic activities themselves as well as with other social and practical activities of those communities. The concept thus probably does not help us to answer too many of our general questions related to aesthetics in music therapy. It could rather help us in developing better questions, and in avoiding unhelpful answers. For instance we are guided to modify our ambitions as to the possibility of developing general theories on meaning and aesthetic quality. *Active meaning-making in con-texts* gain importance, which is one of the reasons why I stress ethnographic perspectives and participatory action research in Part IV of this book, where culture-centered research approaches to music therapy are discussed.

The arguments in this chapter may obviously be read as being in favor of acknowledging the value of a plurality of traditions rather than constructing a linear hierarchy, and the *situated character* of meaning-making and aesthetical judgments has been explored in several angles. Two caveats must be voiced: these arguments do not imply that the qualities of an aesthetic object are unimportant, neither do they imply that the individual level of experience and judgment could be reduced to that of culture and context.

Wittgenstein's later philosophy could be interpreted as a warning against thinking of meaning and aesthetic value as something pregiven or immanent in objects and only moderately moderated by context. The term language game suggests that in relation to meaning and aesthetic value the object does not "exist" independently of the context. For music therapy this does not mean that the object necessarily is a blank screen where client and therapists can project whatever is in their mind. Rather, there is a reciprocal constitution of mind and object. To suggest that agents of meaning games conceive meanings as situated relationships is not to suggest that the relata are insignificant. Meanings, as evolved in phylogeny and cultural history, may reside in the relata, but only a close examination of situations of use will show us whether "slab" is a name or an order, whether a fifth is a triumph, a trite convention, or an arbitrary accident, etc.

This means that to take interest in subcultures is only a necessary, not a sufficient, condition for respecting and acknowledging the cultural world of the client. This world is not only related to traditions and to the history of groups, it is also related to personal history. We therefore need a notion that may include this personal level of experience and expression. Borrowing a term that the literary theorist Mikhail Bakhtin (1929/1984) borrowed from musicology, I propose that *polyphony* may be such a term. Bakhtin, in a discussion of the poetics of Dostoevsky, suggests that one needs to understand the polyphonic character of this author's novels in order to value them properly. From the viewpoint of the traditional monologic canon of the European novel, Dostoevsky's world may seem chaotic and the construction of his novels some sort of conglomerate of disparate materials and incompatible principles for shaping them. Dostoevsky's world is a multivoiced world. The characters of his novels are allowed to voice their own worldviews without being reduced to the unity of a single world and a single consciousness, a phenomenon that is not only philosophical and psychological, but which clearly also affected Dostoevsky's artistic style; his material is heterogeneous and multistyled. I shall not go deep into the poetics of Dostoevsky and the theory of Bakhtin, but Bakhtin's thesis as to what is the major principle behind Dostoevsky's work bears direct relevance for the practice of music therapy: *the affirmation of someone else's consciousness.*

Affirmation of someone else's consciousness is a dialogic enterprise, and this phrase is probably not a bad description of what may be a central element in music therapy. If the consciousness and world experience of both client and therapist are acknowledged, it will be seen that the agents participate and interpret with differences in both starting points and viewpoints. This is why a concept of polyphony may be helpful for the description of music therapy as meaning games. There is not only diversity between aesthetic practices, but also *within* them. If we adopt this conception to music therapy, we can see the value of dialogues and therapeutic interactions in which diverse meanings and values are in action. It is then not a problem if client and therapist have different values and aesthetic preferences. It is in fact inevitable, and in many ways this also can make the interpersonal communication richer and more colorful. To be able to stimulate such polyphonic dialogues, by sharing one's own values and showing respect and interest for those of the client, thus must be an important element of the music therapist's competency.

There might be too much beauty in this contention; polyphonic dialogues are hard to establish and maintain open-ended since established power relations tend to turn them in monologic directions. Music therapy is of course not a context automatically free from such power relations, and polyphonic dialogues may be hard to establish and maintain also in this context. In going back to the discussion of narrative in therapy earlier in this chapter, we see how this links to the issue of opening up a space for different voices to be heard. Essential qualifications for a therapist in opening up possibilities for multivoiced interaction is then the capacity for listening, accepting, and understanding what is being voiced and the meanings of how it is voiced. This challenge is partly covered by terms therapists are well-accustomed with, such as the management of countertransference issues as discussed in the psychodynamic tradition. What needs to be reflected upon is how such issues go beyond intrapersonal and interpersonal processes in that they include the agents' relationships to the musics and cultural contexts they engage in.[10] Aesthetic values, which may be revealed through polyphonic dialogues, must therefore be kept open for critical examination. Reflexivity, the ability to position oneself in a cultural system, is called for.

NOTES

[1] This contention is not equivalent to suggesting that music may not be experienced in privacy. Due to modern technological inventions, such as minidisks and walkmans, music in privacy is quite attainable for many people, but even when a human is alone he is "dialogically" linked to other human beings. As discussed in Chapter 1, co-existence – included awareness of the *virtual other* – may be considered a basic mode of human existence (Bakhtin, 1929/1984; Østerberg, 1997).

[2] See for instance (Bruscia, 1998b; Frohne-Hagemann, 1998; Ruud, 1998; Ansdell, 1999; Bonde, 1999; Aldridge, 2000; Jungaberle et al., 2001; Stige, 2001; Kenny &

Stige, 2002).

[3] See for instance (Kenny, 1982, 1989; Amir, 1992; Aigen, 1995a; Ansdell, 1995; Lee, 1996; Lecourt, 1998; Ruud, 1998; Frohne-Hageman, 2001).

[4] It is, for instance, not probable that to try to detach music therapy improvisations from established *genres* of music automatically makes them more "authentic" or "expressive." To express yourself you need competence and knowledge, as clarified in Wittgenstein's (1953/1967) discussion of language and meaning (to learn a language is to learn a technique). To detach music from genres known by the client therefore might be to *reduce* his possibilities to express himself. Of course, to use a well-known genre and way of music-making could also function as resistance to the therapy process, just as intellectualization might be used in verbal therapy. This does not change the argument, however. Resistance is a frequent element in many forms of therapy, and should be dealt with according to the therapist's understanding of the client and the therapy process.

[5] Framing is a major part of any aesthetic practice. By framing an object or a phenomenon in a specific way, we "color" it and increase or diminish its value. Famous examples from the art scene are Duchamp's *Fontaine* and John Cage's *4:33*. Objects and phenomena (a urinal and silence in the examples above) that people usually do not define as art were by these artists framed as such, and subsequently experienced as such by an audience. This has of course been especially important in the development of conceptual art, but elements of framing are important for any form of art or aesthetic practice.

[6] This is of course not to say that products – including products of the therapy process – are not important in music therapy, cf. the discussion of *artifacts* in Chapter 8.

[7] A note to the reader not familiar with the Greek myths: The term "between Scylla and Charybdis" translates to something like "between two equally hazardous alternatives," and refers to situations and dilemmas where it is impossible – or at least very difficult – to avoid the dangers of one alternative without falling victim of the other.

[8] The later philosophy of Wittgenstein has had a major impact on modern aesthetic theories; see for instance Hagberg (1994, 1995), although Wittgenstein never wrote any systematic work on aesthetics. Some remarks on culture and on his personal (in some ways rather conservative) aesthetic taste were found in his "Nachlass," and published after his death (Wittgenstein, 1980). Also, some of his lectures on aesthetics have later been published (Wittgenstein, 1978). These are interesting enough, but his importance for aesthetic theory is nevertheless mostly related to the general influence of his two major works, *Tractatus Logico-Philosophicus* (1921/1961) and especially *Philosophical Investigations* (1953/1967). This is true even though very little is said – explicitly at least – about aesthetics in these two works. It is Wittgenstein's focus upon language and meaning as a foundation for a discussion of major philosophical problems that has found its way also to aesthetic theory.

[9] His philosophy hardly suggests total relativism. Everything could be different because endless variations of language games and life forms are thinkable. Within each life form, however, agreement on value and values is thinkable, and is often taken for granted.

[10] Therapy, even when understood as a "private space," is only partly bounded by the walls of the music therapy room, since both client and therapist have multiple relations to several cultural contexts. Sometimes, as Chapters 4 and 5 will illuminate, therapeutic interventions are aimed at those cultural contexts themselves. This also relates to the metaphor of "therapy as giving voice," see Chapter 8.

Chapter 3:

THE POWER OF MUSICKING

Performance does not exist in order to present musical works,
but rather, musical works exist in order to give performers
something to perform.
(Christopher Small)

What music therapists have in common is the use of music for some purpose related to health and well-being. A possible implication could be that *musicology* – the disciplined study of music and situations of music use – is a basic discipline for music therapy. So far, though, musicology's impact on music therapy theory has been limited. This chapter examines one possible reason for this, and suggests that two recent trends within contemporary musicology represent an invitation to reevaluate the relationship between music therapy and musicology. These two trends – the study of music as human nature and the study of music as culture – may provide music therapists with fruitful perspectives on their own practice, research, and theory.

TALKING ABOUT MUSIC

As clinicians and scholars music therapists need to be able to communicate in words what happens in music. Clients, relatives, funding agencies, health authorities, and the general public will all ask for verbal and written descriptions of the possibilities and limitations of music therapy practice. Facing this, music therapists often struggle with the elusiveness of music for definition and description. That it is so difficult to talk about music is interesting, if not encouraging at first. Philosophers and musicians have struggled with similar issues for centuries, and it is thought provoking that so many people have been willing to struggle so hard for so long, attempting to find answers to questions about music. There is something *intriguing* about music that asks for closer examination.

From the fact that it may not be possible to translate music into words it does not follow that it is impossible or uninteresting to *talk about* music; one may for instance approach the issue by asking what counts *as* music and what counts *in* music.

Answers to both questions vary over time and between cultures. In modern Western culture much concern has been given to the issue of which *sounds* could count *as* music. For centuries those sounds were mainly modal and tonal, with discrete and fixed pitches, except for the addition of some percussion. As we all know, the twentieth century avant-garde rejected this as a limiting tradition and included all kinds of sounds in their music-making, from concrete sounds of nature and urban life to electronically produced sounds of all sorts. If we turn to other cultures or go back in European history, we can see that what counts as music is a much broader question than which sounds to include. Could, for instance, words and movements count as music? We know that the word music originated from the Greek word *mousiké*, which in early antiquity was related to singing, dancing, and the performance of lyrics and drama. In most European languages a word derived from mousiké is used today, but with a more narrow meaning. In these languages a broader concept was in use before the specialized modern concept took over. In my own language *leik* was such a word, with connotations both to sounds and movements, play, and social gatherings. Similar concepts are found in many non-European languages. In the East-African language Swahili for instance, the term *ngoma* is in use, with connotations similar to those of mousiké and leik, but also with connotations that are specific for those cultures in which Swahili is in use. Ngoma might for instance mean drum, in addition to the social activity of singing and dancing together, and is also used as the name for a tradition of music healing (Janzen, 2000).

If we now turn to the question of what counts *in* music, what makes music special and important, there is also a proliferation of answers. If we again concentrate on European history we can see how ancient Greek ideas about music have lingered on for centuries, such as Pythagoras's ideas about cosmic harmony in relation to mystical numerology and Plato's ideas about ethos and music in education (Barker, 1984). After the renaissance, ideas on what counts in music tended to focus more and more upon music as human expression. In the eighteenth century – the time of rationalism and Enlightenment – music's *limitations* as expression was in focus; the fact that music is not able to designate meaning as accurate as words are. In the nineteenth century – the period of Romanticism – this was turned upside down; music was seen as the richest of all human expressions, in virtue of *not* being figurative or representative in the way that words and pictures are. As in the period of Enlightenment music was considered an expression of emotions, but now in a very different way, as the most sublime of all human expressions (Benestad, 1976). Residues of such ideas have remained influential in contemporary Western cultures, although they have also been under attack.

DEFINING MUSIC

Given all the different practices of and discourses about music, any definition of music may appear as inadequate or problematic. What counts as music for one group may count as noise for another, what is significant form for some is chaos for others, and what is sounding emotion for one individual may for a different person be dry and uninteresting jingle. Maybe there is not much essence shared by all musics; the relationships between different musics may be more like the family resemblance relationships discussed in the previous chapter. With this diversity in mind, it seems reasonable to assume that a common denominator definition of music will be rather abstract. Human perception of music is so strongly influenced by cultural history that any talk about music in the abstract and general – or about "the nature of music" – becomes problematic. Cultural artifacts, such as music, do not constitute natural kinds; they never stop changing. "Nothing guarantees that all the forms of human music contain a nucleus of common properties that would be invariant since the origination of music" the musicologist Jean Molino (2000, p. 169) comments.

Definitions of music therefore hardly make sense except in historical contexts. Consider for instance the definition of music as "organized sound," which was proposed by Edgard Varèse and other pioneers of electronic music in the twentieth century. One may counter that language is also organized sound, and therefore this definition may seem unsatisfactory. The definition, linked to new practices of composition, still played an important historical role, as part of a process of emancipation of dissonance and rhythm in Western music (Benestad, 1976). In fact, music as organized sound is to some extent a relevant definition of music also in music therapy, where the emancipation of dissonance and rhythm as equal musical elements to melody and harmony may be very important. A client may, for instance, at times be especially fascinated by some specific *sounds:* the timbre of a flute in a specific register, the swish of a cymbal, etc. Other times in music therapy the focus may be on how to *organize* sounds: how to build a rhythmic pattern, how to use a scale of tones, etc. A definition of music as organized sound therefore reveals much of relevance for contemporary music therapy. It still must be considered unsatisfactory, however. What about music as *performance* and *expression?* These aspects are deemed important by most therapists and would need to be included in a definition of music of relevance for music therapy.

A concept of music thus relates to a concept of culture, and while a definition hardly could be completely precise or comprehensive it may serve a purpose as clarifying a perspective. While it seems impossible to find *one* way of talking about music that will create consensus, definitions of music may still be helpful, then, not as exact descriptions of a phenomenon, but as pointers suggesting ways and directions of looking and listening. The definition proposed below is created by this author in order to clarify culture-centered premises for music therapy, consistent with the notion of culture developed in Chapter 1. This notion indicates that both human phylogeny and cultural history must be taken into consideration, and I find it necessary to consider music both as event and activity:

> Music may be considered a situated event and activity. As event music is sound-in-time, organized as culturally informed expressions of human protomusicality. As activity music is the act of creating and relating to emerging sounds and expressive gestures.

What is proposed here is that music as event and activity originates from a shared human *protomusicality* developed in human phylogeny. As will be explained, this protomusicality is considered a basic element in humans' capacity for nonverbal communication, as revealed for instance in mother-infant interaction. Such interaction is not music, though. The capacity to music evolves in ontogeny, as expressions become culturally informed, taking the existing cultural plurality of *musics* as departure points. Music therefore is enacted and experienced as *musicking*, that is, as the performed establishment of relationships (between sounds, between sounds and people, between sounds and values, etc.).

This proposal relates to two recent developments within musicology: the study of music and biology, and the study of music in and as culture. To relate a definition of music in music therapy to developments within musicology may seem an obvious thing to do, since musicology is the discipline that traditionally has been most concerned with the issues of defining and describing music. Interestingly enough, however, music therapists only to a limited degree have used the musicological literature. This may be interpreted as a deficiency and imply a critique of the discipline of music therapy, but it may also reveal characteristics of the discipline of musicology as it has traditionally been conceived. Music has to a large degree been studied as formally unique objects of art, and music history has often been detached from society and culture and instead understood as an autonomous evolution of ideas and techniques. Conceived in this way musicology has not contributed much to our understanding of the human and social significance of music (Scott, 2000), and the distance to music therapy has been considerable. Music therapists seem to have been doing the only logical thing when their notions of music have borrowed from psychology rather than musicology.

To speak of music as "free association," as "stimulus," or as an "analogue to mother-infant interaction" appears to have much more clinical relevance than the notions that could be derived from musicological studies of Mozart and Mahler.

As a number of authors have argued, there have been some recent developments within musicology that now suggest that a closer reciprocal relationship between disciplines could be fruitful.[1] Most of these commentators have focused upon new traditions within musicology, such as critical musicology and new musicology, which briefly could be described as the study of music in and as culture. These recent developments are part of the *anthropological turn* discussed in the previous chapter. The line between musicology and ethnomusicology is not as obvious as earlier assumed; the music of the Western classical canon is now considered just as much part of culture as the music of the indigenous people of Australia. The distinction between the disciplines of musicology and ethnomusicology has more or less collapsed, if not always in practice at least in principle. For culture-centered music therapy the relevance of this anthropological turn is indisputable. In line with the discussion of culture given in the first chapter, I will not restrict my focus to this, but also focus upon another recent development in musicology: the evolutionary study of music as human nature.

The three main concepts outlined in the first paragraph following the definition of music above – protomusicality, musics, and musicking – relate to these two recent developments in musicology. Figure 2 communicates the relationships proposed and discussed in this chapter:

Figure 2: Relationships between protomusicality, musics, and musicking.

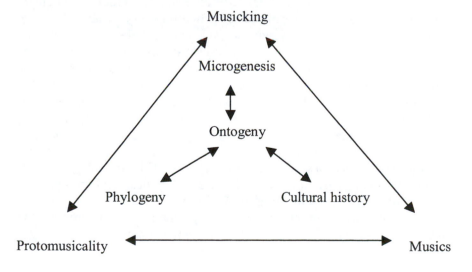

The "music triumvirate" of protomusicality, musics, and musicking may thus be explicated in the following way: *Protomusicality* is music as human capacity, evolved in *phylogeny*. The term *musics* points at music as artifacts produced in *cultural history,* ranging from musical works to musical traditions and subcultures. *Musicking* is music as *microgenesis,* that is, music as situated activity and moment-to-moment lived experience (of culturally informed expressions of human protomusicality). In *ontogeny* individuals therefore engage in musicking based upon their human protomusicality and through use of specific musics.

Ontogeny may be said to be of main interest in therapy, with its focus upon life history and personal development. Ontogeny involves a process of moment-to-moment expression and experience, and my contention is that in studying music in music therapy, *musicking* is an inevitable perspective, that is, music as performed relationships. This contention would be rather empty, though, if not for human protomusicality and for the cultures of music. Protomusicality provides humans with capacities for engaging with expression and communication through sounds, and cultural history provides humans with artifacts that affords, including symbolic tools for communication and for the construction of one's life history. Before discussing the power of musicking I will therefore elaborate on the origins of music and on music in and as culture.

THE ORIGINS OF MUSIC

Music as human capacity has traditionally not been taken very seriously in evolutionary theory. As Geoffrey Miller puts it: "From a pragmatic biological viewpoint, art and music seem like pointless wastes of energy" (Miller, 2000, p. 2). For decades this led to a neglect of these areas of human life more than to a modification of biological theory. While Darwin in his discussion of *The Descent of Man* included sections on the music of birds and on the "musical powers" in gibbons and humans (Darwin, 1871/1998, pp. 379-392 and 586-594), music has not been a mainstream topic in evolutionary biology. The last few decades have seen a slow change in this respect, and the question whether music is a biological adaptation or not is now under debate.[2] There has also been a gradual acknowledgement lately of evolutionary perspectives in musicology. The Swedish musicologist Nils L. Wallin (1991) has been one of the pioneers of this field, and the book *The Origins of Music* (Wallin, Merker & Brown, 2000) will probably be considered one of its milestones. While this volume of essays reveals that much knowledge on the evolution of music already exists, the diversity of proposals made also disclose that there is a long way to go before consensus and establishment of a paradigm is achieved.

In the introduction to the volume, Brown, Merker & Wallin (2000) argue that no account of human evolution is complete without an understanding of how music and dance rituals evolved. They give three main reasons for this: 1) music and dance are essential components of social behaviors of all cultures, 2) the study of the evolution of language has gained importance in evolutionary theory, and it is proposed that music and language share underlying features, 3) the study of music may contribute to our knowledge on human migration and the history of cultural contacts. While I consider these to be three major issues, I will also contend that a fourth is of high relevance for music therapy: the study of protomusicality may reveal information on processes of communication in therapy and everyday situations. Recently a series of articles on the origins of music have been published in the *Nordic Journal of Music Therapy,*[3] and later in this chapter I will focus upon two of these contributions in order to develop a notion of *protomusicality* relevant for music therapy theory.

In the opening paragraphs of this chapter I argued that we should take the non-universality of music seriously. When including a biological perspective this argument is challenged, and I will briefly reconsider the possibility of universals in music. When talking about music as cultural artifact, as product of history, it *is* accurate to speak about *musics*. Multiple traditions exist, and we have no guarantee that there is one common nucleus to them. This is no reason to neglect the shared human capacities developed in phylogeny and the possible biological basis for human behavior. We may then consider both the non-universality of music and the universality of "non-music," as the music anthropologist Kenneth Gourlay (1984) suggests. It is hardly plausible that any specific kind of music is universal (except for a few basic elements as will be discussed below), but rather that expression in sound and the capacity and desire to develop and organize these expressions are universal. These expressions are not music, as developed in cultural history, neither are they just noise or sounds. We may consider them as raw material for the rituals and traditions of music, dance, and drama that have been developed in different cultures. Gourlay also suggests that this allows us to think about music as something belonging to everybody, to the whole community and not only to an elite of that community. Another music anthropologist – John Blacking (1990, p. 71) – has expressed similar ideas by talking about "musics as cultural systems" on one hand and on the other "an innate, species-specific set of cognitive and sensory capacities which human beings are predisposed to use for communication and for making sense of their environment – that is, music as a human capacity."

With this line of reasoning as a backdrop, I will consider some of the arguments about evolved universals related to music. While the diversity of the musics of the world is striking, Brown et al. (2000, p. 13) note that so is the unity of musical practices. These scholars therefore propose that it be about time for musicologists to "reopen" the issue of music origins and universals in music, and to search for a concept of universals that can provide a focus on unity in the great diversity in the world's musical systems and practices. They advocate, for instance, that there is some innateness in human musical processing, one example being that emotional excitement is universally expressed through loud, fast, accelerating, and high-registered sound patterns (Brown et al., 2000, p. 14). Four chapters of *Origins of Music* are devoted to universals in music.

The most cautious author in this section is probably Bruno Nettl, one of the "grand old men" of ethnomusicology. Nettl (2000) suggests that identifications of universals depend on definitions of music, which are cultural, so the conceptual difficulties are obvious right from the beginning. Nettl still proposes that different levels of universals may be explored, and clarifies that we need to study a) the universality of practices of "music," b) universals among musics, and c) universals among musical practices. The *universality of practices* is something most scholars agree upon. Although not all cultures have a concept that would translate to "music," all cultures have shared and patterned sound-making that in an etic perspective could be labeled music. An example of a *universal among musics* is that some intervals, such as the octave and the fifth, seem to be in universal use. One of the *universals among musical practices* is that when making music people are always playing or singing *something,* a particular song or piece, something that resulted from an act of creation.[4]

More radical suggestions are made by Sandra Trehub (2000), who speaks of predispositions in human processing in relation to what she calls musical universals and near-universals. Based upon research on basic principles of auditory pattern perception, she proposes that the perception of music is inherently biased rather than unbiased, as she finds similarities in the perception of musical patterns between adults with extensive exposure to music and infants with minimal exposure. For instance, she finds that both adults and infants when hearing a novel melody focus upon pitch contour and rhythm. They focus upon the relation between pitches more upon than the specific pitches.[5] Trehub also finds that in infants' interval processing there is a preference for and a higher sensitivity to what she calls small-integer frequency ratios, that is, octaves, fifths, and fourths, as opposed to high-integer ratio intervals such as the tritone. Trehub therefore suggests that there is a biological basis for the experience of consonance and dissonance. For instance, infants more readily detect a change from a fifth to a tritone than from a fifth to a fourth, although the difference in interval is larger in the latter case. Trehub explains this by proposing that the first case is a change from a consonant to a dissonant interval.[6]

As we can see, Trehub is more specific than Nettl in the proposal of universals. We need to remember, however, that what she is studying is universals in human musical capacity more than universals in the musics and musical practices of the world. With an ethnographic perspective added, universals are less obvious or dominating or at least integrated with diversity, and this diversity, anthropologists insist, is important. It is a matter of specific sensibilities developed in specific contexts. A simple analogy with language may help. As Geertz (1973/1993, p. 50) notes: "Our capacity to speak is surely innate, our capacity to speak English is surely cultural." The point is that we never just speak, we always speak a language, and a language is a cultural artifact developed through the cultural history of a group of people. Our ability to speak is therefore not only dependent on human capacities developed in phylogeny. It is also closely related to the cultural history and contexts we belong to. Similar comments may be made about music.

This is why we never just play; we always play *something*, as Nettl proposed. This something may be "anti-music," breaching every musical rule we know. We are still musicking in relation to the musics given us by cultural history. It is impossible to go directly from phylogeny to ontogeny. I therefore propose that one needs to be quite careful in proposing musical universals, while it would also be meaningless to neglect the human musical nature developed in phylogeny. Brown et al. (2000) are probably right in asserting that the diversity among musical practices is hardly as extreme as could be imagined, and in cultural history there has been a ubiquitous blending of musical practices and genres. It is reasonable to suggest that there are some species-specific capacities that have made this possible. I have chosen to subsume these capacities under the term *protomusicality*, which I will now elaborate on.

PROTOMUSICALITY

The word "musicality" has often been used to indicate that someone has a special musical talent, while what is to be explored here is the shared human capacity for engaging in communication through sound and movement. A text that has paved the way to this understanding of the concept of musicality is of course John Blacking's (1973) *How Musical Is Man?* Based upon his ethnomusicological studies he objected to the idea that most people are unmusical while musicality is something reserved for a few especially talented people. He called for a reassessment of human musicality and criticized Western psychological tests of musicality as being biased, ethnocentric, and insensitive to cultural issues. Blacking related the question "How musical is man?" to the two more general questions "What is the nature of man?" and "What limits are there to his cultural development?" He argued that there must be a biological basis for music, but that this is always expressed in social contexts through culture:

> There is so much music in the world that it is reasonable to suppose that music, like language and possibly religion, is a species-specific trait of man. Essential physiological and cognitive processes that generate musical composition and performances may even be genetically inherited, and therefore present in almost every human being. An understanding of these and other processes involved in the production of music may provide us with evidence that men are more remarkable and capable creatures than most societies ever allow them to be. This is not the fault of culture itself, but the fault of man, who mistakes the means of culture for the end, and so lives *for* culture and not *beyond* culture (Blacking, 1973, p. 7).

Blacking's text includes many stimulating reflections on music as humanly organized sound, stressing the interrelationships between music, society, and culture. Music is, according to Blacking, a synthesis of cognitive processes present in culture as well as in the human body, and is generated by social experiences in cultural contexts. Questions concerning musical structure may therefore have historical, political, and philosophical answers, as well as answers related to, say, the laws of acoustics. What Blacking therefore proposes is that the rules of music are not arbitrary. They are closely linked to social and cultural life, to human biological capacities, as well as to individual experiences. Blacking's argument has been controversial in some circles, but he has certainly contributed to an understanding of human musicality through integration of biological, psychological, social, and cultural perspectives. His argument will serve as a background as I focus upon two more recent contributions on human musicality, contributions that relate directly to music therapy practice and theory.

Colwyn Trevarthen and Stephen Malloch (2000) suggest that children are born with a uniquely human motivation that makes cultural learning in companionship possible. With reference to Blacking, the authors reflect upon the indications that suggest that humans seem to be able to recognize and sympathize with humanly organized sounds of other cultures. Trevarthen and Malloch suggest that this is because all humans have the capacity to sympathize with rhythmic and melodic movements of both body and voice, with gestures linked to narrative cycles of expression. This capacity is not learned to begin with, albeit it may be cultivated. An infant's sympathy arises from an inborn rhythmic coherence; body movement and modulation of affective expressions are biologically linked. A child is born with a natural talent for the outward signs of human communication, a talent that later in life may be cultivated into conventional musical ability. They conceive of music-making as a human activity that communicates motives, and suggest that music evokes narratives of experience based on humans' innate ability to share the passing of expressive "mind time".[7] This ability, part of our psycho-biological endowment, Trevarthen and Malloch chooses to call *Communicative Musicality*, which they relate to the impulse to move with anticipation of rhythmic sensory consequences and varied emotional evaluations.

As a proposed foundation for a theory of music therapy, the authors outline their theory of Communicative Musicality. The starting point is the increasing amount of research on nonverbal interaction that has demonstrated how humans interact with one another at great speed, synchronizing in subtle and unconscious rhythms of exchange. The authors express dissatisfaction with the term "nonverbal" for this interaction and they state: "Bodily and vocal expression is so powerful in the management of human relations that it deserves a better name. Extending the metaphor, we call it Communicative Musicality" (Trevarthen & Malloch, 2000, p. 5). In clarifying the concept, the authors, with reference to an earlier work of Malloch, identify three dimensions: pulse, quality, and narrative. *Pulse* is the succession of regular and predictable discrete events through time. *Quality* is related to pitch and intonation and consists of the contours of expression moving through time. The third dimension, *narrative*, relates to both individual experiences and experiences of companionship and is built as sequenced units of pulse and quality. These sequences, found in jointly created gestures, are shaped as "phrases" or (proto)-narratives (Trevarthen & Malloch, 2000, pp. 5-9).

The general theoretical relevance of the concept of Communicative Musicality is, according to the authors, increased by the fact that temporal aspects of interpersonal communication are not given the prominence they deserve within much psychological research. The authors propose that satisfying communication, in mother-infant interaction as well as in music therapy, is established through the creation of a coordinated relationship through time (Trevarthen & Malloch, 2000, p. 6). The therapeutic relevance is, again according to the two authors, enhanced by the fact that many therapists, following Freud, have had too rationalistic conceptions of the therapeutic dialogue. Too much stress has been put on language and cognitive appraisal, while not enough attention has been paid to the richness and creativity of the reciprocal structuring of expressive time (Trevarthen & Malloch, 2000, p. 14).

Trevarthen and Malloch challenge mainstream biology and evolutionary psychology in their argument, and Kennair (2001) criticizes the authors for too easily brushing off mainstream biology. There are therefore reasons to believe that this recent contribution to the understanding of human nature will be discussed and challenged in the years to come. I still have chosen to include their notion in this context, because it represents a promising attempt of specifying the biological basis for music-making in ways that are compatible with sensitivity for the importance of cultural learning. This relates to Trevarthen's (1995, 1997) earlier suggestion that a child is born "cultural," that is, born with a disposition for engagement in intense emotional interaction which again is the foundation for symbolizing; the assigning of meaning to things interpreted as signs.

One possible objection to the term Communicative Musicality is that the term music is not defined, so that the distinction between mother-infant communication and the elaborated patterns cultivated in musics becomes too blurred. Ellen Dissanayake, in an article on ethology (behavioral biology) and its relevance to music therapy, has paid more attention to this problem. She proposes the following ethological definition of music: "the capacity to 'artify' and/or respond to the artification by others of various protomusical components, including concurrent vocal, visual, and kinesic elements, whose effects encourage participation and positively affect the participant's sense of well-being" (Dissanayake, 2001, p. 165). Taking the mother-infant research of Trevarthen and others as point of departure (including the concept of Communicative Musicality), she proposes that the behavior of music has evolved from protomusical components first developed in mother-infant interaction. These evolved patterns of interaction had survival value, she argues, in creating and sustaining an emotional bond between ancestral human mothers and their – compared to other animals – immature infants (Dissanayake, 2001, p. 165). The continued argument, then, is that mother-infant interaction includes elements of ritualization (simplification, formalization, exaggeration, repetition, and elaboration), and that this functioned as the basis for the artification (further manipulations) of adult rituals. In this way she is able to describe continuity and connection between mother-infant interaction and cultivated forms of music. To a larger degree than Trevarthen and Malloch (2000), she is also able to distinguish between these. To denote the human capacity that enables humans to participate in nonverbal communication as well as in musical activities, I therefore have chosen to use the term *protomusicality*.

As there is, as yet, no broad consensus on what the origins of music could be, there exist of course alternatives to Dissanayake's (2001) proposal focusing upon the feminine beginnings in mother-infant interaction. Geoffrey Miller (2000), for instance, takes another perspective and elaborates on Darwin's "neglected" theory of sexual selection: music may have evolved as part of ancestral males' competitive sexual display. It is beyond the scope of this chapter to dissolve the differences between Miller and Dissanayake. I have chosen to concentrate on Dissanayake, since she relates her writing directly to the discipline of music therapy and also links her arguments to a tradition of research that over some years have been influential in music therapy theory: the interaction studies conducted by Trevarthen and other mother-infant researchers. At this point it suffices to recognize that music is taken more seriously in biology than before, and that this may provide future music therapy theorists with new perspectives and knowledge on human beings' relationship to music. If there is a specific biological predisposition for music in humans, it remains to be clarified what the exact implications for music therapy may be, and to what degree different theories, such as those of Miller versus Dissanayake, imply differently when it comes to clinical practice and research.

Both Trevarthen and Malloch (2000) and Dissanayake (2001) explicitly argue that biological perspectives on music may add to an understanding of the music therapy process. Trevarthen and Malloch, for instance, consider Communicative Musicality to be the source of the music therapeutic experience and its effects:

> That the practice of music therapy depends, consciously, on both musical skill and clinical training is clear, but the features of expression that are managed and transformed in the course of a treatment are also appreciated at an intuitive level that defies rational analysis and that may not be consciously realised. This intuitive appreciation of how music therapy improves the emotional and cognitive well-being of the client can be enriched, we believe, by accurate information on the dimensions of musicality that are inherent in all human motives and feelings, and in their sympathetic sharing. Research on the acoustic features of vocal interactions with infants has brought out these fundamental features. We advocate a comparable analysis of music therapy practice to clarify how motives and feelings of the human mind are engaged and transformed in the course of treatment (Trevarthen & Malloch, 2000, p. 5).

This call for exact research on the interpersonal interactions in music therapy seems justified. It would not be wise to interpret this as an exhaustive prescription for process research in music therapy though. Protomusicality may serve as the biological basis for the rituals and cultures of music that have been developed, and therefore deserves careful attention. The biological need to learn culture implies that people do, in fact, learn culture, and this dimension must also be studied seriously, which is why we will now gradually turn to the terms *musics* and *musicking.*

MUSIC AND CULTURE

The study of *music in culture* has traditionally belonged to disciplines such as cultural anthropology and ethnomusicology. As Alan P. Merriam underlines in his classic work *The Anthropology of Music* (1964) the boundaries between these two disciplines have become increasingly difficult to see, as anthropological and musicological perspectives gradually have merged.[8] A main concern for Merriam was the limitations involved if ethnomusicologists focus too much upon the study of music as sound and structure. He advocated the study of music *in* culture, as opposed to the study of music as an object in itself with no references to the context it belongs to. Merriam advocated that there is a cultural matrix out of which music is produced, and that this must be included in the study of music.

Later scholars in ethnomusicology and cultural studies have developed this notion further, to a study of music *as* culture. In this perspective it is no longer meaningful to separate music and context: the entity to be studied must be *music-in-context*. It is then argued that cultural context is not just a matrix shaping the music; the shaping is more reciprocal. Music and context do not exist as individual entities but are reciprocally constitutive. When we talk of "music in itself" this is an abstraction, based on an act of taking actions out of context and reifying them in the shape of musical works or traditions. The simple fact that concepts of what is musical and what is extra-musical have changed over time and differ between societies could be an illumination of this line of argument. To really understand music, and music's function and meaning, it is argued we need to examine concrete situations of use.

Since music in the Western world often is considered to be one of the temporal *arts,* one may be led to associate music with the normative use of the word culture. Music therapists are rarely completely comfortable with this though, since what is considered first-rate in arts, manners, and scholarly pursuits is linked to power and privilege while music therapists often work with people in little power living quite unprivileged lives. The unconventional – and sometimes quite unpretentious – character of music typically heard in music therapy sessions may even lead some to separate the sounds of music therapy from culture.[9] As a growing body of literature on music and cultural studies shows, however, the descriptive or "anthropological" concept of culture is essential when studying music. This insight is, as already mentioned, the basis for the development of the so-called new musicology. In this perspective classical music is not different from any other tradition of music; it is embedded in culture(s) and it carries certain cultural values, etc. This line of reasoning also makes it possible to look at music therapy from fresh perspectives. In a recent ethnographic study of music in everyday life, for instance, Tia DeNora (2000) discusses music therapy sessions as well as aerobics classes, karaoke evenings, the personal use of music in romantic situations, and the public use of background music in the retail sector.

Cultural studies on music have contributed with an increased understanding of how individuals are not only passive consumers of music, but in fact active users of the tools and artifacts provided by cultural history. For instance, several authors have shown how people use music actively to build identity and give meaning to their everyday lives, see for instance (Small, 1987, 1998; Willis, 1990; Keil & Feld, 1994; Frith, 1996; Ruud, 1997; DeNora, 2000). Such processes not only involve situations were people are *active* in music in a traditional sense of that word; the musics produced by the music industry or the musics of the concert halls may also be used in flexible and creative ways to serve the needs of groups and individuals.

There is no reason to believe that people who come to music therapy do *not* use music in this way, on the contrary. And if they do not, that may be part of the reason why they search and need music therapy. Sometimes the clients' problems are related to the fact that they are not able to take full advantage of this potential in music as culture, and the therapy process may aim at helping them to develop the abilities, skills, and relationships required for doing so. Chapters 4 to 6 in this book partly illuminate this, and I clearly suggest that music therapists need to relate their practices to the practices of music-making and listening in society. As DeNora's (2000) book shows, this includes "low-status" practices such as karaoke events, but it also includes more prestigious concert events, in comparable ways as dramatherapy must relate its practices to that of the theater (Jennings, 1992, 1997). This is one of the reasons why music therapists need to have a reflected relationship to the context-sensitive issues of meaning, narrative, and aesthetics, as discussed in the previous chapter. Music therapists need to be able to relate to a plurality of musics in order to meet the individual needs of clients coming from different backgrounds with different histories of music use.

PLURALITY OF MUSICS

The notion of *musics* in plural may be compared to that of cultures in plural. Early pioneers of anthropology, such as Edward B. Tylor, thought of cultural development as a linear process, and concentrated on the use of the term *culture* in singular. The obvious diversity of cultural practices that could be observed around the world he then interpreted as stages in an hierarchical evolution (Eriksen, 1995). Later anthropologists, with Franz Boas as one of the pioneers, advocated that it is necessary to speak of *cultures* in plural, in order to avoid ethnocentric neglect of the value of diversity, and in order to acknowledge the possibility that several different but equally complex cultural systems exist side by side.

The concept of *musics* has been especially developed and focused upon among ethnomusicologists (May, 1983), who have demonstrated that the Western tendency of talking about music in the abstract and general is based upon an ethnocentric bias. Although the possibility of universals in music should not be neglected, the traditions of music-making around the world are so diverse that it is meaningful and necessary to talk about musics in plural.[10] The relevance of this has been illustrated in relation to music therapy recently, in discussions of different traditions of music therapy and music healing in history (Horden, 2000) and in different cultural contexts (Gouk, 2000). In the context of this chapter I will restrict myself to the illumination of two points that I find crucial for a better understanding of music in music therapy. First, different musics may represent different possibilities of meaning-making. Second, musics may be decontextualized and recontextualized, that is, appropriated in new settings. Albeit historically developed in concrete social settings, their appropriation is not limited to these settings. In the process of building a personal identity, people thus may use several musics, including musics that are not linked to their immediate geographical or cultural context. This second point then suggests that the concept of context needs to be explored.

Let us first consider the differences in possibilities of meaning-making. Charles Keil, a student of Leonard Meyer, has produced two thought-provoking essays (Keil, 1994a, b) that challenge some concepts of musical meaning the way this issue has been approached in traditional musicology. Meyer's (1956) renowned discussion of music, emotion, and meaning takes classical Western music as a departure point. What Keil does is to illuminate how Meyer's concepts are not so helpful in discussing meaning in popular music and jazz. Keil focuses upon "motion and feeling" instead of Meyer's "emotion and meaning," and he develops the term *participatory discrepancies* as a tool for illuminating this. Keil's main idea is that rock and other popular music forms signify in different ways than classical music by stressing "how-aspects" more than "what-aspects." While complex melodic and harmonic syntax (development of motifs, etc.), as well as norm-deviation and tendency-inhibition (such as in a disappointing cadence), is essential in our experience of classical music, we find little of this in rock, pop, and jazz. These "what-elements" are simply not very developed in these genres, with the possible exception of advanced harmony in some sub-genres of jazz. This lack of complexity in the "what-elements" has led some to suggest that rock, pop, and jazz is of less value than classical music: "it's all trite melodies and the same three chords over and over again."

Keil draws our attention to the complexities of the "how-we-play-what-we-play" aspects of popular music and jazz. His focus is on the ongoing musical process, engendered feeling, more than on the object or the structures built through this process. When we listen to rock (and some music therapy improvisations) it is not the intervals, scales, and chords that usually interest us. More often it is the grain of the voice and the *participatory discrepancies;* the "out-of time-and-out-of-tune" aspects. Examples may be a singer or guitarist playing with the pitch by bending the tone up and down, or a percussionist playing with the beat by playing laid back or on top of it. Keil suggests that popular music and jazz is not about development of motifs, and thus not about variability in melody and harmony: it's about "getting into the groove" through the advanced play with participatory discrepancies. Keil thus illuminates that Meyer's concepts to a high degree are limited to the tradition of classical music. As with Meyer, he acknowledges that there is "something in the music" that needs to be paid attention to when musical meaning is to be discussed, however. We cannot only concentrate on the social situation and its effect on the experience, rather the musical elements and the situation constitute each other in a complex interplay.

It is important to note that Leonard Meyer's (1956) discussion is all but simplistic. He clarified that there is no direct path from the structure of music – its sounds, rhythms, melodies, etc. – to musical experience. Keil's criticism of Meyer is therefore an important one, by supplementing Meyer's understanding of meaning and of this "something in the music," through examining some *different musics* than those studied by Meyer. This should not be interpreted as "there are no participatory discrepancies in classical music." Of course there are; differences in phrasing and intonation may be extremely important for the experience of a musical performance. Keil's argument should still illustrate how different musics may represent different possibilities of meaning-making.

Let us turn to the other point I wanted to illuminate: how musics may be decontextualized and recontextualized, that is, appropriated in new settings. A starting point for this discussion could be to reconsider our concept of context. As Cole (1996) has demonstrated, it is too limited to consider context as "that which surrounds." True, musicking and other human activities always have an immediate context surrounding the actions themselves, and this context is surrounded by other context. We *may,* then, conceive of contexts as "concentric circles" surrounding acts and agents. Cole (1996) also underlines, though, that another concept of context sometimes is illuminating: context as *"that which connects."* Agents do not restrict themselves to the immediate surroundings when they link events and experiences to other events and experiences. This process of *linking* constitutes a high degree of flexibility in meaning-making. Appropriation of different musics is therefore not restricted to the immediate surroundings of the concrete historical and social setting. An individual thus may use several musics, not necessarily linked to his immediate geographical, social, or cultural context. In building a personal and social identity a person thus may choose to relate to, use, and adopt several musics (Ruud, 1997). This suggests that we need to transcend the idea of culture and context as a frame surrounding the individual, and also that we need to transcend the dichotomy sometimes assumed between the individual and the collective level. Musics exists as situated traditions of musicking in which individual agents interact. Also, musics exist as artifacts and traditions that may be decontextualized and recontextualized, as the growing interest for World Music so effectively has demonstrated.

This also suggests that music-in-context at times may be a limiting perspective in understanding person-music relationships. Music-*as*-context is a complementary perspective. Musics provide people with *artifacts* of various sorts, such as musical works (from songs to symphonies) and musical instruments, and this suggests that the *relationships* between artifacts and actors are of interest. Artifacts, provided by cultural history, are tools people may use in processes of enculturation and individualization. The concept of *affordance,* originally developed by James J. Gibson (1979/1986) in a discussion of visual perception in animals, may offer some assistance in describing this, and has been appropriated by several cultural theorists. As originally used by Gibson, the notion describes the *complementarity* between environment and animal:

> The *affordances* of the environment are what it *offers* the animal, what it *provides* or furnishes, either for good or ill. The verb *to afford* is found in the dictionary, but the noun *affordance* is not. I have made it up. I mean by it something that refers to both the environment and the animal in a way that no existing term does. It implies the complementarity of the animal and the environment. ...
> If a terrestrial surface is nearly horizontal (instead of slanted), nearly flat (instead of convex or concave), and sufficiently extended

(relative to the size of the animal), and if its substance is rigid (relative to the weight of the animal), then the surface *affords support*. It is a surface of support, and we call it a substratum, ground, or floor. It is stand-on-able, permitting an upright posture for quadrupeds and bipeds. It is therefore walk-on-able and run-over-able. It is not sink-into-able like a surface of water or a swamp, that is, not for heavy terrestrial animals. Support for water bugs is different.

Note that the four properties listed – horizontal, flat, extended, and rigid – would be *physical* properties of a surface if they were measured with the scales and standard units used in physics. As an affordance of support for a species of animal, however, they have to be measured *relative to the animal*. They are unique for that animal. They are not just abstract physical properties. They have unity relative to the posture and behavior of the animal being considered (Gibson, 1979/1986, pp. 127-128).

In introducing the term, Gibson also gives a few other examples. For humans a surface of support, with the four properties listed above and the additional feature of being approximately knee-high above the ground, affords *sitting*, at least in cultures that have established the habit of sitting as distinguished from kneeling or squatting. Such a surface then constitutes a *seat,* and has meaning as such.[11] For humans one of the major questions in life is what other humans afford. This constitutes the whole domain of social significance, and is closely linked to culture and communication.

Several theorists have proposed that affordance may be a relevant concept in describing meaningful relationships between human agents and cultural artifacts. Meanings are not immanent in objects nor are they simply projected upon objects as empty semiotic spaces. There is a complementarity involved. A chair affords sitting for most people in most situations, but in specific situations with specific people it may afford something completely different, such as breaking a window. More conventionally, different chairs afford different ways of sitting. Similarly, musics as artifacts afford differently. They lend themselves more easily to some uses than to others, but use is still relative to person and situation.

Tia DeNora (2000) has utilized the notion of *affordance* in relation to meanings of music in everyday situations, and proposes that it is possible to treat music as situated event and activity without overlooking the meaning potential of the musical material used. Based on an ethnographic study of how people use music in their everyday lives, with case examples from aerobic sessions, private romantic situations, shopping centers, and music therapy sessions, DeNora advocates that music is a powerful tool in constructing meaning in everyday life. Different musics *afford* differently, however. Specific genres or musical pieces or ways of musicking may give specific possibilities for relating to the world:

> Meaning, or semiotic force, is not an inherent property of cultural material, whether those materials are linguistic, technological or aesthetic. At the same time, material are by no means empty semiotic spaces ... the human sciences must avoid the twin explanatory errors of technologism and sociologism and to look instead at the ways in which people, things and meanings come to be clustered within particular socially located scenes (DeNora, 2000, p. 38).

The affordance of, say, a song is linked to its structure (for instance, tempo or chord sequence), but could not be equaled to its musical structure. Affordance is a *relationship* between person and music, and what counts then is *perceived affordance,* which again is linked to human nature as well as to personal and cultural history (the history of interpretation and use of that structure). Such a perspective – which is compatible with the concept of meaning games explored in the previous chapter – opens up for an understanding that goes beyond reducing music to a stimulus on the one side or a socially constructed sign on the other. A more integrative perspective may be developed. Music – as related to biological capacity, personal and cultural history, and the immediate social situation – is multilayered and polysemic. Any listening or interpretation must take that into consideration, by acknowledging the partiality of just that listening or interpretation, which on the other side could not be considered arbitrary or reduced to accidental circumstance. Implications for music therapy may include viewing the therapy process as shared exploration of new affordances in the musics used.

One of the things that could be learned from this brief reflection is that when looking for differences between musics we cannot look for structural differences only, but must look for differences between musics as situated *cultural systems.* Musics as cultural systems relate to values and practices that go beyond sound-making. As Blacking (1973) emphasized: music is generated by social experiences in cultural contexts and questions concerning musical structure may therefore also have historical, political, and philosophical answers. The rules of music are linked to social and cultural life. If we add to Blacking's argument the possibility that musics also may be decontexualized and recontextualized, as discussed above, we have a tool for understanding how musics seem to be flexible systems that lend themselves for use in specific situations. I will therefore now turn to a discussion of music as performance and activity.

TO MUSIC

The last few years there has been a growing concern within musicology for musical *performance*. The word performance is then used with a broad meaning that includes, say, improvisation and everyday use of music. The perspective taken is *music as action and interaction in social and cultural contexts*. Christopher Small (1998) has, in his book *Musicking,* made one of the most influential and clear articulations of this perspective, and we may take his ideas as a starting point for reflecting upon music as a *verb* instead of as a noun. Small, who earlier has published on topics as diverse as music, society, and education; Schönberg; and African American music, starts his discussion of music as a verb by iterating a common observation: after more than 2000 years of philosophical discussion in Western culture no one seem to have been able to give satisfactory answers to questions such as "What is the meaning of music?" and, "What is the function of music in human life?" No wonder that this is so, says Small, and suggests that those are the wrong questions to ask. "There is no such thing as music" (Small, 1998, p. 2). What he then suggests, and uses the rest of the book to demonstrate, is that music is not a thing but an activity.

Musicking, understood in this way, is of course no new thing. What has been Small's (1998) main contribution is to produce an articulation of this perspective that has been read and acknowledged by a comparatively large group of scholars. Before Small, ethnomusicologists have been promoting similar perspectives based on their studies of music in and as culture. Many scholars in popular music studies have also been interested in studying music as social practice in cultural contexts. Similarly, music therapy may be considered a culture of musicking. Music as action and interaction in context has for instance been the focus of Even Ruud's (1987/1990, 1998) discussions of the concept of music in music therapy. One of the challenging qualities of Small's input, apart from being erudite and articulate, is his choice of case for exemplification. Instead of folk music or popular music or any other oral tradition, he focuses on a classical symphony concert, in many ways the emblem of the view that the notable thing with music is music as a thing, that is, music as a *work of art*.

The Western focus upon autonomous works of art is connected to the idea of immanent meaning (the idea that the meaning of music is to be found in the object and originates from its structures). Small (1998, pp. 5-7) suggests that this idea comes with a few corollaries, such as reducing performance to a medium through which self-contained works of art have to pass, and viewing performances as a one-way systems of communication. In this way it is maintained that what is really interesting and important in art is the *work* itself, with its structures, complexities, and immanent meanings. A simple counterexample to this one-sided focus, Small suggests, is some artists' ability to turn trivial material into great performances. Small therefore turns his focus away from the musical work and toward the performance, and introduces the word "musicking," as the present participle of the verb "to music," a verb that may be found in some larger dictionaries but which has not been much in use in the English language. He then suggests that:

> To music is to take part, in any capacity, in a musical performance, whether by performing, by listening, by rehearsing or practicing, by providing material for performance (what is called composing), or by dancing (Small, 1998, p. 9).

Small's concept of musicking is thus a broad one. He even suggests that it may be useful to extend the meaning of "to music" to the actions of other participants in the performance situation, such as the practice of selling tickets, of setting up instruments and equipment, and of cleaning up when everyone else has gone. In making no principal distinction between what the performers do and what the other people in the setting do, Small wants to communicate that musicking is an activity in which all those present are involved and share responsibility for its characteristics and qualities. A main point for Small, then, is to present an alternative perspective on the question of the meaning of music, which he rephrases as the question of *meanings of performances*. These meanings do not simply reside inside the works themselves, but are produced through shared action in context. In developing this perspective Small is theoretically influenced by Bateson's (1972) ecology of mind; mind not as entity but as process and *relationships* to the world:

> The act of musicking establishes in the place where it is happening a set of relationships, and it is in those relationships that the meaning of the act lies. They are to be found not only between those organized sounds which are conventionally thought of as being the stuff of musical meaning but also between the people who are taking part, in whatever capacity, in the performance; and they model, or stand as metaphor for, ideal relationships as the participants in the performance imagine them to be: relationships between person and person, between individual and society, between humanity and the natural world and even perhaps the supernatural world (Small, 1998, p. 13).

The concept of *musicking* has not been unsuccessful among music therapists; it has been advocated by Ruud (2000), Ansdell (2001), and others, and quite a few music therapists have started to use the term. An interesting observation is that the International Association of Nordoff-Robbins Music Therapists has re-named its newsletter, calling it *Musicing,* based on a term advocated by David E. Elliott (1995), I assume. Like Small, Elliott has proposed that the basic reality of music is not music as object but music as action. To treat music as a verb and activity – like Small and Elliott do – finds many music therapists at home. While music arguably could be viewed both as product and process, music therapists have tended to stress the *process aspects* and underlined that being involved in music is being involved in *musical, personal, and interpersonal processes.* They have proposed that music as process is the experience of mind time; a constant ebb and flow that gives both therapist and client chances to give and take, to care and be near, and to experience both gravity and levity. In other words, music therapists typically have advocated the view that music is activity and relationships. In the term *musicking* a suitable conception of this perspective may be found. What remains to be seen is what theoretical and practical consequences will be drawn from choosing to use the term. In my interpretation, at least one major implication should be clear for the discipline and profession of music therapy. In searching for the meanings of music in music therapy we need to develop a theoretical perspective that allows for viewing meaning as situated use, which again suggests that an ethnographic approach to the study of music therapy becomes vital.

I consider the concept of musicking as potentially useful and helpful for the theory and practice of music therapy. This is obviously so in the improvisational approaches to music therapy, but probably just as much when music therapists appropriate the canonical works of art in the tradition of Western classical music, such as the GIM therapists do. The "objects," or work of arts, are experienced through performances, as events in time and context, and the concept of musicking should be relevant also in these practices of music therapy. Some caveats and criticisms concerning the concept should be given, though, in order to stimulate further reflection and refinement. One of the criticisms that may be voiced is the following: Why – apart from the joy of innovation – do we actually need this "new" word, music as a verb in the present participle? Why not stick to the noun? It is not correct to assume that nouns necessarily function as names labeling *things.* They may just as well denote processes, so it would be possible to talk about music as action, interaction, and relationships without coining a new word.

This criticism I believe at least is a relevant reminder of the limitations of renaming. There is little reason to believe that changing nouns into verbs will solve too many of our problems. After a few years of talking about musicking, healthing, therapying, and so forth, most of us will have enough, I assume, and will not necessarily be in a new place. To Small's defense it could be said that a new word was needed in this specific case, since music as a noun has been linked to a tradition of thinking that has been dominating and limiting for centuries: music as denoting a thing or an object. In fact, Small's concept already seems to have brought some music therapists and scholars of music to a somewhat new place, by stimulating the search for alternative entry points in the discourse about music. This is so even though the word musicking may be used as a gerund and therefore given the function of a noun. Musicking as a gerund, which in fact is how the term is often used, at least clearly labels an activity, not an object.

Another criticism, or at least problem, is related to language. Small's argument is strongly connected to the English language, where music as a verb has not been much in use. In other languages this has been different. For instance, the German and Scandinavian languages already have music very well established as a verb, used in the vernacular.[12] This verb is used in a much more restricted meaning than Small's, though. Usually it denotes the act of playing or singing (together). The broad connotations suggested by Small are usually not covered in this everyday language use. To establish a new verb in these languages or to try to broaden the meanings of the established verb may be possible strategies, although both may create some confusion. This translation problem is a practical one, one may say, but it also hints at the vagueness involved when Small chooses to define his concept as broadly as he does. There *are* good reasons to extend our understanding of making music beyond sound-making. Movements, body posture, and words are essential aspects of the communication process, as illuminated also in the concept of Communicative Musicality discussed earlier. We are therefore reminded about the cultural specificity of the Western concept of music. When to sell tickets and to wash floors also is to music, the concept is getting rather broad and vague though, many would say. A logical continuation of the argument would be that the printer producing the tickets is also musicking, as is the lumberjack cutting the trees that the tickets are made of. In other words, everyone and everything is musicking. The concept decomposes.

It must be acknowledged, however, that some of the criticism in the last paragraph is not paying enough attention to the details of Small's argument. Since he is not discussing music as an abstract and generalized phenomenon, but as a situated practice, what to include then must be considered locally. The suggestion that the printer and lumberjack are musicking and that this decomposes the whole concept may therefore miss the point somewhat. Although Small does not discuss this himself, I propose that musicking as situated practice may be compared to Wittgenstein's (1953/1967) concept of *language game*. In similar ways as we need to pay attention to the concrete situations of social use in order to understand the meaning and function of words, Small's concept of musicking points not only to music as a verb but even more to *music-in-context*. What a context is may be difficult to define in theory, and extensions of context may logically be suggested into eternity. In relation to concrete events and activities it is usually more clear what constitutes the situation of use, and therefore also who participates in the musicking and how.

THE POWER OF MUSICKING

Some of the early modern pioneers of music therapy made very optimistic claims about *the power of music*, and many of them tried to understand their remarkable musical-clinical experiences in the light of ancient philosophy. As is well known, Pythagoras and other philosophers in ancient Greece thought of music as something very important; in fact they built their cosmology on music, a tradition that was brought forward to the thinkers of the middle ages through the works of St. Augustine and Boethius. Some music therapy pioneers linked their work, directly or indirectly, to this tradition. Consider for instance this epigraph found in one of Nordoff and Robbins' books:

> Music is a moral law. It gives a soul to the universe, wings to the mind, flight to the imagination, a charm to sadness, and life to everything (Plato, quoted from Nordoff & Robbins, 1971/1983).

The beauty of this statement is striking, but the use of it could not – and was not intended to, I presume – convince those who ask for a more scientific evaluation of the power of music in music therapy. "If music works then show it, do not kill me with poetry," is a possible response from a skeptical empirical colleague.

The discussions of this chapter have been related to the question if music therapists have anything to learn from musicology or if they should turn to psychology and other behavioral sciences in trying to understand music therapy. In my judgment it should clearly *not* be a question of either/or. The relevance of psychological theory for music therapy was reflected upon in Chapter 1, while the outline made in this chapter suggests the relevance of contemporary musicology for music therapy. We are then talking about a "new" musicology, with for instance open boundaries to and interaction with disciplines such as biology and ethnomusicology.

What remains difficult is to account for the power of music in therapy. To go beyond the idealistic and romantic use of ancient Greek philosophy about music is unavoidable for a contemporary discipline and profession, but what alternatives may be developed for conceptualizing the power of music? I am not asking this question by suggesting that this power should be taken for granted. It is experienced by a large number of clinicians I have spoken with and listened to. It is described in many case studies available in the literature. Still, I would agree with those who suggest that it is something to be studied and explored empirically. Such investigations must be informed by and interpreted in relation to viable theories though, in order to contribute to the development of the discipline and in order to be of any help for the clinician. The purpose of the following paragraphs is to outline how the concepts of protomusicality, musics, and musicking together may establish a possible starting point for the development of such a theory.

As we have seen, Trevarthen and Malloch (2000) and Dissanayake (2001) propose the concepts of *communicative musicality* and *protomusicality* as a basis for a theory on the therapeutical effect of music. These suggestions are interesting and should be explored further, while they to my judgment could not be taken as arguments for biology as the sole foundation of music therapy. The notion of culture outlined in Chapter 1 suggests that human nature is "essentially nonessential," to put it a little awkwardly. While culture is not independent of biology and while in some respects there are biological constraints on culture, music as culture is more than a reflection of biology, it is also a result of social and cultural history. The capacity for cultural learning to some degree enables humans to "wag the dog"; meanings are *mediated* and cannot be grasped by the senses only. Perception is colored by cultural learning. We need to take cultural history into consideration in order to understand humankind.

Music in music therapy is constituted as acts of *musicking*, inevitably related to *protomusicality* as a human capacity developed in phylogeny as well as to *musics* developed in cultural history. Musicking in music therapy may then be understood as available for the individual in a *Zone of Proximal Development*, and may be seen as constitutive of agency through interactions and interpersonal relationships. Music is obviously experienced strongly in the here and now, as shared and evolving time. It is therefore a commonplace suggestion that music may be a powerful tool for the experience of social integration, of *shared focus* and *shared experience*. This is implicit in Trevarthen and Malloch's (2000) concept of communicative musicality in mother-infant interaction, but music seems to have powerful functions of *integration* also in larger social contexts; in communities and possibly in societies at large (Østerberg, 1997). What needs to be accounted for is how this power is constituted, and how music also at times may attain powers of *differentiation* rather than integration.

The concept of protomusicality illuminates why musicking may be powerful in work with in principle any client,[13] from prelinguistic infants to elderly people with, for example, Alzheimer's disease. As Trevarthen and Malloch (2000) elaborates, interaction through sound and movement is a basic human motivation. My main point in concluding this chapter is that this human capacity is inevitably *cultivated* in ontogeny, and that there is no legitimate foundation for a music therapy theory neglecting the conventional and social aspects of musicking. It is not possible to go directly from phylogeny to ontogeny, and it is not helpful to consider music as "natural" or "preverbal" or "preconventional" communication only. This is sometimes confusing in music therapy practice, because the spontaneity of improvisation is given high value, and because so many clients come to music therapy with minimal conventional music training. It is then tempting to suggest that the spontaneity achieved in music therapy sessions is *preconventional*. While I will not neglect the possibility of preconventional aspects in interaction based on the shared human capacity for interaction through sound and movement, I suggest we will have a much better notion of the power of musicking if we are sensitized to the *conventional and postconventional aspects* of music therapy musicking also.

The process of cultural learning starts day one in a child's interactions with an adult human being. Any client coming to therapy is then a child of culture, a cultivated human being. A consequence of this insight is that spontaneous expressions and unconventional musicking is rarely a-cultural. They could for instance be countercultural or subcultural, but will usually in some way or another relate to *genres of expression*. Usually then it will be clarifying to think of unconventional music as *cross- or postconventional* rather than as preconventional. Even though expressions may be within a subgenre or tradition that favors spontaneity, such as music therapy, there is usually some artification involved, such as formalization, exaggeration, repetition, and/or elaboration. Even the most spontaneous of acts is channeled through some socially and culturally defined mode of expression in order to be comprehensible as communication. That unconventional thinking and acting is postconventional rather than a-conventional is for instance illuminated by the tradition of free improvisation in jazz. Conventions of other genres of musicking may be actively avoided, but that is already a new convention, then. Even a so-called free improvisation in jazz is dependent on some rituals, routines, and other social and musical conventions of different types. Similar reflections may be made on free improvisations and other forms of musicking in music therapy.

Musical conventions are not to be avoided in music therapy. They are, in fact, inevitable. To state this is not to neglect the importance of spontaneity, creativity, and individuality in music, but rather to take into consideration the possibility that the path to human individuality goes through social and cultural learning. Usually preconventional, conventional, and postconventional elements go together and interact in therapy. I will for instance speculate that postconventional musicking, animated by the spontaneity of preconventional "whims," may work well as strategies of individual identity building, while conventional musicking is highly important in the development of sociocultural identity. Conventional musicking, then, may play an important part in music therapy processes, while it may in some cases be a straitjacket preventing creativity.

The conventional aspects of musicking underlined above do not mean that the power of musicking is experienced at a conscious and rational level only. Subconscious processes, vitality affects, and strong emotions are part of the music experience. What is provided here is a possibility to acknowledge this without reducing the discourse to a metaphysical focus on works of art or to a sociological focus on context only. With music-in-context as the object of study we may – through an ethnographically informed methodology – study how people, artifacts, and meanings are clustered within particular socially located scenes. The multi-layered character of musicking in music therapy may contribute significantly to its power, then. The agents enter the scene with communicative protomusicality as well as with a personal history of relationship to musics and people. The artifacts, such as the instruments and the musics, may have been attributed meanings through cultural history. New meanings are established as new relationships between people and artifacts are built through the act of musicking in the specific social and cultural contexts of the therapy process.

The discussion above suggests that the term musicking could become a central concept in music therapy theory, at least if we go beyond just thinking about music as a verb and draw the implication that meanings of music should be studied as use and relationships in context. Actions and interactions do not exist in a vacuum, and music-in-context will have to be the unit of study. The acts of musicking therefore necessarily relate to musics as cultural systems. This links to the discussion in Chapter 1 concerning the relationships between phylogeny, ontogeny, and cultural history. No person moves directly from protomusicality to musicking. Musicking, based on human protomusicality involves appropriation of music as culture. When people are musicking they relate to some tradition(s) of music-making, and may relate to and borrow from previous works, or fragments of them. Cultural history is available and indispensable as tools individuals use when engaging in the microgenesis of communicating and creating.

I may sum up the argument by developing the figure presented earlier in the chapter, showing the relationships between protomusicality, musics, and musicking. Figure 2 did this by using concepts developed in Chapter 1. In Figure 3 the relationships are reviewed through the use of notions developed in this chapter:

Figure 3: Relationships between protomusicality, musics, and musicking; expressed through use of the notions developed in this chapter.

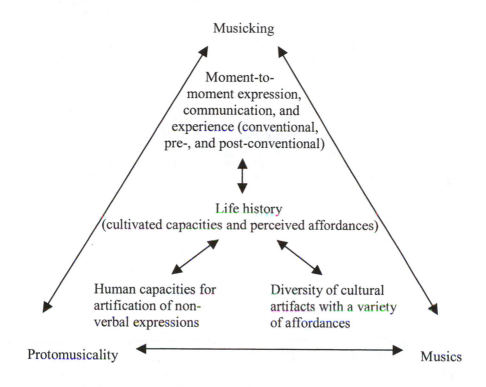

NOTES

[1] See for instance Ansdell (1997, 2001), Ruud (1998), Vink (2001).

[2] Consider the differences between Pinker (1997) and Miller (2000).

[3] Cf. a series of articles and essays on evolutionary perspectives on music, published in *Nordic Journal of Music Therapy*: (Grinde, 2000; Merker, 2000; Christensen, 2000; Kennair, 2000, 2001; Trevarthen & Malloch, 2000; Dissanayake, 2001) and a concurrent Forum-discussion on the origins of music in the journal's web site: www.njmt.no

[4] Two possible exceptions to this last universal proposed by Nettl could be free jazz and free improvisation in music therapy. In defense of Nettl's suggestion it could be argued though that so-called free improvisation is always intertextual, in some way reflecting and commenting upon previously produced music (see later about post-conventional musicking).

---

[5] As readers of the history of psychology will know, perception of melody – which is experienced as the same irrespectively of transpositions – was one of the earliest objects of study when von Ehrenfels more than 100 years ago explored the concept of gestalts in perception. What is new with Trehub's research is that she has developed a methodology that enables her to show that this perception of melody as gestalt exists in infants; see also the Quality dimension of Trevarthen and Malloch's (2000) concept of Communicative Musicality presented later in this chapter.

[6] These ratios were already explored by Pythagoras. The intervals mentioned have these ratios: octave (2:1), fifth (3:2), fourth (4:3), and tritone (45:32). The argument delivered by Trehub is of course obscured by the fact that in the tempered scale used in modern Western music the fifth is lowered and therefore has a very high-integer frequency ratio (much higher than that of the tritone).

[7] Cf. the term "proto-narrative envelope" suggested by Daniel Stern with reference to research made by Trevarthen in the 1980s. In Stern's words: "The basic idea is that certain interactive human events are directly perceived and apprehended right away in terms of meanings, even primitive ones. These meanings do not have to be constructed from diverse pieces but emerge from global intuitive parsing of experience" (Stern, 1995, p. 89).

[8] If this was true in 1964 it is of course much more true today, with the development of new musicology.

[9] In the music therapy literature it is possible to find statements like the following, made by an influential researcher in the field:

> Originally I used the words "sound" and "sound progression" to illustrate that single sounds as well as combinations of sounds can have significance, and to make clear that in therapy not "music" as a cultural/artistic phenomenon is relevant, but sounds and sound progressions as psychological parameters ...
>
> ...music therapists are well aware that the word "music" in "music therapy" does not refer to the cultural/artistic phenomenon which can be heard in concert halls (Smeijsters, 1998, p. 1).

The perspective on music advocated in this book differs from Smeijsters's suggestions in at least three ways: a) I propose that music in music therapy in many ways refers to and is linked to music as cultural and artistic phenomenon, b) I do *not* think sounds or significance can be separated from culture, and c) neither do I think psychological parameters can be separated from culture.

[10] The term *musics* is rarely defined in any accurate way. Bruno Nettl, for instance, admits that ethnomusicologists have not been able to discriminate between different musics in ways as specific as linguists have discriminated between *languages* (Nettl, 1983). I am not sure how substantial a problem this vagueness of meaning should be, and parenthetically, how accurately is it actually possible to define a language and separate it from other languages. One language, for instance Mandarin, may well contain dialects and variants that are more diverse than what is usually considered two different languages, say Norwegian and Danish. The dividing line for languages seems less to be structural qualities of the languages themselves than the

political contexts they are embedded in. A language usually has an army and a government, to exaggerate this point somewhat. Governments, if not armies, usually tend to discipline languages through different types of regulations. The same could usually not be said about musics, which may be one of the reasons why we find it easier to clarify differences between languages than between musics.

[11] Gibson's (1979/1986) description of affordance in relation to meaning is, to my judgment, related to Heidegger's (1927/1962) discussion of how meaning and knowledge may be established *through use*:

> Equipment can genuinely show itself only in dealings cut to its own measure (hammering with a hammer, for example); but in such dealings an entity is not *grasped* thematically as an occurring Thing, nor is the equipment-structure known as such even in the using. The hammering does not simply have knowledge about [um] the hammer's character as equipment, but it has appropriated this equipment in a way which could not possible be more suitable. In dealings such as this, where something is put to use, our concern subordinates itself to the "in-order-to" which is constitutive for the equipment we are employing at the time; the less we just stare at the hammer-Thing, and the more we seize hold of it and use it, the more primordial does our relationship to it become, and the more unveiledly is it encountered as that which it is – as equipment. The hammering itself uncovers the specific "manipulability" ["Handlichkeit"] of the hammer. The Kind of Being which equipment possesses – in which it manifests itself in its own right – we call *"readiness-to-hand"* [*Zuhandenheit*] (Heidegger, 1927/1962, p. 69).

This example and understanding of *meaning as use* is compatible with the discussion of meaning games in Chapter 2, and sheds light on some important processes of meaning in music therapy. Consider for instance the meaning of instruments as tools for sound production and expression.

[12] In German this verb is "musizieren."

[13] This is not to say that it is unnecessary to clarify contraindications in music therapy, but – except for rare cases of neurological damage – rather through differentiating between the value of different forms of musicking than through excluding the possibility of musicking altogether.

Part II:

PRACTICES

At some point, questioning must come to an end, in order for us to act.
(Ludwig Wittgenstein)

Part II highlights how culture-centered music therapy may be practiced. The scope varies from community music therapy with cultural change in the community as part of the aim, to ecological music therapy focusing on the communication at micro- and mesosystem levels, to individual music psychotherapy with focus upon the individual in cultural context. The three chapters therefore focus differently concerning the intrapersonal, interpersonal, and cultural processes that ecologically interact in music therapy. The three clinical populations involved are mentally challenged adults, children with social problems, and adults with psychiatric problems. The immediate contexts surrounding the work are in the first case the community of a town, in the second a kindergarten in relationship to the family of the client, and in the third a small psychiatric clinic. The stories told are of course situated in the concrete cultural contexts of this author's clinical work. The intention here is therefore not to outline general guidelines or *the* practical implications of the premises discussed in Part I, but rather to give examples of how a culture-centered music therapy *may* be practiced. Other therapists musicking with other clients in other contexts will develop other ways of working. This relates to the distinction made in Chapter 1, where I clarified that culture-centered music therapy necessarily also is culture-specific.

This may be illustrated by a brief comparison between the cases that will be presented. While all three cases reflect culture-specific work at the *local level*, this is maybe most obvious and important in Chapter 4. When Knut (whom we met in the Introduction) and the other members of Upbeat wanted to play together with the local brass band, several *community rituals* became important vehicles in process. It was, for instance, possible to use the marching parades and concerts given at seasonal celebrations as arenas of collaboration. Culture-specific elements at a *national level* are obvious in all three cases, and include the fact that the music therapists worked within a welfare system where services were paid by public authorities. This context of public welfare has been typical of the Scandinavian countries, and may be described by the sociological term *decommodification*, which denotes the degree to which welfare services are free of the market (Giddens, 2001, p. 686). An example of culture-specific adjustments on a *regional level* is given in Chapter 6, where the term *hypertextuality* will be is used as metaphor for description of the process. This focus does not reflect local or national culture, but elements that are typical in almost all contemporary industrialized and late modern countries.

The three chapters of Part II are based on presentations made on the World Congresses of Music Therapy in 1993, 1996, and 1999, and they represent a span of seventeen years of clinical practice. I have chosen to keep the general tone and argument of each paper, as originally written, although elements in my thinking have changed somewhat. The rest of the chapters of the book should clarify that. Endnotes with some comments and with reference to more recent ideas are provided, especially in Chapters 4 and 5. In converting these three congress papers into book chapters an introduction situating each paper has also been added, as well as a postscript with some afterthoughts. Since these chapters reflect a development of ideas over years, some reiteration of themes developed in Part I is unavoidable. Early versions of ideas that will be developed in Part III and IV will also be found. For a large part the concepts outlined in Part I may be understood as metatheory for the three cases in Part II. The more immediate theoretical contexts of the clinical work as it was done are presented in each chapter.

Chapter 4:

COMMUNITY MUSIC THERAPY
AS CULTURAL ENGAGEMENT

We are feeling, in other words, a need to re-create community.
This can't be done by going historically backwards, back to
the land, tribe, or village. In the same ways we have had to
redefine what constitutes a family in this decidedly
non-Ozzie-and-Harriet age, we are searching for new
forms of community. Many of the major strands of contemporary
political and social movements may be seen as part of a general
search for individual and community identity.
(Scott Walker)

This chapter – presenting a case study on the work with a group of adult
mentally challenged clients – deals with community music therapy in the
sense that the local community is not only a context *for* the work but also a
context to be worked *with*. At one level the aims of the work were related to
social and cultural mainstreaming; the starting point being that a group of
individuals of a community were excluded from participation in the cultural
life of that community. As this problem results in social and cultural isolation, which is conceived as a potential health threat, a health promotion approach was chosen with development of social networks and of personal
experiences of quality of life as main goals. The music therapy process could
then no longer be framed by the walls of a music therapy room of a clinic or
institution; much of the process evolved in other contexts, in collaboration
with local agents such as teachers of the community music school, musicians
in local bands and choirs, social workers and nurses of the homes of the clients, and local politicians. Public performances were part of the process, as
interventions and goals related to changes in community, groups, and individual clients. This chapter therefore conveys a way of working that is more
public and political than what is conventional for music therapy.

INTRODUCTION

The clinical work that is to be described was part of a project running from 1983-1986. The project was funded by the Norwegian national council of culture in collaboration with the county and municipality that the town of Sandane in Western Norway belongs to. The political context included the changes in Norwegian cultural politics that had taken place in the 1970s (in the direction of more inclusive conceptions and priorities) and the focus United Nations in 1981 put on the needs and rights of handicapped people. The project was therefore established as a pilot project in the Norwegian context, with the ambition of testing out and evaluating possibilities for using music and musical activities as tools for giving handicapped people options for social and cultural participation in their local community. The experiences and results were first published in some articles and a book (Kleive & Stige, 1988), written in the Norwegian language. I was then given a new possibility to reflect upon these questions again in the 1990s, as I got involved in a national project focused upon the implementation of these and some other pilot project experiences on a nationwide scale (Stige, 1992, 1995, 1996).

This chapter is based on a paper presented at the 7th World Congress of Music Therapy in Vitoria-Gasteiz, Spain, 1993. An abbreviated and somewhat altered version of the paper was later published in David Aldridge's *Info CD II* (Stige, 1993/1999). In this chapter some of the paragraphs from the original version of the paper are reintegrated and some other information and details of the music therapy process have been added to make the approach clearer and more understandable. Some of the English language has also been improved. Except for these changes the argument is kept as it was, in spite of any temptation to update and develop it.

MUSIC THERAPY AS CULTURAL ENGAGEMENT

Two main fields of music therapy are often referred to as Educational and Psychotherapeutic practices. Client populations, goals, clinical settings, and treatment theories are very differentiated, both *between* and *within* the two fields, and there have been rather hard discussions between representatives of the two areas, often seen as representatives of "two fighting camps." The development in the last years, however, has given a positive tendency of more communication and understanding between the two traditions. There is also a tendency of more and more differentiated work, in populations, goals etc. The field of music therapy is growing in diverse directions.

In his book *Defining Music Therapy,* Kenneth Bruscia (1989) is showing this by describing eleven different *areas* of music therapy practice. In this chapter I am going to discuss topics of an area that in *some* aspects is related to what Bruscia defines as Recreational Music Therapy. My discussion will use projects done in Sandane, Norway, as a starting point. These projects have given practical experiences combined with theoretical considerations. This work is maybe best described as Music Therapy as Cultural Engagement, an area somewhat larger than Recreational Music Therapy.[1] Cultural activities connected to leisure time may be an ingredient, but is not the defining element. The basis is the conception that an individual is a part of a *community*, and that this community is *cultural* in nature. The concept of culture is here used both in a narrow sense (art, music, etc.) and a wide, descriptive sense (tradition, values, etc.) (Klausen, 1970). The development of modern Western societies makes cultural activities important as paths to integration and participation in communities.

Music Therapy as Cultural Engagement has been integrated since 1988 as a part of the music therapy education program in Sandane. The music therapists working in Sandane are and have been developing the area of practice. Also, the county where Sandane is located now pays two music therapists to work in this area, by collaborating with and guiding professionals of the health and cultural systems in the whole county.[2] I will outline a context for understanding *why* this field of work has been given this priority.

MUSIC THERAPY, HEALTH PROMOTION, AND CULTURAL LIFE

After World War II technology and economy have gone through a fast development in many countries. The individual's possibility to choose education, job, and place to live is much larger than before. But, there are some dark sides of the road. The gap between the rich and the poor – both countries and individuals – seems to be increasing, and the technological development has become a threat to the ecological balance of nature. There are also some other, maybe less dramatic but still very important, dark sides of the road: stress problems, weakening of communities, and a splitting of areas of life which used to belong together. In this situation many persons experience their feeling of identity as threatened. The social networks are changed, and often weakened. Quite a few people experience loneliness and isolation. This situation is bound to have consequences on these individuals' health and quality of life (Dalgard & Sørensen, 1988). It has been suggested that the development of the society produces new clients in a speed that clearly exceeds the pace of the (strong) growth in the modern health systems (Bø, 1989).

In Norway and in many other countries one has attempted to meet this situation by reforms of the health systems and in social reforms aiming at community development, especially since the 1970s. More decentralized and democratic communities are among the goals stated for these reforms, and many of them focus on developing increased possibilities for participation for those who for some reason have been excluded, such as persons with handicaps or mental problems. The institutions have been closed and the municipalities have been given responsibility for providing education, jobs, a place to live, as well as cultural and leisure-time activities for all members of the community. However; political and bureaucratic decisions can never make a human being become an integrated member of a community, or make him *feel* included. These decisions must be combined with empathic *social action*. To move out of an institution and into an apartment in an ordinary living-quarter does *not* automatically create a new social network. Neighbors and fellow citizens need to take responsibility and action to make integration and participation for these people possible, and in some cases professional help is necessary to support the process (Kleive & Stige, 1988).

A mentally retarded person[3] experiences a two-fold problem in this process. He must – as all of us – walk on the "dark sides of the modern road," and he has a starting point as a segregated individual with limited personal resources for changing his own situation. The task to create a positive social network, then, must be very demanding, and the isolation that often follows may represent a health threat. The World Health Organization (WHO) has stressed the connection between health and quality of life and has also put focus on the value of health promotion and prophylactic health work. Health is certainly more than just "not being sick." Health is related to the person's experience of quality of life. Important criteria of quality of life is: the individual's *ability to be active*, his *self-esteem*, his *relationships to other people,* and his *experience of life as meaningful* (Rustøen, 1991). Thus health is a *process*, it is not a state or condition.[4]

An important way to strengthen and improve the social networks is *engagement in cultural activities* (Bø, 1989). These activities will give possibilities for a development of contact and relationships, social learning, and the experience of self-esteem and self-realization. In other words, engagement in such activities may be important for a person's quality of life, and thus his health. Such connections between health, quality of life, and cultural activities seem to be an important background for the growing interest for music therapy in Norway in the 1970s. In the same decade there was an important public discussion on cultural politics. Main issues were how to make the cultural life in the society more decentralized and democratic. The *everyday culture* of the people was given more attention, and cultural *activity* was given more priority than before. Thus, the concept of quality no longer should be attached only to cultural products, but also to the *cultural processes.*[5] This opened up for a broader understanding of the concept of cultural life (Stortingsmelding nr. 52, 1973-74), an understanding in which the field of music therapy could find its place.

A NOTE ON THEORY, GOALS AND METHOD

I will suggest therefore that Music Therapy as Cultural Engagement is an important area for the music therapist. This suggestion is in line with Even Ruud's definition of music therapy (1981, 1987/1990).[6] Ruud suggests that health problems must be regarded as "limited options for action," and that these do not belong to the individual only, they are often (co)created by society. Music therapy – as Ruud defines it – is then connected to a concept of sickness and health that stresses the relationships between the individual and his context, which then again suggests a strong focus upon health promotion and prophylactic health work. The development of the area of Music Therapy as Cultural Engagement may be seen as a way of putting this definition "into action." The case presented in this chapter is from work with mentally handicapped persons, but this way of working could be as relevant for other groups "in risk" in a society: the elderly, people with psychiatric problems, etc.[7] I therefore want to present some thoughts on theory, goals, and method that I consider crucial for all these populations.

It seems clear that the health system and the professions of therapy no longer can work as if health problem(s) only exist inside the client. A family and community perspective seems essential in many cases. The concept of social network, borrowed from anthropology, is a useful tool for understanding and working with many clients. An ecological and system theoretical orientation will be necessary to meet the new challenges (Skårderud, 1984; Dalgard & Sørensen, 1988). Knowledge and theory of individual treatment therefore must be combined with social educational, social psychological, and social psychiatric approaches. Theories focusing on the individual and theories focusing on the social level may here be seen as thesis and antithesis. The challenge must be to develop a useful synthesis (Bø, 1989). Communication is a very important aspect of this. The growth and development of every person depends on communication, and so does the development of the community. The Norwegian philosopher Nina Karin Monsen (1987) states that only when we see and hear the others and are seen and heard by them – that is, only when we communicate – are we able to be them – that is, only when we communicate – are we able to be ourselves and learn who we are. Community *is* communication, as the words themselves tell us. Only when we are able to communicate do the social networks achieve positive values in our lives (Schjødt & Egeland, 1989).

Ruud (1987/1990) states that the music therapist must consider the individual both as an organism, an individual (a person), and a member of society. This point of view I find relevant also in Music Therapy as Cultural Engagement, but it is of specific importance to see the client as a cultural individual in the community. In fact, goals should be defined both for the individual, the music group (if the format is group), the organizations in the community, the public institutions that are involved, the clients' neighborhood, etc.[8] Of course these goals will be on very different levels. The point is that it is not possible to work with the client as an isolated individual. Working *in and with the community* the music therapist will have to be adaptable and to use a broad approach. He may need to combine music therapy models with approaches developed in related fields, such as music education, performance, and counseling. As long as participation in culture is the aim, it is also essential to take the musical codes that are known and preferred by the client as starting point in the process (Ruud, 1987/1990). The work will therefore be open, flexible, and partly public. While working directly with the individual and/or group, crucial interventions in the process may also be directed toward the community itself, for instance in order to work with attitudes and traditions that create barriers in the community. Very often also lack of economic priorities given by the municipality or other funding agents limit the clients' possibilities for growth and development. The work of the music therapists therefore also has a political dimension to it; they cannot be indifferent about the political discussion of education, health, and culture.

Very important aspects of the music therapist's work, then, are the actions taken before and after the traditional music therapy sessions. In order to be able to work in and with a community the music therapist must for instance be given opportunity to work in close collaboration with institutions and organizations of the community and with other professionals working with the client. In the project to be described here, this need was taken care of through conscious use of *combined posts* for the music therapists. The music therapist – instead of being linked to just *one* institution or having a set of fragmented part time jobs – was employed in a full-time position by the municipality, and then a carefully planned schedule was worked out, connected to different institutions, organizations, and arenas considered to be of key importance in order to achieve the goals formulated. In my own case this meant working two days a week in a special school, one day a week in the community music school, one day a week in collaboration with the choirs and brass bands of the community, and one day a week with consultation of other professionals. If the composition of a combined post is more than an arbitrary collection of bits and pieces but reflects a conscious choice of arenas in relation to the tasks and goals given priority, the music therapist is given new options for working with the culture of systems. Having legitimate access to and a defined role in a set of arenas, the music therapist is given possibilities for working with the establishment of contact and communication *between* systems, and in this way try and build down barriers hindering participation for the individual or group in question (Kleive & Stige, 1988).

- MAY WE TOO PLAY IN THE BRASS BAND?

My own first experience with music therapy as cultural engagement in and with a community was the "Sandane-project" (1983-86), funded by the state, the county, and the municipality in collaboration. As described in the introduction to this chapter, this project was established in the context of national political ambitions on developing more inclusive communities and increased possibilities for cultural participation for individuals with handicaps and health problems. I will here tell the story of "Upbeat," one of the many groups we worked with in the project.

The members of Upbeat were in their thirties and forties. They all had Down's syndrome and were all moderately mentally retarded. At the start of the project they lived in an institution where my colleague Ingunn Byrkjedal worked in a part of her combined post. When the project was set up in the autumn of 1983, the members of Upbeat were accepted as the very first handicapped students in the Community Music School in Sandane. They were given priority for several reasons. First, some of them had demonstrated an interest for music, for instance by spontaneously taking over the role as conductor when choirs had visited the institution where they lived. Second, none of them had any other possibility to develop this interest for music. Third, none of them had any activity outside the institution where they lived. Fourth, plans for moving out of the institution and into separate apartments in the community town existed for three of the members of the group. The second, third, and fourth reasons made the issue of developing options for community participation pressing, while the first suggested that music could be a vehicle for this.

The Community Music School in Sandane, being one of the very first in Norway to do so, therefore established its first group for handicapped students. The two music therapists in the project were engaged to work with the students. A broader community perspective was then implicit, but not clearly articulated, since it was felt that some practical experiences were necessary before a strategy could be developed. The paragraph to follow describes the opening minutes of Upbeat's first session:

> Slowly, with their eyes and ears open, they come into the music room. They know nothing about being pioneers, but they know that this is new – and exciting! They have come here after a long walk from Nordfjordheimen, the institution for mentally handicapped were they all live.
>
> Besides Reidar and Gunnar, the group consists of Solveig, Jon, Knut, and Solbjørg. Reidar was able to play a little on a recorder. The others had very little or no experience of making music. But they have an interest of music, and the pictures on the wall soon awaken their interest further. They see pictures of the local brass band, with uniforms and horns. After a few minutes we sit down and talk together.
>
> The atmosphere changes and becomes more relaxed. Knut asks: "May we too play in the brass band (Kleive & Stige, 1988, p. 20)?"[9]

These few notes from the first session show that just to *change arena*, from working in the institution to working in the Community Music School, made an important difference. The pictures on the wall helped Knut to put to words an old dream of his: to play in the local brass band. On different occasions, like every year's celebration of May 17th, the Norwegian National Day, he had heard and seen the brass band playing in the streets. And he had liked it! When seeing the pictures on the wall he was able to *voice* his dream. "May we too play in the brass band?" As music therapists we did not know any answer to that question. We immediately felt that it was important, though. While our training in music therapy had not prepared us for walking out of the music therapy room in search for a brass band to play with, the relevance of the question could not be neglected. The rationale for giving Upbeat music therapy was partly related to visions about developing possibilities for community participation, so how *could* we neglect the question?

We could not, but still we did not know what to answer. We knew little about the attitudes and traditions of the brass band, and even less about the musical aptitudes of the members of Upbeat. We therefore decided that the first thing we had to do was to make music together, the six members of Upbeat and the two music therapists. Knut and the five others were invited to choose an instrument each. They did so; all choosing drums and percussion instruments. I sat at the piano, and my colleague Ingunn assisted and facilitated the playing by conducting a clear and steady basic beat. When we started to play together, the music therapists soon realized that there was a huge gap between the dream voiced and the experience and competency of the group members. The members of the group had never played together before. Some of them had hardly played a musical instrument at all, and it was not even possible to establish a basic beat. Many members of the group were not in contact with either their own beating or the beating of the others. The result was chaos. After some minutes of this the music therapists decided to change approach. To start with structured and conducted activities did not seem to be helpful. Instead we decided that we wanted to explore how contact and communication could be developed through musical improvisation, in the formats of individual improvisations, duets, and group improvisations. We then used the model of *Creative Music Therapy* (Nordoff & Robbins, 1977; Bruscia, 1987) as a starting point, accommodated to the group situation. This improvisational way of working immediately made more sense. The interest of the members of the group was heightened and we felt that we had a less chaotic and more promising atmosphere to work in.

This improvisational approach then was our main method of working for most of the first year of music therapy. Gradually, after some months, we could start to introduce structure, rules, and signs for how to play, as preparations for developing skills that could later be used in making special arrangements of music:

> Gradually signs meaning "fast," "slow," "hard," and "soft" were introduced and mastered. The group members are becoming more coordinated and collaborative. The musicians[10] become more aware and in contact with themselves, each other, the instruments and the music therapists. We now start to try activities with a clear and simple structure. At a sign given by the leader (one of the music therapists) each musician plays his often rather free part. We are able to do such activities after some months. But is this music that others would like to hear (Kleive & Stige, 1988, p. 21)?

This last question became important. Eight months after we started to work with the group, three of its members were about to move out of the institution and into apartments in an ordinary living quarter in town. The music activities in the Community Music School were in continuous development, but this was still only an organizational integration. There was no social or psychological integration, that is, the members of the group had not been given new opportunities for the *experience of belonging* to sociocultural contexts other than that of the institution where they lived. Would it be possible to use music therapy as contribution to a process that could enable them to take part in activities together with other members of the community? We decided to intensify those elements of the work that were geared to change of attitudes and breaking down of barriers in the community.

First we used the local newspaper rather consciously as a tool in this process. We knew that a few articles there would help in increasing the local people's awareness about the situation and preparedness for entering negotiations about steps to be taken. The matter was then discussed with the collaborators involved in the project, and it was concluded that we should start a systematic process of communication with the public choirs and brass bands of the community. These organizations coordinated themselves in a local council of music. We contacted the council, and were invited to their meetings. Through that association general information about the project was given: the political context, the main goals of the overall project, and the new and concrete situation related to the fact that some of the members of Upbeat were about to settle down in apartments in town. Knut's question was of course also communicated to the council. This worked as a foundation for discussion and negotiation about possible action.

WITH LONGING, LIFE, AND SONG!

What problems and possibilities did the music organizations see? Would any of these organizations be interested in any form of contact with the members of Upbeat? The response was in fact quite positive, although mostly at a general level. Few organizations were very eager in binding themselves to any particular collaboration. *One* choir took a different approach, though, and made a suggestion voiced by one of the more influential and well-known men of the community. This choir had for years had a May 17th tradition of entertaining and singing at the institution where the members of Upbeat lived. What about preparing something to perform together on the next National Day, only two months ahead? The music therapists responded positively to the suggestion, thinking about it as a possible point of entry for realizing some of the more ambitious goals of the project: to establish arenas where people that previously had been excluded could participate.

While the scope of the work had been widened, methodological challenges of the music therapy sessions themselves remained important and needed attention. In preparing the May 17th performance, for instance, the music therapists discovered how skills in improvisation also were needed when working with musical arrangements. After eight months of improvisational work the group was now able to play in a shared basic beat. Since simple signs of start, stop, fast, slow, loud, and soft also were mastered, possibilities for writing arrangements of songs and musical pieces now existed.

These arrangements, of course, had to have a clear and simple structure. At this point in the process usually only *one* member at the time was playing a special part in a musical arrangement, in addition to the basic beat kept by the other group members. At a sign given, each musician in turn could play his part, which was tailored to the skills and preferences that he or she had demonstrated through months of improvisation. Even when taking all this care in providing suitable challenges for each group member, the music produced often was quite different than what had been planned for when writing an arrangement. Group members might pop up with spontaneous new ideas, the music therapists might discover new possibilities on the spot, an interesting misunderstanding in the process of playing and conducting might occur, etc. There were always some accommodations to be made, and we decided to include improvisation as elements in the arrangements to be performed:

> The musicians were asked to improvise different atmospheres on their instruments, like "sad," "happy," or "strong." They did this with great interest. We found out that we wanted to improvise together with the choir. Two traditional Norwegian songs were taken as a departure point. One of these songs – a spring song – was arranged with a long improvisational introduction. Bird flutes, percussion instruments, and voices created the atmosphere of spring. In this music-making the members of Upbeat were the skilled ones. They had more experience in improvisation than the members of the choir. Instead of being "handicapped and unskilled" they could experience themselves as skilled musicians (Kleive & Stige, 1988, pp. 25-27)!"

The May 17th outdoor collaborative performance went well. Upbeat and the choir played and sang together. They improvised, smiled, and laughed. It was sunshine and springtime! The spring song mentioned in the quote above included a line that became sort of an epigraph for the continuing process: "With longing, life, and song!" For this first collaborative performance a day more symbolic than May 17th could hardly have been chosen. The National Day symbolizes *hope* for most Norwegians, because it is a celebration of springtime after a long winter, and also because it is used to commemorate the liberation from Denmark in 1814 and from Germany in 1945. This specific May 17th, in 1984, the music therapists and the members of Upbeat were especially happy, and we soon learned that the event actually was our first experience with a way of working that we later chose to call *period-collaboration*.[11]

In the period-collaborations that we developed a group of handicapped musicians worked out musical products together with a choir, a brass band, or another musical organization in the community. In this process the social interaction between the musicians was seen as very important, and this included shared activities such as preparing the room before rehearsals, making and drinking coffee in breaks, etc.[12] The musical products that evolved out of the processes of collaboration were usually a synthesis of the musical competency and tradition of the two "partners" (the music organizations of the community therefore to some degree had to change their concepts of aesthetic quality, while the members of Upbeat had to learn about conventional ways of making music that still were new and different for them). A period-collaboration was always defined as a time-limited mini-project and given direction through the definition of a concrete goal, such as a public performance.

The second year of work with Upbeat included the elements now mentioned; individual and group improvisations in the music therapy sessions combined with concentrated work on musical arrangements. Our approach to this part of the work was very much inspired by Nordoff and Robbins (1971/1983, 1977). In addition there was a continuous process of working with public relations in the community. Public performances were part of the process, sometimes with Upbeat as a separate group, sometimes in period-collaboration with a local choir. Upbeat was now a well-known group in town. The enthusiasm expressed in the description of the first public performance lived on, but was also gradually tempered by new and more varied experiences. Some of the members of Upbeat wanted full assimilation in a choir, which turned out not to be possible at this point. Also, we learned more about the dangers of overenthusiasm. When the local newspaper wrote about Upbeat's performances there was a certain lack of nuance; everything was just fantastic. In the long run we felt that this way of writing was *not* in the interest of the group. It could in fact contribute to stigmatization instead of reducing it.

One of the new musical elements in the second year of work was the inclusion of classical music in the repertoire. The pieces and songs we had been working with up to this point were favorites we knew the members of Upbeat liked, or well-known traditional songs belonging to the repertoire of the local choirs. To include classical music was not something actually planned for. It just kind of happened, and turned out to give us some new possibilities. The pictures on the wall of the music room had originally stimulated Knut to ask: "May we too play with the brass band?" After more than a year this question was not forgotten, but we felt time was not right yet. One day in the second year of work some *other* pictures also came to the attention of the group members. On the opposite wall to the pictures of the brass band hang all the composers of the canon of Western classical music: Bach, Mozart, Beethoven, Brahms, etc. Since this was in Norway, a picture of Edvard Grieg was also included, and *he* was the one that caught the group's attention. Not because of any patriotism, I assume: Upbeat did not know who these guys were, but of the men on the wall Grieg was certainly the one with the nicest mustache! Again Knut was the one to ask a question: "Who is that man?" We explained, and added the fact that Grieg was born in Bergen. That got the group going! Most of them had lived in Bergen in their adolescence, in the central institution for mentally retarded people in Western Norway. Only later had they moved to the local institution in the town of Sandane. In order to acknowledge this renewed interest for Bergen, the music therapists decided that we should include in our repertoire some of Grieg's lyrical pieces for piano. We arranged them for Upbeat, only to discover that the group members liked this music a lot. The pieces turned out to be rather well suited for this kind of work also. Being based upon folk music they are melodic but also repetitive and simple in form and structure, for instance by allowing for the use of drones.[13]

One element in the overall community project that Upbeat's process was part of, was, as briefly mentioned before, to collaborate with and give consultations to other institutions and communities. Consultation-collaboration relationships with professionals who wanted to build up community music activities for mentally retarded people were established. A component in this work was to arrange some new collaborative concerts, where groups from other towns and districts of the county were invited to come and perform, separately and together with Upbeat. This also contributed to a new awareness among local people about "something" happening concerning the rights and possibilities for handicapped people for cultural participation.

GO DOWN, MOSES

As the work proceeded and we entered the third and last year of the project period, we asked ourselves: "How then, could we make Upbeat's first dream come true, to play with the brass band?" After two years with practice in improvisation and structured activities, and after quite a few concerts and period-collaborations we thought that the time possibly was right. Again the issue was discussed in the local council of music, and an agreement about a period-collaboration was made. This time there was more reluctance in the air than what we were used to; the brass band was more geared toward conventional quality of product than what many of the local choirs were. The headmaster of the Community Music School was also conductor of the brass band, and this helped in building the connection:

He [the headmaster] suggested a period-collaboration between Up-beat and the brass band. "Kum ba yah, My Lord" and "Go Down, Moses" were now dressed in some new musical clothes.

"The People's Voice," a concert where the audience was asked to sing along, was on the brass band's schedule later that winter. Up-beat could play together with the brass band on that occasion! We couldn't quite believe it ...

The rehearsals began. Quite proud we saw how six mentally handicapped musicians had "climbed mountains." The pictures on the wall in the music room had now become a natural part of their lives, in more than one way. Under these rehearsals – and in the breaks filled with talking and coffee drinking – these musicians be-came a part of the musical and social community. And, the uniforms, the uniforms ...

The concert at "The People's Voice" was a kind of final break-through for Upbeat. Reidar played "Kum ba yah" on the recorder. Together with him the head of the administration of the municipality, who was one of the members of the brass band, played his clarinet. The contact between the two of them was not to be doubted. This we could see; they poked and teased each other, and smiled the whole time. When playing "Go Down Moses" Solbjørg played a tremolo on the drum. She did this with such enthusiasm that the audience ap-plauded and she herself stood up and shouted in triumph, her arms up in the air (Kleive & Stige, 1988, pp. 30-32)!

For years Knut and some of the other members of Upbeat had been listening to, marching besides, and dreaming about taking part in the music of the brass band. Finally this dream had been transformed to reality. Some of the other group members probably had not had the same dream in such a clear manner. They too had very positive experiences with this specific period-collaboration. The power of the brass instruments and the rhythms of the drums stimulated them to take new steps. Take Solbjørg, mentioned above; her tremolo and fortissimo finale of "Go Down, Moses" must be seen in the light of her improvisations in the music therapy room two years earlier. At that time she had restricted her playing to the softest of the soft sounds you could make on a frame-drum, in a rigid and slow tempo. Steps had been taken indeed, both musically and socially.

One question, of course, remained to be asked. What were the more last-ing effects for Upbeat's members of such a period-collaboration? In closing the project after three years of work, we had to ask ourselves to what degree we had achieved our goal of increasing the possibilities for participation in the local community for the members of Upbeat. We did not have many research resources available to examine the question in detail, but our observations suggested that it was reasonable to conclude that new potentials were established. New contacts had been formed between the members of Upbeat, the brass band, and the choirs. While arranged contacts are different from a social network, we learned that the contacts established in fact to some degree could and would be kept alive after the period-collaborations. As the members of Upbeat were moving out of the institution and starting to live in their own apartments they also had to start moving around in town more than before, in order to buy food, visit public offices, etc. We knew then that they would meet the brass band players and choir singers "everywhere" in town. Since Sandane is a small town and a community where "everybody" sings in a choir or plays in the brass band, the possibilities for meeting fellow musicians increases to quite high levels if you participate in the musical life of the community, what Upbeat now did.

At a cultural level the premises of narrow effect questions could be questioned. Part of the value of the work was that memories for life had been produced. Some of us dream of climbing mountains, others of playing with the local brass band, and for our life histories the memories of our achievements and failures in relation to such dreams are important. Also, the people in town had been shown that music could be something more and different from what they had been used to thinking. In other words: barriers for participation had been reduced, with promising prospects not only for the members of Upbeat, but for other people with special needs in this community.

SOME CONSEQUENCES FOR RESEARCH AND ETHICS

Research on music therapy as cultural engagement in and with communities is needed. We need to know more about what kind of health problems exist for whom, where, and when, and the possible contribution of music therapy interventions should be evaluated. To do research in an area like this will require varied and flexible approaches in which both quantitative and qualitative methods for collecting, analyzing, and interpreting data will be relevant (Hammersley & Atkinson, 1983/1987), as will be the combination of these (triangulation). It will not be a good idea to try to give very specific norms for research in the area, but I will underline three points of view that I find important:

- In assessing health and quality of life, *the individual's own experience and description* of his life situation is very important. The phenomenological perspective should therefore be included in the research.[14]

- Many clients experience that their alternatives for choice and action are limited and restricted because of attitudes or practical and economical limitations in the community. Research should have as one aim to *contribute to changes* in these conditions. Research that carries on the best from the "action research" tradition therefore will be to the benefit of the clients.
- Research on humans cannot be separated from *ethics* (Fjelland & Gjengedal, 1990). In Music Therapy as Cultural Engagement this is of outmost importance. Much of the time the therapist will move in a borderland between cultural activities, health promotion, prophylactic health work, and therapy. How clear is this for the client? How clear could it and should it be? How could one ensure the rights of those clients that have no language and thus cannot discuss this in words?

A critical question could be voiced: how helpful is it to meet a "client-producing" development in the society with more professional help, as exemplified in this paper? There are no simple answers to this. For many people help is needed now, not after a long political process to change society and build better communities. Music Therapy as Cultural Engagement in fact includes the possibility of integrating the two perspectives. The music therapist could try to help clients through changing the world, if only a bit. The changes may be small, and the part of the world where the therapist is working may be very small indeed, but social change could be part of the therapist's agenda.[15] If this is accepted we get a therapist-role that is broader and more political than a traditional therapist-role; see (Haaland, 1991).

In this area of music therapy we not only need action researchers then, but in fact also "action therapists." The music therapist should help the client to clarify his identity in the community through cultural participation. This may be done in many different ways. In working with Upbeat it was important that the music therapists communicated to the members of the community, exemplified by the members of the local music council, that these people were not primarily handicapped but persons longing for possibilities of making music and willing to contribute with their own song. The members of Upbeat were persons with dreams to be pursued, which is not too different from anyone. They were musicians that wanted to take part in the cultural life of the community.

Other times the communication may go further, or offer more specific possibilities for the participants *to voice their dreams directly to be community*. For instance, when performing songs, the lyrics may voice how the participants experience their participation, their contacts, and their responsibilities in the community.

POSTSCRIPT: FROM MICRO TO MACRO

This was the end of the 1993-paper, and the work described here – possibly in a slightly overenthusiastic voice since Upbeat's own enthusiasm was contagious and since this project was crucial in the development of my ideas on community music therapy – may be framed in several ways. Some of these have been mentioned, such as music as *health promotion* and *prophylactic health work through strengthening of social networks*. The project also illuminates dilemmas concerning what values count in the music life of a community, and how "normalization" of excluded individuals may be achieved through the mastery of valued social roles (Stige, 1995). I also want to point at the personal development through music achieved by the members of Upbeat. This may be described as a process of enculturation or of being *inscribed* in a culture. From free improvisation to the more structured playing with the brass band there is a process of learning a musical technique and "language," a process making cultural and social participation possible; see also (Rolvsjord, 1998, 2002).

With the insight that hindsight gives; what I today feel is most striking with the work discussed in this chapter is its *ecological* character. This project paved the way for the more explicitly ecological perspective taken in the next chapter. I first read Urie Bronfenbrenner's (1979) *The Ecology of Human Development* in the early 1980s and this way of thinking influenced my perceptions of the community music therapy project Upbeat's process was a part of. In rereading the description of the work, I strongly feel that this aspect should be clarified, and I will use this postscript to briefly outline some of Bronfenbrenner's (1979) concepts for description of the ecology of human development, and to see how these concepts may throw light on the process described. Bronfenbrenner defines the ecology of human development in the following manner:

> The ecology of human development involves the scientific study of the progressive, mutual accommodation between an active, growing human being and the changing properties of the immediate settings in which the developing person lives, as this process is affected by relations between these settings, and by the larger contexts in which the settings are embedded (Bronfenbrenner, 1979, p. 21).

Four layers of context or ecology are considered:

- *Microsystem* – a pattern of activities, roles, and interpersonal relations experienced by the developing person in a given setting (such as a family or a peer group)
- *Mesosystem* – the interrelations among two or more settings in which the developing person actively participates (such as the relations among home, school, and neighborhood peer group for a child)
- Exosystem – settings that do not involve the active participation of the developing person, but which influence (or are influenced by) what happens in the settings containing the developing person (such as a local council or a school administration)
- Macrosystem – consistencies, in the form and content of the three lower-order systems outlined above, at the level of the subculture or the culture as a whole (after [Bronfenbrenner, 1979, pp. 16-42])

Bronfenbrenner (1979) hypothesized that an individual's thinking, feeling, and willing – as well as overt behavior – develop as a result of *transactions* among the various components of the individual as influenced by biological maturation and bodily functioning, as well as by transactions within and among the settings the individual participates in. Stimuli from the environment, feedback from the environment as a result of an individual's overt behavior, and the reciprocal influences between individual and environment are all involved in this.

To work with Upbeat gave the music therapists a rare opportunity to work on all the levels suggested by Bronfenbrenner, with the aim of stimulating the development of the members of the group. As is usual in therapy, interventions on a *microsystem* level were crucial. Weekly sessions of music therapy were conducted, and the activities, roles, and relationships were explored within that context. Important issues were for instance the clients' relationship to the music improvised, to each other, and to the two therapists. *Mesosystem* aspects of this soon came to be important, as the members of Upbeat were "pioneers" in a community music school with no experience of having handicapped students, at the same time as they were about to move out of an institution and into a community neighborhood. Work at this level included interventions well beyond the walls of the therapy room, in building connections between teachers of the community music school and the personnel of the institution, as well as connections with choirs and members of the local music council.

In order to ensure the quality of this process, quite a lot of effort was also put into working at the *exosystem* level. This involved working with information and the establishment of connections – between, for instance, the top administrator, the chairman, and the rector of the community music school –

to ensure that this school was given the resources it needed, and that they were used in ways that served Upbeat. Working at the exosystem level was time consuming, and also quite demanding, since it broke very clearly with the expected role of a more traditional "microsystem music therapist." We considered this to be a necessary element of the project, however, and the local music council's central role in this project should be quite clear from the description given in this chapter.

Usually few possibilities for going beyond the exosystem level are given, at least at the level of practice or action (it is of course always relevant to *reflect* upon *macrosystem* processes). In this specific project the work was from day one embedded in a discussion of national politics on community, music life, and the inclusion of handicapped people. After the work described in this chapter was finished, and the documentation of it published, I was given the possibility to extend the scope to the macrosystem level. The music therapy training in Sandane was invited to be part of a national project aimed at helping community music schools to establish activities for handicapped students, with the experiences of Upbeat as part of the frame of reference (Stige, 1992, 1995, 1996).

In the particular case of Upbeat, then, interventions were developed for all the four layers of ecology described by Bronfenbrenner. This is usually not possible or required. One of the premises of ecological thinking is that changes in one system may lead to changes in another, which leads to a possible "economy" of ecological interventions. What needs to be evaluated, in each case, is which layers should be worked with, how, and when. The rationale for ecological music therapy is that it is not always enough or effective to work on a microsystem level. That may be due to limitations in the growing person or to barriers in the meso- and exosystems. To go from micro to macro is not always adequate, though. What typically characterizes practices that may be labeled as ecological, such as the process to be described in the next chapter, is that microsystem interventions are extended to the mesosystem level. Exo- and macrosystem interventions represent politicization of the role of the therapist, a possibility that should not be neglected when necessary, nor should it be insisted upon in all cases.

NOTES

[1] When writing this paper for the World Congress in Spain in 1993 I used the term Music Therapy as Cultural Engagement to communicate that the target of intervention was not restricted to the individual or group, but in fact included the culture of the community. At the congress I discussed the approach with Leslie Bunt, Kenneth Bruscia, and other colleagues with better knowledge of the English language than

me, and I decided to start using the term Community Music Therapy. This change in terms I have chosen to communicate by using Community Music Therapy in the chapter title and the original formulation in the text.

[2] This aspect of the work, which may be labeled consultation-collaboration music therapy, I consider important even though there has been no space for a careful discussion of it in this book. Fragments of this issue are touched upon later in this chapter as well as in Chapters 5 and 8.

[3] I am here using a translated version of the term that was politically correct in Norway at the time, being well aware of the fact that what is politically correct concerning such terms vary over time and between countries.

[4] Implicit in this last statement – when written in 1993 – was a criticism of Kenneth Bruscia's (1989) definition of health as a state of well-being. It is worth noting that Bruscia (1998a) in the second version of *Defining Music Therapy* changed his definition of health giving more attention to the process aspects. For a further discussion of the concept of health, see Chapter 7.

[5] Cf. the concept of *musicking* explored in Chapter 3. Note also that the term *cultural* here is used with reference to the normative meaning of it (see Chapter 1), but with links to the broader culture of the community.

[6] A definition that Ruud also uses in his more recent book (1998): *Music Therapy: Improvisation, Communication, and Culture.*

[7] When this was written in 1993, few examples of similar work existed in Norway. Today a number of approaches have been explored, such as the development of inclusive community choirs for isolated elderly people, the establishment of inclusive "music cafés," etc.

[8] The music therapist's authority in defining goals on all these levels and for all these systems and organizations could of course be questioned. The project to be described was informed by action research methodology stressing communal reflections and communicatively established goals, see Chapter 11.

[9] This quote, and those to follow, are (rather free) translations made by this author.

[10] Note the rhetoric of the 1988 text. In order to challenge established values and notions, as part of the process of changing attitudes and breaking down barriers, we tried to avoid terms such as patient and some times even client, and used a broad spectrum of more open terms, such as group member, musician and student.

[11] Today I find the term "period-collaboration" somewhat clumsy, although it should be noted that the translation to English makes it even clumsier than the Norwegian original. See also Chapter 9, where this form of working is seen in relation to a local tradition of "dugnad" (working bee). This term has more recently been applied locally on collaborations such as "The People's Voice" described later in this chapter.

[12] Cf. the discussion in Chapter 3 of Small's (1998) broad concept of musicking.

[13] Cf. the notion of *affordance* discussed in Chapter 3. Grieg's lyrical pieces turned out to afford richly in at least three ways in relation to this group: a) The music linked geographically to the life history of the members of the group, and therefore played a role in personal and cultural identity development, b) The musical structures were very well suited for musicking adapted to the needs and capacities of the group, c) Grieg's music is revered highly by most Norwegians, and public perform-

ances of it therefore contributed to local changes in attitudes to the members of Upbeat as musicians in the community.

[14] This statement should probably be specified, since the term "phenomenological" is used in so many ways. I have used it here not in the original specific meaning given by Husserl but rather in the more open, "vernacular" meaning referring to participants' own experiences. This overlaps with the "emic perspective" of an ethnographic study; see Chapter 10.

[15] This statement is related to the fact that the project described was informed by action research theory; see Chapter 11.

Chapter 5:

ECOLOGICAL MUSIC THERAPY
AND
MEDIATED LEARNING

an organism can learn only that which it is taught by
the circumstances of living and the experiences of
exchanging messages with those around him.
(Gregory Bateson)

This chapter deals with ecological music therapy. A case study on the work with the problems of a child with Asperger's syndrome will be presented, and the music therapy process is described as a *transactional process* of learning in social contexts, conceptualized as *mediated learning experiences* (MLE). This is framed in an ecological perspective based on Bronfenbrenner's concepts. Compared to the case presented in Chapter 4, this chapter describes a process with more elaborate interventions at a mesosystem level and less focus upon the exo- or macrosystem levels.

INTRODUCTION

The case story of this chapter originates from a project that ran from 1992-1994, as collaboration between the music therapy education in Sandane and a regional center for special education and assessment. The aim of the project was to explore new approaches to music therapy assessment and consultation. Based upon the clinical experiences and the theoretical ideas described in Chapter 4, I chose to concentrate my efforts on developing an ecological approach. This chapter is based upon a paper presented at the 8th World Congress of Music Therapy in Hamburg, Germany, 1996. The text is published with only small changes from the 1996 version. As in Chapter 4, some sentences have been added or altered to enhance the clarity, and the case is framed by the addition of endnotes and a postscript.

– I DON'T LIKE MUSIC

The main purpose of this paper is to explore implications for music therapy assessment, intervention, and evaluation of taking a transactional and eco-logical perspective on child development. The discussion will be related to my work with children with learning problems and difficulties with social interaction. Fragments of a case study will be given, to clarify my sugges-tions. I will start by telling you about my first encounter with a six-year-old boy visiting the center for special education and assessment where I was working. The boy, named Paul, was to stay at the center for an assessment period of two weeks. The reason for referral was social difficulties, and also some language and learning problems, as experienced by his parents and the teachers of his kindergarten. I met Paul the first day he stayed at the center. He was inside a playing room, with his mother sitting in a corner watching, and he was doing some quite advanced building and construction at the mo-ment I came in. Standing in the doorway, I tried to make contact:

– Hey, Paul!
 Paul just keeps on building, as if I wasn't there. I try again:
 – Hey, Paul! My name is Brynjulf. We could make some music together.
 There is still no answer. No reaction. He doesn't even look at me. I feel a bit helpless. I move toward him, kneeling in front of him. His mother approaches, saying:
 – It's not always so very easy …
 Well, who said this was going be easy? I make one more try:
 – Hey! I'm Brynjulf. We could make some music together. Do you like to sing? Do you want to play the drum?
 Without moving his eyes from the building bricks, Paul finally gives me an answer. He mumbles with a quiet flat voice, and with almost no facial expression:
 – I don't like music.

I remember this first encounter with Paul quite well. It gave me a few things to work on. First, I did not exactly feel very successful in my attempts of making contact. In psychodynamic language it could be said that there were some countertransference issues that I realized I had to deal with. Second, how should I interpret Paul's behavior? He did not look at me once. He hardly spoke at all. He had almost no facial expression. Maybe this boy just did not like music? On the other side, there was something in this boy's behavior that went beyond communication of preferences. In fact, it was the *lack* of communication that was striking. Taking this lack of communication into consideration, how representative were the behaviors I had seen? In other words, how ecologically valid were the observations? Were Paul's behaviors mostly connected to the situation of being in a strange place with a strange man? In reflecting upon such questions I remembered Bronfenbrenner's words:

> it can be said that much of developmental psychology, as it now exists, is the science of the strange behavior of children in strange situations with strange adults for the briefest possible periods of time (Bronfenbrenner, 1979, p. 19).

Could this "explain" what I had seen? Or, did the reactions of Paul show me that he was a "strange" boy, with severe problems of communication? Or was the truth something in the middle, Paul being "strange" enough to have more than usual problems with handling this, for him, strange situation?

A TRANSACTIONAL AND ECOLOGICAL PERSPECTIVE

To take a transactional perspective on child development is to take an inclusive view. It encompasses functioning determined by the person, the environment, or both. Development is not seen as individual adjustments and changes caused by *personal variables* such as biological processes, neither as the individual's reactions to *environmental variables*. The transactional perspective takes into consideration *both* individual and environmental variables, as well as the *interaction* between them, and this interaction is seen as *mediated* (socially and culturally). Such a *transactional perspective* is developed for instance in Leontjew's (1979) Activity Theory, and is found in the writings of other Russian psychologists, such as Vygotsky and Elkonin. In Western psychology, Kurt Lewin probably was the first to develop theories in such a perspective. Today, a transactional perspective on development is suggested by psychologists belonging to miscellaneous schools of psychology (Adelman, 1995). This is an interesting development, but could also be confusing. To clarify my own perspective a little bit, I will point out two characteristics of how I use the term "transactional perspective on development":

- There is an interplay between the individual and the environment, and this interplay has a reciprocal impact on both the individual and the environment (both will change)

- Culturally informed social interaction is part of this interplay, and is a major feature (a third factor) in the child's development.

Many music therapists have been inspired by the work of Daniel Stern (1985/1998). As far as I can see, his description of the interpersonal world of the infant is in accordance with these characteristics of a transactional perspective. His perspective could be criticized for being a "microsystem theory," though, focusing mostly on the interaction between the child and an adult. At the very least we need supplemental theories that also include the environmental and cultural factors in the meso-, exo-, and macrosystems. This calls for an ecological perspective on child development, as advocated by Urie Bronfenbrenner (1979). He suggested that the microsystems indeed *are* very important, with the *activities, relationships,* and *roles* that they can offer the developing child. But a child participates in more than one microsystem (for instance in the family *and* the kindergarten systems), and the importance of the mesosystems – the interaction between different microsystems – should not be underestimated. Also the exo- and macrosystems are "framing" the micro- and mesosystem interaction, often with quite some impact on it. Human development, then, according to Bronfenbrenner, could be defined in this way:

> Human development is the process through which the growing person acquires a more extended, differentiated, and valid conception of the ecological environment, and becomes motivated and able to engage in activities that reveal the properties of, sustain, or restructure that environment at levels of similar or greater complexity in form and content (Bronfenbrenner, 1979, p. 27).

The statements I have made on a transactional and ecological perspective on development will, according to my judgment, have some implications for music therapy theory and practice. The first and most general implication is:

- Assessment, interventions and evaluation should not be restricted to personal variables (potentials and problems), but should include the environment and the interplay between the child and the environment.

Three other, more specific, implications could be:

- Assessment should be carried through in different situations (familiar and strange to the child) in an attempt to clarify individual and environment variables and the interplay between them.

- Since social interplay and the daily environment of the child is of utmost importance for the child's development, traditional interventions of music therapy could be insufficient (although they may be important or even necessary).
- Music therapists therefore could help parents, teachers, etc. in their daily communication with the child (for instance through consultation).
- Evaluation of interventions should focus not only on individual changes, but also on changes in the interplay between the child and the environment.

Many music therapists would agree that a transactional and ecological perspective on development sounds reasonable, but would add: "This is too broad a perspective to have any implications for my practice. It becomes overwhelming. How, for instance, could I as a music therapist change the conditions of the client at a meso-, exo-, or macrosystem level?" In telling the story of Paul, which I soon will return to, I will share how I myself have tried to be inspired by and not overwhelmed by this perspective. First I will illuminate how my way of thinking about Paul's problem was informed by taking a transactional and ecological perspective. Both his learning problems and social problems could be explored as *problems in social interaction*.

LEARNING AS SOCIAL INTERACTION

A transactional and ecological perspective on development suggests that learning is not only individual actions and discoveries, or reactions to environmental stimuli, but to a large degree social interaction. Such a perspective was advocated by the Israeli researcher Reuven Feuerstein in the 1970s, and developed by Pnina Klein (1989) and others. Feuerstein's main concept is *mediated learning experience* (MLE), defined as "a quality of interaction between the organism and its environment. This quality is ensured by the interposition of an initiated, intentional human being who mediates the stimuli impinging on the organism" (Feuerstein & Feuerstein, 1991). Feuerstein questioned the single modality theories of learning, focusing on the *direct exposure* of stimuli as the source of cognitive development (the behavioral S-R and the Piagetian S-O-R formulas). The concept of MLE (with the S-H-O-H-R formula) suggests that *social interaction* often is a very important part of the learning process. When learning is part of a social process a human mediator (H) mediates some stimuli, giving them salience and importance. Feuerstein therefore advocated a *two-modalities hypothesis*: direct exposure to stimuli and MLE coexist. He suggests that MLE, as a quality of interaction, is responsible for the modifiability and diversity seen in human development. Feuerstein argued that mediated learning experiences can be described by twelve different parameters, four of them being critical and necessary: Focusing, Affecting, Expanding, and Rewarding (Klein, 1989).

Focusing (intentionality and reciprocity) is defined as the main condition of an MLE interaction. The content of the interaction is shaped by the intention to mediate, and this intention is shared with the mediatee. The intention transforms the three components of the interaction: the stimuli, the mediator, and the mediatee. This is done by establishing a *focus;* the amplitude, tonality, salience, and rhythm of a stimulus are modified in order to make sure it is observed and perceived.

Affecting (mediation of meaning) deals with the energetic dimensions of the interaction, the *why?* and *what for?* Mediation of meaning starts on the preverbal level, the mediator using paralinguistic modes of communication: body language, changes in the amplitude of the voice, etc. As soon as verbal understanding develops, the paralinguistic communication is accompanied with words, designating meaning and significance to certain stimuli and events. This creates in the mediatee an orientation toward the search for "meaning." Mediation of meaning then of course is not value free, but in fact is determined by the cultural heritage of the individuals.

Expanding (transcendence) means going beyond the immediate goals of the interaction. This can for instance be done by adding conceptualizations or aesthetic qualities. Expanding widens the interaction and creates in the mediatee a propensity to enlarge his cognitive and affective repertoire.

Rewarding (mediated feelings of competence) includes any behavior of a mediator that is aimed at communicating approval of the child.

I find the theory of mediated learning experiences, combined with compatible theories of developmental psychology, very helpful in the development of music therapy for children with learning problems and social difficulties, and the concept of MLE is introduced here to show how it informed my thinking of Paul's problems, in seeing them in relation to transactional and ecological perspectives.

MUSIC AND MEANING AS SOCIAL INTERACTION

Music in music therapy very often is understood as communication; nonverbal, creative, and aesthetic. Very few music therapists would disagree on this. Still, a transactional perspective on development might challenge our concept of music, or to be more specific, of musical meaning. If music is communication, the next question is: What could be communicated through music? In music therapy this question often is answered with focus on the syntax of the music. The structure of the music – the musical elements and the relationship between them – is analyzed and forms the basis for interpretation of musical meaning. One important example of this way of thinking is the Improvisation Assessment Profiles as developed by Kenneth Bruscia (1987, pp. 401-496).[1]

When we are focusing on the syntax, the main question is: What does the music of the child sound like? A transactional and ecological perspective suggests a more pragmatic perspective in the analysis of meaning. The main question then becomes: How does the child *use* the music? The question "What does music communicate?" becomes part of the question "How is music a part of the interplay between the individual and the environment?" This does not mean that syntax is unimportant, rather that the structure of the music only carries certain possibilities of meaning; it has a polysemic potential. In fact, this polysemic potential of the music is a very important element of music as an aesthetic phenomenon. Through social interaction this polysemic potential is developed, it is given a direction.

The aesthetics of music, then, is neither the study of an objective nor a subjective phenomenon; aesthetic qualities are developed through social interaction (Ruud, 1987/1990). Musical elements do not *carry* meaning independently of how they are *given* meaning in social contexts. Such a perspective on the meaning of music is inspired by Ludwig Wittgenstein's (1953/1967) theory of language. I cannot give a theoretical discussion of this here, but this concept of musical meaning inspired me in my work with Paul. I did not only try to hear changes in his sounds, in how he sung or played the drum, but also tried to observe changes in how he *used* the music in his interaction with the world, and in how this was given meaning[2].

THE STORY OF PAUL: THE ASSESSMENT PROCESS

Paul was, as I told you, six years old when he came to the center where I was working. The reason for referral was social problems, and some language and learning problems. Paul stayed at the center for two weeks. He was ob-served and tested by different professionals: doctors, psychologists, special teachers, etc. The observations and tests showed a boy with a very good capacity when he was working with visual, cognitive tasks. But he had some problems with language, his understanding being very literal so that humor, sarcasm, and metaphorical use of language often was misunderstood. He also had serious problems in social situations, not being able to follow or even understand the nonverbal and verbal rules. He showed little interest for other people in most of these situations.

According to the first implication of the theory I have presented in this chapter, as a music therapist I wanted to assess the interplay between Paul and his environment, in both strange and well-known situations. I chose four contexts for the study of such situations: a) Paul alone in the music therapy room, b) Paul together with two other children in the music therapy room, c) Paul playing with other children at the center, and d) Paul playing in the kindergarten in his local community.

Although his first words to me had been "I don't like music," he in fact did come to the music therapy room later that day. "I don't like music" did not sound like a very promising start, but what did Paul actually mean with that statement? What was Paul's concept of music? I soon found out that Paul did not engage himself in traditional kindergarten music activities, like singing traditional songs together. He was just silent. Toward the end of the first session, though, he discovered that there were some instruments, sounds, and activities in the music room that he found attractive. He very much liked the sound of the kazoo, for instance, and after two sessions he also began to play the drum, beating a basic beat, although in a clumsy and inaccurate way.

Paul had eight music therapy assessment sessions in the music therapy room through the two weeks at the center. Being together with other children in this room did not change his behavior too much. He wanted to play the kazoo and the drum, but did not engage in interplay with the other children. In addition to the sessions in the music therapy room, I started to observe Paul when playing together with other children at the center. He usually played in the same place and at the same time as the other children, but I rarely found him in interplay. He seemed to be focused on his own things. Usually he was building and constructing something, often at a quite advanced level. The only contacts he had with other children were *conflicts*. Playing in the snow, for instance, he might take the snow other children had gathered, because he needed it for his own building projects. Or, he would find pleasure in throwing snow in other children's faces. Of course such behavior often caused quarrels and fights.

One day, in Paul's second week at the center, I followed the children when they went skiing in the woods surrounding the buildings of the center. I then discovered that Paul, often skiing by himself, in fact also was *singing* to himself. He sang fragments of the traditional songs that he never would sing in the music therapy room. So, here was a boy who did not like music but who liked to sing. Obviously, traditional activities and role expectations in the music therapy room seemed *not* to be the best setting for the discovery and development of Paul's relationship to music. The question was whether it was possible to develop other activities in music that could be more fruitful in relation to the social problems he had.[3]

At this time the psychologists of the center concluded their part of the assessment process. Stressing the personal variables, they suggested that Paul had Asperger's syndrome. The main symptoms of this disorder are, according to DSM-IV (American Psychiatric Association, 1995): severe and sustained problems with social interaction, and the development of restricted, repetitive patterns of behavior, interests, and activities. Some motor clumsiness is often observed. Lorna Wing (1981) also suggests that children with Asperger's syndrome often have some language problems, like literal understanding of language (this is not included in the DSM-IV list of symptoms). Paul's problems fitted these descriptive criteria. At the same time, a shared concern of parents and professionals was that there could be some positive and some negative consequences of giving Paul this diagnosis. Paul "needed" a diagnosis in order to get paid professional help from the municipality, and the diagnosis given should also give some guidelines for defining what kind of help would be required. The same diagnosis could create problems at the micro- and mesosystem level though. One popular way of thinking about people with Asperger's syndrome is that "they don't change much." Their problems with social interaction seem to be lasting. In this way the diagnosis could *decrease expectations for change*, making it less likely that the adults surrounding Paul would initiate mediated learning experiences. This could also create problems in the collaboration between the home and the kindergarten. Some hope for change and development is usually essential in giving meaning to such collaboration. Both Paul's parents and his teachers were concerned about this, and the importance of changing perspective from the individual to the ecological level was highlighted. The "they don't change much" argument could be turned around to a more positive focus upon the environment and the transactional perspective: "This child is more vulnerable to social conditions than other children, and more careful attention from adults will be necessary in order to create mediated learning experiences."

After this, the assessment process moved into a new stage. The defined focus was how to develop an intervention with a realistic perspective on Paul's limitations concerning social interaction. Isolation or conflict were the dominant patterns in his interaction with other children. What kind of conditions, settings, and activities were needed in order to give him a chance to go beyond these patterns? It seemed important to assess Paul's interplay with his daily environment, and to develop an intervention that could give him mediated learning experiences. After his stay at the center I therefore went to his community and visited him in his kindergarten. I observed him there, in play and in different activities, and discussed his situation with his teachers and parents. Paul was more humorous and relaxed in this setting, but my impression of him was not too different compared to the situations at the center, suggesting that the personal variables indeed were important in his case. I also tried to get a picture of how he related to the other children in the kindergarten, and how they related to him. Many of them seemed to avoid him. Again, isolation or conflict seemed to be the two alternatives for Paul. It was decided that the aim of the assessment process now was to develop a setting and a set of activities that he could use differently.

INTERVENTION THROUGH CONSULTATION

As a music therapist I could not work with Paul myself, because he was living too far away from the place I was living. There was no music therapist living in Paul's community either, so it was decided that one of the pre-school teachers should work with him. My role was to be a consultant. This was not necessarily the second-best solution, though, but had some advantages since the intervention we intended to develop was linked to Paul's *interaction in the kindergarten* (and to the interaction between the kindergarten and the home). The preschool teacher's possibility of integrating the activities very carefully with everyday life in the kindergarten could therefore be of outmost importance.

A small music interaction group of three children, including Paul, was established to create a safe and clearly set out situation. The first few sessions the music therapists worked with the group, in order to develop a set of activities that could be useful. It was still a fact that Paul "did not like music." More traditional music activities and songs, whether in the kindergarten tradition or in the music therapy tradition, did not appeal to him at this point. Or, probably more precisely, there was something with the situations created through those activities that he was not able to relate to. I therefore started a process of experiencing with the development of activities tailored to his needs, using the following four criteria: a) The activities should be based on some of Paul's competencies (like his competency in building and construction), b) the music in the activities should be based on Paul's musical preferences (preferred sounds, instruments, and songs), c) sound and music should be used to stimulate social interaction, d) the activities should stimulate play and interplay between the children, making it easier to transfer experiences and competencies to other play situations in the kindergarten.

The goal of working with activities developed after these guidelines was to give Paul positive experiences of learning in social interaction, with concurrent new and different role expectations. This, we hoped, could help him develop more positive relationships to the children and the adults in the kindergarten.

One of the activities developed we named *the airport:* The children were given some toy bricks with the task to build an airplane. Paul's very advanced building competency made him successful in this task. When the plane was finished the three children were given different roles: Two of the children were given instruments, a kazoo and a drum, the third child had the airplane. The simple rules of the game then were as follows: "This part of the floor is the airport. The kazoo is the sound of the engine, and when the engine starts, the plane starts to move. When the plane lifts the sound of the kazoo changes, the pitch moving up and down together with the movements of the plane." The children enjoyed this, and the game could go on for quite a while. The plane and the kazoo sound moved up and down, and the engine roared with dramatic energy. At points there would be more drama; the plane would fall down and be smashed to pieces. This was the time for the drum: explosions and fires burned on the skin of the drum, causing loud and dramatic drumming.

We learned that Paul took *pleasure* in and was able to *participate* in such activities, also with some capacity for adapting his behavior to that of the other children. The focus on social interaction and cooperation was established by the very *concrete connection* between sound and movement. To participate he had to, and was able to, focus on what the other children were doing. The social rules were clear-cut enough for him to be able to understand and follow them. His preference for construction (his abilities being very useful every time the plane fell down) and for the instruments (the kazoo and the drum) made it motivating for him to participate. It was possible for the music therapist – and in fact also for the other children – to engage with him in learning situations characterized by intentionality and reciprocity, and to mediate meanings that included Paul's successful participation.[4] For Paul, then, these experiences must have been different from the isolation-or-conflict-experiences he was used to in the kindergarten.

After a few days we had tried out several activities similar to the one described above, and I knew that we now had an approach that could be potentially helpful for Paul. It was time for the preschool teacher to take over. A major consideration for me in the consultation process was that I did not want the preschool teacher to *copy* my activities, or the way I had used them in any exact way. I did not want the activities to ossify into a rigid set of procedures, but to be part of a living and changing interaction, making transfer to the everyday life of the kindergarten more realistic (cf. the third MLE criteria described above).

My goal in working with the preschool teacher was then *not* to teach him how to use a specific set of activities, but to help him understand the principles of MLE and then to develop his *own* way of working in spontaneous but theoretically informed interaction with the children. The preschool teacher worked with this little group of children two or three times a week. I visited the kindergarten every second week, observed the work and gave consultation and advice. I soon learned that the preschool teacher was able to develop activities and interactions congruent with the parameters of MLE. For instance, he developed a puzzle, taking into account Paul's visual competency as well as his interest for a children's program in TV that included a similar puzzle. This puzzle was used to frame a set of activities, like guessing names of songs, suggesting songs, singing songs, playing songs, or dramatizing songs. The puzzle created a *focus*, and framed interaction where *mediation of meaning* could be developed. The relation to outside contexts contributed to *expanding* beyond the immediate situation, and the relation to Paul's competencies ensured the *rewarding* aspects.

Since the transactional characteristic of the process was considered important, a tool for the preschool teacher to develop his ability to reflect upon his own participation was searched for, and found in the use of *video analysis* of the interactions. This turned out to also become an important part of the ecological framing of the work, by providing the agents with a new possibility to work on mesosystem relationships.

VIDEO EVALUATION AS PART OF
THE CONSULTATION PROCESS

This music interaction group worked together for five months, before Paul moved from kindergarten to school.[5] Evaluation of the process was carried through by video taping the sessions. The tapes were analyzed with focus upon the parameters of MLE and upon changes in the way the participants used music.

In fact, these tapes became an indispensable part of the consultation process also. I must admit that in the beginning I wondered whether I was asking too much when I requested the preschool teacher to tape his sessions. Video taping, analyzing, and interpretation takes time. But I soon learned that the video was very helpful for him. An evaluation in a transactional perspective – as pointed out earlier – is not supposed to focus only on the child's behavior, but on the *interplay* between the child and the environment. And the preschool teacher, himself a part of this interplay, got a lot of information about himself through analyzing and interpreting the tapes. For instance he learned to be more sensitive to Paul's musical participation. Paul, especially in the beginning of the process, quite often seemed not to participate in social interaction through music. But studying the videos, the preschool teacher learned that many times Paul participated in ways that he had not noticed. Paul could tap the rhythm with his foot instead of beating the drum, he could be whispering instead of singing, etc. Discovering this, the preschool teacher became more musically sensitive; he became a better mediator.[6]

Another point must be made; the video tapes turned out to be very helpful in a mesosystem perspective. As is often the case with children like Paul, the relationship between home and kindergarten was somewhat tense and strained. The boy's tendency to create conflicts around him frustrated the adults working in the kindergarten, while Paul's parents did not feel quite sure that the preschool teacher actually *was* doing everything that could be done in order to help Paul. This had created a negative circle of communication, with reciprocal skepticism and suspicion. Such negative circles of communication between the two microsystems of home and kindergarten could be very destructive to a child's development, especially when the child – as in Paul's case – needs special attention, which demands constructive collaboration between the parties involved (Rye, 1993).

An important element of the intervention and the consultation process was therefore to explore if working with the music interaction group could support and develop the communication between the two microsystems involved. We approached this by inviting Paul's mother to be part of the consultation sessions where the videos were analyzed, and this turned out to be very fruitful. She contributed with fresh perspectives on how to interpret the tapes. With the deep knowledge of her child that a mother usually has, she contributed to a shared and enhanced understanding of the observations. She could contextualize them in ways that the preschool teacher or the music therapist were not able to. In turn, by observing the interaction between Paul and the preschool teacher, the mother could see and appreciate the efforts made, and therefore she became less skeptical to the kindergarten. She also expressed that what she saw helped her to see new possibilities in how to interact with Paul at home. These discussions therefore stimulated the communication and cooperation between the home and the kindergarten in a positive direction and the evaluation process became an important part of the mesosystem aspect of the intervention.

These process aspects of the evaluation were complemented by a qualitative investigation of outcome. The approach chosen was participant observation, where the preschool teacher observed Paul both in the music interaction group activities and in the daily life of the kindergarten. These observations were then communicated as summarized statements. After eight weeks, for instance, the preschool teacher's summary was:

> Paul is not so impatient in the music sessions as he used to be. Turn-taking with the other children is easier, and he doesn't want to finish off the activities all the time anymore. Before he used to shrink from new activities, but this is not so common anymore. He is even taking some initiatives in the group, participating in new ways. In the beginning he would never sing a song together with the others. After a period of whispering to a few songs, he now can suggest one of his (few) favorite songs and sing along (although often without using words).
>
> His very intense interest in building and construction still quite often creates problems in the group. He starts building, "forgetting" the other children in the group. But I have learned something about how to create activities which help him interact with the other children. And Paul is more spontaneous than before, telling us about things happening to him outside the group. One day, for instance, he started telling us about a visit to the theater. Another day he started telling about the music on his father's personal computer, suggesting that we should sing one of the tunes.
>
> The other children seem a bit more attentive to Paul than before. I now would like to try to help Paul transfer these new experiences and competencies to other situations in the kindergarten.

Paul had developed his relationship to music and to other people, and it seemed that the communication was expanding by relating to other contexts and experiences. It is also interesting to see the development in the way Paul uses music. While in the beginning music mostly was used in isolation, he now uses music both for initiating social interaction (suggesting they should sing together) and for expanding (telling about the music at the computer at home). The value of the preschool teacher's statement as (soft) evidence of the efficiency of the intervention is not my main point here though, but more the following: The preschool teacher's development – in self-reflection and in his attitudes toward Paul – is almost as important as Paul's development. This increases the expectations for change, making new mediated learning experiences more likely. A positive circle of transaction could be established. Certainly the preschool teacher also had learned to use music in new ways, and to discover new meanings in the musical interactions.

A BROADER CONCEPT OF MUSIC THERAPY?

I have tried to show how a transactional and ecological perspective on child development has implications for the development of music therapy with children with learning problems and social problems. As far as I can see, to work as music therapist within the pre-school and school system is not limited to what Bruscia (1989) would call Educational Music Therapy.[7] Music therapy within the school system just as well could be classified as *health promotion* and prevention of health problems, for instance connected to the feeling of isolation or of lack of competency. As Adelman (1995) suggests, the school in fact could be seen as one of the more important "health institutions" in the life of children.

The specific implications for music therapy with other client populations must be discussed elsewhere, but I can see some general implications for the concept of music therapy. In these closing statements I will not introduce a new formal definition of music therapy. I just want to suggest that the concept could be broader than what are suggested in most traditional definitions of music therapy; see, for instance, Bruscia (1989). First I would like to clarify that the words "music therapy" cover – as far as I can see – at least two different concepts: a) a discipline and profession related to music and the development of health, and b) a *curative* intervention, as opposed to, for instance, music as health promotion. In my discussion here I will focus on music therapy as a discipline and profession, which then includes different ways of working, with curative interventions as only one of the possibilities.

To define music therapy is not only to describe a practical field, it is also to take a stance in a theoretical discourse. A transactional and ecological perspective on development could be seen as a challenge to our concept of music therapy, which usually is seen as a microsystem phenomenon, connected to the relationship between a client and a therapist. If development is more than a microsystem phenomenon, music therapy could also be defined as a meso-, exo-, and macrosystem phenomenon. The concepts "port of entry" and "time of entry" might clarify this a little bit:

The music therapist, using music to help the client develop health, could – together with the client if possible – choose different *ports of entry*. The traditional therapeutic relationship is a microsystem port of entry. Sometimes it is preferable to enlarge the microsystem port of entry, as for instance is done in family therapy. Other times the perspective should be broadened even more. The interaction at the mesosystem level – for instance between a child's family and his kindergarten – could need support and nurturing. The question then becomes: How could a music therapist create situations which could change the interactions at the mesosystem level? With Paul I worked at this level, giving consultations both to the preschool teacher and to the mother and trying to establish an arena for more positive communication between them. Working at the exo- and macrosystem level might also be relevant, although more difficult to define. Quite a few traditions and political decisions at the exo- and macrosystem levels might have important consequences for the conditions of the client. For instance, societies and communities might discriminate against handicapped people. This is a health problem and could be an area of focus for the music therapist (Stige, 1993/1999).[8]

Just as important is the choice of *time of entry*. A transactional perspective underlines that problems develop over time, and that poor interaction between the individual and the environment could have long-lasting effects. The music therapist – as far as I can see – then should not only focus on curative interventions, working *after* the problems have developed to a certain degree. Very often it is important to work at an *earlier* time of entry. *Prevention* of health problems – and even more important, *health promotion* – becomes a natural part of the music therapy competency (Stige, 1996).

As you will understand, I do not suggest that the theories I have presented in this chapter should be used to prescribe the details of a music therapist's work: the choice of procedures, techniques, etc. The theories are rather perspectives which could help us to look at music therapy in a new way. Changing the way of looking at the world does not mean that every detail changes, though. When humans learnt that the world is round like a ball, the lawn of their backyard could still be flat enough.

POSTSCRIPT: THE CONCEPT OF ECOLOGY

The work described in this chapter could hardly be labeled as "more" eco-logical than that discussed in Chapter 4, but at the time I wrote this in 1996 I was more explicitly framing my work as ecological than what I did in 1993. In the last paragraphs above I am hinting at consequences for how music therapy may be understood as discipline, profession, practice, and discourse. These suggestions will be developed in Part III of the book. In this postscript I will take a step back and look briefly at the concept of ecology and its relevance for music therapy.

As Gadamer (1993/1996, p. 79) reminds us, the concept of ecology has – as might be expected – an etymology that goes back to a Greek word, namely *oikos*, which means household. As a scientific concept ecological analyses were originally developed in biological science, as a tool for description and analysis of processes of interrelationships in nature. The concept of ecology has been very important in biology, and is by some considered to be one of the major concepts of twentieth century thinking. After some time the term ecology started to become used as a metaphor by social researchers. In the 1920s the Chicago school of sociology was probably among the first to do this, with expressions such as "urban ecology," etc. In the 1940s cybernetics and systems theory started to develop as a more general theory on how systems work in general. A thinker that was strongly influenced by this was Gregory Bateson (1972, 1980), who outlined consequences for a new understanding of the concept of mind; mind not as individual entity, but as relational processes.

The 1970s also produced two other publications that brought the concept of ecology to the forefront of psychology. Gibson's (1979/1986) *The Ecological Approach to Visual Perception* was mentioned in Chapter 3 in relation to the concept of *affordance*. Another work that even more greatly influenced the approaches that have been described in this chapter is Urie Bronfenbrenner's (1979) *The Ecology of Human Development* (see postscript, Chapter 4). Bronfenbrenner was inspired by Kurt Lewin's pioneering work on field theory.[9] My own use of the term ecological music therapy was originally inspired by Bronfenbrenner's work, later informed by contributions by Bateson (1972, 1980) and others. Generally speaking, music therapists have been slow in assimilating ecological perspectives and systems theory thinking, one of the notable exceptions being Carolyn Kenny's work (1985, 1989). In the second edition of Bruscia's (1998a) *Defining Music Therapy,* ecological music therapy is acknowledged as one out of six areas of practice. This will probably contribute to a stronger interest for this way of thinking and working in the years to come.

The concept of human or social ecology reminds us of the illusory nature of the autonomous, unitary individual, and it thus challenges some ideas that may have been typical among therapists. As persons we are products of relational and transactional processes, as well as agents in these processes. No man is an island, John Donne wrote, and the folk wisdom of proverbs in many languages tells us the same (the Swahili "Mtu ni watu" being my favorite in being so concise). The concept of ecology enables us to conceptualize social life as dynamic and continuously changing. It is important to remember, though, that different levels are involved when biologists and social researchers use the concept of ecology. In the latter case the ecological model is used as a metaphor, and – as with all metaphors – some aspects are illuminated while other aspects are cast more in the shadow. Some of the criticisms against Bateson and other proponents of ecological thinking and systems theory in relation to human interaction have been that issues of *power* and *intentionality* are underestimated and even difficult to account for in this perspective.

Another typical criticism is that too much stress is put on the collective level. This criticism I find less relevant, however. As the stories of Upbeat in Chapter 4 and of Paul in this chapter tell us, ecological thinking does not mean that the individual level is left out, only that the individual must be understood in relation to the social contexts that she is a part of. Paul's case is illuminating in this respect. As a child diagnosed as having Asperger's syndrome, it is obvious that some of his problems originated at an individual and biological level. Life consequences showed themselves on different levels, including the psychological and social, and it would be a mistake to think that therapeutic interventions should be restricted to an individual level. On the contrary, this boy was more sensitive and vulnerable in social and cultural contexts than most children, so that special care was needed to form and develop these contexts so that nurturing transactional processes between the individual and the environment could be expected.

The relevance of working at a mesosystem level is especially large when working with children or other clients that are very dependent on their social contexts, with limited power or possibility to change or choose the contexts of their life. With adults this is sometimes different, and to work at a micro-system level with awareness about culture and context may be a fruitful alternative. This will be the focus of Chapter 6.

NOTES

[1] For a discussion of IAP, see the Forum of *Nordic Journal of Music Therapy:* www.njmt.no.

[2] As the reader will understand; working with Paul was part of what led to the development of the theoretical perspectives on meaning and aesthetics outlined in Chapter 2.

[3] With the concepts developed in Chapter 3, one may say that other forms of musicking were suggested. The capacities of Paul's protomusicality were to some degree challenged, and there were clear limitations concerning perceived affordances. There were certain musics and forms of musicking he was not able to relate to (such as the songs of the gatherings in the kindergarten), while he had a stronger relationship to other forms, such as music he heard on television and the music of the data games of his father's computer.

[4] Cf. the criteria for Mediated Learning Experiences described above.

[5] Such a move is what Bronfenbrenner (1979, p. 26) calls an ecological transition. I later gave consultations to Paul's school teachers also, which gave me an interesting possibility to compare the school and the kindergarten systems. In many ways Paul's options for MLE were reduced in school compared to kindergarten, but it would

take too long to discuss this here.

[6] I have touched upon the issue of video evaluation in a later chapter on music therapy supervision (Stige, 2001).

[7] When writing this in 1996 I felt that the work did not fit in as Educational Music Therapy, as defined by Bruscia (1989). With the categories that Bruscia (1998a) later developed, Ecological Music Therapy would be a more suitable term.

[8] The paper that is referred to here is in a revised version republished as Chapter 4 of this book.

[9] See Chapter 11 for a discussion of Lewin's action research, which also is informed by his field theory.

Chapter 6:

HYPERTEXTUALITY
IN INDIVIDUAL MUSIC PSYCHOTHERAPY

Any utterance is a link in a very complexly organized
chain of utterances.
(Mikhail Bakhtin)

This chapter is meant to illuminate how cultural issues may play a part in individual music psychotherapy. Compared to the two previous chapters the format and form of therapy is more conventional in this chapter. While the interventions described in Chapter 4 and 5 included the sociocultural or community level, the case described in the pages to come is from individual music psychotherapy where interventions are kept on a microsystem level. By this I hope to show the relevance of culture-centered perspectives for more conventional areas and formats of music therapy, without restricting myself to conventional conceptualizations of the therapy process. This ambition is based in the premises outlined in Part I of the book, where the suggestion that personal development include internalization of culture is defended.

INTRODUCTION

The case example described in this chapter stems from an ongoing qualitative research project on meaning-making in music therapy, connected to my position as a research fellow at the University of Oslo. The study is an ethnographically informed qualitative investigation of my own clinical practice in a psychiatric clinic, and the main sources of data are field observations combined with qualitative interviews of the clients. The focus is meaning-making in a culture-centered perspective. This chapter is based upon a paper presented at the 9th World Congress in Music Therapy in Washington, D.C. 1999, on *hypertexts* in music therapy. In the version that is presented here some alterations and clarifications have been made, including the addition of a postscript.

THE TEXT ANALOGY IN MUSIC THERAPY

All discussions of meaning are complex, and the discussion of meanings in music therapy certainly is no exception. Such a discussion must embrace the meaning of music, of body language, and of verbal language, as well as the *relationships* between these meanings. Then there is the problem of how to understand the relationship between personal and public meaning, and the relationship between text (including acts and music) and context. A discussion of the meaning of meaning in therapy must also be added, that is, what kinds of meanings are essential to change in therapy?

The last couple of decades have seen an increasing interest for the text analogy in psychotherapy. Users of this analogy usually focus upon narrative and storytelling, the basic idea being that people's problems are constructed as performances of oppressive, dominant stories of knowledge. Therapy then means to help the client to (co)author and perform alternative and liberating stories (White & Epston, 1990; McLeod, 1997). The text analogy has not been very influential in music therapy, although *some* examples of researchers that have taken interest in the analogy do exist. An early example is Carolyn Kenny's (1982) treatment of music as analogous to myths. Even Ruud's (1997) work on music and identity treats identity as continuous construction of a life narrative through the use of music and activities and relationships developed through music. Ruud has later related this to questions on health and quality of life and to music therapy (Ruud, 1998). The construction of a life narrative through use of music is also Isabelle Frohne-Hagemann's (1998) focus in her approach "Music Life Panorama" (MLP). While Ruud's discussion is more theoretical, Frohne-Hagemann offers a clinical model of how to use music life narrative in therapy. There are also some other researchers who from different perspectives have touched upon discourse, narrative, and the text analogy in music therapy.[1]

While I acknowledge the relevance of the focus upon the *story* often taken when the text analogy is discussed, I will focus upon *hypertextuality* as a metaphor for the music therapy process, a metaphor that can illuminate the relevance of culture-centered perspectives in individual music therapy. *Hypertexts* challenge our traditional ideas of texts as linear narratives, structured in sequences by having a beginning, middle, and end. The focus I have chosen therefore also questions the dominating story on the dominance of the story often found in the literature on narrative therapy. There are other literary genres, such as poetry, that deserve attention. This is especially relevant for *music* therapy, since it is possible to argue that music is closer to poetry than to storytelling. Poetry and storytelling are not only different literary genres, they are different strategies of meaning-making, and it is probable that humans have developed these and other strategies because they can be used differently and serve different functions. If music therapists choose to examine the text analogy, it should therefore not be reduced to a focus upon the story. Other, less linear ways of meaning-making deserve our attention, poetry and hypertexts being two possible examples. This proposal has of course its own historical context; a glance at the history of the arts tells us that deconstruction of linear narrativity has been a major project within some traditions of literature, art, and music of the twentieth century.[2]

I will explore *hypertextuality* as a potential helpful metaphor in music therapy. This suggestion was originally a vague idea based on some patterns I discovered in one of my client's use of music and in my own interpretation of these patterns. I started to realize that the text analogy in music therapy could suggest much more than reading music as a story. I became highly interested in elements of *intertextuality* in music therapy sessions.[3] This came up at the same time that I as a researcher explored the possibilities of Internet, web sites, and electronic databases, and the idea of using *hypertextuality* as a metaphor for description of the music therapy process emerged. My willingness to *explore* this idea and investigate possible implications reflects one of my presuppositions to the study of music therapy; that the relevance of contemporary cultural developments should be examined. The fact that very many people today use computers and hypertexts to construct their own texts should influence our music therapy practice. This chapter includes no discussion of the use of information technology and Internet in music therapy, though, and I do not have access to such technology in the music therapy room I am using. My intention is broader, since I think technology is more than a thing you have or have not, but is also a cultural process through which we live and change as human beings.

Hypertext and hypertext theory is still in a state of becoming. Most of us have only recently become aware of the concept, and we tend to relate it to information technology and postmodern tendencies in cultural development. Hypertextuality might also be seen as something old. As a child I enjoyed very much reading in my parent's encyclopedia. One entry usually suggested several others, and I could create a web of threads through the huge amount of texts in these books. I was enjoying an experience of hypertext, defined as a text that does not form a single sequence and that may be read in various orders so that the reader can discontinue reading a document at certain points in order to consult other related material. I therefore do not want to restrict the discussion of hypertext to a celebration of postmodernism, although I do link it to what we could call postmodern sensitivities. A celebration of postmodernism would already be somewhat behind the times, but I think we need postmodernism, if not as a dominant story then as a continuous challenge to pre-modern and modern traditions in culture and society.

If there is something in my suggestion that hypertextuality might be a helpful metaphor in music therapy theory, this will not only be relevant when working with clients that are computer freaks, or have their musical identity connected to genres such as ambient, techno, and hip hop. Some clients may enjoy these genres of music or read hypermedia literary journals such as *BeeHive,* but my intention is not primarily to suggest a metaphor that reflects the language developed by clients that have and use information technology. Rather, I will attempt to develop a notion that can sensitize therapists to hypermedia qualities in music therapy processes, possibly of special relevance for the understanding of music therapy in late capitalist societies.

TEXTS AND HYPERTEXTS

The first suggestion that might need a defense, before discussing hypertextuality in music therapy, is the idea that music could be treated as a text. That this is not obvious may be one of the reasons why the text analogy has not been very influential in music therapy. An argument for treating music as a text could be developed on the basis of Ricoeur's (1986/1991) work *From Text to Action,* where the idea that meaningful actions might be interpreted as texts is defended. Ricoeur thus suggests that hermeneutics is a basic discipline for the understanding of human action and interaction, a suggestion that is developed in Nerheim's (1995) discussion of theories of health science. I accept Ricoeur's suggestion as a starting point, although I am well aware that it is not unproblematic (Grimen, 1992). There seems to be a common problem of meaning in texts, actions, and music, although it remains to be explored how far this suggestion goes. Music is process; it is a flow of meaningful (inter)actions and sounds. And music is product; it is often objectified in recordings and/or notations. To treat music as a text hardly captures all there is to music, but as far as I can see, both elements of the process and of the product might be treated as a text, that is, as a web of signs.

The word *text* comes from Latin, and originally meant web. Reminiscences of this original meaning are found in words such as textile and texture. Our understanding of the concept of text is usually connected to the technology of writing and later printing. The *sequence,* one word at a time, is basic to this technology, and we tend to conceive of texts as linear. This conception is also found in much of the literature on the text analogy in therapy (McLeod, 1997), where there is a focus upon the story or narrative. The term *hypertext* has been developed to convey an explicit alternative to the linear text. Theodor Holm Nelson, who on his Internet homepage presents himself as "Designer, Generalist, Contrarian," coined the term in 1963, defining hypertext as "fully non-sequential writing." Of course Nelson did not "invent" hypertext as a phenomenon. As mentioned earlier, there are hypertext elements in encyclopedias, and when mathematicians in the eighteenth century worked with ideas on geometry in a hyperbolic room their ideas might be seen as related to the recent concept of hypertext.

Hypertext, as popularly conceived – and that will do for now – is a series of text chunks or nodes that are connected by links that offer different pathways to the reader. In the same way as our understanding of the concept of text is influenced by the technology of printing, computer technology influences our understanding of the concept of hypertext, especially because of the multiple links possibilities of this technology. It may be said that the most important qualitative transition to nonlinear hypertextuality in contemporary societies occurs in the World Wide Web. A premise for this chapter, though, is that texts are more than books and hypertexts more than computers, and an understanding of hypertextuality relevant for music therapy is enhanced by contributions in *literary* theory on hypertext.[4]

The non-sequential writing in hypertext is of course relative. Hypertexts have linear components, within chunks and between chunks, but the possibility of moving back and forth between chunks in several directions opens up for multidimensional reading and writing. We read no longer in two dimensions, but in (at least) three. While some might say that the book standardizes our knowledge, hypertexts to some degree individualize it. "To some degree" only, because in many hypertexts the links are preconstructed by the author, giving the reader a limited room to move in. These systems are often classified as *passive* (from the reader's perspective). The author is then still a powerful guide in the reading process. The alternative is *interactive* systems of hypertext, where the reader has the possibility to edit the text and to add new texts and links. In the world of computer technology this is not yet always possible, while I would suggest this to be central to clinical music therapy practice.

Hypertext functions may also be classified as *internal* and *external*. Some of these functions one may find also in traditional texts. *Internal* hypertext functions in traditional texts are for instance pagination, lists of contents, footnotes, and indexes. *External* hypertext functions could for instance be found in traditional library catalogues. With these functions already established in conventional texts there will be blurry borders between more traditional texts and hypertexts, and one may even ask if we need the concept of hypertext. I think we do, because hypertexts offer possibilities that are not sufficiently conceptualized by words like "indexes" and "catalogues." The links found in computer hypertexts open up a freedom of choice and a speed of movement between chunks not imagined in the reading and writing of traditional texts. So hypertexts do more than challenge the idea of linearity in texts. Several other themes present themselves, the relationship between the author and the reader being one of the more important. When the reader has the possibility to move freely between chunks that are not structured in a hierarchy and that are linked with other chunks that again are linked to additional chunks, the idea of the text as a separate and formed entity is also challenged.

HYPERTEXTUALITY IN MUSIC

The term *hypermedia* has increasingly come to use. A hypermedia document could for instance include text, graphics, sound, and animation. Many hypertext documents include sounds and graphics, and the distinction between hypertext and hypermedia is so blurry that some authors call them both hypertext, which I think also is in line with Ricoeur's (1986/1991) argument on the extension of the concept of text. Hypertexts then frequently overlap with hypermedia, and music is of course a part of this picture. While music in hypertexts and hypermedia is a pretty obvious phenomenon, do we find hypertextuality in music? The Norwegian musicologist Petter Dyndahl (1998) discusses this question, and approaches it by focusing upon the question of linearity in music, and the question of the relationship between the composer, performer, and listener.

The tradition of classical European music and also much popular music share several features with the tradition of written texts. Linearity is a basic quality in this music. It has a beginning, middle, and end; harmony builds tension over time and asks for release; themes are developed; melodies are formed in phrases, etc. We actually can see that there is a "proto-narrativity" in this music. As Dyndahl (1998) shows, other music traditions are different and closer to the nonlinear qualities found in hypertexts, examples being techno music and the ambient music of Brian Eno, characterized by *layers of sound* more than melodies and harmonic development. This music creates a feeling of space with no time; there is no linear direction, rather a feeling of vertigo. The music consists of multiple layers of sound structures with no clear beginning or end. Already at this point I find the discussion of hypertextuality in music helpful for the discipline of music therapy. Some music therapists when discussing musical *form* tend to stress a linear conception of this concept.[5] This might be due to the dominance of linear traditions in Western music, and could be a bias when working with clients that have other cultural points of reference, for instance techno, ambience, hip hop, and rap, or for that matter Stockhausen (which I suppose is more rare).

The other question discussed by Dyndahl in his paper, the relationship between the composer, performer, and listener, might be even more relevant in this context. Computer hypertexts challenge our traditional view of the relationship between author and reader. Similar tendencies might be seen in music. Dyndahl chooses his example from (hip hop) rap, where the DJ has been acknowledged as a creator. Originally the DJ would be a qualified listener, or at best an editor, choosing the music to be heard. In rap music the DJ is a *creator* and *performer*. By sampling sounds and "break beats" and by mixing layers of sounds and beats, new grooves are created, often combined with "scratching" (an effect created by moving the record back and forth). On top of the groove created in this way the characteristic rhythmic rap monologue is added.

Most of Dyndahl's examples of hypertextuality in music are taken from recent genres of popular music, but some of the aspects that we consider essential to hypertextuality in music – such as nonlinearity and intertextuality – is not something completely new. Non-linearity is found in many kinds of minimalist traditions in music, and intertextuality has been a basic element of musical practice for centuries, for example in the use of a *cantus firmus* as the basis for improvisation or composition of new melodies in polyphonic music. In a similar vein the concept of hypertextuality in music also could shed light on the creative process in music therapy improvisations. Music as and in therapy is usually understood mostly as a function of intra- and interpersonal processes, and the literature tends to focus upon what is considered spontaneous and preconventional expressions and to downplay cultural influences and intertextuality in the music. Musicians, including clients and therapists in music therapy, borrow consciously and unconsciously from other musicians and musics, though, and the use of conventional and post-conventional elements of music must therefore be taken into consideration when interpreting music.[6]

To what degree hypertextuality might be a helpful metaphor for an understanding of the music therapy *process* I will discuss after having presented a synopsis of one year of a therapy process and some statements given by the client on her experience of this process. The synopsis is based on my clinical notes made after therapy sessions, while the presentation of the client's statements on the process are based upon qualitative research interviews.

SYNOPSIS OF A YEAR IN MUSIC THERAPY

Ramona was a woman of middle age when she referred herself to music therapy. She had lived a difficult adult life where she had been working extremely hard as mother and volunteer social worker. She was living in a relationship where she was not happy, and she was kept down as a woman. The community she lived in to some degree accepted and legitimized this oppression. A few years before she came to music therapy she had a crisis, since one of her two children had a serious illness. For a while there were grim prospects for the life of the child. The daughter survived, but was seriously handicapped. After this episode Ramona's struggle to survive psychologically became even tougher. She first went at the situation with fighting spirit; then she collapsed. She was confused and depressed, suicidal at times, and no longer able to function in her roles as mother and volunteer. Ramona then asked for psychiatric help and was offered anti-psychotic medication, milieu therapy, and individual verbal psychotherapy.

When referring herself to music therapy three years later she still was receiving these services, and she felt that she needed them, although she also regretted the new problems she ascribed to her role as client. By now Ramona was an outpatient most of the time, only going to the clinic to have therapy. One or two times a year her problems would overwhelm her and she would ask for status as an inpatient for some weeks. When Ramona first came to music therapy she was in the middle of one of her inpatient periods. In the first assessment session Ramona told me that she wanted to learn some new songs: "Ordinary songs, songs that ordinary people sing." The songs she knew were mostly hymns, and she stated: "I don't feel they're true anymore, but I want to be able to sing again. I have not been able to do that the last years." As soon as she had stated this wish, she legitimated it by adding: "You know, if you teach me some chords on the guitar and things like that, I may help my children if they want to play and sing."

Her idea of what music therapy could be for her was, as can be seen, not expansive. I suggested four sessions of assessment before we decided if we should collaborate for a longer period of time. In this period of assessment I asked her, as I do with most of my clients, to try out a broad range of activities. I invited her to participate in several improvisations where she tried the piano and the djembe,[7] in solo and dyadic improvisations, with and without a verbal given. I also suggested we could do some work with music and movement, but she refused: "That's absolutely out of the question. Just by mentioning the word 'movement' you make me feel extremely anxious." During these sessions of assessment we also looked through a songbook of well-known Norwegian songs, and I asked Ramona to choose songs we could sing. She hardly knew any of the songs, and was not knowledgeable of the Norwegian cultural heritage to the extent her age and intelligence would suggest. She said that her lack of knowledge was due to the fact that she had been living several years abroad, but also that: "I didn't learn these songs as a child."

Although she did not know any of the songs in the book, she picked songs with titles she liked, and wanted to give them a try. She learned chords, melodies, and lyrics quite fast, and was moved by some of the lyrics. In the second session, for instance, when working with a seemingly straight-forward and trite song with lyrics about a "happy child in a tough world," she suddenly discovered that she had emotions that drew her energy in other directions than the "wish to learn new songs." She was filled with very strong feelings of grief for her daughter. After singing the song she told me that in the years after her daughter's illness she had not allowed herself to be much in contact with the grief, not even in verbal therapy. She started to cry. After some seconds of silence she expressed that it surprised her that music in music therapy could create such strong feelings.

When the four assessment sessions were evaluated we agreed to continue to work together. I felt that she had showed motivation and ability to use music as a way of working with herself. Ramona herself expressed a wish to continue, and stated:

> When I came to you three weeks ago I thought you just could teach me some songs and that you didn't need to know anything about me. I can see now that I made a miscalculation. ... I came to you because I wanted to find my way back to the music, back to the beauty. I can see now that the grief I have repressed has stopped me from finding this way.

We agreed to focus our work on songs as she originally had suggested and on improvisation on instruments as I had introduced, with weekly sessions of one hour. In the beginning we mostly worked with songs. Ramona brought with her some hymns she knew and wanted to work with. "I cannot sing them properly, there's a ball in my throat." We also worked with songs that were new to her. She expressed that it gave her a feeling of getting access to a "new world" to learn these new songs.

An issue in this early phase of therapy was *freedom* in her use of the sessions. In the first sessions she would enter the music therapy room and ask me: "What have you been planning for today?" My answer was that I had no fixed plan and that I was ready to work with what she felt were her needs. She said that she was not quite sure what I meant by that, but that she would take the challenge. We worked with this for a long time, and in several sessions she told me either that she wanted me to suggest something – which I then usually did – or that she was stressed because she was not able to suggest anything. The first time Ramona found the freedom to briefly use the music according to her own needs was in session six. Ramona came into the room and said; "Today I need to *make noise.*" She played the drums and percussion instruments while I played the piano. Afterward she was surprised when I called what we had done music. "To me it's only noise," she would say, adding politely that she of course only was talking about her own contribution. The naming of the game was a topic of discussion for a period of several sessions.

Gradually *programmatic* improvisations became a larger part of the therapy process. Most of the improvisations were related to a theme or playing rule that had been crystallized through verbal conversation. "Saying no," "harmony," "interaction," "intrusion," are examples of such themes. Some sessions she came and stated that she had a need to *receive* something. She felt need for nourishment of some kind, and *music listening* started to become a part of the sessions. I played the piano for her, we listened to a CD together, or we listened to an earlier improvisation we had made. Quite often when listening she developed visual imagery, often related to topics that she was working with in verbal therapy. In session eighteen, for instance, when we listened to "Prelude to Act I," in the opera *Traviata* by Verdi, she had imagery of being on a mountain pasture. She saw a lamb that needed protection; it was threatened and prosecuted by a big black raven. After she had processed the experience through writing we chose to listen to the music once more. She then stated: "There is a lamb – a little girl – within myself that needs protection. I want to pick it up and protect it, as I did when listening to this music."

In the following sessions Ramona quite actively used the music as *texts* she could interpret. Other times the act of *playing* – not the interpretation of it but the (inter)activity itself – was in the center of the work. Ramona expressed that to play gave her a feeling of being alive, of being connected to another person. Before session twenty-two Ramona had a very difficult life situation. She came to the sessions in a depressed state, and she told me that she had suicidal thoughts. When coming to the next session she told me that she did not want to come, but that she felt obliged to. She had questions like "Does this help?" "Is there any hope for me?" "Do I deserve the place you have given me here?" She explained her situation and feelings by referring to the lack of understanding and support she experienced in her family and also in her community. This situation lasted for several sessions, and music listening was the main activity in these sessions. Since Ramona needed to work through the question as to whether she deserved her place in music therapy, these sessions also came to include thinking back on the sessions she had had. In session twenty-four Ramona remembered one of her first piano improvisations, where the high number of keys and possibilities found on a keyboard had struck her as especially encouraging. "Eighty-eight keys, that's a lot of possibilities indeed."

In session twenty-five we listened to Gabriel Fauré's *Sicilienne,* from *Pelléas et Mélisande.* After the music was finished Ramona expressed: "That was *harmony.* People *played* together, *listened* to each other. It *is* possible!" Some hope was being born in her. We also listened to some earlier recordings of Ramona's improvisations. She was surprised by the vitality in the playing and expressed: "Is that me? I took a chance there." Ramona chose to continue in music therapy, and said in session twenty-seven: "Therapy is the chance I *have* to make a space for myself." So we started to improvise in the sessions again. She tried some new instruments, and she was fascinated of the sounds produced by them, while at the same time she often gave metaphorical descriptions of the music that we made. "The xylophone is so warm," or, in a different vein: "I'm just like one of those small hailstones in the ocean drum, I move automatically," "To play the pipe chimes was risky, it put me in front of the music so that you could hear me."

A difference from earlier in the process was that she now started to appreciate interaction in music as being something more and different than traditional harmony and synchronized rhythms. In session thirty-one we listened to an improvisation we had made in the previous session, where the verbal given I had suggested was: "You will be in charge, and you will decide what the music will be like." She played the drums and xylophone and I played the piano. When listening to this music she enjoyed the creativity, vitality, and playful character it had. She then put her eyes on a large and colorful painting on the wall, a painting that had been made by a group of patients sitting around the four sides of an enormous canvas. She expressed: "This music is like that picture; there are different perspectives, different ideas, different colors and figures, but they all work together in a funny way."

After session thirty-three there was a summer vacation for four weeks. When she came back she was troubled because the relationship with her partner was very strained. Again she had strong suicidal thoughts. At the same time she seemed very determined. During the summer she had met a woman that also had been abused, and who had impressed her by sharing her process of trying to become friends with her own body. In the therapy session she stated that she wanted to work with her relationship to her body. One year after she so strongly had refused my suggestion on working with music and movement she now felt she was ready; she wanted me to help her develop her ability to care for and enjoy her own body. In addition to singing, improvising, and listening, we therefore started working with movement to music.

TALKING ABOUT MUSIC THERAPY

My narrative of the first year of Ramona's therapy process ends here,[8] and provides a context for presentation of the statements she herself made on her experience of music therapy in two qualitative research interviews, the first of them after session thirty-eight, the other after session thirty-nine. Both interviews were recorded and transcribed and then given back to her with an invitation to make any correction, comment, and elaboration she wanted. Based on my experience in previous interviews with clients, I chose not to ask Ramona many research questions. I started the first interview by just asking Ramona to describe her *experience of music in therapy*, and to tell me something about how she felt she was *using the music*.

As expressed in the epigraph to this chapter, any utterance may be considered linked to other utterances and is thus already an *answer* (Bakhtin, 1996). This is of course especially so when I am now about to present utterances given in an *interview*. Since the interview was open-ended, based on a general focus more than on a list of specific questions, I will argue that most of Ramona's utterances here are answers in the more abstract meaning suggested above, not so much concrete answers to concrete questions. I consider Ramona's utterances to be answers to the challenges, experiences, and discourses she had been part of during her first year in music therapy, which again of course was embedded in her life experience.

Some basic metaphors dominated in Ramona's utterances on her experience of and use of music in music therapy. One group of metaphors was connected to *space* and *room,*[9] another group to *traveling*. Both when describing music as a space and as a travel, she stressed the experience of being in charge and of feeling the freedom of choice. Her very first utterance, after my brief introduction, was:

> When I asked to start in music therapy I thought: "Now I will at any rate have a chance to *learn some music*." But I have discovered that the main thing would not be to *learn* music, but to have the possibility to be *in charge* of the sounds myself. How should I explain? The alphabet has letters that can be made into words. It is me who decides *what* words. I had a picture of music as being a ready-made world, something I had to learn and memorize; to learn chords, to learn where I could find the different sounds. But you have contri-

buted to making it into *another world* than what I had thought of. The sounds have become mine, I can put together the sounds I want, I can say that this is to "play music," even though it's nothing that I've been taught. It's impulsive, it's the *use of sounds.*

Ramona then explored her suggestion on having found "another world":

> Music is for me a world without words, with interaction of tones and sounds. It has become so even more during music therapy. In my adult life I have been feeling that my position is at the back of the queue of people who dominate and master music. But – this [music therapy] has given me an entrance to a *new* music room, to say it this way.

Ramona here played with double meanings. She used the very concrete expression "music room," but in the context of the utterance it was obvious that she also was talking about a room in an abstract sense; a "music space." She soon would elaborate on this more metaphorical meaning:

> There is a music room here at the clinic, which is my point of departure. It includes many instruments. According to your[10] own needs and the shape you're in that particular day I have been allowed to choose the instrument I have wanted to use. Well, I have experienced that there is a very large spectrum here, and possibilities too. The music room of my life, well, that also has to do with expressions and impressions, It's in a way quite hard to put words on music.

What we can see here is that very concrete experiences of the variety of possibilities found in the "real" music room at the clinic form the basis for her use of "room"/"space" as metaphor. This experience has been expanded to an experience of a more personal space, a space that has given her some new awareness on her possibilities to shape her own life. This space was not created all in a sudden, it was more a matter of a slow and gradual process:

> Well, there has been a development where I have started to trust that it's OK that I just make sounds. It does not have to be a known song or phrase; I do not need to copy. It's actually you who have created that impulse. I have named it noise; I say "to ravage and make noise," you call it "to play [music]." So – well that has made an impression, little by little. I can feel that. And maybe that way I have

come into a room in the music world that has expanded something. Developed me maybe ...

Something inside me has been expanded, through learning that music can be so many things ... It has to do with the lack of limitations, the possibility to *use* things you did not know of. The experience of *harmony,* although we had not been practicing [playing just this music]. And the experience of interplay,[11] although nothing was arranged or agreed upon before we started. There is something in the experience ... that my own contribution gives our music *depth*. This experience of being able to contribute in a positive way has given me a stronger will *not* to give up in my crisis, to put it this way. ... It feels good to be able to contribute in a positive way. I feel I have found that I have a right to live, a right to take space.

During the year Ramona had been going to music therapy she had been suicidal several times, so the conversation dwelled at this point, on the role of music in relation to her wish to live:

Quite often I have come to the sessions with flat batteries. Then we just found something to do. Then I have gone from music therapy with the feeling that *it is possible* to do something although you have not planned it, and it can be good for you. ...

Earlier my life used to be that I needed to have everything under control, I had to know what each thing would bring. It took a crisis to learn how to move into an unknown arena. I have been feeling that I have had nothing to lose, I have lost everything already. When the situation have been this fatal I have thought that it doesn't matter if I make a fool of myself. And then – instead of fatal things – music therapy has brought something positive. ...

I feel safer now. I have started to trust that the goals are not pre-defined, that there is room for my "making noise," to put it that way. I have understood that that was not to misuse music therapy. I have experienced that there is room for more than what I have given room for myself. There is a lot of space in music therapy, a lot more than what I have had inside myself. ... Now I am in a phase where I find this exciting and thrilling. I have come to a point in my life where I can say [that] I learn to know my self through music. ...

I think this space has been built slowly during this year. It's quite recently that I have been able to say that it's a space. It has been an experience,[12] gradually I have started to feel that these experiences are enclosed in a room.[13]

She then elaborated on her feelings in the experience of building this room. And she introduces a new metaphor to help her describe this:

> I have not always known where the walls have been, or if there were any walls. To stretch out for something that you don't know, that's like putting your boat on the water without bringing the oars with you. ... You feel that the boat is floating, it's not sinking, but how should one be able to move forwards? Maybe you don't know that.

She explored this new metaphor, suggesting that sometimes she maybe felt she had an oar, but was not sure if it was the right one. Maybe it was one for a canoe instead of a rowing boat? And what would people say if they saw her rowing with a paddle?

> I have been feeling that I do not know what boat I'm entering, I do not know what tool to use, but I have been able to move, I have had the courage to try... But if my parents had seen this they would be shaking their heads saying: "What kind of foolish behavior is this?"

Ramona stated that maybe she would not be able to answer such a question. When she had started in music therapy she had had some clear-cut objectives. She had wanted to challenge herself by learning some new songs. Now maybe she could not state very clearly what her objectives were, but she had learned that she longed for a personal space.

At this moment I chose to share some of my own associations to the boat metaphor she had just introduced, and suggested that maybe music therapy is similar to entering a boat on a river. You cannot plan beforehand how to row or where to row. You need to follow the river and pay attention to the stones in the water and to the way the river bends before you choose how to row. Ramona accepted this image of the therapy process, and asked the following question in a way that to me suggested that the idea was new to her:

> Does that mean that you are saying that you too have been on some kind of journey, that you have been experiencing interesting things and that you could not plan the details of what we should do?

I confirmed, and she stated:

> Sometimes I feel a need to have some kind of overview: "What can music therapy be?" Maybe my horizon is too narrow so that I am not using all the possibilities...

I communicated that I understood her wish, while at the same time I re-minded her about the river image and the importance of working with the things she felt for at any time. This introduced a new sequence of comments on our work on music and movement, and Ramona asked me if I remem-bered how she reacted when I first introduced the possibility in one of the very first sessions. I told her that my understanding at that time had been that she had fear of the idea of moving, but also that her fear of the possibility of me forcing her was just as important. She confirmed this and stated:

> My earlier experience has been that people have forced me or in some other way made things happen, although I did not want them to ... so it was correct of me to say no at that time. But it creates some hope in me that I am not standing on the same doorstep today.

This was the end of the first research interview with Ramona. In a second interview made nine days later she had read the transcript of the first inter-view, and expressed that the text gave a good impression of her experience of music therapy. The main theme she felt was that she now was on her way to learn more about herself. At the same time she underlined that music ther-apy was not her only support on this journey. Especially she pointed at the importance of verbal psychotherapy.

HYPERTEXTUALITY AS A META-METAPHOR

My discussion now will focus upon to what degree Ramona's metaphors can be reinterpreted by the hypertext analogy. One might ask: Why bother with making a translation of Ramona's interesting metaphors? Her creation of metaphors could be a focus of interest in itself. I agree, but as Frederick Steier (1991, p. 8) suggests, to reflect upon practice allows clinicians and researchers to be aware of what their subjects are telling them, not by impos-ing their own categories, but by trying to see *if* and *how* these categories may or may not fit. The reason for bothering with this then will be to see if these categories can establish useful distinctions in the development of a language for communication with professional colleagues.

Several of Ramona's descriptions lend themselves to a translation into the hypertext analogy. She had only to a little degree used music therapy as a help to retell her complete life narrative. To *this,* verbal psychotherapy probably was more important. Instead she had used music therapy as a means to build a room and a space for herself, she had created something she did not know could exist. Many of the metaphors she used can be seen as analogous to the description I earlier gave of hypertext. She had not been moving in one direction, but in several; she had not been working on one text, but on several. She had been moving from songs to improvisations to conversations and back again to songs. She had asked for the freedom to sit down, listen, and receive, and she had asked for the challenge to stand up and move. These elements in the process can all be interpreted as texts (or chunks or nodes, to use hypertext terms), and they have been linked in several ways. Let us use the songs as an example. When early in the process she stated that she wanted to learn the songs that "ordinary people sing," she used them as a link to the "world out there"; the songs became *external links*. She learned songs in music therapy that she later heard on the radio, and new connections to the cultural world she wanted to be more integrated in were established. Other times the songs became *internal links:* they connected her to a part of her life story that she already knew, but seldom found access to. One example of this was when she in the second session sang the simple song with lyrics about a "happy child in a tough world" and all of a sudden had access to strong feelings of grief for her daughter.

One important thing for me when suggesting that the elements of the therapy process can be described as nodes and links is that it opens up for a more differentiated use of the text analogy in music therapy. To delve into a close reading of every sequence of music, conversation, or movement may not always be very helpful. Sometimes we can learn more from trying to understand how the music links different experiences than from asking what the music means in itself.[14] In Ramona's case we can identify this changing role of the music. Sometimes the music is a node and Ramona interpreted it as a text, as for instance in session eighteen where she listened to the Prelude to Verdi's *Traviata* and worked with verbal and visual imagery on the prosecuted lamb, interpreted by herself as the prosecuted child she once had been. Other times it would be more precise to describe the role of the music as a link between two nodes; for instance when she in session six stated that she needed to make noise. When listening to the music afterward it would have been too restricted to interpret it as an isolated text. Ramona in the second interview underlined the importance of the music as a *connection:*

> I have lived very separated from my own feelings. ... I have placed them in another room within myself ... [In music] I have allowed myself to go back in my own life, I have reached for my childish right to express myself in other ways than with words.

Here we can sense that the music very much is a link; it becomes, to use Ramona's own metaphor, a door into the room where she has hidden her feelings. The music then became a link that made it possible for Ramona to start a process of moving back and forth between her verbal knowledge and her emotional nonverbal knowledge.

There are also other aspects of Ramona's use of metaphors that fit quite nicely with the hypertext metaphor. Her consistent use of the room/space metaphor has already been illuminated. When she at one point in the interview shifts to the rowing boat as a metaphor, she explores a *traveling metaphor*, a metaphor that is much used also in the literature on hypertext. To work with a hypertext is often compared to embarking a journey. You enter a landscape where you can move in several directions. Questions of navigation then arise. In a hypertext you do not always know before you start where to move or how to move. There are several choices to be made during your journey. This creates a need for some kind of navigation tools, which is a well-known theme in the literature of hypertext, and which also came up in Ramona's experience of music therapy.

To sum up so far; I suggest that the hypertext metaphor captures several of the most important elements in Ramona's own description of her experience of music in therapy. It captures the process as interactive, it captures the special multidimensional freedom of being able to move in several directions, and also the possibility to move, via internal or external links, back and forth between chunks of several media (music, conversation, and movement). In session forty I chose to share the association I had made between her metaphors and the hypertext analogy, to check out whether that made any sense to her. She had not heard about hypertext, so I made a short and simple explanation of its function to her, using a computer as an example. She then expressed:

> It's an interesting thought, ... When coming to a link, as you describe it, you have three possibilities: to go on, to change direction, or just stop. In my life I have been aware of only two possibilities: to go on in the same direction or to get stuck. What has been helpful for me in music therapy is just this freedom of choice: you do not have to follow just one text, just one sequence of chords, you can move freely, go wherever you feel it's right to go. This thing about freedom is actually something you could add to the interview [transcript]. I've been thinking about this. Actually I started to discover it early in the music therapy [process]. You remember that time I sat by the piano and discovered that I had the freedom to use any key?

In music therapy the client and the therapist engage in a coprocessing of mutual experience. I think that one of the assets of music therapy is its multimedia character, and that this is illuminated in a new way by the hypertext analogy, since it underlines the importance of the *links*. Flexible moves between sequences in different media are possible to establish. Music therapy has more to offer than just another medium for the coprocessing of experience. The possibility of moving in a flexible way between several media may be just as important. A possible theoretical approach for further elaboration of this suggestion might be literary theories on intertextuality.

A PRECEDING ANALOGOUS CASE?

The reader may ask how generalizable the suggestions made in this chapter are, and may also think that I have been rushing to conclusions. I have just presented *one* case, and this is not necessarily a representative one. My suggestion is not that hypertextuality is the best metaphor for the description of every therapy process, I am just offering *one* new way of looking at such processes. Although I have been discussing only one case here, I have myself experienced this metaphor as useful in other cases. Future exploration is necessary to evaluate when and if these cases will be perceived as *preceding analogous cases* by other music therapists. When evaluating a case a lawyer acknowledges the unique constellations in the case she is facing, while she at the same time looks for preceding analogous cases that she can learn from. In similar ways preceding analogous cases may be used in qualitative research and in the clinician's attempts of making sense of the case he is working with (Kvale, 1996, p. 233).

In the case of Ramona I am suggesting that hypertextuality is the metaphor that best captures her own description of the experience of music therapy in relation to my interpretation of it. It is important for me to underline that whatever metaphor we use we need to explore the potentiality and the limitation of it. Let me start with a possible limitation of the hypertext metaphor. In the second interview Ramona underlined that she in music therapy has allowed her inner child to speak up, even though it did not have any words. She then in a sentence compares this with the fact that a baby communicates very well with her mother or father just by using sounds and no words. This proto-narrative aspect of the music therapy process – including the element of time and timing so important in music – is only partly covered by the metaphor of hypertextuality.

On the other hand, I think Ramona's case has illuminated the strength of the hypertext metaphor compared to some of the more established metaphors in music therapy theory, such as "music as a stimulus," "music as free association," and "music as mother-infant interaction." Music as stimulus is obviously a restricting metaphor since clients do not only react to music; they act through music. What then about the free association metaphor? There are obvious relationships between the idea of links and the idea of free association. To think of musical improvisations as free associations is not very accurate, however. The associations made in improvisation are not so free; they are also directed by cultural tendencies mediated through music as a medium. Quite often also the therapist improvises together with the client and thus acts as a mediator. The idea of working with links thus better describes the active therapist role often found in music therapy, and it can include conscious and unconscious associations made by the client. The mother-infant-interaction metaphor captures the mediating and interactive aspect of the music therapy process, but may restrict our focus when working with older children, adolescents, and adults. For these clients the internalization of cultural products and processes such as language and musical genres is inevitably such an important part of their psychological function that there are limitations to the mother-infant analogy.

Two related functions of metaphors and theoretical constructs are that they can *contain* the experience of the process, and that they can *sensitize* the therapist to the client's experience. These functions are essential for the usefulness of a metaphor, and they are of course based upon the descriptive power of the metaphor. Let me explicate in this case: The hypertext metaphor helped me to contain and acknowledge Ramona's need to work with several media and activities, changing between them over time and working on several levels simultaneously. The metaphor helped me avoid the establishment of dead rituals around certain media, activities, and ways of meaning-making. Of course this could have been contained by other ideas than the hypertext analogy, for instance by humanistic ideas on therapy underlining the value of meeting the client "where he is." The hypertext analogy may – in addition – *sensitize* to the *changing functions* of musics and activities and to the *navigation problems* experienced by the client during the therapy process.

Concerning changing functions, let us take the songs as example. Sometimes Ramona used them as texts to be interpreted, sometimes as links to other texts. These other texts could be very different in nature. It could for instance be her hidden feelings about her daughter or her longing for being part of a larger and more open culture outside her restricted local community. And even more important, some of the chunks that she linked together were not narratives in a traditional way, but wordless experiences: sounds, emotions, body experiences. What she herself in the two interviews stated as important and helpful was the possibility given in music therapy to link these chunks ("to open up doors between rooms").

The navigation problems are not restricted to the feeling of being lost. That *is* a part of it, and something to be worked with when a client experiences that through therapy her world is changing; walls are falling down and new paths and horizons appear. Sometimes the landscape seems to be without paths or the client finds herself in a boat with no oars. The mediating function of the therapist then becomes important. To provide a ready-made map is not possible, because the life-world of the client is changing continuously. The question then is how to help the client by providing new links, and by marking these so that they can be experienced and used by the client. In Ramona's case this *marking of links* was done in several ways. Sometimes the marking was established by giving the improvisations titles, by defining givens before starting to play, or through the verbal processing of the music. Other times the marking of links was done through "sampling," that is, through establishing intertextuality in the music. By using musical genres, specific songs, or just elements and fragments from other musics, I was able to hint at doors and doorsteps that Ramona could choose to use when working with her musical and personal space. A *waltz* improvisation, for instance, did at one point clearly connect to Ramona's negative feelings about her body and about moving to music (as she associated waltz with dance music). These experiences were linked in a new way, though; since Ramona to her surprise discovered that she enjoyed the improvisation and the sound of the music very much, and therefore found the motivation for exploration of new relationships.

Further use and elaboration of the metaphor of hypertextuality is necessary to evaluate if other hypertext-notions than those I have focused upon also can be useful for the understanding of music therapy processes. I am thinking about such notions as *dynamic links* and *variable links,* which may be helpful for the discussion of some specific qualities that "links" in music therapy processes might have.[15] Already though, I think Ramona's case has demonstrated potential as a preceding analogous case from which we can learn about some important aspects of the music therapy process.

POSTSCRIPT: HYPERTEXT NARRATIVES

When it comes to the use of metaphors there is always a problem of model imperialism. Too literal and rigid interpretations of metaphors will limit and not enhance sensitivity in practice. Communities of knowledge sometimes develop a dogmatic relationship to a metaphor, and it may then be a scholarly responsibility to overthrow some tables. Other times tables are overthrown continuously, so that there is a need to stabilize and clarify meanings and uses. One issue to consider, then, is how exact the hypertext metaphor is and should be. In some respects it is quite open-ended in this chapter. This looseness may be due to the fact that my use of the metaphor is quite new, and thus simply represents a deficit. Another possibility is that the looseness in itself represents some of the potential in the metaphor. In Chapter 2 a clinically relevant concept of *narrative* was discussed, and distanced from the clear-cut story written or told by an individual author. Open-ended "inhabited and enacted stories" were put in focus and the perspective taken that human life is to participate in an endless human "performative conversation" involving the constant reworking of stories and dramas. In this perspective the boundaries between stories and hypertexts, as discussed here, are blurred. The qualities of being open-ended, inhabited, and enacted are shared. We could speak of hypertext narratives.

Metaphors have a history of use; their meaning change over time. An open-ended conception of narrative in relation to hypertextuality, as outlined here, could be related to postmodernist sensitivities developed in late capitalist societies. This then stands in contrast to a more modernist and linear conception of narrative, a change that may be related to general cultural changes in many contemporary societies. As Sherry Turkle (1995/1997) suggests, we are moving from a modernist culture of calculation toward a postmodernist culture of simulation. This produces new metaphors for the self and its relationships to the world. *Windows*, for instance, has become a cogent metaphor for thinking about the self as a multiple, distributed system. As Turkle suggests, the self is no longer simply playing different roles in different settings at different times. The "life practice of windows" is that of a decentered self, a self that exists in many worlds and plays many roles at the same time.

Possibly then this captures qualities of enacted hypertextuality, as being even more open-ended and distributed than the enacted narratives discussed in Chapter 2. A postmodern culture of simulation, navigation, and interaction situates the self in several contexts at once. If this is so, life is characterized by hypertextuality even messier than that of therapy, and much more time consuming. As players participate in games of simulation and navigation, they become authors not only of texts and hypertexts but also of themselves, constructing new selves through social interaction. Therapy may then be to provide clients with new and safe options both for simulation and navigation through interaction with the therapist.

It is extremely inaccurate to suggest that we live in a postmodern society, however. Apart from the uneasy use of personal pronoun in such a statement (people live in very different worlds), there are premodern, modern, and postmodern elements to most people's lives, in different blends. This was certainly so in Ramona's case. The therapy process was very much about creating windows and links between such elements. It is therefore no reason to limit the use of the hypertext metaphor to postmodern developments; that just represents a new and enlarged perspective. This may be compared to the hypertext elements in traditional books enlarged and developed by computer technology. Some of the themes touched upon in this chapter, such as music's role as a link between body and "soul," are as old as the documented history of thinking about music (Gouk, 2000, p. 4).

NOTES

[1] See for instance (Bruscia, 1998b; Ansdell, 1999; Bonde, 1999; Aldridge, 2000; Jungaberle et al., 2001).

[2] See the discussion of aesthetics in Chapter 2.

[3] See (Stige, 1999).

[4] One contribution of indirect relevance is Julia Kristeva's (1980) discussion of intertextuality based on the dialogical principle of Mikhail Bakhtin.

[5] See the discussion of aesthetics in Chapter 2.

[6] Cf. the discussion of conventional and post-conventional musicking in Chapter 3.

[7] A West African drum to be played with your hands (without sticks).

[8] Ramona continued in music therapy for another one and a half years, when she decided to terminate the collaboration. Her private life had taken a new direction, she was engaged in a new job, and she was for the first time able to take social advantage of her music interest by joining a local choir. The focus of this chapter is not the effect of the therapy process, though, but the interpretation and understanding of the process itself.

[9] Ramona here used the Norwegian word "rom," which has a double meaning covered in English by the words "space" and "room."

[10] Ramona's language is here changing to the second person, but she is speaking about herself, which is obvious from the rest of the quote.

[11] Here Ramona used the Norwegian word "samspel," which has the double meaning of "interaction in music" and "social interaction."

[12] Alternative translation: "sensation."

[13] "Space" could also have been used as a translation here, cf. footnote 9."

[14] I have touched upon this topic in an earlier article, when discussing my work with another client. He used to play the same instrument every session and the syntax of the music was almost identical for several sessions. Still, the meaning of two sessions could be very different, because the client would *use* the music in different ways, sometimes linking it to experiences of being relaxed and feeling good, other times to difficult emotional memories (Stige, 1999).

[15] "Dynamic links" is a concept used to denote links in texts that change continuously, like music does. *Access* to these links then change in time. "Variable links" are *links* that change. Each time you encounter the "same" chunk the hypertext has changed because it is continuously constructed, and thus also the construction of links changes.

Part III:

IMPLICATIONS

There is nothing as practical as a good theory.
(Kurt Lewin)

In this part of the book I will discuss some implications of culture-centered perspectives for the description and understanding of music therapy as practice and discourse, discipline and profession. In Chapter 7 the issue of *defining music therapy* will be examined, while *a model of the music therapy process* is proposed in Chapter 8, based on the notion of music therapy as situated practice. In Chapter 9 implications of entering *new arenas* for clinical work will be discussed in relation to concurrent *changes in agenda*. The request for increased reflexivity, the ability to reflect upon one's position in a social and cultural system, is at the heart of this discussion and linked to some topics of seminal importance for music therapy, such as the post-colonial challenge. This challenge also highlights one of the continuing themes of this book: the relations and tensions between local and more general perspectives.

Chapter 7:

REDEFINING MUSIC THERAPY

What is music therapy? More than a profession. Scarcely a living.
A way of being, of relating at both non-verbal ends of the
speech scale; sub-vocal relationship at the fumbling pre-ego
depth of being and supra-vocal communication at altitudes
where words no longer suffice. It is rejection and relegation
to the file of "Quackery and Witchcraft" in some circles.
It is a warm welcome into the multi-disciplinary
medical team in others.
(Mary Priestley)

Culture-centered perspectives suggest that music therapy be conceived as a situated practice, which again indicates that no final or universal definition of music therapy will do. There is a request for definition implicit in the development of any discipline and profession, and the issue of redefining music therapy will therefore continuously be on the agenda. This chapter takes as departure point that a distinction of conceptual levels subsumed under the term "music therapy" will be helpful, and proposes definitions that may sensitize music therapists to cultural issues.

- BUT IS IT MUSIC THERAPY?

The community project Upbeat belonged to and the ecological processes worked with in relation to Paul are in some respects different from what is traditionally considered therapy in Western societies. When I have presented these and similar case stories in conferences, a typical response from the audience has been: "This is interesting, but is it music therapy?" One possible answer could be: "Yes, it is music therapy, but maybe it is not therapy." The absurdity of this answer is reduced if one acknowledges that the term therapy is given a variety of meanings in different discourses. "Therapy" is a word that is used in several quite divergent ways, and while this is not a very radical statement it is probably still a fact that many debates on the definition of music therapy have suffered from lack of recognition of this. It makes a difference, for instance, whether the word is used by ordinary people talking about their everyday experiences, by a psychologist in a psychiatric clinic, or by a music therapist engaged in a theoretical discussion about the identity of the discipline and profession. An elaborated version of the imagined answer given above would then be: "Yes, it is music therapy, but maybe it is not *therapy* the way you define the term."

Music therapists also use the term "therapy" in ways that reveal several concepts, on different conceptual levels. Before discussing this in detail, I will briefly illuminate the clinical importance of the differences in meaning involved when the term therapy is used in the vernacular and in a professional context. In the first case the word often means any act, hobby, or experience that relieves tension or increases well-being, in the latter case it usually means treatment of disease or disorder by some systematic curative process. In community work and ecological practices the choice of discourse may be much less obvious than in conventional individual therapy. One illuminative example is given by the Norwegian music therapist Venja Ruud Nilsen who works with women in prison as well as in a project of supervision and after-care, where rock bands and music activities are used to support processes of social integration and adjustment to society (Ruud Nilsen, 1996). In relation to the activities of this project these women commonly described their music experiences in terms such as "this is good, this is therapy for me." At the same time they would object strongly to the term "therapy" when used by the music therapist (Ruud Nilsen, personal communication). This may at first seem odd, but is explainable if one considers the possibility that these women took it for granted that a professional health worker like a music therapist would use the term therapy to denote methodical treatment of disease and disorder.

Sensitivity for context and discourse is then required when the word therapy is used. If we now concentrate on the level of professional discourse, will "treatment of disease and disorder" be a satisfactory delimitation of the last word of the combination term music therapy? Few music therapists would suggest that. It is obvious that a high number of music therapists work in ways that could not be categorized as treatment; they may for instance work with habilitation, rehabilitation, health promotion, or palliative care. A way of dealing with this dilemma would be to try and stretch the range of meanings connected to the term therapy. By studying the etymological roots of the word one may for instance find that therapy is derived from the Greek word *therapeia*, with a broad range of meanings related to service, including conscientious care. "Caring service" or "conscientious care" may be more descriptive umbrellas than "treatment" for the coverage of what music therapists do, but communication problems would not be solved by this. What term should then be used in those cases music therapists in fact *do* work with treatment: "music *therapy*," or maybe "music therapy therapy?"

The original meaning of the word therapeia is related to *care,* but the modern meaning of the word therapy is in professional contexts more often related to *cure.* Even in contexts where the term therapy is taken to denote treatment and cure it is still a rather inclusive label, both denotatively and connotatively. A broad range of qualifiers are therefore in use when professionals speak about therapy, such as shock therapy, aversion therapy, inhalation therapy, sex therapy, behavior therapy, Gestalt therapy, group therapy, speech therapy, and occupational therapy. Some of these qualifiers denote techniques, methods, or models of therapy, others denote targets of intervention, and others again denote formats of therapy. Some qualifiers denote forms of therapy that have developed their own education programs, research traditions, academic journals, ethical guidelines, etc. In other words, these therapy forms are linked to professions or semiprofessions which again are linked to bodies of knowledge that approach the status of being disciplines (branches of learning).

This chapter will deal with the issue of (re)defining music therapy, which – according to the brief tour around the issue made above – relates to questions of practice, discourse, profession, and discipline. My interest for the issue of redefining music therapy was originally fueled by the fact that when I first read Bruscia's (1989) *Defining Music Therapy* I realized that the community practices that I had worked with in the 1980s did not fit well with the definition given in this book. This could of course be interpreted in different ways; maybe the community practices I had been part of should not be considered music therapy, or maybe Bruscia's definition was too narrow? Obviously the latter view has been held by Bruscia since the second edition of his important book included the area of Ecological Music Therapy (Bruscia, 1998a). In a more principal vein this experience could suggest that music therapy will have to be redefined continuously, as new practices and perspectives are developed. In the long run this may give us more inclusive definitions, although there may be areas that will be left behind, and the issue of defining boundaries will always be relevant.

There are some obvious philosophical and practical problems concerning attempts of developing definitions of music therapy. In addition to the breadth of possible meanings of the term therapy, the qualifier in this case – music – does not specify clinical population, approach, or target of intervention in any way, so that the total range of practices subsumed under the term music therapy is broad indeed. All this taken together suggests that music therapy is a family resemblances category, with similarities existing between subsets, but not necessarily with much core shared. Anyone who has had the courage and patience to try and define music therapy, with global or local ambitions, has experienced how any such definition easily becomes object for dissension and disagreement. This might be linked to the understanding of the aim of the work (cure, care, creative growth, personality development, health promotion, etc.) and to what this is related to (disease, disability, personal suffering, problems related to quality of life, social or cultural breach to life of a community, etc.). It might also be connected to the choice of term for the person going to therapy (client, patient, child, consumer, etc.). In addition, the disagreement might be about the role of music (music in therapy or therapy in music) or what competencies are needed for the music therapist (musical, clinical, personal, theoretical, scientific, etc.). These are more than picky disagreements on language details as they usually reveal differences in world-view and metatheory. Each word chosen in a definition have more or less specific connotations to other words, that is; they belong to discourses and value systems. Music therapy is in a pre-paradigmatic, or maybe rather a multiparadigmatic, situation. Several worldviews and metatheories are operating within the field. Not only are music therapy practices extremely diverse, then, there is also much diversity in conceptualization.

Definitions are needed for the development of professional identity and as tools in the processes of critical discussion and reflexivity, and music therapists need definitions for communication with other professionals, with clients, parents or caretakers, and with policy-makers. What I propose is therefore not that the problems of definition outlined so far should keep scholars away from defining music therapy, but from seeing these definitions as accurate and objective descriptions, revealing what is as it is. It may be helpful to think of definitions as *tools* in the process of constructing the discipline and/or professional identities. One of the jobs that can be done with the help of a good definition is to reflect upon the suggested boundaries and connections between music therapy and other disciplines. This job is especially necessary in the pioneering years of a discipline, but becomes important in certain time intervals, as social and cultural changes in a society alters the relationship between disciplines and professions and repeatedly create needs for reflections upon boundaries and overlapping fields.

If disciplines have overlapping fields, the metaphor of family resemblances may help us to relate to the fact that a field of practice may be conceptualized under the umbrella of more than one family resemblance category (in a similar way as one person may "belong" to several families, the mother's family, the father's family, etc.). To redefine music therapy is therefore to engage in dialogues and debates on identity, in which "But is it music therapy?" is a natural question. I will nevertheless argue that this question also may have authoritarian functions that could limit the exploration of new fields and approaches. Two typical foundations for asking may then be: a) this practice is not similar to this (or that) *exemplar* of music therapy, or b) it does not fit with contemporary professional use of the term therapy. To my judgment neither of these objections represent good arguments for suggesting that a practice should *not* be subsumed under the umbrella music therapy. Exemplars – such as the pioneering work of Nordoff and Robbins, Mary Priestley, and Helen Bonny – have been extremely important for *expanding* our understanding of what music therapy can be. Will these exemplars be equally helpful in defining *limits* for what should be considered music therapy? I can see no good reasons why they would. The second objection may at first seem more substantial. There will of course be problems of professional communication if music therapists have their own way of defining therapy which is very different from how for instance a psychologist or an occupational therapist thinks.

There *is* a discrepancy between typical language use of the term therapy among most professional therapists today and some of the typical practices music therapists engage in. For instance, fields like *health promotion* and *palliative care* already have been cultivated under the umbrella of music therapy for years. I welcome this development warmly, while I find it somewhat confusing to label palliative care as therapy. The reflections above run into the same paradox of language use as I started the chapter with. How can I argue that there are music therapy practices that should not be considered therapy? Is music therapy currently sailing under the right flag? By exploring another metaphor, an answer could be suggested: If we do not consider the term music therapy to be an exact label naming a predefined territory, but rather a banner that a group of people with shared interests have chosen to hold up while marching, we may understand that as they march both the landscape and the members of the group may change considerably. The group learns new things and sees new things, as response to the changing landscape, while they may still be carrying their good old banner.

MUSIC AND HEALTH

In order to move beyond illumination of paradoxes of language use, I think it will be helpful to reflect upon this *shared interest* that music therapy practices evolve around, which I propose may be conceptualized as *music and* health. Whether the focus is promotion of resources, prevention of problems, cure, rehabilitation, or palliative care, some health concern will guide and influence the process of musicking. I will therefore briefly explicate a concept of health that may be compatible with the culture-centered perspective that I try to develop in this book.

The concept of health has been subject to much philosophical discussion (Gadamer, 1993/1996; Jensen & Andersen, 1994). In fact, health is a concern for most people. Health is related to life and death, as well as to quality of life. Our ability to deal with these issues is not that obvious, while our interest in them is. Health issues are important for our everyday life as well as for the economical and political development of communities and societies. No wonder then that health issues are the focus of a plethora of public debates and personal dialogues. In modern societies people live longer than before and they have access to therapies and health services that nobody in the generations before could even dream of. This new situation has not reduced peoples' need for talking about health issues, but rather the opposite. Some suggest that this interest for thinking and talking about health is becoming unhealthy, and they may even paraphrase Plato who more than 2000 years ago is supposed to have uttered that to be concerned about health is the most important hindrance for anyone who wants to live a good life. Such caveats should not be neglected, rather integrated, in music therapists' concern about issues and concepts of health.

In biomedicine sickness to a large degree is seen as a result of biological processes which could be scientifically explained. Most health workers and scholars would agree, though, that health is something more than not being sick. It has for instance been suggested that the health system only influences 10 percent of those factors that are connected to health (Hjort, 1989). If one wants to challenge the medical tradition and explore the possibilities for focusing upon health promotion in wider contexts, the question is; what is this "more than not being sick?" How can we account for the fact that an individual is more than a biological being; that she is also a psychological, social, and cultural-historical being? These have in fact been important issues for the World Health Organization (WHO). As early as in 1946 WHO made a definition of health which is far more ambitious – some would also say unrealistic – than the traditional medical concept of health:

> Health is a state of complete physical, mental and social well-being and not merely the absence of disease or infirmity (World Health Organization, 1946).

This definition has been important in the health discourse after World War II, and as it makes health a concern not only for health professionals but also for society and politics in general it has a considerable sociological touch to it. Paradoxically the definition could be criticized for being too individual and "psychological," focusing upon harmony in the experiencing person. Complete well-being, of course, is impossible. Being human means to live with ups and downs. Some times health is to be patient, to realize that life is not a state of complete well-being. Other times health is to rebel, to protest against injustice and suppression. To be healthy, then, is not to be free from loss and limitations, it is more about being able to accept and handle loss and limitation, even seeing that sometimes loss also is liberation. The concept of health as a *process*, with ups and downs, will then be more instructive than the notion of health as a state of well-being.

The Danish philosopher Uffe Juul Jensen (1994) thus argues that health is not only well-being, but well-being experienced in relationship to the suffering that life gives. Health, as Juul Jensen sees it, is a set of *personal qualifications for participation in a community*, connected to *care and communication between people*. Jensen then builds upon a hermeneutic and dialectic theory of knowledge, suggesting that it is not given that it is the health professionals that know the answers to the issues that arise out of health problems. The answers must be sought in a process of communication *between* professionals and patients. Of course health problems differ. There *are* problems that relate more to humans as biological beings. Then the health professional is the expert; she knows how to repair a broken leg. But very many problems are due to complex interactions between biological, psychological, social, and cultural factors. The answers, the hermeneutics of the situation, then must be produced in a dialogue between the professional and the patient (Nerheim, 1995). Such an approach to health issues has important implications for health politics, making health not only a field for specialists but also an area for cooperation between people. Not only processes of sickness and of cure, but also processes of health and health-promotion become important. This hermeneutic approach has been influential in my search for a conception of health that I find relevant for culture-centered music therapy. In the following paragraphs I will give a brief review of some concepts of health given in the music therapy literature. The review is not at all meant to be comprehensive. Rather, I will discuss a few conceptions and see them in relation to the view that has been outlined in this paragraph.

Even Ruud (1987/1990, 1998) stresses the need for what he calls a hu-manized concept of health. Health is something more and different than "not being sick," he argues. We therefore need a broader concept of health than what is typically found within medicine. He relates the concept of health to the concept of *quality of life*, and he also suggests that health extends beyond the individual to include community and culture. He is arguing that there is a reciprocal influence between the individual and collective levels, and that the health of either will influence the other. Hence his definition of music therapy (which he formulated as early as in the late 1970s): music therapy is an effort to increase a person's possibilities for action (Ruud, 1998, p. 52). This definition – linking health to possibilities of action – has a clear flavor of sociological thinking. To increase a person's possibilities for action could mean empowerment, but also alleviation of some of the material, psychological, or social forces that keep a person in a handicapped or disfavored role. Ruud admits that this definition is rather broad, and that it therefore does not give a very precise picture of what a therapist can do. Precise pictures are not always what we need, though. Sometimes we need pictures that show us broader connections, and I consider Ruud's definition to be an important reminder of the relationships between therapy and society.

David Aldridge (1996) – in a discussion of health as performance – makes an effort to link perception and performance of music to health. He focuses upon features of modern societies, and suggests that health is related to process and identity:

> In modern times, health is no longer a state of not being sick. Individuals are choosing to become healthy and, in some cases, declare themselves as pursuing the activity of being well. This change, from attributing the status "being sick" to engaging in the activity of "becoming well," is a reflection of a modern trend whereby individuals are taking the definitions of themselves into their own hands rather than relying upon an identity being imposed by another (Aldridge, 1996, p. 20).

Aldridge adds that clients, as a consequence of this, have begun to demand that their understandings about health play a role in their care. When health is subject to social and individual definition, professional practitioners will start to seek complementary understandings, he suggests. Aldridge also advocates the need for a phenomenological understanding of music and its relationship to health, focusing upon the expressive body and music as identity, indicating that expression of health is something that could better be sung or played than spoken.

In the second edition of *Defining Music Therapy*, Kenneth Bruscia (1998a) advocates a different conception of health then what he did in the first edition of that book. In the first edition Bruscia (1989) treats health as a state of well-being, with a dichotomy involved; either you have health or you don't. In the second edition he gives a criticism of this view, and adopts Antonovsky's (1987/1991) "salutogenic" orientation, where a person's health can be described along a continuum, depending on how well he or she is resisting or coping with health threats. Health is then not a state, but a process of building (resistance) resources. Bruscia also draws on the contributions given by Ruud and Aldridge, that health is related to the social and that health is a way of being-in-the-world (it is not something you have or don't). Based on these premises, Bruscia then gives this definition of health:

Health is the process of becoming one's fullest potential for individual and ecological wholeness (Bruscia, 1998a, p. 84).

I sympathize with these three attempts of developing a conception of health that is relevant for music therapy. To illustrate how complex this issue is I will briefly mention a few critical comments to these conceptions. Since my intention here is not to end up with a "final" definition, I will not go into a thorough discussion of this criticism. Instead I will use the three definitions given and the criticism suggested to highlight a conception of health based on the cultural perspectives developed in this book.

I identify with Ruud's reminder about the social aspects of health, and about the possibility of developing a music therapy that is not only focusing upon the individual, but upon its context. There are some implicit problems in defining health as possibilities of action, however; who is given the authority to define which actions deserve to be promoted and which do not? Another basic question is: How *culturally biased* is the phrase "possibilities for action"? Is it based upon a typical Western value (the primacy of the autonomous individual with a high degree of agency), so that this definition of health is less relevant for people in other cultures? Similarly Aldridge's conception of health is based on ideas about modern humans concerned with self-definition and active construction of identity. Again this is probably mostly a late modern concern. Not all clients will identify with this, and the focus may also be too optimistic concerning any individual's freedom to choose identity. Bruscia's definition may run into similar problems. Who is supposed to define what is meant with fullest potential for wholeness?

Such questions are not easily resolved, as what we grapple with here is navigation between Scylla and Charibdys; biological or sociocultural determinism on one side and humanistic ideas about the autonomous and self-sufficient individual on the other. The latter position, although much more appealing than any version of determinism, is no solution, because it leads into creating a dichotomy between the individual and the collective. Other persons, at least if we *need* them in one way or another, then become a threat toward an individual's autonomy. I consider this to be a relevant criticism of Antonovsky's (1987/1991) conception of health; it is too concerned with the autonomous individual and does not take sufficiently into consideration the dialectics between the individual and the collective levels of human existence. A salutogenic orientation, as promoted by Antonovsky, will therefore be problematic in a culture-centered perspective if it is linked to a conception of the self-sufficient individual rather than to a focus upon human coexistence.

One attempt of coming to grips with this dilemma is developed by the Danish philosopher Ole Dreier (1994). Taking the cultural psychology of

Vygotsky and the activity theory of Leontjew as a departure point, he attempts to outline a dialectical conception of health. He acknowledges the individual aspects of health, as personal conditions and qualifications for *participation in social life*, but stresses that health also concerns people's *mutual care* to ensure the development of the conditions and qualifications of each person:

> Health is neither just my interest for myself or others' interest for me, but the mutual and general interest and care for each person's possibility for participation (Dreier, 1994, p. 199).[1]

In this way Dreier locates health neither in body, person, nor society, but as a quality of the *interaction and activity* that humans engage in. To state this is both more and less than giving an alternative definition of health. Dreier's intention is hardly to "define" health in any exact manner; he is rather suggesting an alternative path to follow. His statements are connected to a specific way of thinking about humans, based upon theoretical assumptions that are compatible with those presented in Part I of this book.

In relation to this a music therapist will have to reflect upon how music and health link. Links may exist on biological, psychological, social, and cultural levels. Exactly how and how much music and health link is partly an empirical question. My errand here is theoretical; what has been outlined above is a relational notion of health, and my theoretical proposal is that this notion is compatible with the relational notion of music(king) discussed in Chapter 3. The music of music therapy is *health musicking*, it is the shared and performed establishment of relationships that may promote health. The mutual interest and care for each person's possibility and participation may be expressed through musicking between client and therapist, as well as in relationships to other people and contexts.

This may throw some light on the *means versus ends* debate that has plagued music therapy. The way the term music therapy has come to use it may be argued that music refers more to the means of the practice than to the ends. Music therapy is usually not first and foremost about developing musical skills or sensitivities, the argument goes. If one compares with physiotherapy or speech therapy – practices that help people with physical problems and speech problems respectively – the term *music* therapy then may even be considered somewhat misleading. An analogy would imply that music therapists should be helping people with developing their *music*.[2] If one maintains a means and ends dichotomy, I agree that this would be a strange description of music therapy, and that it would be more accurate to describe music as means and health as end. As I have tried to show throughout this book, such a conception of means and ends would not do justice to the complex nature of music therapy processes, and I agree with Rudy Garred (1996, 2001) who argues that music in music therapy in most cases could be considered a *dialogic medium* more than a means in any goal-rational conception. The conception I have chosen for music as medium is *musicking,* that is, music as situated practice based upon a shared human protomusicality. In this way I want to suggest that means and ends are not dichotomies in music therapy, but are aspects of the same process in systems of change, and it may make perfect sense to suggest that music therapists work in order to promote musicking.

CONCEPTUAL LEVELS IN DEFINING MUSIC THERAPY

The argument above is based upon the key assumption that definition of practices and disciplines must be understood in historical contexts; they grow out of interests of action and of knowledge situated in specific cultural and social circumstances. In this perspective it must be understood how the label of music therapy is not "natural." It was chosen in a specific historical context of clinical practice with a concept of therapy strongly informed by medical perspectives, or at least addressed to communicate in medical contexts. Today the label has a touch of reductionist anachronism to it. Later developments of both theory and practice suggest that health rather than therapy is the shared focus.[3] This change in focus contributes to the problem of defining music therapy. To this must be added the confusion created when distinctions are not made between definitions of discipline, profession, and practice. Disagreements on definitions may in some cases be based in insufficient distinctions between these conceptual levels. In some other fields this distinction may be more obvious in everyday discourse, because different words are in use for each level. Compare for instance the differences in language between the two following descriptions; a music therapist is doing music therapy after having studied music therapy, while a physician may be doing surgery after having studied medicine. In the latter case three different words distinguish profession, practice, and discipline, while in the first case these three levels are all related to the same term.

If there was no history and we could start all over, I would propose we chose new terms in order to clarify these conceptual levels. We could choose a term different from "music therapy" for the discipline (for instance *health musicology)* and then two other terms for practice and profession. In the present situation of established use of the term music therapy, this probably only would create confusion. Instead I propose that continuous reflection upon the conceptual distinctions between music therapy as discipline, profession, and practice is precious for the development of the field.

It must also be acknowledged that there is a lay everyday discourse and practice related to music as or in therapy. People in every culture and historical epoch seem to have linked music to health in some way or another. We could then go beyond the statement that music therapy is a multivocal term and identify four conceptual levels or domains of use:

- Folk music therapy
- Music therapy as discipline
- Music therapy as profession
- Music therapy as professional practice.[4]

I will briefly explicate this suggestion, before I give a more in-depth discussion of the domains:

Folk music therapy: Folk music therapy is heterodox and/or historical discourses and practices on music and health. As a modern discipline and profession the history of music therapy goes back to World War II only, there is a prehistory of music therapy going back for centuries. While there are different opinions as to the ubiquity and continuity of music therapy in, say, European cultural history, there is little doubt that music has been an important part of the healing rituals of most nontechnological or tribal cultures, and that music is also used by individuals and groups in contemporary late modern societies in order to promote health and well-being. Only if one neglects the cultural aspects of music therapy theory and practice is it possible to argue that modern music therapy could be understood properly if not in the context of this broader picture.

Music therapy as discipline: Music therapy may be considered an evolving discipline, that is, a branch of learning identified by a field of study, a tradition of inquiry, and a disciplined discourse. Usually the place and date of birth of this modern discipline has been ascribed to the United States in the 1940s. Today it is growing on all six continents. What constitutes the discipline is not clear, though; Is music therapy as discipline the study and learning of music therapy professional practice, or should the focus be broader, say the relationship between music and health?

Music therapy as profession: In an increasing number of countries music therapy has become a profession, that is, a vocation requiring training in some defined body of knowledge. The standards of qualification differ dramatically from country to country, as does the definition of the body of knowledge required. Some of the principal questions to ask are: "Is the training to be defined in a disciplinary or interdisciplinary perspective?" "How are theoretical knowledge, practical skills, and personal and ethical qualifications linked?" A profession is not only principally linked to a discipline or an interdisciplinary field, it is also practically and politically linked to a society, through informal and formal regulations of roles and responsibilities.

Music therapy as professional practice: In much of the literature and everyday conversations among music therapists the term music therapy refers not to the discipline or profession, but to professional clinical practice. In this perspective music therapy is a *doing,* that is, an interactive process of making music in the service of health and well-being. Music therapy is then separated from other things music therapists may do, such as research, teaching, writing, consultation, and supervision. One of the questions to be asked is: "What kind of practices are to be included in a notion of music therapy as professional practice?" The relevance of this question has only been increasing as music therapists have engaged in a broader spectrum of activities in a variety of new settings (health promotion in child health centers, didactics and habilitation in community centers, palliative care in hospices, etc.). Some music therapists may argue that the term "music therapy" should be congruent with the conventional meaning of the term "therapy," and that professional practices should be restricted to clinical settings authorized to work with the *cure* of disorders and diseases. While this is an important subfield it would clearly exclude many music therapists and limit the development of the discipline to restrict a definition of music therapy practice to this level, and a more inclusive conception is chosen by this author.

I suggest that we need a deepened understanding of the four domains described here in order to increase our ability to reflect upon and communicate about how to define music therapy. The definitions I will provide as my argument evolves are then not to be viewed as neutral descriptions of a given reality. They are actions that reveal a purpose; I want to illuminate how a culture-centered perspective may inform the understanding of music therapy in relation to the four domains outlined above. I will do so by first discussing folk music therapy, then music therapy as discipline and profession, and finally music therapy as professional practice.

FOLK MUSIC THERAPY

While professional music therapy is a rather new enterprise in most countries, it is quite often stated that there is a prehistory of music therapy going back for centuries and even millenniums. Also, music is and has been an important part of the healing rituals of most nontechnological or tribal cultures. The first written documentation of music in therapy is said to be an

Egyptian medical papyri dating back to 1500 BC (Bunt, 1994, p. 10). Music and health is and has been a cultural theme in most, or maybe even all, cultures that we know of (Gouk, 2000). If music therapy was an applied science only, with practice shaped as the application of knowledge produced in laboratories, then music therapists possibly could leave it to the historians and anthropologists to study and reflect upon how people have used and do use music in the service of health and healing. The argument in this book is that this is not the case. Professional music therapy is embedded in cultural processes. Values, procedures, and theories of music therapy are informed by and informs culture-at-large as well as different subcultures in the specific arena and era of practice. This is not to say that science plays no role, only that it does not cover the whole territory (and that the development of science also is influenced by cultural processes).

In a discussion of music therapy history Peregrine Horden suggests that three "therapeutic territories" are of interest: the heterodox, the professional, and the historical. "The professional is mainstream music therapy in Europe and America; the heterodox represents a variety of non-mainstream currents; history is the domain to which they both variously appeal for precedent and legitimacy" (Horden, 2000, p. 8). Horden's errand is to "save" history from being misused by contemporary professional and heterodox music therapists. The chapters of the book he has edited give documentation for arguing that there is less ubiquity and continuity in the history of music therapy than previously suggested by Kümmel (1977) and later proposed in many music therapy text-books. I respect Horden's argument, while my own errand here is slightly different. I propose that professional music therapy – which now exists on all continents, not only in Europe and North America – will be better understood if seen in relation to both heterodox and historical practices.

I have chosen the generic term "folk music therapy" to characterize this broad domain. In congruence with the cultural perspective taken in this book I suggest that music therapists should take serious interest in folk music therapy, in similar ways as cultural psychologists now start to take folk psychology more seriously than what has been typical within mainstream psychology; see for instance Bruner (1990). In a culture-centered music therapy – as in cultural psychology or psychiatry – *meaning* is a core term, and to construct impermeable walls between professional and folk practices and discourses will then not do any good (except, possibly, for the status of the profession). The term folk music therapy, as I use it here, is rather multivocal. One could argue that there are at least four main subdomains to relate to: historical practices, traditional practices of music healing in cultures around the world, nonexpert and noninstitutionalized uses of music for health in modern societies, and alternative and semi-institutionalized music healing practices in modern societies. To lump all this together in one term, as I do here, will not do for many purposes but hopefully for the purpose I have in this context: to argue that these territories should all be visited and explored by music therapists.

Texts discussing the history of music therapy (Kümmel, 1977; Horden, 2000) and texts discussing music healing in different cultural contexts (Boyce-Tillman, 2000; Gouk, 2000) must therefore be seen in relation to each other and in relation to professional music therapy. In line with my general argument about music therapy's relationship to multidisciplinary fields of knowledge, I also suggest that music therapists should go beyond readings and interpretations of such texts; they should themselves *contribute* with research in the territories outlined above. Such readings and research on the "broader culture of music therapy" would also add to music therapists' reflexivity. By seeing their own practices in the light of other practices they may be able to evaluate assumptions and procedures that have been taken for granted. On a more pragmatic everyday level of clinical practice therapists' ability to understand the expectations of clients coming to therapy could also be enhanced. A therapist's ability to acknowledge and encounter a client with respect will be enhanced if the client's assumptions about music and health are known and understood.

Music therapists belong to a young and relatively weak discipline and profession, and may have been inclined to uncritically celebrate the suggested continuity of music therapy in Western history as well as to reject or neglect contemporary heterodox practices of music and health. To my judgment, alternative strategies should be sought, of which the most immediate challenge is to acknowledge the relationship to contemporary heterodox practices. Even Ruud (1998) is one of the music therapists who explicitly have focused upon music therapy as part of a broader discourse and practice on music and health. He also argues that professional music therapy not only borrows from such discourses and practices, but that music therapists also should contribute to them. Much of Ruud's more recent research, on music and identity and on music and quality of life, is based upon this view. To my judgment, this kind of openness will benefit the development of music therapy as a discipline and profession.

There are some caveats to be made though: In order to be able to interact ethically with clients, colleagues, and authorities there is also a need for boundaries, definitions, and clarification of differences between lay and professional practice. To state that there are relationships between lay and professional practice is not do state that there are no differences. When speaking to an audience of music therapists this is usually not necessary to declare. They are themselves concerned with the issue, for the protection of their trade if not for any other reason. In clinical work it may be very important to note that the distinction between lay and professional practices and discourse may be important to maintain for both parties. While heterodox practices should not be neglected just because they may represent some competition in the market for the music therapist, there may still be cases where criticism is legitimate. For instance, it could be argued that many of the rather strong contentions about the power of music in some heterodox practices are based on wild speculations or biased and uncritical readings of research literature (Summer & Summer, 1996). My intention is not to suggest that music therapists should not allow themselves to engage in critical evaluations of heterodox practices, rather that the same critical light should be used on history as well as on contemporary professional practices. This critical light could also be constructive, aimed at illuminating how the possibilities of music in and as therapy are embedded in different and sometimes incommensurable language games or meaning systems. Folk music therapy may reveal people's dreams about what music and life could be.

MUSIC THERAPY AS DISCIPLINE AND PROFESSION

There is a plethora of music therapy definitions, see for instance the appendix of Bruscia's (1998a) *Defining Music Therapy.* Surprisingly few deal with the discipline and profession of music therapy. It is the *practice* of music therapists that has been defined; music therapy as clinical practice, treatment modality, model of intervention, or therapeutic approach. This probably reflects the history of modern music therapy. It did not grow out of academia as a response to scholars' theoretical questions and research interests, rather it grew out of practical and clinical needs and possibilities in Western societies in the second half of the twentieth century. Modern music therapy first established itself as a multifaceted field of practice. From such clinical and practical starting points a process of formalization of training started, with later establishments of associations, journals, training courses, and research milieus.[5]

A process in the direction of establishment of a new discipline and profession had started. One could argue that this happened due to scientific progress; not before after World War II was the knowledge base secure enough for a modern discipline and profession of music therapy to be established. A more inclusive and probable explanation is that this scholarly development was made possible by processes of modernization of Western societies, with increased *division of expert labor* as one of the main characteristics. The growth of modern professions, which started in the nineteenth century, could then not be described as a result of scientific progress only, rather as part of a process of social and cultural change in which scientific development of knowledge played its role as a condition and catalyst (Abbott, 1988). This perspective means that we cannot study the development of music therapy as discipline and profession in isolation, as a result of progress and internal processes only. We must also pay attention to the growth of music therapy as a field interacting with other fields, and the social and cultural conditions that have supported or countered this development.

The status and identity of music therapy as a discipline is not at all clear at the present. Some would even ask if music therapy *is* a separate discipline, or if it is a multidisciplinary profession, or just a field of interest drawing its theories and concepts from some recognized and well-established disciplines. If music therapy *is* a discipline, it is probably best understood as an *evolving discipline* still in search of identity. One crucial issue then is the role of the profession and of "environmental" pressures in the shaping of this evolving discipline. To my knowledge, this has not been studied extensively. I must therefore restrict myself to some principal reflections.

Universities, colleges, and other institutions training music therapists usually consider music therapy to be more than a collection of techniques and procedures. Although standards of training differ dramatically – with duration of training probably varying on a scale from one to seven, eight, or nine years of full time studies – there seems to be a shared assumption that in order to become a music therapist there is a *body of knowledge* that must be studied. That this body includes theoretical, musical-practical, as well as personal-ethical components is apparently a shared assumption as well. To define this body of knowledge – its focus or borders – seems to be dramatically difficult, however. Few comprehensive attempts of doing so are found in the literature. This may be because the focus has been taken for granted; the body of knowledge should support and inform clinical practice and make the training of professional and competent music therapists possible. My contention is that this may be a restricting conception and starting point.

Let us consider one of the possible problems with such a starting point. As Abbott (1988) and others have shown, one of the problems of the system of professions in modern societies is that each profession develops a tendency to focus upon their own interests as experts in a social field, fighting for dominance and power, better payment, etc. This may be countered, or sometimes concealed, by clinical ideologies that stress client-centered perspectives. In most cases third parties, such as the state and other funding agencies, also play their part in shaping the field. This does not resolve the problem though. While there is no earthly reason to expect that a profession should not be interested in its own interests, there is still a need for a critical self-reflection on any profession's cultural and social role. If the discipline of music therapy is linked too closely to the profession of music therapy and defined by the needs as they are seen from, say, the professional associations, a critical and constructive potential is lost. It will to my judgment therefore be healthy to define the discipline of music therapy *in relation to but not limited by* the existing clinical practices and/or interests of the profession.

The arguments above suggest that a broad conception of music therapy as discipline would be fruitful, and I will propose the following:

> Music therapy as discipline is the study and learning of the relationship between music and health.

I suggest then that music therapy as discipline is better conceptualized as a broad field of study – the relationship between music and health – than as a territory of professional practice. This could open up for the study of several practices – professional and nonprofessional – and the discipline could as such supplement, support, and challenge contemporary and future practices (informed by diachronic and synchronic foci of study). The discipline of music therapy could then be conceived as having several subfields of study, such as:

- Music and health in the perspective of human phylogeny: biological and evolutionary perspectives on the relationship between humans, music, rituals, and health.
- Music and health in the perspective of cultural history: the history of musical healing and music therapy.
- Music and health in the perspective of human ontogeny: life span development to and through music.
- Nonprofessional practices of music healing in cultural contexts, and other everyday health-related uses of music.
- Process and outcome studies of professional practices related to health promotion and palliative care.
- Music therapeutics: process and outcome studies of curative music therapy practices (specified in approaches, clinical populations, clinical contexts, etc.)

This list is not meant to be comprehensive; rather it should illuminate the breadth that could be imagined for the discipline of music therapy. A discipline with such a broad focus would be freed from fruitless negotiations about which clinical practices deserve the label "therapy" and which do not, and should not restrict itself to the task of legitimating professional practices.

I am proposing this definition of the discipline well aware of the fact that many music therapists already take interest in one or more of the subfields mentioned, at the same time as few, if any, academic milieus of music therapy define their field in such a broad perspective as the whole list above suggests. As these milieus today mainly are established as schools for producing professional practitioners, they do not have the size, breadth of competency, or financial resources to do so. The definition above is therefore given as a possible direction for future development more than as a description of status quo. Negotiations with neighboring disciplines – such as medicine, psychology, education, musicology, sociology, and anthropology – will be part of the identity development of the evolving discipline of music therapy. So-called indigenous theories of professional music therapy – "theories that emerge from clinical practices in the field" (Bruscia, 1998a, p. xiii) – could then be cultivated and informed by interaction with neighboring disciplines. In order to achieve this, building of international academic networks – including interdisciplinary networks – will be crucial, as well as inclusive avenues for publication of multicultural and metatheoretical discussions based on diverse forms of inquiry.

Music therapists could then stretch the scholarship of music therapy beyond a narrow clinical focus and develop more critical sensibility and appreciation of the relevance of folk music therapy and everyday aesthetics. It could be argued that such a process includes the possibility of music therapy losing identity or being subsumed under a larger or more developed discipline. I consider it more plausible that the identity would be clarified, and that a context for a critical reevaluation and refinement of professional practice would be created. With the definition outlined above it would be very clear that the fields of interest for the discipline and profession of music therapy do *not* overlap completely. The tension involved should be fruitful, as the possibilities and limits of professional practice could be contextualized in a broader field of knowledge.

MUSIC THERAPY AS PROFESSIONAL PRACTICE

The definition of music therapy as a discipline given above suggests that music therapy as a profession could be freed from the strenuous task of stretching the meaning of the word "therapy" in all kinds of directions in order to defend the diversity of professional practice linked to the discipline. If music therapy as discipline is the study and learning of the relationship between music and health, the health-promoting activities of the profession will belong to several categories, with therapy – in the conventional contemporary sense of that word – as only *one* of the possibilities. Music therapy professional practice may include other types of interventions, such as primary health promotion, prevention of problems, habilitation, rehabilitation, and palliative care. These types of intervention all usually imply direct work with clients. Indirectly, still in relation to clients, music therapists work with research, teaching, supervision, consultation, public information, etc. Also, there are several types of practice in which direct and indirect elements interact closely, such as consultation-collaboration music therapy[6] and participatory action research.

In defining music therapy as professional practice one may then go in two directions; either by providing a "restrictive" definition of music therapy as curative practice or a very wide definition embracing all types of practices a music therapist may engage in, including such "indirect" practices as research and supervision. Focused and restrictive definitions will be important in specific clinical contexts and areas of practice. In the context of this discussion a "middle way" has been chosen; a definition that can illuminate some shared characteristics of practices in which music therapists work directly with clients. According to the argument developed in this book, to define the essence or core of music therapy as professional practice is hardly possible. Any such practice will be situated in historical contexts, and the focus of and approach to the work may vary accordingly. A disciplined and professional practice may be given some formal characteristics, though, and in the paragraphs to follow I will try to outline a suggestion of how these could be described through the lens of a culture-centered perspective. The outline will be based on the following proposed definition of music therapy:

> Music therapy as professional practice is situated health musicking in a planned process of collaboration between client and therapist.

Arguments in support of the main concepts of the definition are developed in various chapters throughout this book, and I will here only briefly comment upon the basic concepts. The terms will not be discussed in order of appearance in the definition, as this order only reflects the grammar of the English language. Instead I will use the sequence of concepts that I think best illuminates the relationships between the notions.

Health: Music therapy as professional practice, based upon the discipline of music therapy as defined above, is under obligation to focus upon health-work. Health is then understood as the mutual and general interest and care for each person's possibility for participation. Individual aspects of health, as personal conditions and qualifications for *participation in sociocultural life,* are then acknowledged, while *mutual care* to ensure the development of the conditions and qualifications of each person is also underlined. Health is therefore not understood as an either-or state, but as a quality of the *inter-actions and activities* that humans engage in. Health is then seen in connection with empowerment, as a major shared theme in processes that in other respects may be labeled differently, such as cure, care, habilitation, etc.

Situated health musicking: While music in music therapy conventionally may be considered a means to therapeutic or health-related ends, the phrase "situated health musicking" is used in this definition to communicate the chosen perspective of music as dialogic medium and situated activity in relation to health. The term "musicking" was explicated in some detail in Chapter 3, and the term "health musicking" will be elaborated upon in the next chapter. The term "situated" has been used in the context of several discussions in the previous chapters. I will briefly here summarize the implications of stressing the *situated* character of music therapy practice: Music therapy must be understood as a process situated in an evolving sociocultural context. Sensitivity to this proposal goes beyond focusing upon how environments influence individuals and groups in the course of development. How individuals and groups select and shape the environments that influence their development must also be considered. There is a reciprocal process of influence involved, of which the term *transaction* sometimes is used. An important element of such transactions is meaning-making. Meanings then are located in time and space and have a history. In addition to any universal "mechanisms" (linked to human nature) of how music works and means, both local and personal sources of meaning-making then must be examined, as processes in which sounds, movements, and linguistic signs interact and affect each other. This all relates to a cultural psychology conception of the relationships between agent, activity, and world, viewing them more or less as mutually constitutive.

Client: The notion of client, as used here, denotes any individual, dyad, group, or community suffering from health problems not possible to deal with in a satisfactory way in everyday contexts, so that the services of a music therapist have been sought. While a client in therapy often is an individual (even when an ecological perspective is chosen), this notion then proposes that in some cases it is legitimate and relevant to define a community as a client in music therapy. This raises some important ethical considerations that will be discussed in Chapter 9.

Therapist: A music therapist is professionally trained in music therapy and relevant aspects of related disciplines, skilled in music therapy techniques, and obliged to a set of ethical principles and values. For a culture-centered music therapist the value of being knowledgeable and sensitive to his own relationship to the client's cultural context is also seen as crucial. In the definition above the term "therapist" is used (instead of "music therapist.") This is done to distinguish between the conceptual levels of profession and professional practice. While I propose that music therapy as professional practice usually requires the competency of a professional music therapist, practices that could be labeled music therapy but which are led by other professionals are imaginable, one example being GIM led by a GIM-trained psychiatrist.

Planned process: For the client the music therapy process may be understood as engagement in health-promoting cultural learning in a zone of proximal development. For the therapist the process involves planned interventions as well as more spontaneous interactions. For both parties the process is part of an overall plan that at some level of specificity defines arena, agenda, and activities. These are relative to the client and his health problems as well as to the therapist and his competency. They are also relative to the context of work.

Collaboration: To define music therapy as a planned process of collaboration underlines both the equality of and the differences between the two agents involved. There is a shared responsibility between the two parties; they work together over time in relation to the goals defined. In this process there is a differentiation in role responsibilities defined by the therapist's higher competency and function as a helper, but *within* this differentiation collaboration and open communication should be given priority in music therapy informed by culture-centered perspectives. This means that to describe music therapy as a systematic process of intervention would only be partly accurate, as it underlines the therapist's role as expert on expense of emphasizing the shared responsibility.

THE PRACTICE OF REDEFINING MUSIC THERAPY

In the epigraph to this chapter one of the major European pioneers of modern music therapy asks: "What is music therapy?" (Priestley, 1975/1985, p. 15). Her answer is not given as a formal definition, but reveals her experience and understanding as related to the attitudes and values of the contexts she had observed and worked in as a music therapist. Her statement was made at a time where idealism was higher and job opportunities lower than in Britain today, so much is obvious. At the same time we are reminded about the possibility that even more formal definitions of music therapy are situated. They are positioned in discourse, and also relate in some ways to eras and cultures of music therapy. Definitions of music therapy are not merely descriptions, then, they are acts of meaning in an evolving field. They are influenced by and in turn influence certain practices and discourses of music therapy. The definitions that I have given in this chapter are of course no different; they communicate a culture-centered perspective. While I agree with Bruscia (1989, 1998a), who argues that definitions of music therapy should be developed at levels that are not exclusively linked to specific clinical theories and populations, I think that definitions inevitably will be informed by metatheoretical assumptions. Metatheoretical awareness will then be part of what will redefine music therapy in the future.

The definition of professional music therapy practice that I have given in this chapter is broad. I do not consider curative practice as the "purest" form of music therapy or as the main exemplar constituting the discipline and profession. Practices of care and prevention, habilitation and rehabilitation, are all related to health and are of principal importance. We are still left with problems of communication, if all these fields of practice are covered by the same term. I consider it rather important that we go beyond "watering down" the notion of therapy in order to make it broad enough for inclusion of other health-related practices. When music therapists actually *are* working with treatment and cure of disease or disorder they will need a language enabling them to communicate that that is what they are doing. The discipline and profession therefore needs to develop language tools for clarifying differences between different areas of practice. Such differences may to some degree be articulated at a discipline-specific level, that is, at a general level in relation to specific contexts of clinical practice. At the same time, the notion of situated practice elaborated upon in this book supports the idea that to define music therapy is also a continuous practice of local redefinition.

A definition – in order to have any effect – is as much about social consensus as about logical delineation. In this respect it is only partly accurate to connect definitions to authors. It is necessary to do so, as agents should be responsible for their actions, but it must also be understood how definitions are only possible in the context of practices and discourses that support them. The practice of redefining music therapy is therefore best understood as collective reflexivity, where individual statements only could be considered as contributions in a continuing dialogue. Such contributions then relate to history and tradition as well as to appraisals of status quo and future possibilities. Criteria for a good definition are related to the degree of resonance with clinical practice and sociocultural developments, but as these *change* continuously, a definition should also be open for reinterpretation. The notion of a concept – which usually is characterized by clarity, precision, simplicity, and maximum definition – could then be reconceived in interconnected, relational terms (Lave & Wenger, 1991, p. 121). As such, definitions make sense in the context of broader discourses and practices. The practice of redefining music therapy is therefore not limited to those who write books and articles. It is a practice all music therapists participate in.

In choosing arena, format, activities, and approach a music therapist is defining music therapy in his or her way. Reflexivity could be developed in communication with colleagues and clients, who may ask questions about the rationales guiding the practice, which for instance may be conceptualized as choice of theoretical targets and targets of intervention. It will be important to be able to communicate whether the purpose of the intervention is health promotion, cure of disorder, or elevation of quality of life. The interventions must also be located within the context of other activities in institution and community. In this way what will be required is a large set of evolving local definitions of music therapy. It may be countered that a set of local definitions may lead to fragmentation of discipline and profession. This is not an inevitable outcome, though, if practitioners relate to and participate in the continuous scholarly dialogue as to how to define and conceptualize the discipline, profession, and practice of music therapy.

In some epochs the identity and boundaries of disciplines may seem rather clear, while in other periods they are not. This – of course – does not necessarily reveal a decline in research or thinking, rather that the relationships to society and to neighboring disciplines change and develop. The situated character of music therapy practice and the culture-centered perspectives advocated in this book may be taken as tokens suggesting that disciplines are arbitrary and socially constructed only. I think that would be a too radical suggestion. In the case of music therapy I think, for instance, that the notion of a shared human protomusicality outlined in Chapter 3 is a reminder about the possibility of some unity in conceptions and practices. Exactly *how* unity in diversity could be conceptualized in relation to music therapy is a much more complex question. An adequate answer requires more knowledge than what we possess at the moment. I still think it is fruitful to try and explicate some (metatheoretically informed) general descriptions of music therapy, which will be done in the following chapter in relation to the music therapy process. Such descriptions could then be used as departure point for future research, reflection, and critique.

NOTES

[1] My translation from Danish.

[2] This argument is somewhat biased. To define a form of therapy by its means is not so unique. A comparable case is psychotherapy, which is not defined by its ends – psychological change – but by its means. Psychotherapy implies the use of psychological means and psychological knowledge. Pharmacological treatment is therefore

usually *not* considered psychotherapy, although it may cause psychological change.

[3] It is not unique that disciplines change focus and function over years. An illuminative case may for instance be anthropology, which at the beginning of the twentieth century often was considered a marginal discipline mostly occupied with exotic cultures, and which at the end of the same century claimed to have something important to say about human life in all societies and cultures.

[4] Music therapy as professional practice could of course be subdivided in many ways. For conceptual clarification it will be important to distinguish between practices where music therapists work in congruence with a conventional ("narrow") conception of the term therapy and practices where they work with health promotion and care in a broader sense (cf. the somewhat misleading but still illuminating cure-care distinction).

[5] In the late 1940s the first American universities started to establish courses in music therapy, and new texts about the field were produced (Schullian & Schoen's *Music and Medicine* in 1948 being one of the first). In 1950 the National Association for Music Therapy was established in the United States. Similar developments saw daylight in Europe and South America a decade or two later, and in the 1960s and 1970s the first research journals were established.

[6] See Chapters 4 and 8.

Chapter 8:

A MODEL OF
THE MUSIC THERAPY PROCESS

*There is, it seems, an inescapable relationship between the
way we configure our inner and outer worlds, not only as
individuals but as larger communities and even nations.
"Music" (and all the activities this term may encompass) is
itself a powerful expression of that configuration, as well as
a means of altering it. Yet although music's cathartic
and transformative powers may be universal, the ways
such powers are harnessed and directed appear to be
culturally specific. Indeed, the forms musical healing may
take within a given community are determined by how its
members conceive of health and illness, as well as their
relationship to the material and spiritual realms.*
(Penelope Gouk)

Based upon the culture-centered premises discussed in Part I and the culture-specific clinical experiences described in the previous chapters, I will now start the process of discussing some possible principles for a culture-centered music therapy. Culture-centered music therapy supports a focus upon individuals and groups in context. Personal, social, and cultural relationships will be at the core of clinical practice, with possibility for cultural engagement and critique kept open.

SITUATED PRACTICE

One of the lessons to be learned from history and anthropology is that what counts as therapy is contingent on time and cultural context. Therapies develop in and into cultures where certain values and practices begin to be taken for granted. Why, for instance, do clinicians usually work with individuals, not so much with collectives? Why do therapists work in special locations and special rooms, using special activities and equipment, in definite formats? In asking these questions I do not want to communicate that there are never good reasons for doing the things implied, but simply that the questions should be asked. We must avoid "naturalization" of music therapy, treating music therapy as x or y in short of discussions of why, where, how, when, and with whom, that is, in short of "contextualization."

This chapter will elaborate on the suggestion that it is fruitful to conceive of music therapy as *situated practice*. Culture-centered music therapy cannot treat culture as a superficial independent variable or as background noise to be filtered out in order to pinpoint universal psychological mechanisms. The cultural psychology discussed in Chapter 1 proposes that culture and mind are constitutive parts of each other and that humans are "biologically pro-grammed" to become cultural beings. To separate the mind from its cultural context is to remove it from what makes it mindful. Thus, we need to move beyond the futile nature versus nurture debate. Instead we could start to ask questions about what is meaningful in the nature-nurture interaction.

This makes it necessary to supersede the metaphors suggested by a natural science way of thinking about music therapy. Music is more than a stimulus or a "drug," and music therapy practice is not a collection of techniques and procedures in a culture-free space. My argument instead focuses upon music therapy as *situated practice;* as health-related rituals embedded in culture and enclosed in social contexts. The term "situated" – connected to learning, activity, etc. – is used to clarify that thoughts and actions are located in time and space. It is also used to clarify that the meanings of thoughts and actions are dependent on the immediate social context they belong to. The term "situated" also links to a theoretical perspective informed by cultural psychology; a perspective that focuses upon the relational character of experience and learning and upon the negotiated character of meaning. All activities are then situated, as they relate to immediate social context and cultural history (Lave & Wenger, 1991).

To state that activities and practices are situated means to acknowledge that the agents are "thrown" into situations of concrete social and historical conditions. At the same time the agents' active meaning-making, say by the constructions of links to aesthetic communities, is of great importance. A discussion of music therapy as situated practice therefore needs to go beyond questions of *what, where,* and *when. Who* are involved as agents and *how* the activities are shaped are among the questions that need to be asked to better understand the relational character of music therapy practice. I will develop the argument by suggesting a context-inclusive model for describing music therapy processes.

SHARED COMPONENTS IN MUSIC THERAPY PRACTICES

What will be presented here is a model of the music therapy process that proposes some shared components in music therapy practices, while at the same time conceptualizing them in ways that may aid the discussion and exploration of music therapy as situated practice.

Figure 4: Shared components in music therapy practices in relation to available resources and contexts.

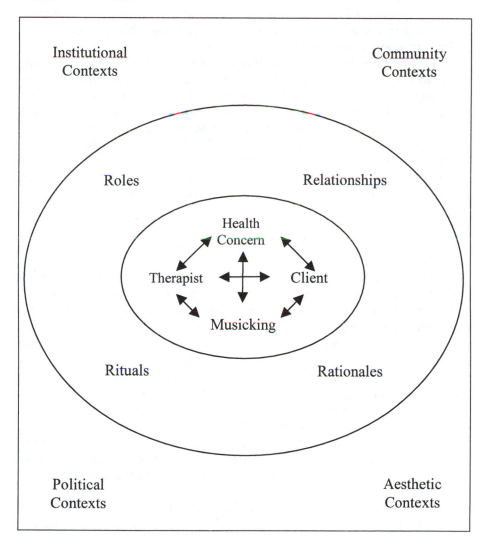

Music therapy practice, as defined in the previous chapter, may be conceived of as situated health musicking in a planned process of collaboration between client and music therapist. The focal point of this practice then is the *musicking* of a *client* and a *therapist* in relation to a *health concern.* This collaboration is embodied in the shape of *rituals* where *roles* and *relationships* are explored and developed, and it is framed by certain *rationales.* These roles, relationships, rituals, and rationales all link to multiple contexts, such as *institutional contexts, community contexts, aesthetic contexts,* and *political contexts.* On this basis, a model of the music therapy process may be conceptualized in relation to notions such as *communitas in context* and *reflexivity in action*, which illuminate health-promoting dynamics between I-Thou encounters and cultural contexts.

This model is based on explications of the clinical experiences communicated in Chapter 4 to 6, as well as upon incorporation of relevant concepts developed in the literature of music therapy and neighboring disciplines. The intention is not to illuminate every dynamic factor or aspect of the therapy process, as this would ask for a more detailed discussion in relation to specific clinical theories.[1] Hopefully the model will reveal some shared principles of relevance for culture-centered music therapy. Further clinical research will be necessary to evaluate to what degree this is the case. In this chapter I will concentrate on explicating the basic terms of the model.

HEALTH MUSICKING

Health musicking was described above as the *musicking* of a *client* and a *therapist* in relation to a *health concern.* In Figure 4 there is a "quadrilateral" then, formed by the four central components in the model. This geometric metaphor has been consciously chosen in contrast to the triadic relation that is often proposed between client, therapist, and music. In music therapy the dialogue between client and therapist is not only mediated by the fact that music is used, it is also mediated by the health concern that legitimates and gives direction to the whole process. While this health concern usually is expressed by and through the client, it could not be equaled to the client. It is a concern that may involve relationships to other individuals, groups, and communities, as well as to cultural values, practices, and narrative representations. In order to conceptualize the music therapy process in a way that allows for a focus upon several relationships, the quadrilateral image has been chosen.

What characterizes musicking in relation to a health concern? Expanding upon the notion of "affordances" outlined in Chapter 3, I will propose the following: *health musicking is characterized by careful assessment and application of the health affordances of arena, agenda, agents, activities, and artifacts.* Such a process of musicking is then relative to client, therapist, and health concern, and it is framed and facilitated by use of a set of resources that I in Figure 4 chose to label roles, relationships, rituals, and rationales. These resources will be discussed later in this chapter, with reference to relevant theoretical contributions in related disciplines. Here I will elaborate upon possible health affordances of arena, agenda, agents, activities, and artifacts, by using examples from the three cases described in Part II of the book.

Arena: Quite often therapy is carried out in a specifically designed setting, a specific music therapy room in a clinic for instance. Frank and Frank (1991) advocate that in psychotherapy this sense of "protected setting" may be very important in order to establish the necessary atmosphere of mutual trust for any in-depth process to develop. In many approaches to music therapy this may be equally important, as illuminated in the case of Ramona. It must be assessed though, in every case, what different arenas may afford. With Upbeat new possibilities grew out of having the sessions in a community music school. The idea of playing with the local brass band originated from this more open setting, which then in turn led to an exploration of other arenas in the local environment, such as "The People's Voice." Similarly, in the ecological approach to Paul's problems it was of outmost importance *not* to limit the arena by concentrating on activities in the music therapy room. Using everyday situations in his kindergarten enhanced his possibilities for development in a social context.

Agenda: The way I use the term agenda here is related to the more common term "therapeutic contract," but goes beyond this to include evolving issues, goals, and themes as conceived consciously and unconsciously by therapist and client. One example is given in Ramona's case story, where a contract of goals and ways of working was established but where the additional theme of *freedom* of how to use sessions soon evolved and turned out to be quite important. The importance and function of such an issue is of course relative to the problematic of the client. Similarly, the process of Upbeat demonstrated the function of an *evolving agenda*. From the first session the dream of playing with the brass band functioned as a main issue of the agenda, but in the process several subissues evolved around being together in music, such as the search for a shared basic beat. Agendas may be intrapersonal or interpersonal and relate to community and culture. Important aspects to consider are what different agendas may afford as well as how negotiations and establishments of agendas may afford. How important was it, for instance, for Upbeat's process that the main issue of the agenda was raised by one of the members of the group and not by one of the therapists?

Agents: As used here, the term refers to human agents involved in the dynamics of a therapy process. The main agents in therapy are conventionally considered to be the therapist and the client. This may be so also in culture-centered approaches, but Chapters 4 and 5 clearly demonstrate the possibility of other agents gaining importance that at points exceed that of the therapist. For Upbeat, the members of the brass band symbolically represented the possibility of belonging to and being part of the community, and their importance increased when direct collaboration and interaction in fact became possible. In the consultation-collaboration phase of the work with Paul, both the preschool teacher and other children became important as the main agents that Paul was interacting with. In a culture-centered approach a music therapist, if possible together with the client, should assess which agents may be important and how. At times the role of the music therapist changes from that of being a conventional therapist to, for instance, becoming a project coordinator or a consultant.

Activities: I propose the following six types of music activities to be vital in music therapy practices: to *listen*, to *play*, to *create*, to *perform*, to *interpret*, and to *reflect* (Stige, 1995). To *listen* is of course more than an activity; it may also be considered a basic attitude to all other music activities. To a somewhat lesser degree the same could be said about to *play* (to amuse oneself and to engage in a game). To *create* may be done systematically, as when composing, or more spontaneously, as when improvising. To *perform* means to take an existing piece of music as point of departure in a performance, while to *interpret,* as used here, means to relate to the sounds of music through another modality, such as movement, art, or poetry. To *reflect* means to put the other activities in perspective, quite often through verbal processing, alternatively through other modalities (see later about reflexivity). Some methods of music therapy, such as *improvisation*, obviously include an integrated range of activities, such as elements of listening, playing, creating, and performing. Usually elements of interpretation and reflection are also added. The range of activities described above is broad, and the descriptions too brief to reveal properly the scope of possible affordances. At this point it should suffice to underline that affordances of each type of activity could not be described comprehensively in a general theory of music therapy. They must be assessed in each specific situation in relation to each client. Small's (1998) broad conception of musicking is of relevance here. As selling tickets could be considered part of the musicking of a symphony concert, skiing in the woods turned out to be part of Paul's singing. While singing in relation to typical music therapy activities in the music therapy room had little to offer this particular child, singing while skiing opened up new possibilities.

Artifacts: Several types of artifacts are in use in a music therapy process, such as instruments, songs, words, and metaphors. The argument in this book has been that cultural artifacts are important in a person's development of self and identity. In line with the cultural psychology tradition outlined in Chapter 1, it may be argued that a person's sense of self and agency is constituted through internalization and creative use of cultural artifacts in social contexts. How artifacts afford is again relative to person and situation, one clear example being the simple song that became so important in the early phase of Ramona's therapy process. The lyrics could in another situation be considered trite and shallow, but in this context they offered Ramona a possibility for exploring and expressing emotions that she had rejected in her life. Artifacts therefore may be one of the more important components in the music therapy process, and it may also be important to pay close attention to artifacts that grow out of the therapy process itself, such as songs, poems, metaphors, and musical arrangements. In Ramona's case, new metaphors were produced in the therapy process, and they enabled her to tell her own story in new ways and with new perspectives on her own life. For Upbeat, musical arrangements grew out of sequences of improvisation and enabled the group to engage in projects of collaboration with several choirs and the brass band of the local community.

The five components discussed above – arena, agenda, agents, activities, and artifacts – all link in various ways and they form a complex web of relationships. What an arena affords is dependent not only upon the client and the therapist in question, but upon how the agenda evolves, upon what other agents will be involved, upon what activities are allowed for in the particular cultural space, and upon what artifacts are accessible. The metaphor of *hypertextuality*, developed in Chapter 6, may offer a way of conceptualizing the flexible and changing relationships between these components.

CLIENT AND THERAPIST LEARNING IN RELATIONSHIP

After this brief discussion of the health-musicking axis of the quadrilateral of Figure 4, I will consider one important aspect of the client-therapist axis, namely *learning in relationship*. Health as mutual interest for each person's possibility for participation suggests an understanding of music therapy that focuses upon *meaning*. It is not that one cannot imagine mechanisms of music therapy,[2] it is more that such mechanisms will always be subject for interpretation by client and therapist. Since humans share a common phylogeny, it is maybe not surprising that researchers on mother-infant interaction find crosscultural patterns of tempi etc. in, for instance, lullabies (Trevarthen

& Malloch, 2000). When working with music in therapy, though, only rarely do we work with the direct effect of music as such. To be biologically programmed to become cultural beings means something more than to be biologically programmed to react in specific ways on specific stimuli. If not the opposite, it means that humans easily are motivated to engage in cultural learning, and through that process human beings develop diverse relationships to stimuli encountered. When clients come to therapy they usually already have a long history of cultural learning.

I therefore maintain *meaning* as a main theme of culture-centered music therapy. As the chapters of Part I make clear, I am not advocating a freewheeling meaning-making though, but meaning-making within biological and social constraints. Human behavior and action is neither completely determined nor completely arbitrary, rather it is culturally mediated through social interaction. There is little reason then to produce dichotomies between the mechanism and meaning aspects of music therapy. I also consider it important to keep in mind that human agency within constraints also may have transformation of conditions as one of its goals, so that we should not understand constraints as something completely static, especially when we are talking about social conditions. These constraints are interpreted and given meaning, not as something revealed in an "archeological" way, but as something discovered through learning and participation in social contexts.

The human path to individuality thus goes through culture and the collective. The implications I draw from this is more than to advocate the relevance of group therapy. We also need to explore other collective forms of therapy, such as milieu therapy and community music therapy in ecological perspectives, and we need to consider the relevance of cultural processes when working individually. The relational notion of health advocated above therefore leads us to an examination of *learning through participation in cultural and social contexts*. Learning, then, is to be understood not as processes happening in the head of individuals only, but as processes situated in social coparticipation and increasing future possibilities for fuller participation in social and cultural performances. Such a perspective on learning is developed in Lave & Wenger's (1991) *Situated learning,* which I find highly relevant for culture-centered music therapy.

A person's relational self-experience in music therapy may be considered learning through legitimate peripheral participation in the role of an apprentice. The planned direction of the process is increased possibilities for participation, in the context of therapy and in the context of a larger community. The foci upon the context of therapy and community sometimes interact and merge, as illuminated in Chapters 4 and 5, while other times they form sequences in time. Learning is then defined relative to actional contexts, in a similar way as meaning is defined relative to language games.

Learning and meaning is then not considered private phenomena, but distributed among coparticipants.[3] The notion of situated learning relates learning to social and cultural participation, and allows for human agency and the development of personal identity. Participation – defined as a process where individuals work together in a socially and culturally organized structure – creates *relationships* of different kinds: relations to the activities, to the artifacts, and to the agents involved. As learners participate in communities of practitioners they then also follow several *trajectories of participation* that relate to each other; personal trajectories as well as trajectories connected to specific institutions, communities, and society at large. The personal trajectory opens up for learning as construction of a new identity, and this links to the other trajectories, where learning related to roles and expectations in institutions, communities, and society is in focus (Lave & Wenger, 1991).

The notion of situated learning implies that learning is developed in relationships between individuals and contexts, and this notion then challenges – or at least supplements – the more mechanistic notions of learning found in much behavioral and cognitive psychology. The notion helps music therapists to see connections that otherwise may be concealed; the relationship between health, learning, and sociocultural participation as well as the relationship between cultural learning and improvisation. While a more mechanistic conception of learning may be difficult to link to the creativity and improvisational qualities often cultivated in music therapy, the notion of situated learning implies a constitutive role in learning for improvisation (Lave & Wenger, 1991). The notion of situated learning may then function as a conceptual bridge that makes it possible for music therapists to view musicking as situated action that may be studied as integrative elements in the process of learning in the direction of full participation, which – as we just saw in Chapter 7 – may be tied to a relational concept of health.

The discussion above suggests that client and therapist are both learners of culture, and that the music therapist may be described as a "more experienced learner" than the client. Therapy is partly about learning how to enter a culture, find your way in it, and sometimes even new ways "beyond" it.[4] Learning in relationship is then not only about learning skills and propositional knowledge. As with the infant interacting spontaneously with her mother, learning is also the learning of "being with" and of operating with the signs of a culture, and these are situated in the same process and context. The notion of learning in relationship may therefore be linked to Vygotsky's concept of *Zone of Proximal Development (ZPD)* discussed in Chapter 1 and the notion of *Mediated Learning Experiences (MLE)* presented in Chapter 5.

ROLES AND RELATIONSHIPS

Above, the music therapy process has been discussed as health musicking in an interpersonal process of cultural learning. This highlights the quadrilateral of the inner circle of Figure 4. Further perspectives will be added by taking a closer look at the resources of the next circle: *roles, relationships, rituals,* and *rationales*. The themes to be developed below all reflect the interplay between therapy as an *interpersonal encounter* and therapy as a *social institution inscribed in cultural contexts*. In other words, the *resources* of the model may be viewed from two perspectives: as *elements in the client-therapist interaction* and as *elements that link to other contexts*. Rituals, for instance, may be a resource *within* a conventional music therapy session as well as a community resource that may be used as *local links* in ecological practices, as was exemplified when Upbeat could participate in seasonal celebrations and in "The People's Voice." When elaborating on the resources of the outer circle of Figure 4 – roles, relationships, rituals, and rationales – I will try to illuminate this double perspective.

When roles and relationships in therapy are discussed, usually the interpersonal encounter between two or more individuals is stressed. I too consider this aspect to be essential, and the reader may notice that all case examples given in Part II included a focus upon such encounters. In addition, though, culture-centered perspectives suggest that the music therapy process may be understood in a broader picture where roles and relationships link to the local community and other relevant contexts. New roles and forms of relationships may then need to be explored. The notion of health explicated above suggests that *partnership* becomes an important descriptive term for the client-therapist relationship. The roles of the two agents will necessarily be differentiated, but music therapy should be understood as a collaborative enterprise.

Partnership and equality has been stressed by several therapeutic approaches before. The added dimension here is that the focus of the clinical dialogue goes beyond the context of the client-therapist relationship, so that relationships to cultural contexts of various sorts may be explored carefully, in action and reflection. This will be clearer, hopefully, after the discussions of communitas and reflexivity later in the chapter. Thinking in this double perspective suggests that the clients' relationships to people other than the therapist may be a direct focus of interest, the support and building of a social network through music activities being one possible example. The role of the therapist then sometimes will be quite different from that of conventional modern forms of therapy. As exemplified in Chapters 4 and 5, the therapist may engage in changing the client-context relationship not only by stimulating changes in the individual, but by working directly with the context or community in question. New roles for the music therapist then will have to be explored. For instance, the therapist will sometimes operate as a *project coordinator.* Other times the establishment of *consultation-collaboration* relationships will be essential.

The role as *project coordinator* is relevant when there is a high degree of concern for how a context or community limits the possibilities of participation for a client, and when there exist options for working directly with these barriers. Sometimes this may be done informally, through the use of existing social networks. Other times this will be formalized, for instance in a participatory action research project. The project may be concerned with the development of new arenas for encounter and interaction, with the modification of limiting negative attitudes in the community, with the stimulation of existing local resources, with the building of helpful social networks, etc.

While the project coordinator aspect of the music therapist role was especially prominent in working with Upbeat, the music therapist's role as *consultant* became equally important in Paul's process. The basic idea when working with consultation-collaboration relationships is that the music therapy process is seen in relation to other processes in systems that the client relates to and is part of. Cross-disciplinary consultation may result in distribution of insight and skills in ways that will stimulate health-promoting changes in these systems. Nurses, teachers, parents, and other partners of the music therapist may have access to arenas and approaches that are closed for the music therapist (for instance due to practical or financial reasons), but the client may still benefit strongly from the competency of a music therapist. Consultations may be organized at regular intervals and/or with response at request. Collaboration activities may include informal consultations and participation in music therapy seminars or teachings, and it may include shared development of interventions with differentiation of roles and responsibilities.

What is asked for in developing consultation-collaboration relationships is related to what I earlier have described as "barefoot supervision" (Stige, 2001). While not every music therapist may be specifically trained in giving supervision, a basic knowledge of supervision combined with local knowledge of needs and resources may at times be what is required when developing context-sensitive approaches. Similar perspectives may be taken when working with cross-disciplinary consultation. For the music therapist this may include sharing of knowledge so that "barefoot" coworkers may qualify themselves in integrating musicking in their way of dealing with a situation.[5]

This will suffice as examples on how roles and relationships in culture-centered practices must be understood in a wide spectrum, from the interpersonal client-therapist encounter to a broad social context. In either case, roles and relationships are framed by *rituals* and *rationales:*

RITUALS AND RATIONALES

I have proposed relationships between musicking, health, and learning, and that music therapy may provide clients with possibilities for legitimate peripheral participation in communities of practice, with gradual increase of options for full participation. Learning in music therapy, then, is closer to a way of being in the social world than to a way of coming to know about it. Clients work with relations to activities, artifacts, and agents in communities of knowledge and practice, with cultural learning and development of identity as possible positive outcomes. If this perspective is pursued, music therapy as a community of knowledge and practice, a context for cultural learning, must be examined. I will try to do so by discussing music therapy as authorized cultural form, with special focus upon the *ritual* elements.[6]

A ritual, as understood here, is a practice regularly repeated in a set or predictable manner. Until quite recently rituals were in the Occidental world conceived of as practices of "the others," that is, of people of so-called primitive cultures. It is today acknowledged, however, that any culture has several types of rituals, magic-religious and/or secularized. Rituals may serve many different functions. They have a potential for both preservation and alteration of the norms and values of a community, and they might also serve important functions for the individual. While some social theorists have suggested that there is a decline of rituals connected to the process of modernization, others suggest that there is a renewed need and interest for rituals in late modernity. In any case, most theorists agree that rituals regulating sex and death are indispensable for the preservation of communities. People build bonds to each other and to the group through rituals such as marriage and funerals. Other important, though not quite so essential, rituals may be linked to seasonal changes, changes in an individual's or group's social role, etc. This view suggests that as communities change rituals will. Rituals are not basically archaic patterns, then, but conventions shaped and reshaped in evolving cultures.

The scholar who more than anyone else has paved the way for such a notion of ritual is Arnold van Gennep, with his famous work *Les Rites de Passage* (Gennep, 1909/1999).[7] Van Gennep suggested that the relationship between religion and magic is the relationship between theory and practice. Religion is the theory about the sacred power, whether defined as dynamism or as animism, while magic is practice (ceremonies, rituals, and cult). This suggestion could be interpreted as a first step in the deconstruction of the difference between "them" and "us," since magic before van Gennep mainly had been interpreted as primitive religion. With this van Gennep also suggested that the difference between magic and other forms of practice is not absolute, but relative, since people's understanding of what is divine or sacred changes over time. Magic becomes a practice among practices. Another practice, supported by another theory, might for instance be science (Gennep, 1909/1999, p. 27).

Van Gennep's understanding of rituals was mainly related to magic-religious practices, as practiced by "the others." His work was done in a time where European colonialism was close to its peak, and he lived in a world where it still made sense to use expressions like "half-civilized people." Van Gennep thus maintained the difference between "them" (the primitive people) and "us" (the people of the Western world). He treated rituals mainly as magic-religious activities, and thought of *rites de passage* as rituals that made the transition from the profane to the sacred (or vice versa) possible. The more recent tendency of studying and acknowledging what could be called secularized rituals does not find direct support in van Gennep's work. He indirectly paved the way for this, however, for instance by deconstructing the difference between religious and magic practices. Typical modern secularized rituals may be education and examination, initiations in clubs and associations, and *therapy*.[8]

This deconstruction and the more recent secularization of the concept of ritual is of interest for music therapy. The history of music therapy, or of music healing practices, is very often told as the history of three different types of practices; the magic, the religious, and the rational; see Kümmel (1977), Ruud (1987/1990), and Bunt (1994). It is then often suggested that the magic and religious practices only have historical interest, while modern music therapy is a new (research based) development of the early attempts of rational practices. When Ruud (1998, Chapter 8) suggests the metaphor "improvisation as liminal experience," based on van Gennep and Victor Turner's (see later) contributions, I choose to interpret this also as an opportunity to take a new look at how we construct the differences between ritual and rational practices. Music therapy may then be studied as rituals authorized by the society they belong to and developed in order to help people with problems in living. In contemporary health services, the authorization of a ritual depends upon its efficiency in promoting health. It also depends upon the degree of congruency between the rationale of the ritual and other influential rationales in the field.[9]

Parallels in practice may at some points be superficial, and to compare healing rituals of other times or cultures with contemporary music therapy practices may end up as rather decontextualized and essentialist interpretations suffering from a lack of reflection upon the problem of etic description. Reinterpretation of local beliefs and practices by translating them into a Western scientific language obviously will be based on a value judgment on which local truth is less local and more truth. Still, I argue that a focus upon ritual may help us to better understand music therapy as situated practice. When van Gennep coined the term *rites de passage* he was not just thinking of personal transformations. To him *social transformations,* the process where individuals and groups developed new social positions in their culture, were of outmost importance. The rituals that were of particular interest to van Gennep are constructed to ensure the transition from one place to another, from one age to another, from one social status or position to another, etc. In sum, these rituals are designed to help the individual and/or group go through a necessary shift, by giving possibilities for meaning and control in the most existential situations in human life. At the same time these rituals serve a *public and social function*, by offering members of the person's community possibilities for giving support, for sharing experiences, and for exercising control, etc. If we consider therapies as *specific authorized rituals,* similar functions may come into question. To look at music therapy as authorized rituals, then, is to focus upon the ritual as a safe container for *personal* experiences *and* to see this in relation to *public and social functions*.

The personal is certainly *one* important aspect; we may call it the internal function of the ritual. A ritual may increase the participants' sense of fitness or mastery, and is often felt to have a symbolic or quasi-symbolic significance. The ritual is a container, a safe environment that provides the participants with continuity and predictability. At the same time the ritual may be experienced as symbolizing transformation (in fact, as symbolizing the therapeutic process), and may as such be a vehicle of keeping the hope alive. The building blocks of rituals are then symbols as much as patterned conduct. Furthermore, *rituals* may have important protective functions related to "travels" into altered states of consciousness. They define the social roles and the concomitant responsibilities, and they may create perspectives by framing the experience of past, present, and future. In this way it may be said that the music therapist's task is to create effective ritual contexts for the development of learning, participation, and performance.

If this was the whole story, we would not need to go to the ethnographic perspectives implied in van Gennep's concept of *rites de passage,* however. While therapy *is* about personal transition, we must also consider the social and cultural role of a ritual; therapy may also represent social and cultural transition. Sometimes therapeutic changes occur in the client's relationship to social and cultural contexts, other times therapy also contributes to social or cultural *change* in these contexts themselves, in direct or indirect ways.

An ecology and dialectics of internal and external functions of rituals is involved, which may be better understood if we link the concept of context to that of *communitas:*

COMMUNITAS IN CONTEXT

In the model of the music therapy process that is proposed in this chapter, four types of contexts have been listed: institutional contexts, community contexts, political contexts, and aesthetic contexts. With the differentiation of the concept of context proposed earlier, it is obvious that this is not a comprehensive list of contexts, although it should cover some of the more important categories. My intention here is not to explicate every kind of possible context, rather to highlight how contexts may be integral to the music therapy process, how there may be a health-promoting dynamic between contexts and the I-Thou of the therapist-client encounter. Contexts then are not "extra" or "outer" layers, but vital elements in the therapy process.

I will approach this question via a discussion of the term *communitas,* which both relates to the issue of ritual discussed above and to the communion of the I-Thou. One of the music therapists that have touched upon music therapy as ritual practice, Even Ruud (1998), has developed an interesting discussion of communitas and of improvisation as liminal experience in music therapy.[10] The term communitas in relation to rituals was originally developed by Victor Turner, which in turn based his work on van Gennep's discussion of rites de passage. In explicating the concept I will therefore start by briefly going back to van Gennep's contribution and then turn to Turner.

In *Les Rites de Passage* van Gennep (1909/1999) made a comparative analysis of transitional rituals in a large number of cultures and eras. Out of a huge amount of data he searched for possible patterns, and developed the concept of *rites de passage.* Van Gennep's focus was diachronic; he was interested in rituals as they proceed in time. He came up with the suggestion that all *rites de passage* can be described as transitions related to three phases: the phase of separation, the threshold phase, and the phase of (re)integration. By using the Latin word for threshold, he also called these three phases for preliminal, liminal, and postliminal. Van Gennep then discussed this model in relation to some major life events most cultures have dealt with through the development of *rites de passage;* transition from one place to another, the integration of a stranger, pregnancy and birth, initiation to new social roles, engagement and marriage, funerals, etc.

Van Gennep's model is quite flexible. Each phase may last for hours, or for days, weeks, months, and even years. The rituals that ensure the transitions may be duplicated in many ways. Each phase can include its own sub-phases with its own *rites de passage*. So he did not propose a rigid schema, but a flexible model capable of detecting similarities and differences between cultures. According to van Gennep, there seem to be commonalties between cultures concerning the structure of the different phases; separation rituals tend to include *breach of established norms*, the threshold phase often includes *elimination of the customs and habits of everyday life* in the community, while rites of integration may be centered around *acts of communion*, such as dancing and eating together. As we will see, the description of characteristics of the threshold (liminal) phase has later been taken up and developed by Victor Turner, and may have relevance for an understanding of strong musical and personal encounters in music therapy.

It is worth noticing that van Gennep's work in large was a reinterpretation of the meaning and function of rituals described by other ethnographers, whom he criticized for describing rituals as isolated events. One of van Gennep's main points was that each ritual must be interpreted in context, and he focused himself mainly on two contexts: a) the context of the total set of rituals in each culture, and b) the context of similar (in purpose) rituals in other cultures. His approach was thus comparative; he negotiated between the cultural specific and the universal. He then ran into the dilemma that more or less constitutes comparative cultural studies: the dilemma of how to bridge emic and etic perspectives. Van Gennep did not discuss this dilemma explicitly, but by interpreting the rituals in the two contexts mentioned he handled it in his way. Van Gennep's project was neither to establish a unified model that neglects differences nor to establish historical relationships between similar rituals in different cultures. By creating his model van Gennep wanted to uncover a pattern that could be used to structure both similarities and differences between rituals in different cultures (Gilhus, 1999).

The simplicity and flexibility of van Gennep's model has made it popular in anthropology, sociology, and cultural studies. A major contribution to the model's prominence in contemporary cultural studies has been the work of the anthropologist Victor W. Turner. While van Gennep mostly studied nonliterate cultures and older literate cultures, Turner has contributed to the contemporary situation where van Gennep's model is used also in attempts of interpreting modern rituals. While van Gennep was especially interested in the transition between the three phases he described in his model, Turner focused upon the *liminal phase* or period, which he thought was the most important. Three core concepts in Turner's writing were *humanitas, societas,* and *communitas*. Humanitas is by Turner used to denote a shared "pre-social" human identity,[11] while societas denotes the social conventions and cultural regulations that separate humans into classes, cultures, etc. Communitas, then, is a concept Turner used to describe situations where the contradictions between humanitas and societas are nullified (Berkaak, 1993, pp. 25-26). Turner himself, in one of his comments on the concept, related these situations and processes to Martin Buber's (1923/1992) famous discussion of the I-Thou relationship:

> Essentially communitas is a relationship between concrete historical idiosyncratic individuals. These individuals are not segmentalized into roles and statuses but confront one another in the manner of Martin Buber's "I" and "Thou." Along with this direct, immediate and total confrontation of human identities there tends to go a model for society as a homogenous unstructured communitas, whose boundaries are ideally coterminous with those of the human species (Turner, 1969, pp. 131-132).

Even Ruud (1998) uses this anthropological notion of communitas as a concept for the understanding of the interpersonal encounter that by many is considered vital in music therapy. He underlines how improvisations in music therapy seek to build strong experiences of equality and being-togetherness through a temporal leveling-out of all social roles. In music therapy, Ruud suggests, improvisation becomes a "joint project" of closeness and mutuality with emotion as the main measure of the credibility of the experience (Ruud, 1998, p. 132). Ruud's discussion points to music as flow and fluidity, to the spontaneous and immediate, to the transcendent as well as to peak experiences and trances. Some practices of music therapy value such experiences strongly, and share this with both ancient rituals and some contemporary art forms such as jazz.

I have no problems in seeing that Ruud points at some values and experiences that are held highly among many music therapists. His discussion of improvisation as liminal experience links music therapy to the cultural development of Western societies, where new forms of liminality have been developed. Liminality – from the Greek word for threshold – was by Turner held as the domain for freedom; the domain for the uncommon, the strange and the new (Turner, 1967a). In liminality there is a certain freedom to juggle with the factors of existence, and there is a particular freedom of action. "Anything" may happen; the rules and norms that usually tie individuals to a social structure are put out of action. Turner's notion of the liminal has shown itself to be suitable also for the discussion of processes of modern culture, as in Berkaak's (1993) investigation of rock music. The liminal, then, may be said to continue to exist in modern culture, maybe in "attenuated" forms compared to traditional rituals of trance and transcendence, although the liminal aspects of free improvisation in certain genres and arenas of performance may challenge that contention.

Interpreters of late modern culture may suggest that ritual aspects have been downplayed seriously, that what is to be found rather are "liminoid activities" in sports and arts – basically activities closer to individual than to collective concerns. My judgment is that if liminal experiences could be properly understood at an individual level, one may indeed ask why we would need the concept. Other concepts covering strong and optimal personal experiences, such as *flow* (Csikszentmihalyi, 1990), could do. What Turner elegantly demonstrates is how individual and interpersonal experiences of a ritual are integrated with economic, political, and cultural processes, even when they seemingly are most separated from society, as in the liminal phase of a rite de passage. Turner's argument is that ritual symbolic actions refer to or imply social relationships, and that they also function as "epitomes" of the wider and spontaneous social processes in which they are embodied. Rituals reveal values in relation to the community or society in which they are performed. In the study of rituals Turner therefore saw a key to an understanding of the constitution of human societies. Rituals articulate social values not mainly as archaic forms but as commentaries to contemporary needs and structures. While social structure tends to become masked and unconscious because "it is there" all the time, rituals may reveal or unmask this structure (Berkaak, 1993).

The communitas of a ritual, for instance of music therapy, must therefore always be seen in relation to the social structures it relates to. The local community may be such a structure, or the society and culture at large, or specific aesthetic contexts that the client or therapist relate to. The therapy process, with its ritual elements, may from one perspective be seen as cultivation of *social cohesion*. Any ritual therapy may serve an instrumental role in conforming the individual to societal expectations. At the same time there is a potential, especially due to its liminal elements, in any ritual for *social critique*. This dual function of the ritual should be considered carefully when discussing the ritual elements of music therapy.

Participation in rituals demands some kind of acceptance of the society or community that sanction and authorize them, so also with music therapy. The therapist to some degree represents the society and its values, and as a more expert learner than the client the interaction will probably hardly ever lose all elements of mediated communication and guided participation. The client, as a neophyte or "candidate of initiation," stands in a relationship to a therapist that in some respects could then be compared to that of the instructors or leaders of the rituals van Gennep and Turner discussed. It must be noted, then, that the relationship to these leaders according to Turner are *not* characterized by equality and reciprocity, rather by authority and obedience. The experience of communitas, as Turner discussed it, is usually developed *among* neophytes, *not* in the relation between neophyte and leader. I think

Ruud may be correct, though, in suggesting that music therapy, understood as ritual, includes strong communal possibilities and may lead to experiences of communitas in the encounter between therapist and client. I would add that the importance of communitas among "neophytes" should not be neglected, and I propose that interpersonal relationships other than that between client and therapist may gain importance in culture-centered approaches to music therapy, as was discussed in relation to Upbeat's and Paul's stories.

To the degree that music therapy enables communitas and represents freedom, it is as counterculture and anti-music, as temporary and relative elimination of customs and habits. The music therapy experience is linked to and framed by "host communities." We must therefore try to avoid romantic and essentialist interpretations of communitas in music therapy as absolute equality and mutuality in music. Communitas is framed by the scripts, rules, and roles of specific communities, and I argue for the need to reflect upon the dynamic relationships between the therapeutic encounter and the contexts it relates to.

REFLEXIVITY IN ACTION

The model elaborated upon above may be summarized in the following way: The musicking of a client and a therapist in relation to a health-concern is framed by certain rationales (clinical theory and folk theory) and is embodied in rituals defining roles and relationships. These roles, relationships, rituals, and rationales link to multiple contexts which must be considered integral elements in the therapy process. The final issue to be discussed in this chapter is how the links between individuals and cultural systems and contexts may be conceptualized in music therapy. I propose that the notion of *reflexivity* may be helpful in this respect.

Reflexivity may be understood as an individual's ability to reflect upon his own position in relation to social and cultural systems. Kirsten Hastrup, a Danish ethnographer, underlines that reflexivity involves the process of moving between a first-person and third-person perspective (Hastrup, 1999). To reflect upon one's position in relation to others implies that the person sees her own actions as if she was in the position of another, while she at the same time acknowledges her role as agent and as a locus of emotion and experience. Reflexivity evolves in dialogue (sometimes intrapersonal but always with some "other" implied) and therefore also involves the second-person perspective.

The ability to reflect is implicit in the notion of *action* that is used throughout this book. While behavior is observable doing (in humans or animals) that originates events, action implies that the actor can reflect upon what he does. The individual *knows* that he acts and he has some image of what he is doing. That image may be inaccurate, and the consequences of his action may be different from what he imagined (because his image of the context of the action may have been inaccurate or because the context may have been difficult to predict). Be that as it may; reflexivity implies human self-regulation that goes beyond learnt behavior. Processes of metacognition enables the person to view a situation from several perspectives, and thus also to choose to transcend the norms he would usually obey.

Jürgen Habermas is, as Fornäs (1995) and several other authors have noted, one of the social theorists that most strongly have underlined the development of rationality and the self-reflexive character of modern life. Modernity is characterized by demystifying and self-reflexive questioning, and may as such be understood as fundamentally ambivalent (Fornäs, 1995, p. 29). This tendency has been intensified by late-modern and postmodern developments, where the individual's self-reflexive search for identity in polysemic social situations has been given much interest. These descriptions capture, to my judgment, crucial elements in human existence in contemporary societies. I do not think they would suffice as satisfactory descriptions of reflexivity in the music therapy process, though, one problem being that the rational and verbal aspects of reflexivity are emphasized to the neglect of other aspects, another that processes of reflexivity in traditional cultures may be overseen. If we again turn to a discussion of rituals, we may discover that an examination of the liminal phase with its exaggerations and temporary upheaval of social norms may furnish us with a broader concept of reflexivity of relevance for music therapy.

Rituals may provide occasions for society to view itself critically. According to Turner (1967a) the chaos of the betwixt and between of the liminal phase may be used to put the elements of culture in perspective and as such to stimulate social and cultural creativity. Turner's discussion of the possibility of reflection given in the liminal phase of rituals is related to what he calls "mediation of *sacra,*" which he considers to be "the heart of the liminal matter." With reference to Jane Harrison he proposes that sacra may be communicated as 1) exhibition (what is shown), 2) actions (what is done), and 3) instructions (what is said) (Turner, 1967a, p. 102). The possibility for reflection is connected to the creative, often absurd, character of the mediation of sacra. Turner notes, for instance, how certain exhibitions and actions represent cultural and natural features in disproportional ways. A head or a nose may be discolored, a lazy man may be figured with an enormous penis but no arms, or a figure of a pregnant woman may picture her carrying four babies at the same time. Turner suggests:

> It seems to me that to enlarge or diminish or discolor in this way is a primordial mode of abstraction. The outstandingly exaggerated feature is made into an object of reflection (Turner, 1967a, p. 103).

In the liminal phase of rites de passage the neophyte may be invited to reflect upon the element that has been manipulated, that is, to reflect upon its place and function in the culture that the candidate of initiation is about to be integrated in. Turner relates this also to another phenomena in such rituals, the use of masks and monstrous symbols. He criticizes earlier researchers who tended to reduce the interpretation of such elements by seeing them as reflections of hallucinations, nightmares, and dreams only. Turner himself gives these monsters an interpretation related to social and cultural processes. Similar to the componential exaggeration described above, these elements may stimulate the neophytes to reflect upon *relationships* (between individuals or groups, between cultural artifacts and social norms of community, etc.). According to Turner, rituals have a potential for leading to "direct apprehension of reality" by pointing to the impulses and conflicts that constitute social interactions (Turner, 1967a). Turner's discussion is compatible with Geertz's (1973/1993, p. 142) contention that it is overconservative to think of rituals as vehicles for the stabilization of traditional social ties. Rituals may at times also function as a driving force of individual or social change. It must also be noted that Turner's discussion of the possibilities for reflection embodied in rituals to some degree is paralleled by Bakhtin's discussion of the European carnival tradition (Morris, 1994) and by Handelman's (1982) discussion of festival and play.

My proposal, then, is that the discussion above suggests a concept of reflexivity that is not limited to the rational and verbal, and that therefore may be very suitable for music therapy. We first may note how the paths of communicating "sacra" suggested by Turner seem to be compatible with typical procedures in a music therapy process. Instruments and other artifacts are *shown* and may be given symbolic meaning, and there are strong elements of both *action* and *"instruction"* (talking). Similarly, therapy processes may, as rituals, deal with the revealing of what is usually hidden in everyday life. One of the things we can learn from the discussion above is that such revealing could be framed as the disclosure of thoughts, emotions, and states in the individual, but also – and at the same time – as certain *relationships;* between individuals, between artifacts and values, between groups and communities, etc.

This may be exemplified by going back to Ramona's descriptions of her own therapy process in Chapter 6. In reading her statements we see that one important thread is how she contextualizes her experiences by *seeing them in relation to her history and her everyday experiences*. The elements of music therapy are given meaning not only because they confirm her earlier experience and thus her expectations, but also because they challenge them, sometimes by being different and absurd. Before coming to music therapy she had been thinking about music as a ready-made world, with herself at the back of the queue of people who dominate and master it. Through the improvisations of music therapy she had been given another entrance. What she usually would call noise was now integrated in a more free musical play with sounds and symbols. Dangers were involved in this; she had to enter a boat without oars, and she knew that if her parents had seen her playing they would have been shaking their heads, saying: "What kind of foolish behavior is this?" So music therapy challenged the actions and values that had shaped her life. The liminal experience of "being in a boat with no oars" had opened up another space in her life, a space in which she could define her relationship to herself and to the subculture and the community she belonged to in new ways. The mutual understanding and reciprocal interaction of the music therapy sessions stood in relationship to the other communities she belonged to. In music therapy she could do "something different," and through that develop and voice new perspectives on her life.

What is different is of course different from case to case. We could for instance use the discussion of reflexivity in the liminal phase of rituals to offer a possible new perspective on the music therapy pioneer Paul Nordoff's experience of successfully applying the Middle Eastern idiom to a inner-city boy from Philadelphia. Nordoff himself suggests that his music goes "beyond culture" and reaches for the archetypal and universal (Robbins & Robbins, 1998). An alternative interpretation would be to suggest that the effect experienced is not due to universal or archetypal qualities intrinsic to the Middle Eastern idiom, but to the fact that this music is exaggerated, different, and strange *compared* to the music usually experienced by such a boy. In the same way as a mask or an exaggerated figure in a ritual may provide the neophyte with new perspectives by being different, this music, and the acts of musicking involved, may provide the music therapy client with new possibilities for experiencing himself in relation to other people. The "absurdity" of the music may then be basic for its therapeutic value. We are then *not* speaking of absurdity as an intrinsic quality of the music, but as a relationship between the musicking and the musics known by the client before entering music therapy, as illuminated by Turner's (1967a) discussion of the liminal phase of a ritual.

Reflexivity then, in music therapy, may be considered to be *reflections in and through actions*. Reflections upon relationships may be seen as a path to individuality, but not to individualism, as social and cultural contexts remain crucial. A ritual may work as an interface between the individual and his culture and community. The ritual elements of music therapy suggest that therapies are not "discovered" or "invented," rather that they grow out of individual and cultural needs. As rituals evolve and change over generations, we should expect music therapy to do so as well.

NOTES

[1] There are, of course, already quite a few theoretical proposals made on the components of therapeutic processes. Most of these contributions are linked to specific approaches to therapy, but some general proposals also exist. In music therapy two important examples are Sears's (1968/1996) discussion of "Processes in Music Therapy" (later taken up by Kenny [1989] and others) and Bruscia's (1987, Chapter 38) discussion of dynamics and process in improvisational music therapy. In the literature of psychotherapy an important discussion of general components has been made by Jerome Frank (Frank, 1982, 1989; Frank & Frank, 1991).

[2] Due to the focus I have chosen I elaborate meanings of the word "meaning" throughout the book, while I use "mechanism" as a more vague, but hopefully not completely inadequate, metaphor for actions and events determined by some regularity or law. For a discussion of root metaphors in world hypotheses, see Pepper (1942).

[3] This argument is compatible with Wittgenstein's (1953/1967) private language argument, see Glossary.

[4] What is proposed here is not the possibility of going beyond culture as such, but of going beyond the limitations of a specific sub-culture.

[5] This proposal of course raises important ethical issues as to what knowledge can be shared between disciplines and coworkers in responsible ways. It is probably not possible to define a set of rules regulating such issues. Choices must be made in relation to the needs of the client, to local resources and limitations, to the status and role of music therapy in the given context, etc.

[6] In focusing upon the ritual elements of therapy I may be construed as going in the direction of suggesting continuity between modern music therapy and the rituals of, say, ngoma healing in South Eastern Africa. This is not quite my intention. The life-world and cosmology of most Sangomas are quite different from that of most modern music therapists. My errand is therefore *not* to promote ideas of continuity through notions such as "the contemporary shaman" (Moreno, 1988) or "the rational shaman" (Bunt, 1994). While I started to take an interest in comparing modern music therapy with ngoma rituals quite a few years ago (Stige, 1983), I have been reluctant in developing the idea of music therapy as ritual because of fear of being misunderstood. I do not think that African rituals can be transplanted to Occidental

contexts, or that the Sangoma has preserved perennial truths lost by modern humans. The contexts and worldviews, as well as the agent's self-understanding and role responsibilities, are too different for that kind of juxtaposition. Still, I acknowledge that a tendency to ritualize certain behaviors and procedures is part of human nature (Dissanayake, 2001) and cultivated in communities, and that rituals form a basic element of music therapy process in all cultures (Kenny, 2002).

[7] Van Gennep wrote in French, and the term *rites de passage* is often used in English also, possibly as a "linguistic homage" to his seminal scholarly contribution. Note also that while the original book was titled *Les Rites de Passage*, the translation I have been using is titled *Rites de Passage*.

[8] The comparison between therapy and ritual is not a new one. From the psychotherapeutic literature Jerome Frank's discussion of components shared by all therapies (Frank, 1982, 1989; Frank & Frank, 1991) is well known and included ritual as one of these components. From the literature of anthropology Victor Turner has contributed to such an understanding.

[9] It is not my task in this context to evaluate the attempts that have been made by music therapists and others to explain the therapeutic value of indigenous rituals by referring to physiological or neurological research, by defining the local beliefs in spirits as metaphors for the unconscious, etc. Some of these attempts are interesting, others are highly speculative; see for instance Summer & Summer (1996). My argument is instead focused upon the contention that there are ritual elements, framed by myths, research, and theoretical rationales, in modern music therapy practices.

[10] Ruud first presented the concept of *communitas* in relation to music therapy in a paper at the 1st Nordic Conference in Music Therapy in Sandane in 1991, and has later published different versions of the paper (Ruud, 1992, 1995, 1998).

[11] If such an identity is even conceivable is a complex discussion, cf. the notion of culture in Chapter 1.

Chapter 9:

NEW ARENAS AND AGENDAS

*for the music therapist, as we have seen, the connection to
direct experience is fundamental. In a sense we must be doing,
or at least vividly remembering, music therapy experience
while designing philosophy and theory. It seems important
that we call forth every resource we know as "memory"
of our moving moments with music and clients, while
creating these more abstract formulations.*
(Carolyn Kenny)

In several chapters I have advocated that it is significant to acknowledge
how music therapy practices are linked to history and cultural context. In the
previous chapter this was explored in relation to professional practice, as a
discussion of a model of the music therapy process. In this chapter implications for discipline and discourse will be examined. It is not possible to define areas of music therapy logically or ahistorically, rather music therapy
practices must be examined in the eras they belong to. This contention
serves as a basis for a discussion of arenas of music therapy in relation to
target and time of interventions and the establishment and use of local links.
The argument of the chapter proceeds by exploring some questions of an
evolving agenda for the discipline, including issues such as context-sensitive
metaphors for music therapy, postcolonial aspects, and ethical challenges.

AREAS AND ERAS OF MUSIC THERAPY

In *Defining Music Therapy*, Bruscia (1989) argued that music therapy
practice is too broad and complex to be defined by a single approach, model,
method, or theoretical orientation: "Music therapy encompasses a wide
range of clinical practices, depending upon the setting in which it is
employed. In an educational setting, for example, music therapy is practiced
quite differently than it would be within a rehabilitative, psychotherapeutic,
or medical setting" (Bruscia, 1989, p. 55). Bruscia continued by arguing that
these variations – which relate to theoretical and empirical foundations as
well as to choice of procedures – have significant implications for achieving

an overall identity of the field. He therefore set out to define *areas of practice,* and suggested that in the late 1980s music therapy included or related to eleven main areas of practice. Each area, according to Bruscia, could be defined by a particular clinical setting, population, goal, and treatment approach. Using these criteria, he proposed the following eleven areas: Educational, Instructional, Behavioral, Psychotherapeutic, Pastoral, Supervisory and Training, Medical, Healing, Recreational, Activity, and Interrelated Arts. Bruscia defined each area and also exemplified at four *levels* of practice: auxiliary, augmentative, intensive, and primary.

I consider Bruscia's definition of areas of music therapy to represent an important theoretical contribution to the field. Music therapists are given access to a system of terms that enable them to classify practices and therefore to compare them by looking at differences and similarities. When I first read Bruscia's book in 1989, I considered it a bit confusing that some areas had their identity linked to setting and others more to goal or approach, but I also felt that one of the strengths of Bruscia's scheme was the broader spectrum of terms it represented. Also, the criteria of the system enabled music therapists to describe *connections* between practices with different populations as well as to outline differences between practices with the same population. In spite of this positive judgment, I struggled with adjusting and using the system in a Norwegian context. Music Therapy as Cultural Engagement (Chapter 4) did not quite fit the label Recreational Music Therapy, and when I later worked with Paul (Chapter 5) I felt that Educational Music Therapy was not quite what I was working with, even though the setting and some of the goals were educational.

After the 1998 revision of Bruscia's book, these concrete problems were "solved." In the second edition of *Defining Music Therapy* the area of Ecological Music Therapy had been included, and I consider it relevant to propose that the music therapy processes of Upbeat and Paul could be subsumed under this area. This does not change the fundamental question raised by my first experience of bad fit between the practices I worked with and the system presented by Bruscia. Is it even possible to develop any general description of areas of music therapy, or are such areas relative to the historical and cultural context of practice? That is, should we rather speak of eras than of areas of practice? The arguments about situated practice developed in this book clearly suggest that it is not unproblematic to formulate definitions of areas of music therapy that would be valid worldwide. Practices of music therapy change and develop in time, as new client populations gain importance, as sites are opened and closed for the profession, and as new clinical foci and approaches are developed. In different times and contexts different possibilities and traditions of practice evolve. In this respect a perspective is added if one describes music therapy in relation to *concrete historical eras.*

To "areafy," then, to some degree is to reify and to "freeze" descriptions to an abstract and ahistorical level instead of situating the descriptions to concrete processes of change.

To be precise, Bruscia (1989, 1998a) does not state that his intention is to produce a static and worldwide system. He categorizes music therapy practices on the basis of a review of the literature of music therapy as it exists at the time of writing the two books. In the second edition of *Defining Music Therapy* he reduces the number of areas from eleven to six: Didactic, Medical, Healing, Psychotherapeutic, Recreational, and Ecological. The main criteria in this revised definition of areas is the *primary clinical focus*, as defined by the priority health concern of the client and the agency serving him, the goal of the music therapist, and the nature of the client-therapist relationship. I therefore propose that awareness of the situated character of music therapy practice does not necessarily require a total rejection of Bruscia's system. All theoretical descriptions unavoidably include elements of abstraction and reduction, and the areas defined by Bruscia – especially in the second edition of the book – to some degree will fit music therapy practices of most modern countries. They relate to institutions – in the sociological meaning of that term – that have been developed in all modern cultures (such as education and medicine), and should therefore have something to offer outside, for example, an American context.

The argument that practices are *situated* still holds, and in addition to describing music therapy in general and theoretically defined areas of practices, concrete ethnographic descriptions will be needed in order to get a better understanding of music therapy practice. Also, the discipline and profession needs to develop terms for description that may sensitize to the situated character of the therapist's choice of arena and agenda for the work. To this issue I will now turn, trying to illuminate how music therapy may be described in relation to *target and time of intervention* and to the establishment and use of *local links*.

TARGET AND TIME OF INTERVENTION

While therapy in the Western world usually is conceived of as a private undertaking – with four walls and double doors as important remedies to ensure privacy – healing practices of other cultures sometimes function as public or semipublic events (Turner, 1967b). There is no basis for directly transplanting such traditional practices to contemporary modern contexts. Public therapy would in many modern contexts come rather close to reality-TV and other exhibitionist-voyeur practices. Examining the practices of other cultures may stimulate our ability to reflect upon ideas taken for granted in our own culture, though, and the idea that therapy primarily is a private thing could be one of those. Chapters 4 and 5 in this book gave examples of more public approaches to music therapy, and other examples of this are described in the literature.[1]

I will here therefore elaborate upon the idea that the relevant *target of intervention* in therapy at times will not be limited to the individual. In Chapter 5 the idea that it may be fruitful to categorize approaches to music therapy in relation to port and time of entry was discussed briefly. Taking an ecological perspective, interventions may be categorized according to target of intervention in relation to the systems perspective proposed by Bronfenbrenner (1979). While modern therapy is usually constructed as a microsystem phenomenon, other systems may be focused upon. The music therapist may choose to work on the meso- and exosystems levels and at times also on the macrosystems levels. Here, this is expressed theoretically, in rather abstract terms. In real-life music therapy the choice will be experienced as a careful choice of target of intervention in a set of available arenas. Instead of taking for granted that music therapy is something conducted in a music therapy room of a clinic or institution, music therapists could actively make reflected choices of targets and sites for their work.

In an everyday clinical situation this is partly a problem of choice of format and arena. Could the health concern in question best be worked with in individual sessions, dyads, groups, or family settings? Should the arena be a closed music therapy room in a clinic, an open-ward milieu, a classroom of a public school, a club, a café, a choir, a community center, etc.? Such choices need to be made in relation to at least two contexts: the clinical needs of the client and the cultural circumstances. Direct or indirect approaches may be chosen, focusing upon individuals as or in systems, upon emotions, behaviors, attitudes, and relationships. Some clients have, for instance, needs that make alternative choices of arena very relevant. If one wants to work with the development of *social networks* in a local community, to choose a variety of sites in that community – preferably sites connected to communal rites and traditions – could be a better choice than to work with the client in isolation in a music therapy room. This is especially clear, of course, if you work with children or other clients with reduced powers to choose and change the arenas where they live their lives. To work *in and with these arenas* may then be a constructive strategy.

There is need for more knowledge on how choice of arenas, with concurrent choices of agendas and activities, may influence the process and effect of music therapy. To try to develop some general descriptions of this, linked to, for instance, diagnoses and client populations, may be one of the necessary steps to take. It will not be a fully satisfactory strategy, however.

Choices of arena, agenda, and activities will be linked to and negotiated in concrete situations, and ethnographic case stories will be needed as part of the basis for informed and reflective future choices. The choice of target of intervention – say, between barriers in individual, group, or community – is therefore best described if we also use *target* as a verb instead of as a noun. While the noun invites us to try and develop general categories for description across contexts, the verb may remind us about the situated character of the process. On the basis of an assessment of how specific arenas, agendas, and activities afford, therapists may target their intervention in relation to the situation at hand.

Similar considerations may be made for the choice of *time of intervention*. Since problems develop over time, there is no reason for the music therapist to only focus on curative interventions, as already argued in previous chapters. Music therapists may go in and work at earlier phases of the life of a problem, in focusing upon health promotion and prevention. Also, beyond the point of any possible cure, music therapists contribute in giving palliative care, etc. Such reflections then may be abstracted to time of intervention in relation to the life of the problem; for instance, prevention, therapy, rehabilitation, and palliative care. Theoretically one may argue that there is much to gain, for the individual as well as for the society, in giving more priority to *early interventions*. For instance, it is suggested that to work with the motherhood constellation in the first year or two of a ("threatened") child's life is much better than giving the same child individual therapy at a later stage (Stern, 1995).[2] Again, the situation at hand is decisive. General descriptions offer possibilities for broad reflections upon this issue, but clinical choices will have to be made in specific situations taking the needs and values of the specific client into consideration. This is maybe self-evident; clinical judgment is always based upon a combination of general knowledge and assessment of the situation at hand. What I try to communicate is that culture-centered perspectives suggest that local knowledge is valued highly and provides a basis for sensitive timing.

If such ideas are to be put in action, access to arenas of practice must be negotiated. Theoretical ideas on how to serve a client population will result in a diversity of practices, due to the fact that they will be situated in different cultural contexts. A therapist's ability to negotiate access to arenas and alterations of agendas will depend upon his cultural sensitivity and reflexivity, as well as upon his ability to use local links when that is relevant.

LOCAL LINKS

Music therapists work with clients that are linked to both personal histories and cultural contexts. Even when clients suffer from diseases of biological origin, these must be understood historically, as they are interpreted and ascribed to the individual by experts who themselves live culturally and historically situated lives. In similar ways the techniques, procedures, and models of therapy must be examined as *situated activities*. Therapies are practiced as cultural forms distributed in certain social groups and conveying certain values, and therapies therefore also are informed and shaped by other social and cultural practices. The cultural perspectives outlined in this book support the idea that cultural borrowings are involved when forms of therapy evolve, at the same time as the shared phylogeny of human beings also suggests that there may be shared factors among various effective therapies.

A critical and constructive examination of what *options* for cultural borrowing exist and of how these borrowings at times may be local in nature is therefore required. Does it, for instance, matter if the work presented in the previous chapters was conducted in Sandane, Santiago, or Santa Barbara? Rather obviously, yes, and I will briefly illuminate how those cases went beyond the "standard repertoire" of models of music therapy by *utilizing rituals and traditions of the local community as resources*. To communicate my point and illuminate an example of local links, I will go back to the story of Upbeat told in Chapter 4, and start with a brief presentation of the community that was the immediate context of that work, in order to see how links between established values and practices in the local community and the music therapy process mattered.

The members of Upbeat lived in Sandane, today a small town, but only a few decades ago just a tiny cluster of houses close to the sands at the end of a fjord arm. For centuries the inhabitants mainly made their living as farmers. At the time Haydn composed his symphonies for the palaces of Europe, the citizens of Sandane barely had bread on the table in their tiny timber huts. The country was poor and had not yet gained its independence from Danish and Swedish domination. In contrast to the situation in many European countries at that time, the people were not tenant farmers dependent on a landlord, however. They were all equally poor but independent. Or: possibly *interdependent* is a better word, which will be clear when the tradition of *dugnad* (working bee) is discussed later. The rapid changes of the nineteenth and twentieth century led to the disappearance of the tiny timber huts of the penniless farmers, except for those now found on the local outdoor museum, and Sandane gradually developed into a modern little town in a quite well-off country. By the time music therapy came to Sandane in the early 1980s, the town had if not a sophisticated high-art cultural life at least quite a high level of popular participation in local cultural activities such as choirs and brass bands. Tradition and Norwegian folk music was and is still strong in this rural part of the country, together with a growing interest for the music styles of other countries and continents, especially North American music. In fact, none of the three musical festivals that are arranged here every year focus upon the music of the Norwegian Harding fiddles: there is a rock music festival, a blues festival, and a country music festival. A little town in Western Norway is then probably also a little bit of Chicago, Minnesota, and New Orleans, possibly of California too, since high tech is strong here.

There is a mixture, then, in this context, of traditional and modern elements as well as ingredients of the information society, a mixture some would prefer to call postmodern. Be that as it may, one of the *traditional* values that has been preserved and cultivated is "solidarity-in-action" in the shape of an old practice called *dugnad*. There is no English word that accurately covers this Norwegian term, but "working bee" – in the meaning of "community social gathering in order to perform a task" – is probably the closest. In Western Norway, especially in the rural areas, the word dugnad is almost magic. There is a strong positive connotation to the practice it denotes. People feel obliged to participate when a dugnad is arranged, and generally they enjoy the communal atmosphere, the shared humor, and the experience of community. Originally, in the old tradition, a dugnad was *not* arranged. There was no leader or organizing committee or anything of that sort. The word just went from mouth to mouth when someone was in need. People then agreed to help, after the principle "one for all and all for one." If someone was ill, for instance, and not able to do the haymaking, the neighboring farmers would turn up and do the job, not asking for anything in return (but knowing – of course – that the practice of dugnad would work as an insurance if they themselves one day would need help of some kind).

The positive connotations to the practice of dugnad have contributed to its ability to survive in modern contexts, in slightly transformed versions. When a kindergarten or a school needs to fix up the yard or when an organization needs to have its clubhouse painted, a dugnad is arranged. If you give such an event the name of dugnad, people tend to show up, and they tend to take pleasure in working together, drinking coffee, talking and laughing together. Looking with hindsight at the process of working with Upbeat, I now strongly think that the "period collaborations" that so successfully were introduced in that type of work did link to the practice of dugnad. The positive attitude people met these projects with, the atmosphere of shared effort within a delimited time frame, and the strong element of social gathering suggests that. At that time (1983-1986) the word dugnad was not yet part of the discourse on music and cultural activities in this town, but a couple of years later it was. The term "dugnadskonsert" (concert working bee) started to be used when choirs or bands worked together in producing a local event, such as "The People's Voice" described in Chapter 4. On several occasions Upbeat or other groups of handicapped people became part of such musical working bees.

This example clearly illuminates how music therapists may link their practice, consciously or unconsciously, to local values, traditions, and practices. In this case the effect of doing this was probably mostly positive. The main goals of the therapy process were to establish arenas where the members of Upbeat could be participators of the cultural life of the local community, in order to build social networks and counter the tendency to isolation that these individuals had experienced. The local practice of dugnad colored the expectations of the members of the local community as well as their general attitude to the project, and helped shape the "period collaborations" into a practical and successful way of working. A logical consequence of this argument is that "period collaborations" may be less easy to establish and possibly also less effective in other contexts, with not so positive values connected to working bees.

The example above is taken from the immediate social and cultural context of a project. It is important to underline again, though, that situated practice and cultural borrowing is *not* limited to such immediate contexts. This point could be exemplified with the same case. In the work with Upbeat important borrowings from the "internal" culture of music therapy took place: Nordoff and Robbins's improvisational approach to music therapy was used and adopted to the specific local needs. In addition, some borrowings from the Norwegian tradition of music education took place, but only some, as certain aspects of that tradition clearly did *not* suit the needs of Upbeat (Stige, 1995). Musically, there were borrowings from the local song tradition, from the standard repertoire of national hymns, from classical music, from international pop, etc.

The idea of music therapy as situated practice is therefore *not* that some practices are situated (by being adjusted to the local environment) and some are not (by being less adjusted). All practices are situated, and the question is in which ways they *are* and how this effects the therapy process. This is maybe especially interesting in music therapy, as compared to many other therapy forms, since music seems to be able to travel so well. The label *World Music* is rather new, but music has always traveled, and even the most local tradition of music typically includes multiple alien influences. A client coming to music therapy is therefore usually musically socialized to a broad spectrum of musical styles, and has already developed relationships to these musics. The argument above suggests the development of a plurality of ways of doing music therapy, not only dependent on the needs of the client and the skills of the therapist, but upon how arena, agenda, agents, activities, and artifacts afford. Modern music therapy being a young and evolving discipline and profession is given a special possibility in that there is not yet too much tradition inhibiting processes of resituating practices to new contexts. To acknowledge that the question "What is music therapy?" to some degree is a new question in each context will be a continuous challenge.

SHARED AGENDA?

When elaborating upon what implications a culture-inclusive conception of humankind may have for our understanding of music therapy, I have been moving between discussions of the general and the particular. A repeated theme may be articulated in the following questions: "How can we negotiate between claims on universal mechanisms on one side and the total relativism of radical local-meaning perspectives on the other?" This is a question culture-centered music therapy shares with clinical ethnography, medical anthropology, and cultural psychiatry. It is related to issues such as gender, ethnicity, migration, and social change, and is therefore of relevance both for homogenous and multicultural contexts in both Western and non-Western societies.[3]

Michael Cole (1996) argues that when psychology tried to become a science, it stopped thinking about the culture in which individuals operate. In much of what exists of clinical research and theory today, culture and cultural differences have been treated as epiphenomena or even irrelevant variables (Littlewood & Dein, 2000). A culture-centered perspective to music therapy illuminates some of the problems inherent in any claim of universal definition of disorder, suffering, health, and therapy. These processes need to be studied in context, and scholarly concepts cannot be dissociated completely from such contexts. To confine concepts to delimited local contexts is just as problematic. In the cultural perspective there is therefore an implicit invitation to do comparative investigations of concepts and practices.[4] One implication, as has been clarified in the previous chapters, is to examine music therapy as situated practice. An understanding of music therapy as situated practice is not equivalent with reducing music therapy to fragmented sets of local practices and local theories, however. The notions advocated in this book as premises, such as the concept of *culture*, the notions of *language game* and *aesthetic practices*, and terms such as *musics* and *musicking* are all generic terms. They suggest diversity to be a basic premise for human existence, but their logical consequence is not radical relativism, rather as conditioned relativism. If nothing else, family resemblances could be sought for. This means that it is meaningful to ask if there are any shared themes to be explored in an agenda for a culture-centered music therapy.

The shared themes to be discussed later in this chapter are not to be considered as proposals for a specific clinical theory for music therapy. Rather they are proposed as "narrative themes," assumptions that clinical theories may be evaluated against. As such they may be used as "metanarratives" or general "narrative themes" against which specific clinical theories may be discussed and reflected upon. The notion of "metanarrative" (and "meta-theory") then taken is a pragmatic one, not an abstract and stable foundation to build theories on, but tools for reflexivity, tools for reflecting upon theories and the practices they are related to. The list of themes to be discussed could have been made quite long. Themes such as social roles, cultural identity, and social networks, and concepts such as performance and relationship all deserve to be examined. I have chosen to focus upon just a few themes as a starting point for this kind of reflection: *metaphors to work by, postcolonial beginnings*, and the *ethics of culturally informed empathy*.

The themes I have chosen to focus upon stress the social, communal, and communicative aspects of therapy. This may be conceived to stand in opposition to much contemporary thinking, where therapy is considered to be a matter of personal choice, or a necessity due to biological processes that need treatment. The individual element seems essential and the social and cultural aspects are maybe not so obvious in many mainstream approaches to therapy. The alternative suggested here is not a return to the ritual collective therapies found in traditional cultures. Rather, I will examine how collective and cultural elements of therapy may be acknowledged also as elements in individuals' process of building identity in relation to diverse contexts.

METAPHORS TO WORK BY

A place to start is to examine the metaphors we use when trying to understand what music as or in therapy can be. A recent text – *Music as Medicine* (Horden, 2000) – discusses the history of music therapy since antiquity, and gives in its title *one* of the metaphors that have been in use. The metaphor "music as medicine" may be apt for some contemporary practices, and may also be a suitable metaphor for much of the prehistory of modern music therapy. As Horden illuminates, after antiquity there were for centuries some fundamentals of medicine and music theory that seemed to go well together. Diseases were considered to be the result of imbalance in the four humors,[5] an imbalance that could be amended by a balanced mind. This connected well to the music theory of the time, where each mode or type of music was thought of as having its specific *ethos* that could induce a specific response in the listener. Throughout European history different variations of a narrative focusing upon music's ability to create harmony and balance in humans flourished (Benestad, 1976; Kümmel, 1977; Ruud, 1987/1990; Horden, 2000).

When Schullian and Schoen published their *Music and Medicine* in 1948, as one of the first major books in the history of modern music therapy, humoral pathology certainly was no longer part of the rationale, but the text was edited with the overall message that there is a history of continuity "from Pythagoras right through to the first professional music therapists, for whose calling the book was evidently to serve as a manifesto" (Horden, 2000, p. 22). This proposed continuity of history has been challenged by Horden's work. Continuity or not, music as medicine obviously is only *one* of the metaphors music therapists work by, and I doubt it will be the metaphor that will help in developing an understanding of music therapy in context. Medicine – both when understood as a substance used in treating a disease and when understood as the science of restoring or preserving health – is hardly the metaphor that leads us in the direction of taking interest for local knowledge and personal meaning. Other metaphors must also be explored. Much of what music therapists do today is obviously not in line with the images of a musical therapy that has dominated in European history. In contemporary music therapy the client is rarely a passive recipient of music.

Music as medicine has music as *external object* in focus. Other metaphors, such as music as free association, may focus upon music as an *intrapersonal process*. Other metaphors again, such as music as analogous to mother-infant interaction, focus upon music as an *interpersonal process*. The metaphor that I developed in Chapter 6, music as hypertext, opens up a *culture-inclusive* discussion of the therapy process, where the use and linking of cultural artifacts, personal experiences, and interpersonal processes comes into focus. The metaphor that I will concentrate on in the following, *musicking as giving voice,* takes these ideas one step further and offers a possibility for seeing music therapy in relation to a *community*. To understand music therapy as situated practice is to focus upon the reciprocal relationship between the individual and the collective. To accentuate this I want to propose that *giving voice* is a core image that can characterize the client-therapist musicking of the music therapy process. I have borrowed the image from John McLeod's (1997) discussion of narrative therapy, and want to elaborate upon this notion to make it relevant for music therapy theory.

Taking a comparative perspective on different forms of therapeutic practices and comparing ways of dealing with life problems, John McLeod suggests that traditional forms (for instance, shaman rituals), modern forms (for instance psychoanalysis), and postmodern forms (for instance, narrative therapy) share a common pattern:

> it can be seen that there exists a common pattern that can be described as a process of giving voice to troubles, having that voice accepted by a representative of the community (priest, shaman, therapist) – having it "authorized"– then being able to use that voice in everyday discourse (McLeod, 1997, p. 96).

McLeod's proposal is made in the context of discussing metaphors for narrative therapy, where the image of therapy as *authoring* has often been used. This image, he suggests, may conceal the coconstructed nature of narration, and he proposes therapy as *giving voice to experiences that have been silenced* as a more open metaphor. The experiences in question may have been silenced by the limitations created by, say, a handicap or a disease, or by the social role or cultural position developed through the ecology of reactions to this in the individual as well as in a community. In the context of McLeod's discussion, sociocultural processes such as silencing due to oppression and execution of power as well as to (inter)personal experiences of shame are focused upon.

Considering the variety of practices found among music therapists, we do well in keeping the possibility for a large scope of silencing processes open. It is then necessary to transcend the focus upon the verbal story implicit in the tradition of narrative therapy that McLeod (1997) takes as a departure point. A person may have a need to express herself through many voices, and the music therapist may listen for not only verbal content, but rhythm in the utterances, for the quality and grain of the voice, etc. The notion of giving voice is then extended. It is not only a matter of telling stories, but of acts of musicking as ways of voicing one's participation in the world.[6] Giving voice, then, includes the therapist's own active participation in polysemic and multimedia dialogues. In line with the practice of narrative therapy, the role of the therapist will not be conceived as passive and/or neutral, but as active, participatory, and self-reflexive.

The processes discussed in Part II may all be understood in this perspective. Upbeat made their voices heard through public performances in the local community and thus communicated their wish and capacity for participation. Paul needed a carefully designed agenda and set of activities in the kindergarten in order to make his voice heard in ways that could give him positive experiences of being with others, while Ramona could use the experiences of participating in shared improvisations in the protected space of the clinic as steps to accepting her own voice in relation to the cultural context that she belonged to. Music therapy should provide a variety of possibilities for participation by giving voices to experiences that have been silenced. In this respect therapy may be considered an emancipatory practice, but it is important to remember that possibilities for giving voice are not free. They are limited by social structures and cultural patterns, as any therapy is a cultural form that in some respect is authorized – and therefore also controlled or at least disciplined – by society.

POSTCOLONIAL BEGINNINGS

The issue of *silencing* of individuals was brought up above, in relation to viewing music therapy as *giving voice*. An evolving discipline such as music therapy also needs to relate to the issue of *silencing of groups* and subcultures, even countries and continents.

Peoples and nations have – more than once in history – developed cultures that have enabled them to dominate other people. This cultural dominance has then often been attributed to racial superiority, which again has been used to justify the imperialistic practice. In the early twentieth century it was not uncommon – at least in Europe – to think of Europeans as belonging to the imperial race, and to speak of the white man's burden of colonial responsibility. The Social Darwinism of the late nineteenth and early twentieth century supported such perspectives by drawing rather direct and unjustified parallels between biological and cultural evolution. A major advocate of this way of thinking was Herbert Spencer.[7] His followers justified politics of competitive individualism and laissez-faire capitalism, convinced that this would be in the service of an inevitable, progressive, and cumulative social change. This way of thinking has certainly been under serious attack, but has also been quite widespread in Western societies. It was, of course, used to legitimate European cultural dominance and the colonial system.

Early scholars within anthropology, such as Edward B. Tylor, offered no direct resistance to this line of thinking. On the contrary; their notion of cultural history was one of unilinear evolution, from primitive to civilized. While this may still be a common assumption in some circles, general theories on the evolution of human thought – often called culture-epoch theories – are misleading in many ways. An interesting early discussion of this problem is provided by Wittgenstein's discussion of James Frazer's (1922/1996) famous work *The Golden Bough*. Frazer's theory was that human thought has evolved from primitive animism to religion to positive science. In contrast to Frazer, Wittgenstein advocated that people with magic practices do not lack rational understanding. They do not use magic because they wrongly believe that magic works as natural science. Frazer gets it wrong,

Wittgenstein suggests, because he is evaluating other practices by criteria of the language game he belongs to himself, instead of taking differences in forms of life into consideration (Fredriksson, 1993, p. 173).

The suggestion that phylogeny and cultural history could be understood as parallel processes – in mechanisms if not in timing – was the main fallacy of Social Darwinism, which was used to legitimate imperialism, colonialism, and eugenics, in addition to the so-called laissez-faire capitalism. The parallels that have been drawn between ontogeny and cultural history are equally problematic. In early twentieth-century European discourse about "the white man's burden" it was, for instance, common to speak of the people of the African colonies as "children." Their culture had not "matured" to the level of European culture, it was suggested. To include a notion of culture as part of one's explanatory repertoire, then, is not exactly a vaccination against discrimination, or plainly, against getting it wrong. *Cultural critique* therefore needs to be an implicit element in culture-centered music therapy. One of the most important developments of cultural critique the last few decades has been *postcolonialism,* with Edward Said's (1978/1995) book *Orientalism* as a milestone in the literature. Said demonstrated how Western attitudes toward the East have been important in Western identity-building, through an active construction of the Orient as "the Others." Part of Said's agenda, then, was to challenge the belief in culture as something positively and ahistorically given; culture evolves out of historical conditions where agents fight for social and economical power. Postcolonialism, as it has evolved after Said's text about orientalism, could then be said to be a (multi)cultural critique of power that uses knowledge in order to advance itself.

This issue has gained importance as music therapy now grows on all continents. Around the world the number of music therapists – and thus therapy contexts – is increasing. Professional music therapy, which originated as a Western enterprise, is now also building a broader foundation internationally. This of course means that it is important that each region has an opportunity to develop its own traditions of music therapy based upon local knowledge. The challenge probably goes deeper than that, though. If we compare to another modern discipline, such as psychology, we see how Western values have entered the practice, theory, and research of the discipline to a degree that has made the separation of Western values and definition of the field difficult. Similar problems may arise in music therapy, and the question is if Western music therapists are willing to enter a dialogue with scholars from other continents on what music therapy is, how it works, what the role of the therapist is, etc. In which ways are the voices of scholars from different contexts heard in creating the international agenda of music therapy?[8]

Take this as a departure point when the following paradoxes are considered. Textbooks in music therapy very often mention African healing rituals as examples of the ubiquity of music therapy in history and diverse cultural contexts, while the voices of the practitioners of such rituals are hardly – if at all – heard in the contemporary international discourse of music therapy. Many Western music therapists are influenced by African music; they tend to play the djembe, teach themselves some African songs, etc. At the same time, there are few tracks of African influence in texts written by the Western-trained pioneers of the modern South African tradition of music therapy, as described for instance in Maranto's (1993) *Music Therapy. International Perspectives*. This probably reveals that some "deep culture" issues are involved. To borrow songs and rhythms from an alien culture is one thing, to adapt to foreign basic beliefs about humans, music, health, and therapy something different. Mercédès Pavlicevic touches upon this in a recent essay:

> My neighbour at Pretoria University Music Department is Meki Nzewi. Master drummer and music ethnologist, he speaks with passion and authority as befits an elder in Africa. We disagree on many things. And the more I listen to what it is that I disagree with, the more I think he has a point or two. Meki, who hails from Nigeria, maintains that music in Africa is healing, and what is music therapy other than some colonial import? Why is music therapy separate from music-making? Why is it calling itself thus in South Africa, instead of imbibing African music-healing traditions? My blood pressure rises instantly, and I suggest to him that perhaps African music-healing, too, might absorb something from music therapy. This is where Meki and I are at the moment. I think that this is where music therapy in South Africa – and much of Africa – is at the moment (Pavlicevic, 2001).

It remains to be seen then, how modern music therapy practices will be able to negotiate with the traditional healing rituals of Africa. Pavlicevic does not suggest that a synthesis is close:

> in Africa there is a long tradition of music healing. Can there be a synthesis of these two music-based practices towards something new? Would this be a compromise, resulting in a thinner practice or a richer one? As a Western-trained improvisational music therapist, having listened to and partaken in healing rites, I am not altogether convinced that African music healing and music therapy are especially closely related. But I am utterly convinced that music therapy

can learn an enormous amount from the African worldview and from music-making in Africa – rather than from African music-healing as such (Pavlicevic, 2001).

David Akombo, pioneer of Kenyan music therapy, is closer to suggesting that a synthesis is possible. In describing the East African developments, he writes:

> The interest is not particularly related to the two fundamental traditions; the reason for this is [that] there has been a great deal of cultural diffusion that has had a great impact on the authentic cultural values of the people. The initial significance of music therapy as viewed from the African traditions has faded with time, and due to a recent growth in research in music therapy, now the focus is on both idioms, and how the multi-cultural approach can enhance the objectives of music therapy as an independent discipline has become a central issue (Akombo, 2000).

How silenced will African voices be in modern music therapy? South African professional music therapy of today is not very African, according to Pavlicevic's colleague in Pretoria. The African healing rituals are not music therapy, according to Pavlicevic and most professional music therapists. Whether a synthesis of these two traditions is possible or not is of course not the only possible question. One could also ask how these traditions could *complement* each other and develop a division of labor (while possibly also learn from each other). There is today a division of labor between Western medicine and traditional herbal medicine in most parts of Africa. Could – and should – a division of labor also be negotiated between modern music therapy and traditional healing rituals? The arguments above illuminate that there are probably more than financial reasons, though these certainly also exist, behind the fact that Africa today is the continent with fewest initiatives to the establishment of music therapy as a modern discipline and profession. Traditional African thinking about music and healing does not, in most cases, support the separation of music-making and music therapy.[9]

My own evaluation of the situation described above is that a division of labor is a more probable development than a synthesis of the two traditions, although Akombo's argument about cultural diffusion at least suggests that the future picture will be complex and multifaceted. One of the questions is: Could a division of labor develop as a result of a reciprocal dialogue informed by cultural understanding? Or; will it mainly be a result of power struggles where each group takes as much as it can of the cake and leaves the rest to the others? The situation described here probably makes Africa one of the most important and interesting continents for contemporary music therapy. It highlights that to sensitize music therapists to the fact that their practices are situated involves something more and different than learning local songs and traditions of music-making. It involves deep engagement with and critical review of notions that we take for granted in our everyday lives: what music is, what health is, what therapy is, what it means to be a human being, etc. Music therapy is not a natural thing; it is a cultivated tradition, albeit possibly based upon shared principles of human protomusicality.

The combination of the terms "music" and "therapy" is a pleonasm in some circles and a catachresis in others. It will not be possible for music therapists to develop an open and reflective attitude to these dilemmas if there is no ethnographical tradition of research and reflection within the discipline and profession. Postcolonial beginnings in music therapy could imply critical examination of knowledge bases and cultures of the discipline, in order to assess if and how knowledge is used to advance certain ways of life for the benefit of certain groups of people and disadvantage of others. The challenge is therefore related to the broader issue of ethics and cultural sensitivity. If there is not a space for cultural critique some clients will be discriminated against and some countries or regions marginalized in the discourse of music therapy. There is thus, as outlined above, a multicultural and postcolonial challenge to meet for contemporary music therapy. Music therapy practices interact with other practices in culture and society, and music therapy is different in different places at different times, not just because science moves forward. Therapy also plays a cultural and social role in society, in supporting or challenging certain values and practices. There is therefore a politics of music therapy to monitor, internally as well as in relation to different cultures.

ETHICS OF CULTURALLY INFORMED EMPATHY

A general formulation of a politics of music therapy in relation to the world would of course be problematic, to say the least. One could, at best, formulate certain values such politics could be based upon, such as critique of power and privilege. Such general formulations easily turn into numb political correctness if they are not developed and modified in specific contexts. To formulate values is of course to engage in an ethical discourse, and I will close this chapter with a few reflections on *ethical implications* of a culture-centered perspective.

The primary ethical considerations for a music therapist are based on the responsibility and respect for the individual client, and ethical guidelines developed by national professional associations usually stress this quite clearly, although obligations to profession and society may also be under-lined (Dileo, 2001). Adding a culture-centered perspective means that the issue of *cultural sensitivity* gains importance. It is not enough to try and show empathy and respect for another human being. This must be culturally informed, as empathy may have different forms of expression and meaning in different cultures (Brown, 2001). Empathy and respect must then be ex-pressed in relation to an individual's position in a cultural context, that is, *the client's relationship to specific cultural values* must be taken into con-sideration (one may of course not take for granted that clients from similar subcultures share similar values).

For most of us it is easy to agree with the above contentions, although practical implementation is more challenging. Guidelines for the ethics of *being with* another person in a culture-sensitive way are hard to develop, except at a very general level. In interaction with persons with very different cultural values one's own taken-for-granted values and ways of being may no longer work, and that could at times be surprisingly difficult to handle. Difficulties increase because ethical dilemmas clearly go beyond the prob-lem of adjusting one's own ways to another person. Multicultural contexts are typically characterized by *conflict* of values. For instance, if a father due to religion or cultural background does not want his handicapped girl to par-ticipate in a music therapy group, and the music therapist has informed rea-sons to believe that this would be helpful for her, what is more important, the father's values or the girl's possibilities for development? The challenge of developing cultural sensitivity means to work with one's own flexibility and understanding, but clearly does not mean to accept everything or agree with everybody. There will be plenty of situations were the music therapist needs to take a stance and has to engage in negotiations in relation to conflicts of interest. Community music therapy practices are probably especially com-plicated in this respect, as the music therapist frequently gets involved in multiple roles (therapist, project coordinator, and consultant, for example) and as the process usually involves large groups of people with which there will always be differences in opinion and values.

The Norwegian philosopher Arne Johan Vetlesen (1994) offers a discus-sion of ethics that is of interest here. He proposes that the question of moral performance too often has been focused upon "not doing wrong," while the issue of "doing good" should be given equal interest. In a dominating tradi-tion of Western philosophy (influenced by Kant and others) the foundation of ethics has been considered to be humans' capacity for reason, and the concurrent ability to act out of duty. As a supplement of equal importance

Vetlesen promotes the importance of the human capacity for emotion and empathy as a precondition for moral performance. Moral performance then is something more than showing respect for another human being; it is also to show *concern*. According to Vetlesen, moral performance runs through a sequence of three levels: perception, judgment, and action. Emotions, through the human capacity for empathy, thus anchor ethical judgments and moral performances. Emotions and empathy provide agents with an entry into the moral domain. In this domain judgments will have to be made, often in the tension between the universalism of the human rights and the specificity of cultural traditions.[10] Moral performance, then, concerned about both woe and weal of the other, will include a range of actions, from showing respect and concern in interpersonal dialogues to political engagement and critique.

A comment must then be made on ethics in relation to the development of theory and practice. This book has given theoretical arguments that may be used in the *expansion* of music therapy practice. Such an expansion of music therapy practices is not per definition a blessing for clients or communities. This depends, among other things, on the therapist's ability to define and reflect upon the limits of one's competency and the boundaries of the work to be done. Not least in ecological approaches to music therapy, problems of competency and boundaries become crucial. When, for instance, does health musicking as "musicalization" of a community turn into "medicalization," where the music therapist's focus upon health and quality of life is experienced as invading the freedom each individual wants to have in defining his own focus when being in music? In order to deal with such questions, concepts for reflection will be needed. It is obvious that *theory development* is much more than a tool for advancement of the discipline, it is also an ethical obligation in relation to clinical practice.

Culture-centered perspectives do *not* go well with monologic traditions of knowledge. A self-reflexive move for dialogic pluralism is a more promising alternative, for both research and theory development. The internal politics of the discipline of music therapy would then be on a healthy track if a self-consciously polyphonic music therapy tradition was sought for. This ultimately also implies the development of a *poetics* of music therapy that allows for the development of *diversity* in scholarly discourse, while at the same time also avoiding fragmentation of it. For this to happen, broad and inclusive arenas for international discussion and development of music therapy will be needed. For example, it will be important to have scholarly journals that do not totalize either empirical, theoretical, or metatheoretical articles, but which present the readers with a mix of these, combined with discussion and critique, in order to develop a discourse where these sources of understanding may challenge each other.

NOTES

[1] Consider for instance Ingunn Byrkjedal's (1992) work with the social climate of school classes, Trygve Aasgaard's (1999, 2000) milieu-oriented work in hospital wards, or Gary Ansdell's (2002) discussion of community music therapy in the British context.

[2] For a recent treatment of early intervention in relation to music therapy, see Jónsdóttir (2002).

[3] Some may question why I separate Western societies in the argument above. There are four corners to the world, and one may speak of Western, Eastern, Northern, and Southern societies. A separation of Western societies may be legitimized by the fact that modern music therapy, as we know it today, evolved in Western contexts. This constitutes a concrete historical context for the discussion but should not be interpreted as a hierarchy or a static priority of contexts.

[4] See (Gouk, 2000) and (Horden, 2000) for examples of this in the music therapy literature.

[5] The four humors of this theory were blood, phlegm, yellow bile, and black bile.

[6] See the notion of *polyphonic dialogues* discussed in Chapter 3.

[7] Spencer was the one who coined the expression "survival of the fittest," an expression Darwin later adopted.

[8] *Voices: A World Forum for Music Therapy,* www.voices.no, was established in 2001 to stimulate these kind of intercultural dialogues in music therapy.

[9] "Traditional African thinking" is of course an extremely inaccurate term, as the continent consists of a plethora of diverse cultures. With J. H. Kwabena Nketia, Ghanian pioneer of African musicology, I suggest that African "musical cultures not only have their historical roots in the soil of Africa, but ... also form a network of distinct yet related traditions which overlap in certain aspects of style, practice, or usage, and share common features of internal pattern, basic procedure, and contextual similarities. These related musical traditions constitute a family distinct from those of the West or the Orient in their area of emphasis" (Nketia, 1974, p. 4). Note the similarity between Nketia's description and Wittgenstein's (1953/1967) concept of "family resemblances."

[10] To equate the human rights with universalism is not completely unproblematic, of course. These rights – as they are articulated today – may be said to be influenced by Western values. I still consider the human rights to be an indispensable tool for criticism and change of repressive practices. To give an example in European history: While Aristotle could develop his ethics by excluding women and slaves, such an approach was made impossible by the universalism that grew out of the Enlightenment, which in principle granted equal rights to all individuals.

Part IV:

INVESTIGATIONS

Every science, like every person, has a duty toward its
neighbors, not perhaps to love them as itself, but still to lend
them its tools, to borrow tools from them, and, generally,
to keep the neighboring sciences straight.
(Gregory Bateson)

Part IV includes some suggestions for music therapy research. The approaches discussed are considered especially important for a culture-centered music therapy, by offering collaborative and critical perspectives. Chapter 10 and 11 describe two approaches to research that in this author's opinion deserve more attention than what they have received so far in our discipline. The approaches discussed here, ethnographically informed inquiry (Chapter 10) and participatory action research (Chapter 11), constitute in no way a comprehensive record over approaches possible for a culture-centered music therapy. Other options are available, such as biographic research, narrative analysis, and dialogical phenomenology. The two approaches outlined here are chosen because they provide clear examples of what seems to be a logical consequence of a culture-centered perspective: the proclivity to conduct research in natural-occurring social settings rather than in experimental laboratories, and to take agents and their meanings and goals as a departure point. Naturalism (as the term has been used by some qualitative researchers) is not what is advocated, though, but rather a culture-sensitive form of *reflexivity*. The focus upon interpretive and critical approaches in the first two chapters to follow is not to exclude approaches cultivated in the nomothetic and empirical research traditions, and in Chapter 12 possibilities of reconciling the two dominant cultures in music therapy research are examined.

Chapter 10:

ETHNOGRAPHICALLY INFORMED
CLINICAL RESEARCH

*First, all social research has a necessarily cultural, ethnographic
or "anthropological" aspect to it. This is an expression of
what I call the double hermeneutic which characterizes social
science. The sociologist has as a field of study phenomena
which are already constituted as meaningful. The condition of
"entry" to this field is getting to know what actors already know,
and have to know, to "go on" in the daily activities of social life.*
(Anthony Giddens)

As shown throughout this book, the intra- and interpersonal processes of
health-related musicking are social and cultural processes, and the issue of
meaning comes into focus. As the discussion of meaning has been linked to
use in meaning games embedded in forms of life, it follows that clinical
research could be informed by ethnography. This chapter explores an interpretive approach to ethnography that draws on narrative, cultural studies,
and anthropology. Writing – seen in the light of a concept of dialogic aspect
seeing – is considered to be a central aspect of the research process.

CLINICAL RESEARCH

Before elaborating on the suggestion that clinical research in music therapy
could be strengthened by learning from ethnography, I will briefly clarify
how I use the term "clinical research." Several uses are found in the literature, such as a) clinical research is applied research (as opposed to basic
research), and b) clinical research is observation (for research purposes) of
your own clinical work. While the last suggestion usually is leaning toward
an interpretive and qualitative paradigm of research, the first – almost per
definition – is leaning toward an empirical and quantitative paradigm. Both
traditions of use of the term "clinical research" have something to offer, but I
also find them somewhat problematic and unsatisfactory.

Applied research is usually defined as research performed to solve practical problems, as opposed to basic research, which is conducted primarily to

increase the scientific body of knowledge without having in mind any specific application of the research findings. This distinction has proved helpful in disciplines such as physics and chemistry, where basic research in the laboratory in principle may be conducted with no practical usage in mind. Sooner or later, however, much basic research ends up with results that are converted to practical technology. Basic knowledge may be developed in a laboratory and applied to solve real world problems, or (depending on perspective) *create* such problems for that matter. Ever since the development of the atomic bomb – if not before – no researcher can ignore the application aspect of the knowledge developed. Be that as it may, in this context I will focus upon another question: Does the *distinction* between basic and applied research make sense in a discipline like music therapy?

One argument in favor of the relevance of the distinction could be that basic research – for instance on music psychology – may be conducted in a laboratory and then applied in music therapy.[1] This argument, in my judgment, relates to the language of biomedicine, where basic knowledge is developed through laboratory research and then applied through clinical research. The question is to what degree laboratory research on how people react to music has enough of ecological validity to be of much value for the understanding of how people act through music in the context of therapy. If music therapy is a situated practice, and if culture and context is considered essential for the understanding of people's relationship to music, then it is not so obvious that a distinction between basic and applied research is clarifying. In fact this distinction could suggest that research in the discipline of music therapy generally is applied, since the discipline is related to a helping profession. Basic research is then seen as something done by music psychologists and others outside the discipline, and all music therapy research is lumped together as applied research, which – as we remember – is another name for clinical research. This is not very elucidatory, and it also suggests that the logic of the experiment is the basic tradition to build music therapy research upon. *That* may be relevant for specific areas of music therapy practice, such as medical music therapy, but it is not a valid guideline for the whole field. As I will elaborate in Chapter 12, I think music therapists need both quantitative and qualitative research methods.

To define clinical research as applied research I do not find satisfying then. It is not a very illuminating distinction for a situated practice, and it invites us to consider experimental research to be a matrix for all research in music therapy. If we turn to the alternative mentioned above, to define clinical research as the study of one's own clinical work,[2] we also run into some problems. To conduct clinical research should then mean to work directly with a client and observe one's work as it is happening, and to study these observations for research purposes. This definition is in line with the clinical research that is the foundation for Chapters 4 to 6 of this book, and it should not be in conflict with the ethnographic perspective outlined in this chapter. I still do not consider it to be a satisfactory definition of clinical research; it is too narrowly connected to participant observation.

A more satisfying use of the term *clinical research* is simply "process and outcome research on clinical practice." Clinical research may then aim at improving practice through the development of theories on practice, and at supporting practice through documentation of its effect and value. In this way the possibility for constructive collaboration between quantitative and qualitative researchers at least is kept open. This simple definition I think also is more in line with the use of the term in related disciplines such as psychology, medicine, and in the other arts therapies (see for instance Lewith & Aldridge, 1993). Sometimes the term is defined even more broadly, and may also include epidemiological studies and health services research (Lippe, 1988; National Institutes of Health, 1997/2001). I find the implications these definitions may have for the discipline's self-understanding to be an important issue. To define clinical research as applied research may limit our understanding of the discipline in the direction of being a practical field applying knowledge developed in other fields, while defining clinical research as participant observation of one's own clinical work may limit the research aspirations of music therapists.

The broad and simple definition of clinical research as research on clinical practice asks for a clarification of the concept of clinical practice, which I – according to the discussions in Part III – suggest may be understood as health-related professional practice, in clinics and other traditional clinical settings as well as in community settings. The obvious fact that clinical practice is conducted in a setting or arena reminds us about the sometimes forgotten fact that clinical practice is social practice. According to the perspective outlined in this book, any social practice is also a cultural practice, which invites us to reflect upon what could be learned from ethnography, the scholarly approach to the study of culture. All social research has a cultural and ethnographic aspect to it, as Giddens (1986/1989, p. 284) argues in the paragraph that is used as epigraph to this chapter.

To study clinical practice is necessarily to study a social and cultural practice, and the researcher is *not* alone in doing interpretations. The researcher needs to know (as much as possible of) what the actors know. The agents of the therapeutic situation are necessarily already involved in processes of interpretation and meaning production. Hermeneutics – both as an interpretive research method and as a philosophical discourse on interpretation as a basic human condition – gains importance as all agents are involved in acts of meaning-making and interpretation. The double hermeneutic Giddens (1986/1989) speaks of may in fact be seen as *multiple hermeneutics:*

the clinical researcher interprets agents that already are involved in interpretations of the same situation, and who also may engage in interpretations of the researcher and of the researcher's interpretations, etc. There are ethnographic aspects to these processes, no doubt, and clinical researchers may develop their competency by learning from ethnographers. Metareflections among ethnographers concerning their own research could also be very relevant. In this chapter I will focus upon reflections on ethno*graphy*, including the *writing* aspect of research.

ETHNOGRAPHY

Ethnography is a tradition of social research, and may be understood as a scholarly approach to the study and learning about the culture of a person or – more frequently – a group of people. There are of course several sub-traditions of ethnography, such as inductive (empirical) ethnography, interpretive ethnography, critical ethnography, and postmodern ethnography (Alvesson & Sköldberg, 2000). In this chapter I will focus upon insights developed within interpretive, critical, and postmodern perspectives, without neglecting the need for sound data as a foundation for interpretation and critique. While much quantitative research focuses upon a small set of variables and a large number of subjects, the ethnographer attempts to get an in-depth understanding of subjects in context, of their life-world and culture.[3] Participant observation in the milieu of the subject is therefore essential to this tradition of research, and ethnographic accounts are both descriptive and interpretive. Interpretive because ethnographers search for the meaning of what they observe, descriptive because interpretations need to be based on some kind of evidence. Sometimes quite detailed information about a culture might be necessary as a foundation for interpretations.

Ethnography is often considered a branch of anthropology, but is also a strong research tradition within sociology. Other disciplines have developed ethnographic research traditions as well, and it is probably correct to consider ethnography to be a cross-disciplinary tradition of research. Originally ethnography grew out of the colonial powers' need to describe and understand the natives of their colonies, and ethnographers have therefore been criticized for serving colonial powers. The once quite common Eurocentric division of peoples with and without history could be seen in this perspective. Only people constituted with a *history* were in colonial times considered to have the right to establish nations. This division of political power was in fact, if indirectly, also connected to a division of labor among disciplines. The prehistoric and historic development of *nations* was studied by archeologists and historians, while the indigenous people of, for example, Africa, Australasia, and America were studied by ethnographers. These people were then constructed as living in "timeless" stable traditions, and ethnographers thus in some ways contributed to the political processes that made repression of the "Others" possible (Clifford & Marcus, 1986; Denzin & Lincoln, 1998).

This not so respectful history of ethnography is important to remember. It reminds us about the relationship between power and knowledge, and it also serves as a backdrop for understanding the strong focus upon self-criticism and reflexivity in contemporary ethnography. As there are several traditions of psychology and music therapy, there are also several perspectives to ethnography.[4] The more empirical or naturalist approaches to ethnography will not be examined here, rather the more reflexive and critical traditions. Criticism of ethnocentric perspectives in scholarly works have flourished in modern ethnography, and the relationships between insider (emic) perspectives and outsider (etic) perspectives have been examined carefully. Among ethnographers there is an increasing awareness about issues such as the researcher's self-presentation in the field he studies, and his self-representation in the text he produces.

Some of the late nineteenth- and early twentieth-century pioneers of modern ethnography – such as Franz Boas and Bronislaw Malinowsky – tried, with more or less success, to breach with the servile tradition of earlier ethnography. Malinowsky is also often considered the pioneer of *prolonged field observation* as the preferred method of research in anthropology. In the nineteenth-century, "armchair" ethnographers – studying and comparing documents produced by others – were not rare at all. Malinowsky considered that to be an unsatisfactory approach to ethnography, because it so easily led to ethnocentric judgments. The researcher's world would not be challenged enough by the "Others." Malinowsky emphasized participant observation and detailed description, and also advocated that the researcher's task was to understand the world as it was seen by the "Others." In this perspective, the goal of ethnography was to grasp the native's point of view and his relation to life; in other words, to realize his vision of his world (Eriksen, 1995).

The twentieth century gradually saw a widening of the settings in which the ethnographic approach was applied. Ethnographers going to the South Pacific and other remote places (seen with Occidental eyes) were supplemented by ethnographers working in their own city. The "Others" of European and American societies became a focus of interest. In the 1920s and 1930s the Chicago school of sociology took an ethnographic approach to the study of subcultures of urban America. In more recent times the construction of "Others" has been put under debate, and the types of context studied in ethnographic perspectives have been broadened to include any setting where a group of people interact and thus are embedded in culture. A strong ethnographic research tradition has been developed within education, where researchers have studied the social life of the classroom, the staff room, the schoolyard, etc. My proposal is that it would serve the self-understanding and sensitivity of music therapists if an ethnographic research tradition was established and cultivated also in the discipline of music therapy.

Let me at once comment upon a possible objection: Most music therapy researchers are not ethnographers, so how could they possibly do ethnography? Is it not disrespect for the knowledge base of different disciplines and underestimation of professional competency to conceive music therapy research as ethnography? Is not interdisciplinary competency so difficult to establish in modern societies that attempts of developing such competency are bound to end up as either disciplinary imperialism or as dilettantism? I think the dangers of imperialism are important to consider, but the alternative to interdisciplinary studies of humankind is unwarranted reductionism. And we should not be too quick to dismiss "interdisciplinarians" as dilettantes. When I propose a close relationship between clinical research in music therapy and ethnography, I am doing more than using ethnography as a loose metaphor, but I am not suggesting that clinical researchers should or could be professional ethnographers. I am rather suggesting that clinical research needs to be *informed* by ethnography, and I am suggesting that music therapists should take interest in other relevant ethnographically informed research, such as ethnomusicology.[5]

Ethnographic perspectives are present in some music therapy literature, such as in Sekeles' (1996) and Moreno's (1995) interest for indigenous healing rituals, in Akombo's (2000) description of pioneering music therapy in Kenya, and in Carolyn Kenny's (1982, 1989) discussions of music therapy theory. Similarly Even Ruud (1987/1990, 1998) has argued for the relevance of anthropology for music therapy, and David Aldridge (1998, 2000) has conducted studies with ethnographic aspects to it. Generally, though, I do not think ethnographic perspectives are integrated in music therapy clinical research. I think they should be, not as the only approach to clinical research, but as an important one sensitizing the researcher to the meaning construction of the agents involved in the therapeutic process. I will elaborate on this suggestion by first presenting some ethnographic research techniques and some reflections on methodology, before I exemplify the necessary self-reflexivity of ethnography by examining the role of writing in ethnographically informed clinical research.

ETHNOGRAPHIC RESEARCH TECHNIQUES

Ethnography is hardly a well-defined and prescriptive set of techniques for collection and analysis of empirical data. That would in fact be counterproductive to the sensitivity for context that is a basic asset of any ethnographic endeavor. Ethnography is very much about judgment in context, and context sensitivity is the golden rule more than anything else. Preconditions for good research include solid training in theory as well as development of the everyday sensitivity of social communication that we all possess (Hammersley & Atkinson, 1983/1995). Such criteria may seem vague, but given the complexity of the situations ethnographic researchers meet, it would be unhelpful – to say the least – to produce fixed rules of research procedure. Still, there are some techniques that typically are in use among ethnographers, and I will briefly comment upon their relevance for clinical research in music therapy.[6]

One ideal sometimes conveyed is that ethnographers do not study people, but try to *learn* from them. To state it this way to some degree conceals important aspects of the relationships involved; the researcher has some specific interests that differ from those of a student or learner in general. This ideal communicates some of the *respect and humility* for other ways of life that is a necessary precondition for productive ethnography, however. Put this way, ethnographers learn from what people *do*, what they *say*, and what they *make* (and use). The three main ethnographic techniques are therefore often considered to be *participant observation, interviews*, and *interpretation of artifacts:*

Participant observation through prolonged participation and observation in the setting of interest is often considered to be the main approach to ethnography. An ethnographic account should include concrete observations as well as appropriate quotations of spontaneous dialogues, etc. This means that an ethnographer needs to visit his site often, or stay and live there for a long time. In some way he then needs to record his findings, through field notes, photographs, audio recordings, video recordings, etc. A clinical researcher in music therapy could use participant observation, for instance, by following a therapy process over time and/or by following clients or therapists in daily life activities. The first choice to be made would be setting. This could be the place where the researcher works himself or a setting chosen by some other criteria, ideally a setting that is considered particularly suitable to the problem one wants to investigate. Settings differ in how they allow a researcher to gain access to specific empirical material. More practical concerns obviously also count when choosing setting, such as travel distance to the setting and financial costs for the researcher.

Once in the setting, the researcher will have to choose a role, which of course is not something he does freely, but in negotiation with the other agents of the setting. One extreme is the ideal of the complete *participant,* another the complete *observer.* A clinician researcher studying his own therapy may be close to a complete participant, a researcher behind a one-way mirror closer to a complete observer. As different as these roles seem, they paradoxically share some of the same advantages and disadvantages. They may minimize the subject's reactivity to being studied, but they also limit what can be studied and how, since these roles are not very flexible and give little room for role extension (Hammersley & Atkinson, 1983/1995, p. 107). Usually therefore an ethnographically informed clinical researcher would do well in supplementing such roles with variants of *participant as observer* or *observer as participant*, in such a way that it is possible to extend and modify roles to serve research needs. Clinical researchers may, for instance, choose to observe clients in other settings than their therapy settings, or they may choose to conduct interviews, etc.

Participant observation was an important element in the research supporting the cases described in Chapters 4 to 6. Working with Upbeat (Chapter 4) I had a role quite close to the complete participant. As active music therapist I observed the work in the music therapy room. This role was then extended and supplemented with observation of the clients in the community and with conversations with staff working with them, etc. My role working with Ramona (Chapter 6) was also as a complete participant. The extension of the role was here first and foremost through the added element of interviewing her about her experience. The most creative and varied use of participant observation was conducted in the case of Paul (Chapter 5). Here I tried a range of roles from complete participant to complete observer, and conducted observation in several very different contexts: in the music therapy room, in his home, in the woods, and in the kindergarten (in free play, in open groups, and in specially designed groups). This variation of roles and contexts was chosen to ensure as much ecological validity to the observations as possible.

Interviews give the researcher access to *insider accounts* and may be of outmost importance for an ethnographically informed researcher. Conducting an interview demands negotiation of roles in ways that may be similar to those of the participant observer. How formalized and structured should the interview be? In one extreme interviews are conducted in separate and "protected" settings and are structured and focused by the researcher, in another extreme interviews are not very much different from any spontaneous conversation and come close to participant observation. Interviews, providing insider accounts, give information both on the phenomena under scrutiny and on the subject presenting the accounts (what he says and how he says it).

Both perspectives are valid, and a process of interpretation or thick description will be involved (see later).

Music therapy researchers may have interest in having insider accounts from clients, family members, therapists and other professionals, as well as people of the community, depending upon the research question. Sometimes music therapy researchers are skeptical to the idea of conducting interviews, either because it is considered impossible to describe music experiences in words or because it is suggested that such descriptions require a specific competency most clients do not have. I take a different perspective; it may be impossible to translate music to words, but it is still meaningful to talk about music.[7] Of the three cases presented in Part II of this book, interviews were used most systematically in the work with Ramona. The methodology of this approach is described in a previous publication (Stige, 1998). Based upon concepts developed by Steinar Kvale (1996), the process of doing semistructured qualitative interviews were organized in seven interacting steps: *thematizing, designing, interviewing, transcribing, analyzing, verifying,* and *reporting.* Several interviews were conducted, in early, intermediate, and late phases of the therapy process, as well as after the therapy was finished. The element of time is often crucial in ethnographically informed research, since both the phenomena under study and the insider accounts of them may develop over time. The clinical relevance of such insider accounts I have discussed in another publication (Stige, 1999).

The third main ethnographic technique to mention here is *interpretation of artifacts.* In music therapy this may include analysis and interpretations of music as recorded, or the study of musicking as memorized activity. Other options are analysis and interpretation of diaries, poems, and drawings produced by clients, therapists, and other agents the researcher learn from. Cultural artifacts must be understood in the context of their social use, and the interpretation must be examined in the light of the researcher's own pre-understanding, which obviously influences the interpretation. These are issues of hermeneutics. If we go back to Part II, we may see how different the contexts of use were in the interpretation of the music and musicking involved. With Upbeat the music's main function was to serve as a port of entry to social and cultural integration in the local community. The music was therefore listened to in the perspective of how it could make musical interaction with choirs and brass bands of the community feasible, while at the same time paying respect to the expressive quality of each member's musicking. With Paul the musicking more than the music was analyzed, and the main issue was what social rules the musicking conveyed, and whether these were understandable or not for Paul. In the case of Ramona the metaphorical interpretation of both the music and the musicking was of main interest, for the client and for the clinician-researcher. These examples illustrate some of the *diversity of use* necessary to consider in the interpretation of artifacts produced in music therapy.

The three techniques described here – participant observation, interviews, and interpretation of artifacts – are the most common among ethnographers. There is no reason for not using other techniques, however, such as questionnaires, polls, and even projective tests. One advantage with surveys is that they may provide the researcher with information from more informants, and sometimes it is important for the researcher to have response from a representative sample. While a representative sample is a pretty obvious requirement in much empirical research, this is not necessarily so in ethnography. Just as often it is important to choose informants strategically. One looks for informants that are willing and able to give information, and subjects that are more interesting than others because they may be especially insightful, or because their role and history may be different or especially rich, etc. The possibility of using several techniques when conducting ethnography invites the researcher to explore triangulation and to develop a multiperspective understanding of the phenomenon under scrutiny (Hammersley & Atkinson, 1983/1995, pp. 230-232). Other researchers advocate that triangulation not necessarily gives a more complete picture of one phenomenon, rather that different techniques illuminate different aspects (see later).

In any case, ethnography is not first and foremost about research techniques for the gathering of data. That is a necessary first step, but sensitivity in the process of interpreting data is crucial. Two aspects of ethnographic research – the role of the researcher in the field and the writing aspects of doing ethnography – may illuminate this.

THE RESEARCHER IN THE FIELD

Two fundamental problems in all research are the status of the data collected and of the instrument used to collect it. Ethnographers generally use emergent designs; the method of engagement and the procedures for data collection and interpretation emerge as the research progresses. One collects data through prolonged participant observation, takes field notes, and makes recordings and in-depth interviews. Along the road preliminary analyses are conducted in order to give the research the necessary focus and specificity. The researcher's subjectivity is inevitably essential in such a process.

Broadly speaking, there have been two main ways of dealing with this among ethnographers (the problem is shared with many other qualitative researchers also). One strategy is to minimize subjectivity, the other is to acknowledge it and reflect upon its role in the research process. The first strategy has been characteristic of approaches that have labeled themselves as "naturalistic." Based upon a criticism of dominant quantitative and positivistic traditions of social research, naturalistic inquirers have advocated the relevance of the study of particular phenomena in their natural contexts. The possible confusion created by the use of the term naturalistic (which also is used in the natural sciences) may be illustrative, since naturalistic inquiry inherited some of the presuppositions from the positivists they criticized, one of them being the viability of minimizing subjectivity. The alternative is to acknowledge that the researcher influences the informants in some way or another. If this perspective is taken, *reflexivity* throughout the research process is what is asked for, not techniques of minimizing subjectivity (Hammersley & Atkinson, 1983/1995). In line with the general argument of this book, I prefer the second strategy, and propose that clinical researchers need to work seriously with the issue of reflexivity. In relation to research, reflexivity is sometimes understood as the researcher's exploration of his own role in the research process, sometimes as his exploration of his own role in the society he is living in. In this chapter I will focus upon the first aspect.

This asks for reflection upon the role of the researcher-as-instrument. I will discuss the role of the researcher – as instrument and (co)actor – in the field of clinical music therapy by first examining some of the recent literature on qualitative music therapy research, where the *researcher-as-instrument* has been under discussion, under headings such as *authenticity* and *integrity*. These concepts I find relevant for any clinical researcher, although the ethnographically informed researcher may choose to stress the somewhat broader concept of *reflexivity*. I will come back to this, but let us start by seeing what we may learn from the music therapy literature on qualitative research.

It has been suggested that in qualitative research the method is no guarantor or arbiter of truth, the focus of interest becomes the researcher-as-instrument. Kenneth Aigen puts it this way: "... it is ultimately the open-mindedness, insight and thoroughness of the *researcher* that ensures the production of interesting and useful findings" (Aigen, 1995b, p. 296). This inevitably raises questions on the quality of the researcher-as-instrument, and the literature suggests several steps to minimize biasing factors, like the use of reflexive journals, consultation and communication, and other procedures of self-inquiry. Kenneth Bruscia (1995c-e, 1996, 1998c) has presented one of the more elaborated discussions of the researcher-as-instrument, and I will refer to some of his ideas. In three chapters in Barbara Wheeler's book, *Music Therapy Research. Quantitative and Qualitative Perspectives,* Bruscia (1995c-e) explores the process of doing qualitative research. He presents a circular model illustrating the process and the interaction between its elements. Several of these elements – like self-inquire, communicate, and consult – are related to the development of the researcher-as-instrument. At the heart of the model Bruscia puts "appraise," which he argues is crucial in every step of the process. He states that continuous critique and appraise is a condition for achieving the necessary degree of trustworthiness in qualitative research.

Bruscia (1995d) underlines the human side of this: "The challenge is not so much doing qualitative research correctly but rather understanding what is involved in being a qualitative researcher." He goes on by stating that this involves "being fully human." "To deny who we are in order to understand who we are simply makes no sense. One must be at least human to understand humans." Based on this he gives his own definition of qualitative research as "a process wherein one human being genuinely attempts to understand something about another human being or about the conditions of being human by using approaches which take full advantage of being human" (Bruscia, 1995d, p. 426).

This human side of the process of doing qualitative research Bruscia continues to explore in a chapter in Langenberg, Aigen, and Frommer's (1996) book *Qualitative Music Therapy Research. Beginning Dialogues.* In this text he discusses "authenticity" in the research process.[8] He suggests that "When I am authentic as a researcher I bring into awareness whatever is possible for me to bring into it regarding my study; I act in a way that is consistent with what is in my awareness; and, I take responsibility not only for what is and is not in my awareness, but also for what I do and do not in relation to it" Bruscia (1996, p. 82). He then states carefully that his conceptualization of authenticity has two distinctive features: it is an *intra*subjective standard which governs the researcher's relationship to himself, and it is an ongoing *process*, not something to be evaluated after the research project has been completed. The researcher is responsible for his ability to remain open and nonbiased in the research process, which involves a process of self-inquiry and self development, since research on therapy processes inevitably involves research on personal and emotional issues that involve processes of resistance, transference, and countertransference. Bruscia argues that this kind of authenticity is foundational to all other standards of integrity, and concludes by quoting Dag Hammarskjöld: "The more faithfully you listen to the voice within you, the better you will hear what is sounding outside" (Hammarskjöld, in Bruscia, 1996, p. 106).

In a later publication Bruscia expands this discussion, and develops standards of *integrity* in qualitative music therapy research. He defines these as "ideals of quality towards which researchers strive" (Bruscia, 1998c, p. 178). Compared to his discussion of authenticity, the article on integrity to a larger degree stresses interpersonal aspects:

[In qualitative inquiry] the challenges are experiential rather than technological: how does one human being gain access to, understand, and make meaning of another person's experience? There a researcher inevitably has to enter into interpersonal experiences and explore identity issues to drag the tiniest morsel of insight into consciousness. There the purpose of the research is multifaceted: to enlarge our construction of the world and to find and create individual meanings therein (Bruscia, 1998c, p. 176).

According to Bruscia, standards of qualitative research have been slow in developing, and he argues that this is because they are difficult to formulate. Qualitative researchers subscribe to significantly different positions on epistemology, as Even Ruud (1996) has illuminated, and this makes agreement on common standards rather difficult to attain. Taking a relativist position and acknowledging multiple realities and truths, Bruscia (1998c) then underlines that the standards of integrity that he proposes are not meant to be universal or consensual but suggestions that could be applied when relevant. Some of them are related to methodological issues, other to personal, interpersonal, or aesthetic issues.

Bruscia's discussion of the researcher-as-instrument, using concepts like authenticity and integrity, to a large degree focuses upon the *psychological aspects* of the research process. The personal and interpersonal challenges are central to his discussion, illuminating the challenges of the researcher as an involved, empathic, and respectful human being. When discussing clinical research, where the researcher engages in situations of suffering and emotional communication, the relevance and importance of such a focus cannot be overestimated, and Bruscia's discussion invites the researcher to explore his needs for self-inquiry, communication, and supervision. When taking an ethnographically informed perspective, this psychological focus is necessary, but needs to be supplemented by a broader culture-sensitive perspective. Even Ruud (1998), one of very few music therapy researchers to use and discuss the concept of *reflexivity,* advocates the importance of a broader perspective. He argues that there is a correspondence between our values and interests and our perceptions of the world, and he therefore suggests that research should include metacritique. *Reflexivity* then to Ruud (1998, p. 17) includes awareness of our presuppositions and values as researchers. With reference to Anthony Giddens (1991) he also connects this to a concept of identity: "... what characterizes identity in our (post)modern culture is, in large part, reflexivity." "Identity no longer comes to us ready-made, because identity is a process, something never fulfilled" (Ruud, 1998, p. 37).

What Ruud suggests could be described as "culturally informed herme-neutics." Practically speaking this means that researchers need to develop their awareness about how their own values and cultural heritage influence the choices they make in the field, as well as their ability to negotiate their roles with other agents in the field (Stige, 1999). For instance: Clients may have completely different attitudes to music than the researcher. Gatekeep-ers, such as doctors in a clinic, may have prejudices toward music therapists, etc. All such factors influence the role of the researcher in the field. No field is free of barriers; cultural and social barriers are shaped by power relation-ships, roles and responsibilities, customs and traditions. In clinical music therapy research it will therefore often be necessary to reflect upon the inter-action of different *levels* of self-inquiry and reflexivity. A psychological process of self-inquiry and a culturally informed critical hermeneutics are both essential aspects of the clinical research process, and they will influence the researcher's descriptions, analyses, and interpretations, topics we now will turn to.

THICK DESCRIPTION

Ethnographic fieldwork involves the disciplined study of what the world is like to people who have learned to see, hear, think, speak, and act in ways that are different than our own ways. Whether it is even possible to convey such insider perspectives is disputed (see later). In any case, the world does not present itself for the ethnographer in ready-made anthropological or clinical concepts. Rather, what the researcher usually has is a messy heap of data, expressions, field notes, and recordings. Some kind of order and struc-ture will grow out of – or be superimposed upon – this heap, and the *writing aspect* of doing ethnography has been given more and more consideration lately. In writing, the ethnographer decontextualizes and recontextualizes, which in many ways is identical to analysis and interpretation, and writing has thus come to be seen as a core element in the research process. As a first step to a discussion of this, I will here briefly present Clifford Geertz's (1973/1993) concept of *thick description* before focusing upon the so-called *representation crisis* within social research.

The term *thick description* is quite illustrative of the interaction of de-scription and interpretation typical in ethnographic methodology. Geertz borrows the term and the example to illuminate it from the Oxford philo-sopher Gilbert Ryle. Imagine you see someone contracting the eyelids of his right eye. How should you interpret this? It could be an involuntary twitch, a wink as a signal to a friend, a parody of another wink, a rehearsal of a parody, etc. "Complexities are possible, if not practically without end, at least logically so" (Geertz, 1973/1993, p. 7). When researching culture and the meaning of acts, expressions and artifacts, it is *not* enough to give descriptions of what is seen or heard. To add details to such descriptions does not automatically add to our understanding. You need to add descriptions of contexts (situations of use) in which the event can be understood. This is not to say that details are irrelevant. In the example above for instance, very frequent twitches probably more likely would be interpreted as involuntary than less frequent ones. A detailed description of this, with the frequency counted and means and variation calculated, would still be a "thin" description, however. Contexts of use must be added in order to make a sound interpretation. A high frequency of twitches could for instance belong to an exaggerated parody.

To give a thick description is to capture as many as possible or relevant contexts of use, as a basis for the process of guessing meanings and assessing the guesses. For music therapists, for example, this suggests that analysis and interpretation of music as heard is insufficient. The meaning of music cannot be understood if isolated from the meaning game it is part of.[9] To give a thick description is to try to capture possible meanings. Geertz (1973/1993), then, argues that our data on meaning are our own constructions of other people's constructions. All we have are winks upon winks upon winks. This sounds rather discouraging. How could we ever find a way through all the layers of possible meanings? Thick descriptions must be given some kind of specification, not through reliance on general or context-independent theories of meaning, but through *situating* the process of guessing meanings and assessing guesses. This is one of the reasons why we may need to use several of the three main ethnographic research techniques described above. Sometimes, for instance, it is not enough to observe a client to understand, we also need to talk to him or listen to his music, and vice versa.

If our task is to guess meanings, and assess these guesses, on what foundation do we operate? Obviously the empirical material is important. There are no good interpretations without good observations and descriptions. But this is not solely an empirical problem. Geertz (1973/1993) is one of many contemporary ethnographers who have realized that the tradition of *hermeneutics* is of high relevance for ethnographic research.

THE REPRESENTATION CRISIS

Geertz's term *thick description* reminds us about how intertwined the processes of description and interpretation are. We are here touching upon issues that more generally have been named the *representation crisis* in social research. It is no longer taken for granted that the research text mirrors the field studied. The researcher is hardly just presenting facts of the field through language as a transparent medium. Rather the narrative elements of representing the field have come under scrutiny. The research report is, if not science fiction, to some degree "art faction." It is cultivated as the art of telling stories grounded in experience. The examination of ethnography as acts of "writing culture" (Clifford & Marcus, 1986) is therefore of high relevance for the music therapy clinical researcher.

As we have seen, when studying clinical practice as culture researchers put themselves in positions where they have to abolish the idea of being neutral and objective. In order to have any rapport and anything to report they will need to interact closely with the informants involved, and therefore of course will influence the field they are studying. This situation is a challenge, and researchers will at times feel their scholarly integrity and the trustworthiness of their findings challenged. For instance, how does one achieve clarity of voice? How can one ensure that the findings presented differentiate one's own voice from those of the informants in a satisfactory way? We are here touching upon issues that are related to an epistemological crisis experienced by contemporary ethnographers. At least after Said's (1978/1995) *Orientalism* the days are gone when Western writers could portray non-Western peoples with unchallenged authority. It is now generally stated that accounts of culture are contingent, historical, and contestable (Clifford & Marcus, 1986).

Similarly the authority of the clinical researcher describing the world of the client will be questioned. In this situation it may be fruitful to take serious interest in the *writing aspects* of doing research. Again, there is much to learn from contemporary ethnography. The term ethnography is in fact used both for the process of studying culture and for the scientific products of that process. The scientific products are – as in any discipline – usually texts, and it may be argued that the process of studying culture basically is *writing*. "Ethnographers write," Clifford Geertz (1988/1997) states. They usually do quite a few other things too – such as designing their studies and working with access and field relations – but more than once lately has it been suggested that writing is at the center of ethnographic research. This interest for ethnographic writing is multifaceted indeed. It is concerned with the "internal" debate on *ethnographic methodology*, questioning the traditional idea that writing is something you do to report your research, when the real research is done, so to say. It is concerned with *ethical issues*, as for instance ethical aspects in the relationship between those who tell and those who write (between the informants and the researcher). It is concerned with *philosophical issues*, for instance regarding the historical situatedness of the author and the text. And it is concerned with *political issues* related to ethnography's role in society, for instance the debates about ethnography's historical complicity with colonialism and imperialism (Clifford & Marcus, 1986).

This could all be summarized by the following statement: the suggestion that language mirrors reality is seriously challenged and this in turn constitutes a serious challenge for the ethnographically informed researcher.[10] Norman K. Denzin (1997) approaches the representation crisis by evoking a postmodern ethnography and a focus upon experiential texts. James Clifford (1986) offers a somewhat different response to the challenge, by combining awareness of the literary aspects of ethnography with a request for rigor and responsibility. Language is not a transparent medium showing us how the world is, but neither is it a sign system with a life of its own, independent of realities of the world. Clifford advocates a self-conscious *serious partiality;* the reflexive acknowledgement of the partiality of any account on culture, a position he illuminates very well with the following allegory:

> Ethnographers are more and more like the Cree hunter who (the story goes) came to Montreal to testify in court concerning the fate of his hunting lands in the new James Bay hydroelectric scheme. He would describe his way of life. But when administered the oath he hesitated: "I am not sure I can tell the truth... I can only tell what I know" (Clifford, 1986, p. 8).

It is interesting to notice that the question of research as writing and the researcher as author has been discussed especially vividly within ethnography (it should be relevant for all qualitative research). One explanation may be that the amount of data and the richness of the material collected is so overwhelming in ethnographic research, which makes it very hard to defend the proposal that the research report is merely a picture of the field that has been studied. It is obvious that the researcher's *presentation* of the material is of utmost importance (Alvesson & Sköldberg, 2000). This I think is often the case for the music therapy clinical researchers who might be dealing with music recordings, field notes of their own experiences, transcriptions of interviews, and observations of nonverbal behavior. Music therapy is a multimedia experience and the study of it soon creates huge amounts of data.

We may therefore regard *writing* to be a key element in clinical research. This may be seen from several angles. Writing – as decontextualization and recontextualization – is an integrated part of the description, analysis, and interpretation throughout the research process. Writing is a way of communicating with the scholarly community, in ways that provoke response and critique, or to say it more "Bakhtinian"; in ways that stimulate a more dialogical understanding of the issues under scrutiny. It is also important to remember that the subjects studied quite often are themselves literate. The clinical researcher therefore should not iterate the one-sided synchronic focus and the neglect of diachronic aspects (and literary sources) found in much earlier anthropological research. The clinical researcher should not study clients as if they were individuals without personal and cultural history and as if there were no written sources available. Instead, music therapy researchers could find inspiration in the increasing interdisciplinary interest for biography, narrative, temporality, and memory, and the intersection of the personal and social worlds (Hammersley & Atkinson, 1983/1995, p. 161).

WRITING AS DIALOGIC ASPECT SEEING

I suggest that one way of practicing the self-conscious serious partiality advocated by Clifford (1986) is *writing as dialogic aspect seeing*. To illuminate this, I will go back to the case of Ramona described in Chapter 6.[11]

When interpreting the two interviews Ramona gave I focused upon *hypertext* as a possible metaphor for her experience and use of music in therapy. She had been using music therapy as a means to build a virtual room and space for herself. She had not been moving in one direction, trying to rework her personal history in any chronological order. Instead she had been moving in several directions, sometimes focusing upon the joy of playing, sometimes upon the sound and beauty of the music, sometimes upon metaphoric content, etc. I felt that several of her descriptions did lend themselves to a translation into the hypertext analogy. She had not been working on one text in one direction, but on several texts in several directions. She had been moving from songs to improvisations to conversations and back again to songs. She had asked for the freedom just to sit down, listen, and receive, and she had asked for the challenge to stand up and move. These elements in the process could all be thought of as chunks or nodes that had been linked in several new ways. My interpretation therefore suggested that the hypertext metaphor could capture several of the most important elements in Ramona's own description of her experience of music in therapy. I chose to share the association I had made between her metaphors and the hypertext analogy, to see if that had any meaning to her. She had not heard about hypertext, so I made a short and simple explanation of its function, and she then immediately was able to relate to the image, adding a new perspective by linking it to her own personal story: "When coming to a link, as you describe it, you have three possibilities: to go on, to change direction, or just stop. In my life I have been aware of only two possibilities: to go on in the same direction or to get stuck."

The case of Ramona should illustrate quite well some problems of representation in music therapy clinical research. We could start with an obvious one: What do we count as data, which data do we choose to analyze and interpret, and how do we present these data in a research text? I have not included any description of body language or music, but have limited myself to a presentation of the client's own words about her experience, and of these words I have chosen to present only a few statements. It would not be irrelevant for readers to ask for more evidence (for thicker descriptions). I could have provided more statements, but how many would be needed? I could have added more information on contexts to interpret these statements against, such as information about the therapy process, about the life history and pathology of the client, etc. When does a reader have reasons to trust that the researcher has made a reasonable interpretation?

This reflects a basic discussion on the interdependence between data, instrument, and theory. I will exemplify by briefly referring to Wittgenstein's (1953/1967, p. 193ff) discussion of *seeing aspects* of objects. Wittgenstein suggests that we see as we interpret. He illustrates this with his famous discussion of the duck-rabbit, which can be seen as a rabbit's head or as a duck's head (the "ears of the rabbit" then interpreted as the "beak of the duck"). When asked what we see in the figure, Wittgenstein argues that we tend to say either "It's a rabbit" or "It's a duck." We do not say "Now I see it as a rabbit," just as little as when seeing a fork we would say "Now it's a fork. It can be a fork too." We tend to see one aspect at a time, and the context of course is of paramount importance.

Wittgenstein's arguments have been used to support the statement that data and theory cannot be separated. The collection of data is already an interpretation. I support this suggestion, and do not find help in the idea of an inductive approach with concepts developed from a collection of "clean" data. Clinical research in music therapy may at first seem to be rather different than looking for ducks and rabbits in pictures. But Wittgenstein's simple example may help us to see how writing may be integrated in the research process understood as aspect seeing and aspect expression. A classic dilemma in ethnography is the tension between emic and etic perspectives. The etic perspective is the outsider view that the researcher brings with him, while the emic perspective is the native view, the insider way of seeing and understanding. Colonial and modernist ethnography has been criticized for ethnocentrism and unreflective use of etic descriptions, while emic description is seen as the ideal to pursue in much contemporary ethnography. The problem is of course that the preunderstanding of the researcher may make this ideal rather illusory: the researcher will never be a native, and will hardly be able to see the world as the native sees it. An alternative strategy is to engage in some kind of emic-etic dialectics, that is, to let the different perspectives inform each other in a dialogical search for understanding and meaning. The music therapy clinical researcher may not even be able to see the duck that the client sees. The client may have to point out the beak of the duck, while the researcher may have to point out the ears of the rabbit.

The "object" of research in the study that the example of Ramona is taken from is the experience of music in music therapy. Based on the theories I have outlined earlier in the book, I consider this to be an object in potential flux. Meaning is not fixed; it changes over time. In sharing perspectives, the participant and the researcher therefore may transform the object together, so that after a while they see more than rabbits or ducks, maybe duckrabbits or something completely different. I suggest that writing may be an essential research tool in achieving this. Writing may be an impetus for flux, paradoxically – one may think – since writing is fixation. The writing may give an *image*, and the interesting thing to consider is perhaps not its correspondence with the facts of the world but its expression of an aspect of it, an aspect that the reader may relate to and explore. *One* aspect of Ramona's experience of music therapy was by the researcher described as hypertextuality; the possibility to engage in an interactive process with the freedom of linking and moving between expressions in several media. This suggestion is obviously not written as an emic description. Her own description was based on metaphors such as room, space, freedom, choice, doorsteps, journey, navigation, and navigation problems. Certain emic-etic dialectics were involved, though, in that I as a researcher shared my interpretation with the participant. I consider this to be dialogic aspect seeing, and it expresses features of a *situated discourse*.

A research report is not necessarily a Z with a dot; it may as well be an A with a colon. Writing may sum up, but maybe only some aspects, and it just as often challenges and suggests new readings and writings. The suggestions I have made in this chapter are that *through writing* findings are not only reported; they are sometimes also established. I am not advocating constructionism that cuts the relationship between the text and the world, but the perspectives advocated here indicate humility on behalf of the researcher. His authority is questioned, his text does not tell it as it is. It may – at best – contribute to aspect seeing. There are possibilities in this humility, however.

Writing may be seen as a method of inquiry, and as a support in the search for reflexivity, that is, for situating oneself in relationship to the field one is studying. Through a gradual process of writing and rewriting, in dialogue with the participants, the clinical researcher may discover and explore new aspects of the field he studies.

While quantitative clinical researchers want to be able to tell stories about the effect of music therapy, qualitative researchers may be concerned about being able to tell an effective story. This may sound bad, but does not need to be. It depends on the researcher's ability to acknowledge the partiality of his account. Who speaks? Who writes? When and where? With or to whom? Under what structural and historical constraints (Clifford, 1986, p. 13)? Such "rigorous" partiality I consider to be an important part of the role responsibility of the music therapy clinical researcher, also because stories about music therapy are starting to interest ethnographers that study everyday use of music (DeNora, 2000), and thus more than before are going to circulate in a broader scholarly community.

The humility of the researcher and the partiality of the account advocated here may seem discouraging compared to the rigor and the proposed certainty of quantitative clinical research. On the other side, some may feel tempted to write off quantitative research as being too rigid for the study of clinical work. To do so would not necessarily be a very good choice, since therapists *do* have some obligation to answer the "does it work?" question. This question is – according to my view – inseparable from questions of meaning and motivation in each case, which is why I earlier in this chapter insisted on a definition of clinical research that could include quantitative *and* qualitative perspectives. We must keep in mind that the quantitative researcher too is invited to test out his humility. In an article about clinical research in psychology von der Lippe (1988, p. 27) reminds us about G. L. Paul's classic article from 1967, where he states that any research on effect must specify to the level of which treatment given by which therapist to which individual with which problems under which conditions. Tendencies at group level may tell us something about probability, and that may be important knowledge, but there is no certainty for the individual case. The clinical researcher – as well as the clinician – needs to develop his *sensitivity for each case*. In this process sensitizing concepts developed through ethnographic writing may be useful.

INTERACTING VOICES

There are several ethnographic traditions, and the goal of the ethnographer – as of the clinical researcher – may be of different types. Some researchers aim at producing descriptions, other at theory generation, and some at theory testing through comparative methods. What is shared is the challenge of combining context sensitivity and responsiveness to emic perspectives with the ability to produce knowledge that is of interest for a broader scholarly community. In order to achieve this, reflections on how voices interact are essential. Any thick description of utterances of agents in the field must include contexts such as: What were the "questions" or challenges that produced these utterances and what new utterances followed? Ethnographic texts therefore must aim at reproducing the voices of the agents in a field. This is not possible to do in a transparent way, and the dialogic influences must be acknowledged and reflected upon.

Clinical research informed by interpretive and critical ethnography – as stories on interacting voices – then to some degree may transcend the radical distinction between *observer* and *observed*. Only to some degree, though; the clinical researcher must acknowledge the partiality of the research report. As there is no innocent hearing there is no innocent writing.[12] In the next chapter another step will be taken. In *participatory action research* the voice of the subject is not only heard in the research report but throughout the research process. The possibility of developing research that constitutes the participants as responsible co-agents contributing to the definition of aim and scope of the research is examined. In other words: May research be done by a group of people in a community, for the benefit of that community?

NOTES

[1] An example of an argument in favor of this view is Wheeler's (1995b, pp. 8-9) discussion of types of research, where clinical research is treated as applied research.
[2] An example of an argument in favor of this view is Bruscia's (1995a, pp. 22-23) discussion of research versus practice, where clinical research is treated as the study of one's own clinical work.
[3] Ethnography is usually qualitative and interpretive, but quantitative techniques are sometimes also applied.
[4] For overviews of traditions of ethnography; see for instance Hammersley and Atkinson (1983/1995), and Alvesson and Sköldberg (2000).
[5] An example of such research with relevance for music therapy is Hans Weisethaunet's (1999) study of musical improvisation.
[6] The format of this chapter only allows for a brief discussion of techniques and methodology. I refer readers who want to learn more about ethnography to introduc-

tory textbooks, such as Hammersley and Atkinson (1983/1995): *Ethnography. Principles in Practice.*

[7] See Chapter 3 for a discussion of this.

[8] If sensitized to social constructionist ideas on constructed and flexible identities, skepticism toward terms such as "authenticity" is warranted (even if one does not subscribe to the perspectives of social constructionists in general, one may be sensitized by their critique). Concepts of authenticity are sometimes problematic, especially when used to denote spontaneity and heartfelt expression as opposed to judgment and reflexivity. Bruscia does not construct such contrasts or dichotomies, and I think his discussion of authenticity is highly relevant for the music therapy researcher since it illuminates personal and interpersonal issues that need to be closely examined in clinical research.

[9] Consider the discussion of Wittgenstein's (1953/1967) notion of language game in Chapter 2.

[10] I take this problem as a reminder of the more general representation crisis in qualitative research, where the suggestion that language just mirrors reality is seriously challenged; consider Ludwig Wittgenstein's (1953/1967) discussion of meaning and language (see Chapter 2).

[11] The case descriptions of Chapters 4-6 are *not* given as examples of research reports, even though they are based upon research projects. These three chapters are clinical descriptions included to illuminate possible relationships between clinical practice and the theoretical and metatheoretical ideas discussed in this book.

[12] This contention implies some ethical challenges too. If reading the research report, the subject may recognize his own voice and perhaps feel that something precious to him is treated like an instance of a class.

Chapter 11:

PARTICIPATORY ACTION RESEARCH

If you want truly to understand something, try to change it.
(Kurt Lewin)

While the term action research sometimes is used broadly, to denote any research related to practice, a particular tradition of research is discussed in this chapter. Participatory action research not only involves active lay participation in the research process, it also involves shared ownership of the research. Participatory action research is not only done *with* a group of participants, it is aimed at solving problems as they are experienced by a group or community.

RESEARCH AND SOCIAL CHANGE

A miscellaneous array of research types falls under the term *action research*. The term is often used broadly to cover all kinds of research aimed at informing or improving practice; in the case of music therapy, usually clinical practice. This is the use of the term in two influential textbooks on music therapy research (Wheeler, 1995a; Smeijsters, 1997). In this chapter I will follow another path, focusing upon the researcher's social responsibility. Three dimensions are in focus: a) research *for* change, b) participatory influence, and c) empowerment. To clarify the focus I use the term *participatory action research*, which has come into use to denote situated research advocating the primacy of the voices and goals of the participants themselves. Participatory action research is aiming at achieving planned change in the setting of the subjects involved, and change in their relationship to it. In this conception, action research may also be seen as a case countering the criticism sometimes raised concerning the lack of impact of (social) research. Contemporary action researchers in this tradition stress the participatory element very strongly, through a dialogic development of goals and strategies aimed at giving community members the possibility to improve some aspects of their life.

Should music therapy researchers contribute to social change? Some would be quick to offer a negative answer to this question, not necessarily because they reject the importance of social change, but because they suggest this to be beyond the responsibility and competence of a music therapist or clinical researcher. Working for social change involves making political judgments and the result, the argument goes, may be that professional therapists and researchers risk losing their focus. Instead of focusing upon the health of clients they start concentrating on choosing sides in political struggles. Others would stress the point that a profession focusing upon health and well-being of people cannot neglect the issue of social change. People live their lives in social contexts, and these contexts obviously contribute to the mastery or misery experienced by each individual. Social change – as empowerment and emancipation of oppressed and disempowered groups or individuals – should then be part of music therapists' responsibility. In this perspective the alternative to social change is not equilibrium, but injustice, social control, and subjugation. Music therapy is part of society and as such, it is suggested, will either contribute to social control or to social and cultural change – at its best to empowerment and emancipation.

The tradition of participatory action research may be regarded as solidarity in action, and should thus to be closer to the point of view that music therapists and researchers *do* have some political and social responsibility. It is worth underlining that saving the world is unlikely to be a very productive goal, however. Usually rather more modest tasks are at hand. When people face problems, folk wisdom suggests that you may talk about them, think about them, or do something about them. Participatory action research in many ways brings these possibilities together. It is a communicative approach, where collective reflections identifying problems and possible solutions are essential. But the process does not stop with talking and thinking; practical actions are implemented and evaluated, as basis for new collective reflection. Participatory action research in music therapy would therefore be something different than developing rhetoric capacity to express the importance of music therapy for social change. It would mean to go beyond general statements on music as freedom, choice, and diversity, and instead examine music therapy's concrete possibilities and limitations in concrete settings.

Participatory action research – informed by critical reflection – is an approach to research that so far has been given little attention by music therapists, but which I suggest should be highly relevant, at least if a culture-centered perspective is taken. Participatory action research, as we know it today, is a tradition growing out of several different influences, of which two streams have been vital for my own understanding: the pioneering work of the German/American social psychologist Kurt Lewin, and the Critical Theory of the Frankfurt School.

PIONEERS OF ACTION RESEARCH

Kurt Lewin is often credited as having coined the term *action research*, in his 1946 article "Action Research and Minority Problems." He was quite certainly not the first to use the term; his contribution was rather to give it a definition and a theoretical content. Lewin developed his ideas on action research on the foundation of his field theory and his strong interest for group dynamics. Other pioneers of action research have also been suggested. Some advocate that Jacob Moreno is the true pioneer of action research, and he might indeed have been one of the first to use terms such as interaction research and action research. As early as in 1913, when working with prostitutes in a Vienna suburb, he thought of group participants as co-researchers. Moreno insisted on principles such as field-based research, participant observation, participation of concerned lay people, and improvement of social situations as an aim of the research (Altrichter & Gstettner, 1997, p. 48).

Lewin and Moreno knew each other, and it seems reasonable to count Moreno as one of the influences leading to the development of contemporary participatory action research. As a matter of fact, the focus on Kurt Lewin as *the* pioneer of action research is probably quite misleading. It is more reasonable to view this tradition as a convergence of several intellectual traditions, including both American pragmatism and German Critical Theory. I still choose to concentrate on Lewin's work in this section, since he was the first to present a theory of action research, and since his thinking has influenced so many scholars interested in this research tradition. Many of Lewin's ideas are also relevant for a contemporary concept of participatory action research.

Lewin was born in Germany in 1890. He fled Germany in 1933, as did many other prominent German scholars at that time, and he settled in the United States where he worked until his death in 1947. Lewin delivered sharp criticism of the atomistic psychology of Wundt,[1] and was himself more influenced by the Gestalt movement within German psychology. In the United States most of his work focused upon social psychology. He did some important work on group dynamics, leadership, and intergroup relations, and he is counted among the founding pioneers of social psychology as well as of organization and work psychology. He was one of the first to conduct more systematic analyses of the relative importance of personality and environment factors on the individual's behavior, and his concepts of field theory and life space have inspired many scholars. Lewin is, for instance, a major influence for Urie Bronfenbrenner's (1979) seminal work on ecological developmental psychology. Many historians of psychology thus put Lewin in the ranks of influential writers like Freud and Skinner.

In the mid 1940s Lewin constructed a theory of action research that described it as proceeding in a *spiral of steps*, each of which is composed of a sequence of *planning, action,* and *evaluation* and guided by an overall idea and specific goals that may be reformulated in the course of the spiral. Lewin also argued that in order to understand and change social practices, researchers have to include practitioners from the real social world in all phases of inquiry. This construction of action research contributed to its acceptance as a method of inquiry, and has been influential on later action researchers. Lewin (1946/1948) clearly articulated his vision of bridging social action and social theory through social research. Focusing on inter-group relations, he asked:

> How is economic and social discrimination to be attacked if we think not in terms of generalities but in terms of the inhabitants of that particular main street and those side and end streets which make up the small or large town in which the individual group worker is supposed to do his job? (Lewin, 1946/1948, pp. 201-202).

He realized that the question "What to do?" is a new question in each new context. What Lewin suggested thus was very far from traditional scientific experiments that can be replicated by any competent researcher at any time (and any place). Questions like "Where?" "When?" and "By whom?" were considered essential to the research process. Lewin asked for a comparative research on the conditions and effects of various forms of social action, and for research leading to social action. He also expressed the need for an integrated approach:

> We are beginning to see that it is hopeless to attack any one of these aspects of inter-group relations without considering the others. This holds equally for the practical and the scientific sides of the question. Psychology, sociology, and cultural anthropology each have begun to realize that without the help of the other neither of them will be able to proceed very far (Lewin, 1946/1948, p. 203).

Lewin did *not* argue against the tradition of nomothetic science. He suggested that there are two types of research objectives: the study of general laws and the diagnosis of a specific situation:

> To act correctly, it does not suffice, however, if the engineer or the surgeon knows the general laws of physics or physiology. He has to know too the specific character of the situation at hand. This character is determined by a scientific fact-finding called diagnosis. For any

field of action both types of scientific research are needed (Lewin, 1946/1948, p. 204).

Lewin argued then that minority problems are majority problems; the minority groups tend to accept the implicit judgment given by those who have status, even where the judgment is directed against themselves:

> the ideologies and stereotypes which govern inter-group relations should not be viewed as individual character traits but that they are anchored in cultural standards, that their stability and their change depend largely in the happenings in groups as groups (Lewin, 1946/1948, p. 208).

> It should be clear to the social scientist that it is hopeless to cope with this problem by providing sufficient self-esteem for members of a minority group as individuals (Lewin, 1946/1948, p. 214).

Minority groups often experience problems of status and caste, housing and family relations, legal structure of the community, etc. In Lewin's conceptualization, minority groups experience especially strong *barriers* in their life space; they experience that their space of free movement is severely restricted by social structure, discrimination, and prejudice. In order to raise the self-esteem of a minority group, Lewin advocated that both interactive groups have to be studied and worked with. Intergroup relations are two-way affairs. Political aspects and areas of conflict are obvious, and Lewin suggested that the social scientist will need an outmost amount of courage, in the way Plato defined it; wisdom concerning dangers. Dangers and resistance exist when one tries to break down barriers in the life space of minority groups.

Lewin argued that research that results in books and articles is not enough. But what difference may researchers make through action research? A criticism toward Lewin's notion of action research has been that his ideas are optimistic and visionary, but not very specific. Although he briefly outlined the process of doing action research – a topic I will return to later in this chapter – he did not present very accurate guidelines for this kind of research. Partly it may be countered that this must necessarily be so, because action research is about context sensitivity. Also we must remember that the article referred above was written one year before Lewin's death. He was in the process of widening his program for research, but did not live to develop the details. Lewin's importance for later participatory action research is beyond doubt, though, although his contribution for quite some years was marginalized in the United States due to the dominance of positivist theory of science. This approach to social research did not gain strength until the 1960s, and – at least in Europe – a very strong influence then was the Critical Theory of the Frankfurt School.

THE LEGACY OF CRITICAL THEORY

There was a strong and sudden growth of interest for action research in the 1960s and 1970s. Action researchers from this period often referred to Lewin's pioneering contribution, but the direct influence of his work was not always so strong. At least in Europe the influence from Critical Theory was more important. While the term "critical theory" sometimes refers to German nineteenth-century idealism based on Kant's three critiques, other times to all kinds of nonconformist contemporary theory, more often – and in this text – the term is used to denote the approach to social thought developed by the Frankfurt School since the late 1920s. Pioneers of Critical Theory in the 1930s and 1940s were Max Horkheimer, Walter Benjamin, and Theodor W. Adorno. The Institute of Social Research at the University of Frankfurt established a unique interdisciplinary milieu of social research, integrating perspectives from sociology, psychoanalysis, philosophy, economy, and aesthetics. When Hitler came to power in Germany most of the critical theorists fled to the United States, and the "school" became less a scholarly milieu and more a shared intellectual orientation.[2] In postwar Germany, especially in the 1960s, the Frankfurt School again had very influential thinkers, among whom Jürgen Habermas has been one of the most important.

Critical Theory may be seen as a revision and criticism of Marxism, with influences from both humanist thinking and psychoanalysis. Compared to some orthodox readings of Marx, the Critical Theorists strongly emphasize the possibility of *human agency*. The transactional perspective pioneered by Vygotsky concerning the relationship between individual and society is thus compatible with Critical Theory, and among some contemporary Critical Theorists there has been a renewed interest for cultural psychology. The movement of Critical Theory is stressing the social responsibility of scholars; its advocates suggest that research and theory should not only give scientific explanations, but should also be normative, practical, and self-reflexive. Emancipation and empowerment of individuals in social contexts is a main objective. While natural scientists search for nomothetic knowledge and scholars in the humanities search for understanding of idiographic cases, the Critical Theorists advocate that social researchers should focus upon the social conditions connected to the production and application of knowledge. Knowledge is related to power, and to social and material conditions. The social researcher therefore needs to take an active political stand; to be neutral is less of an option.

Groups and classes in social and economic power will – according to the Frankfurt School – strongly influence what counts as knowledge and reason. The term *ideology* – developed from Marxist thinking – is used to conceptualize the result of such a process. While the term ideology in the vernacular may denote the body of myth, symbol, or doctrine of a group or class of people, ideology in Critical Theory refers to *repressive trains of thought*. Ideology is what makes it possible for subordinates to accept their social position as "natural" or "inevitable"; they have accepted the worldview of those who are in power. People in dominating roles and positions seek to communicate that things are necessary and normal; they are simply the way they *need to be* and *should be.* Ideology thus conceals the power relations involved and the exploitation connected to that. The oppressed persons start to define themselves in ways first defined by their masters. In this perspective the Critical Theorists advocate that the main task of the social researcher is *social critique* of ideology.

In his influential work *Knowledge and Human Interests*, Jürgen Habermas (1968/1971) explores the relationships between thought and action, that is, knowledge and human activities. The book may be read as a critique of the narrow instrumental conception of rationality dominating in modern societies and supported by empirical research. Habermas – as Critical Theorists in general – argues against positivist ideas on research as an objective and neutral search for knowledge based on a straightforward correspondence conception of truth. Habermas is not satisfied with the humanities and "apolitical" hermeneutics as an alternative to this dominating tradition of research, however. What he suggests is that social research should be political and critical, guided by an emancipatory interest. Habermas thus proposes that humans' search for knowledge is guided by three main interests, or to be more precise, humans are engaged in three main types of activities that correspond to three main interests of knowledge. The two types of activities and interests of knowledge that typically have been discussed, at least since the days of Descartes and Vico, are the instrumental and the communicative. Habermas insists that a *third activity* and interest needs to be taken into consideration, namely emancipation:

> While *instrumental action* corresponds to the constraint of external nature and the level of the forces of production determines the extent of technical control over natural forces, *communicative action* stands in correspondence to the suppression of man's own nature. The institutional framework determines the extent of repression by the unreflected, "natural" force of social dependence and political power,

which is rooted in prior history and tradition. A society owes emancipation from the external forces of nature to labor processes (including "the transformation of the natural sciences into machinery"). Emancipation from the compulsion of internal nature succeeds to the degree that institutions based on force are replaced by an organization of social relations that is bound only to communication free from domination. This does not occur directly through productive activity, but rather through the revolutionary activity of struggling classes (including the critical activity of reflective sciences) (Habermas, 1968/1971, p. 53).

In this paragraph Habermas also implies some other influential concepts of his theory, such as the problem of *colonization of the life-world* and the possibility of *undistorted communication free of domination.* The concept of life-world is borrowed from Husserl, and has been important in twentieth-century German phenomenology and hermeneutics. Habermas' concern is that the individual's life-world – the context of meaning that people use to interpret and understand the situations they find themselves in – is challenged by "the system." The institutions of the society tend to take control and colonize the life-world. In modern societies this could for instance mean that technology, science, and administration is "taking over" or getting too dominating. Science in itself thus may function as ideology, if it is linked to a narrow logic of means and ends. Emancipation is therefore a continuous human activity and interest, and the path is to be found through undistorted communication and ideology critique.

By focusing strongly upon communication and emancipation Habermas avoids presenting a social theory where the individual is just counted as a member of a class. Habermas is thus critical to any reading of Marx in such directions, and he is critical to Marx's own neglect of the difference between work and interaction, which made Marx conceal the difference between rigorous empirical science and social critique (Habermas, 1968/1971, p. 62). Habermas' solution – social critique through a process of undistorted communication – has been criticized as being too rationalistic as well as too optimistic and naïve. Nevertheless, Habermas has continued to stimulate social researchers, even though postmodern critiques have seriously challenged the grand narratives that have informed him, such as Marxism and psychoanalysis. One of the pertinent questions today is to what degree the scope of Critical Theory may be enlarged. Alvesson and Sköldberg advocate the possibility of a more general usage of Critical Theory – not only for leftist political critique but for a broader cultural critique – and comment:

What is important in using critical theory is that problems are not treated as discrete phenomena which could be tackled with a bit of social engineering; rather they are viewed in light of the totality-subjectivity combination, that is, critical theory sees society in terms of culturally shared forms of consciousness and communication (Alvesson & Sköldberg, 2000, p. 127).

Real world problems then – in this perspective – are not seen in isolation but in relation to cultural norms, social processes, and structures of power. So, while agents and ideologies of capitalism traditionally have been the targets of critique among Critical Theorists, it is possible to imagine the Frankfurt School as a source of inspiration for researchers focusing on other – more limited – issues, such as for instance the culture and norms of public or private health services, to mention a field of relevance for the music therapist. Such more moderate aspirations in the direction of social change – with the purpose of overcoming the barriers of established institutions and modes of thought – may be relevant in many situations. An even more "minimal version" of critical research would be to try to prevent research from contributing to dominance without actually trying to overcome it (Alvesson & Sköldberg, 2000, pp. 128-129).

Methodological implications of this perspective would be to pay more attention to critical interpretation and consideration of broader contexts than what for instance typically is suggested in a Grounded Theory perspective. The specific object of cultural critique – say a community music school not interested in developing activities for handicapped children – is seen in relation to broader social and cultural contexts, such as values dominating the training of music educators, the municipality's economic support of the school, etc. There is then less focus upon the collection and analysis of data (although that is important enough) and more openness for creativity and critical interpretation in the research process. These elements are important already in choice of question and research context, since questions always support and reflect certain values. Researchers, no less than others, struggle with the problem of uncritically adopting conventional views, and critical researchers try to pay attention to the problem of ideology when choosing research questions.

The legacy of Critical Theory could therefore be said to be the challenge to produce "dangerous knowledge"; "the kind of information and insight that upsets institutions and threatens to overturn sovereign regimes of truth" (Kincheloe & McLaren, 1998, p. 260). As such, Critical Theory has been – and still is – influential on many action researchers, who want research to make a difference, not only for themselves but for all the participants of the research project. This legacy has thus been quite an important foundation for the growth of action research in many countries, even though Habermas himself – at least during the German action research boom of the 1960s and 1970s – was rather negative to this approach to research. His skepticism was methodological and related to the (traditional) fear that to merge social research and social action produces uncontrolled change and thus pollutes the collection of data. Habermas pictured critical research as traditional methodology with a strengthened element of critical reflection, while action researchers take one more step and suggest that the researcher's interaction with the field also is political in character, and that methodological innovations are necessary (Altrichter & Gstettner, 1997, p. 47).

CONTEMPORARY TRENDS IN ACTION RESEARCH

After strong growth, partly due to the political radical climate of the 1960s and 1970s in many countries, action research seemed to be out of fashion or to have outplayed its role by the early 1980s. More than one social researcher suggested that action researchers had been too keen on action and too relaxed on the obligation to produce qualified research results. Authors of textbooks on social research would again state that the only value central to research is truth, and disapprove of action researchers' preoccupation with social justice. Throughout the 1980s there were many signs of new beginnings though, and fresh approaches to action research started to gain strength. These approaches often had less overt and systematic critical and theoretical baggage than those of the preceding decades, but stressed other elements, such as practical judgment in context, methodological creativity and flexibility, the problem of participation, and the influence of factors such as gender, sexuality, race, and ethnicity. Such tendencies were fueled by developments in feminism and alternative movements such as environmentalism, and were often also informed by postmodern sensitivities.

Action research no longer was synonymous with leftist politics; in fact, many commercial companies also started to try out action research in order to improve their services. Within professions of health and education interest was given to action research as an alternative to traditional quantitative approaches to research, which typically are hard to adjust to the real-world irregularities of professional practice. An example of the latter is British curriculum research. This tradition has been more pragmatic and less critical than earlier German approaches to action research (Altrichter & Gstettner, 1997). In addition to this, government-initiated evaluation, community projects, etc., also started to be framed as action research projects. There are thus today a variety of action research approaches. If we use Habermas's

(1968/1971) conception of interests of knowledge as a departure point, it may be reasonable to suggest that there are three main traditions: scientific-technical action research, collaborative-communicative action research, and critical-emancipatory action research.

Scientific-technical action research is induced by a particular person or team who – because of experience or qualifications – are regarded as experts. Technical action research promotes better and more efficient practice, as defined by the experts in collaboration with practitioners in the process of improvement. This approach to action research aims at practical improvement and accumulation of knowledge through falsification or refinement of existing theories.

Collaborative-communicative action research is characterized by a more reciprocal and equal relationship between researchers and practitioners who come together to identify potential problems, underlying causes, and possible interventions. Dialogue and negotiated definitions of problems and interventions are stressed and methodological rigor downplayed, compared to scientific-technical action research. While these approaches to action research have become strong within health (Morton-Cooper, 2000) and education (McTaggart, 1997), few examples are found in the music therapy literature. One of the exceptions is Henk Smeijsters' (1997) approach, where a professional researcher collaborates with a music therapist in order to suggest better concepts, procedures, and techniques in the clinical work with a specific client population. Smeijsters' approach includes – to my judgment – elements of both the scientific-technical and collaborative-communicative approach.

In *critical-emancipatory action research* a third element is added to the research process: the empowerment of participants in relation to goals defined through collective discussions and reflection. Such research informed by the legacy of Critical Theory promotes critical consciousness among the participants and aims at ideology critique as well as at changes in repressive conditions (Greenwood & Levin, 1998). These conditions may be material as well as cultural, and may include barriers such as noninclusive rules and negative attitudes toward minority groups. The community music therapy project presented in Chapter 4 was informed by critical-emancipatory action research, as well as by ethnographic principles (Kleive & Stige, 1988), and will be used as example later in this chapter when the problem of participation will be illuminated.

MUSIC THERAPY:
A CASE OF FIDDLING WHILE THE WORLD BURNS?

What is the value of playing or listening to music, compared to medicines, cognitive-behavioral therapy, or other evidence-based interventions? This question is sometimes raised by influential – albeit sometimes also uninformed – voices, both among professional colleagues and funding agencies. Music therapists cannot but relate to such questions. Responses typically divide into two groups: those who suggest music therapy needs *quantitative research* in order to build up more evidence for its efficiency, and those who suggest that what we really need is *qualitative and interpretive research* in order to *understand* the experiential value of music therapy. (The latter response may include the extra challenge of educating the critical voices in order to have them recognize the value of qualitative research.)

While I acknowledge the relevance of both responses, I will propose that the tradition of participatory action research provides the discipline with a third option in response to this challenge, an option that has yet to be explored extensively by music therapy practitioners and researchers. While many researchers tend to treat the music therapy intervention as an isolated independent variable that can be studied separately, the entity to be studied could be defined in a larger scope, namely music therapy in context. This also links to another important question: How do music therapists relate to the social and cultural contexts in which they work and in which clients live their lives? I propose that there are at least three types of situations when action research – as a way of studying music therapy in context – is especially germane. That is when the *client's context-dependency*, the *therapist's context-sensitivity*, or the *practice's context-transforming power* is of special relevance. Let us look briefly at these three possibilities:

The *client's context-dependency* is an extremely relevant factor, for instance when working with children, some groups of elderly people, and some people with neuropsychological problems. Their power and ability to move freely from context to context is limited, and their ability to manage a broad range of contexts may be limited. In other words, there is a narrow spectrum of contexts that is helpful or meaningful for them, and they may be "thrown" into contexts that they have little power to reshape or few possibilities to leave. Consider for instance the situation of Upbeat (Chapter 4) and Paul (Chapter 5). Traditional individual therapy, with one session a week, has its limitations in such cases. The empowerment and development of the client achieved in the therapy context may not be satisfactory generalized to other contexts, and further development is very dependent on the inputs of the 168 minus 1 hours of everyday life of an average week. Community music therapy and ecological music therapy were chosen as the clinical approaches in the two cases described in this book. Action research could be a natural choice of approach to the *study* of such practices.

The *therapist's context-sensitivity* is for instance especially important in situations of multicultural tension or conflict. Lewin's famous words, used as the epigraph to this chapter, are pertinent here: "If you want truly to understand something, try to change it." By engaging in a participatory action research project, the music therapist is given options for *learning* from the participants, who in many cases will know the cultural context better than the therapist. In this way action research in fact may increase the therapist's sensitivity, which will prepare him for better clinical work. A caveat must be voiced here; participatory action research projects in situations of tension or conflict may or may not contribute to reduction of the problems in questions. To what degree the outcome will be positive depends, among other things, upon the cultural sensitivity of the music therapist. In developing this, the education and training of music therapists of course is an important factor (Troppozada, 1995). Cultivation of context-sensitivity through training and supervision, as well as the development of a critical discourse within the discipline, should increase the probability that music therapists qualify themselves for approaches such as collaborative and/or emancipatory action research.

Music therapy's context-transforming power is especially relevant in ecological and milieu-oriented approaches. This was evident in Chapters 4 and 5, where the music therapy practice included interventions on barriers such as attitudes of the local community, rules and practices of schools and kindergartens, and the quality of interactions between contexts (meso- and exosystem aspects). Another relevant example is Trygve Aasgaard's (1999) work in a hospital environment with children with cancer. The whole hospital post was transformed – musicalized, so to say – by the music therapy intervention of public musicking, which should make action research a relevant research strategy.

These and other examples suggest that participatory action research deserve more interest in the discipline of music therapy than what has been the case up till now. Music therapy is a young profession, and action research may turn out to be an interesting context-sensitive alternative for music therapists who want to document the value of their work. The relevance is enhanced by the fact that most music therapists practice music therapy not as manualized procedures, but as flexible approaches that may be adjusted to different social contexts. More in line with the critical tradition it should be noted that music therapists often work with clients that are suppressed or at least experience major barriers in their life space, and the possibility of empowerment through participatory action research should be explored.

Contemporary social and intellectual developments, such as postcolonialism and feminism, will probably become more influential in music therapy in the future than what they are today. This will also increase the relevance of participatory action research. The future of music therapy therefore probably – personally I would add hopefully – will include the development of socially conscious action research, as has already happened in other professions of health and education. It is therefore relevant to look more closely into the process of doing participatory action research.

THE PROCESS OF DOING
PARTICIPATORY ACTION RESEARCH

The process of doing participatory action research may be described with the spiral or repeated cycle as a guiding metaphor. The process starts with some regulating values and ideas that give direction to the work, while the concrete steps in the process – as originally described by Kurt Lewin (1946/1948) – include these sequences: 1) the definition of an objective (based on values and a general idea, that is, a general understanding of a situation and problem), 2) fact-finding (examining the general idea and the means to reach the objective), 3) the making of an overall plan (modifying the general idea), 4) action (first step of the overall plan), and 5) evaluation. The evaluation should serve four functions: a) to evaluate the action, b) to learn, c) to gain information for planning the next step, and d) to create a basis for modifying the overall plan. Lewin thus argued for a circular process of planning, fact-finding, acting, and evaluating, with an ongoing possibility for modification of the original general idea and the overall plan.

Later articulations of the process of participatory action research are usually variants of the ideas developed by Lewin, although the punctuation of the elements of the cycles, as well as the terms used for describing them, may differ somewhat. To some degree this process is similar to how we solve our everyday problems. We stop to think now and then because we have observed something with which we are not happy. Then we make a plan, try it out, and evaluate if our goals were realized. In the tradition of participatory action research, the relation between research and everyday activities is conceived as a continuum. Research is not something completely different from everyday activities, but is characterized by being systematic and reflexive, and better informed by theory.

I will formulate some descriptors and guiding principles for engagement in such collaborative research activities. These are informed by literature on participatory action research in health (Morton-Cooper, 2000) and education

(McTaggart, 1997) as well as by some of the basic culture-centered theoretical assumptions discussed earlier in this book, and then adopted to the discipline of music therapy. Participatory action research in music therapy, as the present author understands it, is:

- workplace and/or community oriented
- geared at solving problems as experienced by practitioners, clients, and/or members of a community
- sensitive to how *musicking* may create and change cultural and social relationships in the workplace/community
- oriented toward improvement of situated practice
- creative and flexible in the development and implementation of research techniques (in relation to goals, local conditions, etc.)
- guided by critical awareness and collective reflections.

The process of doing participatory action research in music therapy may be described as a reflexive development through a series of cycles including the elements of reflection, diagnosis, plan, action, and evaluation. The "spiral" mentioned above is constituted by cycles of collaborative research activities developing in time, aimed at producing knowledge and social change in concrete setting.

- *Reflection:* A thematic concern relevant for music therapy is identified. This may for instance be a case where barriers for participation in music exist in a community or a case where the indication of music therapy in relation to health problems is questioned. The concerned agents (clients, practitioners, community members, etc.) are identified and brought together, with the aim of building a team, or in other ways develop arenas for dialogue, discussion, planning, and evaluation of a research project.
- *Diagnosis:* The team/collaborators engage in a process of examining the thematic concern more carefully, in order to refine and specify it in the direction of more concrete questions and research problems. This involves seeing it in relation to the social and cultural situation and critically inspecting the basic values and assumptions informing the thematic concern. The diagnosis may therefore include fact-finding through the use of empirical methods as well as self-inquiry and hermeneutic exploration of the preunderstanding of the collaborators.
- *Plan:* Based upon the knowledge established in the phase of diagnosis, and a refined understanding of the thematic concern, a plan for how to solve the problem identified is made. Roles and responsibilities among participants are negotiated, as well as intended outcomes and timelines.

The plan may include a spectrum of situated music therapy interventions and research techniques.

- *Action:* The plan is put into action. This action is at the heart of the process, contributes to the production of refined diagnoses and plans, and feeds the elements of evaluation and reflection. Practitioners and researchers may here choose to engage in activities that go beyond the traditional scope of their roles, such as contributing to information sessions and establishing training workshops in a workplace or community. Action always includes elements of trial and error. Some stumbling and fumbling is unavoidable since no diagnosis and plan could account for all the changing factors and conditions met in concrete action. This phase therefore immediately leads into the next, that of evaluation.
- *Evaluation:* The team/collaborators gather data (again roles, responsibilities, and methods may be differentiated) in order to be able to assess the results of the actions implemented, in relation to the goals that were defined at the outset. Unintended and surprising outcomes are of course also examined, and their positive or negative value evaluated.

The steps described above define *one* cycle while the whole idea is that a research project consists of a series of such cycles, with continuous refinement of diagnosis, plan, and action through evaluation and reflection. The description given here – limited by the linearity of language – may suggest that the elements are more discrete than what they usually are. In a research process the steps described above mingle and merge. One needs some kind of plan in order to make a diagnosis. The process of making a diagnosis and a plan is already an action in the field. Evaluation and reflection are continuous elements in the process. Etc. These elements are therefore not to be understood as fully discrete steps, but rather as moves that interact and inform each other. Hopefully a definition of the elements, as given above, may counteract too much confusion and disorientation in the process.

The practitioner-researcher in this research tradition is not only a field-researcher focused upon studying and understanding a field. He is also engaged in collaborative action aimed at *changing* the field. Given the collaborative nature of participatory action research, the research process is necessarily also a *group process*. To use terms developed by Kurt Lewin; the collaborators and team of co-researchers are likely to experience phases such as *forming* and *storming*, and if successful, *norming* and *performing*. As plans are put into action and experiences made, discussions and debates will challenge values and put the different participants' preunderstanding under critical scrutiny. Ethical concerns and interpersonal qualifications are therefore crucial in the process of doing participatory action research.

To sum up the description so far, the process of doing participatory action research may be conceptualized as a cycle of collaborative activities that starts with a thematic concern. There is a problem situation that needs to be understood and transformed. The research process maintains a purposeful change focus, committed to the social context under scrutiny rather than the researchers' enthusiasm for particular research methodologies or theoretical problems. Team building and development of arenas for reflection and discussion may continue throughout the research process. Collective evaluation and reflection based upon negotiated role definitions are continuous elements in the process and form the basis for refined diagnosis of the situation of concern and for the development of new plans of action.

Since the process is defined as a series of cycles and relates to social and cultural contexts in development, there are in principle no final answers to the questions asked. The closing of a research project is therefore defined by the overall plan, and – of course – the practical and financial conditions given. What are then possible outcomes of such research processes? The outcomes are defined by the characteristics of the process: empowerment of participants, collaboration through participation, social change, and acquisition of knowledge. While there is a continuous commitment to the social context of scrutiny, knowledge and experiences that possibly could be transferred to other contexts are of course also of interest. Knowledge diffusion and replication of ideas that work are therefore important elements not to be neglected. This also illuminates the value of Kurt Lewin's (1946/1948) idea that action research involves the integration of social action, research, and training/supervision.

THE PROBLEM OF PARTICIPATION

Participatory action research has gained increasing support and acceptance as a legitimate approach, although critical voices are still heard. "Exactly what is the knowledge produced?" would be one of the quite typical questions asked. The critics then suggest that there is not enough rigor in the process of collecting and analyzing data. Such critique may be countered at an epistemological level, by underlining the situated character of knowledge (see Lave & Wenger, 1991), as well as at a methodological level. Participatory action researchers share the epistemological and methodological concerns developed in Critical Theory, where rigor in data-collection and analysis may be downplayed somewhat and critical reflection emphasized and refined (Alvesson & Sköldberg, 2000). The generalizability of the knowledge produced is another issue under debate. Again, this goes back to the premise of situated knowledge. There is no need to totalize this perspective though. As Lewin (1946/1948) in the original formulation of action research acknowledged different research traditions, there is of course no reason not to use knowledge produced in other contexts, as long as the criteria of ecological validity is met. Similarly, any participatory action research project, situated as it is in a concrete context, could function as a "preceding analogous case"[3] for other researchers in similar contexts.

Although the criticism must be taken seriously, participatory action research therefore should have a legitimate position in a music therapist's research palette. As outlined above, the most powerful potential as well as the most serious problem is probably related to the issue of *participation* itself. I will therefore close this chapter with some reflections on this issue. How do we actually ensure that the result of the process is empowerment of participants and not social engineering in new clothes? Let us start with the question of ownership.

There is no direct relationship between knowledge and behavior, a fact that professionals working with health promotion are well aware of; information about what is good and what is not so good for our health does not necessarily change people's health behavior. In that respect, humans are not fully rational. Or maybe it is better to put it this way: rationality is not fully human. When people are given the possibility to participate in the production of knowledge, the link between knowledge and behavior is strengthened. This in many ways illuminates both the potential and problem in doing action research; there is a considerable potential for change in the participation itself, if you are able to reach to the level of participation, that is. It may be said then that the first challenge is to bring people together, but this is also where the process perhaps already goes wrong. What ownership do the participants have to the research project and to the reasons for implementing it? If they feel that the research belongs to the researcher, and not to them, their involvement will be at a level that does not qualify for the term participation, as it is used in this context.

The process of participatory action research starts with someone stopping. Someone is not quite happy with status quo, with the order of things. There is a beginning before the beginning, then. A project of participatory action research is born out of an emerging critical awareness, which is based on some values and a specific position in a discourse. A project may have different starting points. It may be a grass-root initiative or the initial proposal may come from a researcher or group of researchers, or the idea may be connected to programs initiated by local or national authorities. There is also a fourth possibility: the research project may be practitioner-generated. These differences in starting may influence the process in profound ways.

The main problem, seen in a power perspective, is that both experts and authorities may try to use action research projects as a way of promoting their own ideas and values in ways that lead the participants to believe that these are actually their own when they are not. In other words, we are back to the issue of ideology, in the Critical Theory meaning of that term. There is of course no easy way out of this. Subtle mechanisms of power are ubiquitous in human interaction. I can see no other option than paying serious attention to the legacy of Critical Theory. While this does not mean that all participatory action research projects should be leftist, the term "participatory" at least implies a commitment to values supporting a "minimal version" of critical research (Alvesson & Sköldberg, 2000); the research should be actively monitored with the aim of at least not *contributing* to dominance.

The challenge of participatory action researchers then is to be able to situate the project in its context and to engage a group of people in an endeavor characterized by critical collective reflections and shared responsibilities (Adelman, 1997). To counter some of the possible limitations and ethical problems of this approach, the development of teams and supportive arenas that make collective as well as self-critical reflections possible is then crucial. Which voices are heard? Which voices run the risk of being neglected? A specific problem of participation that music therapy researchers may meet quite often is that some of the participants would be much less articulate that some of the others. Some client participants may have very limited language skills, for instance, or even no such skills. To imagine these people then as participants in a research project is rather problematic. Of course parents or probation officers may be invited to participate on behalf of them, but then the idea of participation is already stretched somewhat.

In the project described in Chapter 4, a sort of combined solution was sought concerning client participation. As much as possible the voices of the clients were heard. Remember, for instance, how Knut's question "May we too play in the brass band?" was influential for the development of the project. For Knut and the other members of Upbeat to participate in formal meetings or discussions about the project was not possible, though, and in order to assess the importance of his request, information from alternative sources was also gathered. By discussing the project with professionals of the institution where the members of Upbeat lived, for instance, we learned that one of the members of Upbeat had established the tradition of marching along with the brass band every time the band would perform, with his recorder in a bag. Another member had the habit of conducting the band when it performed. In other words, Knut's question reflected a dream and a goal that seemed to be shared by several members of the group, although they could not articulate it in words, a fact that contributed to the effort that was made in order to find ways of realizing this dream.

The problem of participation also means that researchers must engage in critical self-reflection. They must remember that they do not enter the arena out of mere academic curiosity only. In case they do, they clearly run the risk of *using* people. As researchers they are committed to a problem situation in a real community, and how the project affects people's lives directly. Change is not sought for its own sake, but in order to "make the world a better place," if only in a small scale in a small place. Who, then, defines what better means? The ethos of participatory action research put great demands on all participants. Creativity and the ability to see new possibilities, as well as openness to accept new ways, could be some of the important stepping-stones. Such things do not always come easy. Skills in communication and negotiation will be needed, the ability to share visions, and – not least – to both give and take in a dialogue. Tolerance for conflicts and disagreements as part of the process will also be required, together with a decent dose of patience. It takes time to negotiate on values and ways of being and doing, especially when old ways are about to be changed. There will always be resistance in some elements of an organization or of a community. These elements of a participatory action research project do not boil down to a set of skills in negotiation and communication, however. Individual *reflexivity* cultivated through collective reflections is seminal in order to counteract the possibility of participatory action research developing into a refined version of expert dominance. Reflexivity in relation to research will be further elaborated upon in the final chapter.

NOTES

[1] Wundt was a psychologist of two "faces"; he also developed a strong interest for what has later been known as cultural psychology (Cole, 1996). This part of Wundt's work should be closer to Lewin's interests, but I have no information on Lewin's appraisal of it.

[2] While the term "Frankfurt *School*" is much used, Critical Theory is closer to a movement than to a school. Critical Theorists do not represent a unified school of thought, rather a shared concern on power, repression, and mutating forms of dominance.

[3] I am borrowing this term from Steinar Kvale (1996); see also Chapter 6.

Chapter 12:

TOWARD A THIRD CULTURE
OF MUSIC THERAPY RESEARCH?

*There is widespread agreement today that reason has to
be understood as embodied, culturally mediated, and
interwoven with social practice. The embeddedness and
variability of basic categories, principles, rules, and
procedures mean that the critique of reason has henceforth
to be carried out in conjunction with social, cultural,
and historical analysis.*
(Thomas McCarthy)

This chapter addresses issues concerning how to position music therapy research methodologically, theoretically, and metatheoretically. These issues have been under lively debate lately. Some suggest that we should identify music therapy research with the "harder" sciences in order to document the efficacy of the interventions. Others suggest that we need to go in a different direction and that the "softer" humanities convey the real identity of music therapy research. These debates reflect the science debates that have been part of academia since at least the days of Descartes and Vico, and which at times have been heated enough to suggest the term "science wars." More than one scholar has proposed that it is time that oppositions constructed between objectivism and relativism and between quantitative and qualitative methods of research be superseded. Toward the end of the chapter the concept of *reflexivity* is presented and clarified, not as a solution to the dilemmas outlined, but as a constructive strategy for approaching them.

THE TWO CULTURES

Often it has been suggested that Western societies are, and have been, characterized by a split in the concept of knowledge; there is a cleft between the arts and humanities on one hand and the sciences on the other. Stefan Collini puts it this way:

Certainly, there have been, from the Greek dawn of Western thought onwards, distinct domains of human knowledge, and at different times reflective minds have pondered the dangers involved when one branch or "discipline" of enquiry comes to be either threateningly dominant or inaccessibly recondite (Collini, 1998, p. ix).

In more modern times this anxiety was made prominent in the Romanticism of the nineteenth century, where fragmentation of knowledge was seen as an increasing danger. In the mid-twentieth century the issue was vitalized by debates on positivism fueled by criticism from the humanities and interpretive traditions within sociology and anthropology. From another perspective, discussions on the academic schism also grew out of scientists' critique of literary intellectuals. When the English novelist and scientist Charles P. Snow (1905-1980) held his famous Rede-lecture "The Two Cultures" in 1959, focusing upon the role of science and the intellectuals in society, he therefore touched upon an old theme in Occidental civilization. Snow's lecture articulated this problem in a fresh way and stimulated a public debate that raged for years.

Snow (1959/1998) could not accept the legitimacy of the gap and split between the literary intellectuals and the scientists that he found in Britain. He noted with deep skepticism and concern that during the 1930s the literary intellectuals had taken to referring to themselves as *the* intellectuals, as though the scientists were not intellectuals. Snow thus opposed the humanities' self-understanding as highbrow and high culture, and to the traditional literary hegemony in the British society. Instead he communicated *science* as the great hope in a world that had been mismanaged and misruled by the traditional elite. Science was a true meritocracy in his eyes. This he thought to be of high value and he argued that literary intellectuals were too closely connected to the heritage of the higher social classes of the British society. Snow advocated the importance of the cultural role and political impact of science. In fact he promoted the rule of a scientific elite instead of the traditional elite. In addition to regretting the split between cultures, he therefore also recommended a shift in balance of power and influence.

This brief description of Snow's lecture should illuminate how his arguments, in addition to relating to an ancient theme in Western cultures, clearly were situated in a specific British context. In other times and other countries, with less tradition for aristocracy and literary elitism, there would perhaps be more concerns about the dominating role of science. My intention is therefore not to adopt Snow's arguments as a general foundation, rather to use them as a starting point for reflecting upon the relationship between cultures of research. To what degree, for instance, does it make sense to speak of two cultures of research in music therapy? To my mind this makes sense, rather evidently and equally unfortunately. "Research in music therapy, quantitative or qualitative?" is the title of an article Dorit Amir published in 1993. This question has dominated the debate on music therapy research, especially maybe in the late 1980s and early 1990s.

As the young discipline of music therapy developed in America in the 1960s and 1970s, a research tradition that was inspired by positivism and the quantitative traditions of psychology and the natural sciences grew strong. Nomothetic research has been the dominating tradition in American music therapy, a fact that any reader of *Journal of Music Therapy* will be well aware of. Generally speaking, the purpose of this tradition has been to establish knowledge about the effects of music on human behavior, and thus to legitimize music therapy practice. In E. T. Gaston's (1968) influential textbook *Music in Therapy* – which for many years was *the* textbook, the *one* source of academic knowledge on music therapy – there are three chapters on research. In these chapters it is just a "fact," not even discussed or questioned, that research is based on nomothetic ideals of science.

Many music therapists feel that the body of knowledge produced in this research tradition has been essential for the growing acceptance of music therapy. Others state that the relevance and validity of this research is questionable, and argue that the methodological requirements of quantitative research bring most of this research to a distance to the living and unpredictable nature of the musical and interpersonal processes of music therapy. An alternative tradition of research in music therapy then started to grow in the mid-eighties. This "new" tradition, often named *qualitative research,* was featured in several publications on music therapy research in the 1990s, as in Wheeler (1995a), Langenberg, Aigen and Frommer (1996), and Smeijsters (1997). While qualitative research may be said to have roots going back for centuries, to the traditions of hermeneutics and the humanities, to Giambattista Vico's *New Science* of 1744, as well as to the interpretive traditions of ethnography of the nineteenth and twentieth centuries, it was often conceived of as something new when it gained foothold in music therapy in the 1980s and 1990s. This probably contributed to a polarization of the two traditions of research in this discipline.

Music therapy research; quantitative or qualitative? Do we have to choose, and if so, why? Several scholarly arguments related to this question have been presented, and it also seems reasonable to suggest that this debate has had important sociological aspects to it; which voices were to define what counts as research in music therapy? Attempts of treating both the quantitative and the qualitative approach as legitimate have of course also been made. Generally speaking, though, there is still often a considerable distance and reciprocal suspicion between researchers relating to the two traditions. Such suspicion did not, as we saw above, exactly come with music therapy. It has in different variants been part of Western cultural history for centuries. With moderate ambitions of solving age-old dilemmas in a few pages, I will approach the issue of how one could imagine a third culture of music therapy research.

SCIENCE AND SUCCESS

Since Francis Bacon, who stated that the book of nature is written in the language of mathematics, there has been a tradition within natural sciences to let count those things that can be counted. Since his days, the natural sciences have been extremely successful, due to the adherence to empiricist principles. Through the use of refined and controlled methods, with possibilities for replication and testing of results, a large body of accumulated knowledge has been built. In the early nineteenth century this success of the natural sciences stimulated French sociologist Auguste Comte to coin the term positivism, and to propose that the social sciences should adhere to the same empiricist principles as the natural sciences, in order to get beyond what he conceived of as futile speculation. To varying degrees the social sciences have followed Comte's advice, psychology being a significant case in point. The success of this young discipline in modern societies, with a concurrent establishment of a strong profession, is probably to a high degree related to its willingness and ability to establish itself as a science.

Positivism has been a success then, at least practically. Philosophically the situation is somewhat different, although things looked good for a long time. The beginning of the twentieth century saw a strong development of the theory of science, through the establishment of the Vienna Circle, which developed the school of *logical positivism* through a refinement of nineteenth-century ideas on positivism. According to the logical positivists, science is based on controlled observations and inductive reasoning. Through carefully monitored observations and experiments, with isolation and manipulation of variables, positive and verifiable knowledge of the world should be possible to achieve. Control of observations requires, according to this view, rejection of theoretical preconceptions. Observations should be made independently of any theory. It should then be possible to develop a universal theory of science; *unity of science* was advocated. Since metaphysics and philosophy generally is not constituted of verifiable statements these discourses could literally be considered meaningless, the logical positivists advocated (Nerheim, 1995).[1]

Today, after decades of fierce philosophical criticism, positivists exist mostly as straw men that scholars of the humanities love to shoot at. Critique of this version of the philosophy of science has not only come from the humanities and interpretive traditions of research, however. Serious critique has also been given to the position of logical positivism from theorists of science who advocate nomothetic empirical research. One of the most important criticisms came from Karl Popper (1959/1992), in *The Logic of Scientific Discovery*. He refused to accept the idea that it is even possible to observe anything independently of theory; to some degree all perception is directed and informed by preconceptions. Neither did he accept the logic of inductive reasoning as a sound foundation for science. Instead he advocated the hypothetico-deductive approach. As a consequence of this critique Popper introduced *falsification* instead of *verification* as a major principle for the scientific enterprise. While the inductive approach of the logical positivists suggested that a researcher should search for verification of findings and theorems, Popper suggested that to be scientific is to search for falsification. That a statement is verified is hardly a good reason for considering it true. After one hundred verifications only one falsification alters its status.[2] Falsification, not verification, should then be considered the demarcation principle for the scientific enterprise and only statements that are possible to falsify could be considered scientific, Popper advocated. It follows that statements that are possible to falsify are not necessarily *true*, even though they are not falsified yet. They may represent the best knowledge available at that time, though.[3]

Popper's critique of logical positivism has been important for the refinement of a postpositivist theory of contemporary empirical research. A refined postpositivist conception of science does not necessarily reveal a changed ontology and epistemology, compared to the realism of the logical positivists. Language is still mostly considered a transparent medium for description of an objective reality. A more radical suggestion would be that science is not a universal practice governed by logical rules exclusively, it is a set of practices based upon premises that may not be explicit and which cannot be proved or made self-evident. In other words, science is also culture; it is situated practices and ways of seeing and listening. Such claims are often based on the work of Thomas Kuhn (1970) who found support in the later philosophy of Ludwig Wittgenstein (1953/1967). Taking this more radical stance, research is not and cannot be an objective and value-free enterprise. Kuhn's (1970) concept of research *paradigms* may be understood as expressions of *cultures of science,* developed by communities of researchers. Such cultures and paradigms may be incompatible or incommensurable; one cannot decide by logic or empirical proof which one is correct.

Kuhn's arguments could suggest that any claim made by scientists is relative to the context of the paradigm it is representing. Taken to its extreme, the critique could thus undermine the whole scientific enterprise. This has hardly happened; the practical success of scientific discoveries has far outweighed the strength of any philosophical argument. It may even be argued that a discipline such as psychology hardly has taken the critique of positivism seriously (Saugstad, 1998).[4] To adhere to positivist and post-positivist principles seems to have been a reliable route to practical success. It is possible to argue, though, that practical success is not the only measure. What difference does it make that the objects of scientific study are humans? What *is* actually success for a discipline concerned with human beings? Is it even possible to ask this question without also asking success for *whom*? This last question brings in the objects of study as potential subjects in the study, and we are left with some nagging questions that the tradition of hermeneutics has tried to deal with.

THE HERMENEUTIC CHALLENGE

One important discussion on the idea of studying humans scientifically has been developed by the Norwegian philosopher Hans Skjervheim (1959/ 2000). His *Objectivism and the Study of Man* was, as Jürgen Habermas (1981/1987) and others have pointed out, one of the first systematic philosophical discussions of the positivistic tradition within social sciences. Skjervheim's agenda was to illuminate the serious fallacy committed when social scientists apply the logic of natural science to the study of humans. Informed by phenomenology and existentialist hermeneutics Skjervheim illuminated how empirical social researchers run the risk of reducing the people they study to objects without agency or capacity for meaning-making.

It is important to clarify that Skjervheim's argument is not anti-empirical. Rather he wanted to illuminate that if social researchers uncritically adopt the philosophy of the natural sciences, they misunderstand and miss their objects of study. Human life is embedded in culture and social structures and will not be understood properly if the researcher does not see himself as part of the same field as the object of study. Social phenomena have meanings that are constituted in social fields, and in order to develop any true understanding researchers must grasp how the people they study perceive themselves and their situations. Skjervheim's critique had an important impact on the Scandinavian debate on social research in the 1960s, which of course also was fueled by the so-called "Positivismusstreit" initiated by the attacks on positivism among German Critical Theorists and others. Within social sciences an increasing acceptance of the relevance of hermeneutics and qualitative research therefore developed, after decades of strong positivistic dominance.[5]

The relevance and importance of hermeneutics was touched upon in Chapter 10, in relation to Giddens's proposal that social research necessarily implies the logic of a double hermeneutic; the researcher is studying a field that is already interpreted by the social agents of that field. Of special relevance here is the tradition of *philosophical hermeneutics*, which goes beyond treating hermeneutics as a research method. Wilhelm Dilthey and other late nineteenth- and early twentieth-century scholars focused upon hermeneutics as an alternative *research method,* different from that of the natural sciences but with its own rigor and value. The twentieth century philosophical hermeneutics, following Heidegger, Gadamer, and Ricoeur, has been less concerned with hermeneutics as a research method and more concerned with the general philosophical issue of *interpretation as a basic human condition.* To be human, these philosophers suggest, is to be involved in interpretation – of events, of fellow humans, of signs, etc. These philosophers therefore advocate the basic and existential relevance of hermeneutic issues (Alvesson & Sköldberg, 2000).

In a discussion of research in the health disciplines, Hjördis Nerheim (1995) takes the arguments of the tradition of philosophical hermeneutics as departure point, and she argues that while the health disciplines require both nomothetic and idiographic research, hermeneutics may serve as a basic discipline or metatheory for these disciplines. This suggestion is met with skepticism in many scientifically inclined milieus; they associate hermeneutics with the arts and humanities and consider empirical experimental research to be the only possible sound foundation for the health disciplines. In the long run it is hard to neglect the strength of Nerheim's basic argument, though. Hermeneutics – oriented toward the existential condition of the Other – must have a basic legitimacy in disciplines that focus upon health, which is not a thing but a quality of human coexistence.[6]

PEACEFUL COEXISTENCE?

Some scientists condemn scholars in the humanities because they think that their works are merely comments upon comments, and are not based in any empirical knowledge about the world. Similarly one finds scholars within the humanities expressing scorn about scientists' epistemological naïveté and their preoccupation with facts. Humans know no facts without a process of interpretation, the critique goes, so one might as well focus upon interpretation, which is a lot about commenting comments. Such reciprocal condemnation makes communication less than easy, and cultures of scholars today fight for hegemony in ways that probably hinder effective transmission and development of existing knowledge. To position oneself in one of the existing camps seems to be the safest option. Whether it is productive for the development of scholarly disciplines is a different question.

One of the necessary conditions for scholarly progress is theoretical development. In the natural sciences a theory usually is considered to be a consistent body of statements that can be verified and which have not yet been falsified, at least not in a way and to a degree that has been accepted as fatal. Such ideas about theories are based in a *correspondence theory* about truth. A statement is true (and meaningful) only to the degree it is in concordance with what the early Wittgenstein (1921/1961) called "Tatsache," the facts (not things) of the world. In contrast to this perspective, a constructionist perspective has been more common within the humanities, especially among scholars subscribing to postmodernist ideas about knowledge. Within this perspective, made famous by Berger and Luckman (1966), our "reality" is socially constructed and our interest should thus be in the processes and products of social construction.

In the 1990s these differences in perspective fueled some heated debates (sometimes termed the "Science War") between scholars in cultural studies and in the natural sciences. Public awareness of these debates was created by the legendary hoax of Alan D. Sokal, a New York professor in physics, who wrote a parody of postmodern science criticism entitled "Transgressing the Boundaries: Toward a Transformative Hermeneutics of Quantum Gravity" (Sokal, 1996a). The article was submitted to the cultural studies journal *Social Text*, accepted as a serious article, and published. Three weeks later Sokal revealed the hoax in an article in *Lingua Franca*, and asked: "Is it now dogma in Cultural Studies that there exists no external world? Or that there exists an external world but science obtains no knowledge of it" (Sokal, 1996b)? In his hoax article he had declared, without evidence or argument, that physical reality is basically a social and linguistic construct. When revealing the hoax he wrote:

> Fair enough: anyone who believes that the laws of physics are mere social conventions is invited to try transgressing those conventions from the windows of my apartment. (I live on the twenty-first floor.) (Sokal, 1996b).

Several similar challenges have been given to the social constructionists: What about riding ninety miles an hour down a dead-end street to test the validity of the social construction of the reality? Behind such aggressive, albeit humorous, proposals lies the assumption that it is through empirical testing that the validity of a theory is decided. These Sokal-like challenges may be less relevant, though, if one sees that the task of the social scientist is not to challenge natural science but to understand humans and cultures in social contexts. The perspectives advocated by social constructionists may for instance be helpful and important for the deconstruction of disempowering ideas about social realities as "natural" or unavoidable. That social realities may be *real* in their own way is also beyond doubt, however. Consider the possibility that we decided to test the laws of physics in the second way prescribed above, and then were stopped by the police:

> to ignore the institutionalized meanings attributed to human acts is about as effective as ignoring the state trooper who stands coolly by our car window and informs us that we have been traveling recklessly at ninety miles an hour and asks to see our license. "Reckless," "license," "state trooper" – all derive from the institutional matrix that society constructs to enforce a particular version of what constitutes reality. They are cultural meanings that guide and control our individual acts (Bruner, 1990, p. 38).

Bruner's example is taken from an account of cultural psychology, and is not specifically related to the science wars referred to above, but to an argument about the relevance of cultural meanings for the study of humans. The example is relevant in this context too, however. Music therapy, it seems, can neither neglect facts of science nor processes of social construction.

So far I have illuminated differences between traditions of research, where oppositions such as science versus the humanities, quantitative research versus qualitative research, nomothetic studies versus ideographic studies, and positivism versus hermeneutics have been outlined. Another classic opposition typically used to denote two main approaches to knowledge in Western cultures is objectivism versus relativism. The relationships between these concepts are of course much more complex than what have been revealed here, but the description above suffices to highlight how cultures of knowledge and research have opposed each other. Possibilities for more peaceful coexistence seem rather slim. At the same time, it is not unproblematic if a discipline such as music therapy develops two separate cultures of research. I will try to illuminate this from two angles, first with a philosophical argument and then with a more practical consideration in relation to the obligations of a music therapist in clinical practice.

The first argument to consider is that it is not necessary to be captured by polarities such as those constructed between the social constructionists and the natural scientists. If the objectivism of natural science is problematic in the study of humans, the alternative is not necessarily social constructionism or relativism. Human rationality develops as practical discourse and judgment in communities of practice, Richard Bernstein (1983) argues, and he proposes that this may establish a foundation for moving beyond objectivism and relativism. Within philosophy and the theory of science there have been numerous criticisms of the notion held by the logical positivists that data and theory could and should be separated. One argument has for instance been developed on the basis of Wittgenstein's (1953/1967, 193ff) discussion of seeing aspects of objects. Wittgenstein suggests that we see as we interpret. He illustrates this with his famous discussion of the duck-rabbit, which can be seen as a rabbit's head or as a duck's head (see Chapter 10). Data and theory can in principle not be separated completely; the collection of data is already to some degree an interpretation. This insight counteracts naïve inductive approaches based on the idea that concepts may be developed from a collection of "clean" data, but it will be to neglect the shared human rationality advocated by Bernstein (1983) to drive this insight to the extreme level of proposing that reality is social construction only. There is some interdependence between the data, the research instrument, and the involved theory, while empirical material is still not left for free construction.

It should therefore be possible to draw on an epistemological position that tries to avoid polarization of empiricist and constructionist positions. Both views build on assumptions on the nature of language that are difficult to defend in social research and the humanities. The correspondence theory on truth assumes that language mirrors reality without or with minimal distortion, while a radical constructionist position leads to nominalism; language and world become disconnected. The Danish ethnographer Kirsten Hastrup (1999) has, with reference to Charles Taylor (1985), suggested an alternative or middle ground that I find helpful. The theories and concepts developed need not to be limited to a designative function or be left for "free" construction; they may be *expressive*. With that term she suggests that theories instead of picturing the world "as it is" could express specific *aspects* of it, aspects that would not otherwise have found an expression. In this way theories actually add something to the world, by being a specific and new "answer" to the challenge of the aspect seen (Hastrup, 1999, p. 193). This proposal I find relevant for clinical research in music therapy, and I will illuminate problems of polarization of positions through some reflections on conditions of the therapeutic endeavor.

There is a tension implicit in any therapeutic endeavor. The therapist is working to help his client change, and this process must take the client's narrative as a departure point. Concepts of health and well-being are cultural and constructed, and the client's perspective is decisive in choosing goals and approach. There are limits to this, though; all goals, developments, and changes cannot be considered equal. When discussing therapy I cannot see that we are any better off with linguistic reductionism than with the biological reductionism that has dominated the field of psychiatry. A consequent relativist epistemology and a concept of "multiple truths" is not at all unproblematic for the field of music therapy. Sometimes we encounter situations where the correspondence theory of truth is highly relevant, that is, situations when searching for clear answers such as "yes" and "no" is essential: "Is my client so depressed that she is in risk of committing suicide?" Other times we ask more pragmatic questions: "How can the client use this music?" Of course we also ask questions related to meaning, with the possibility for "multiple truths": "What does this song mean for this client in this situation, as opposed to other clients or other situations?"

I conclude then, that the practice and study of music therapy needs an inclusive and eclectic concept of truth, acknowledging the relevance of at least three perspectives: the empiricist perspective (correspondence), the hermeneutic perspective (coherence/meaning), and the pragmatist perspective (application/effect). I am well aware of the complex nature of this issue, and that there are many more problems to discuss than what has been outlined here. At the same time I will argue that while it is too restricted to talk about truth as correspondence when you discuss a multifaceted phenomenon like music therapy, it may also be an oversimplification to restrict the discourse to a notion of multiple truths. The concept of "multiple truths" could in fact be seen as a one-dimensional concept of truth, stressing meaning only, while we might need a three-lateral concept and a mixed strategy in search for truth (Alvesson & Sköldberg, 1994).

Such a mixed strategy might involve interaction of the perspectives mentioned above. The culture-centered argument of this book suggests that each particular context becomes a focus of interest in research. To state that all knowledge is local knowledge is of course somewhat self-contradictory, though, by being itself a general statement. My subscription to a three-lateral concept of truth suggests an epistemological position closer to *relationism* than relativism, which again suggests that I acknowledge the possibility of family resemblances or even universals between the language games of meaning-making. Theories of music therapy therefore need to include general principles, or else we have little to guide us when trying to deal with individual cases. As Lerner (1998, p. 8) states in a discussion of relationism in developmental psychology: "The attribute is given its functional meaning only by virtue of its relation to a specific context." If and how a principle operates depends upon the situation.

Taken together these arguments suggest that music therapists could make their voices heard among those who try to link science and the humanities in some way or another. As I argue in the Introduction to this book; the goal envisioned could hardly be a merging of perspectives, but the value of poly-phonic dialogue and crossing of cultures should be explored.

RESEARCH AND REFLEXIVITY

When I argue for the relevance of a three-lateral concept of truth and a mixed strategy in search for it, this has implications for my understanding of *reflexivity* in relation to research. A three-lateral concept of truth suggests an *eclectic* approach to reflexivity, integrating concerns about the solidity of empirical material, about the problems of interpretation, as well as about issues of social critique and self-critical examination. Such an approach to reflexive methodology is discussed by Alvesson and Sköldberg (2000), and I will briefly refer to their ideas. Their argument has been developed in rela-tion to qualitative research. The implications for quantitative research could be somewhat different, but in my judgment the issue of reflexivity should be relevant to this tradition of research also.[7]

Alvesson and Sköldberg (2000) accept the primacy of interpretations. The conception of data as reflections of the world is rejected. In order to communicate this reservation, these authors therefore tend to use the term *empirical material* instead of data. Reflexivity in the research process, then, is interpretation of one's interpretations of the empirical material. To be reflexive in relation to research means to reflect upon the preconditions of one's own activity and on how one's own personal and professional in-volvement influences the interaction with the phenomenon under scrutiny. With reference to Steier (1991) Alvesson and Sköldberg also suggest that a central aspect of reflexivity is the awareness that we construct ourselves while constructing the objects or phenomena that we study, which then sug-gests that self-reflexivity and reflexivity converge. Alvesson and Sköldberg (2000, pp. 7-8) then propose four elements in reflective research:

- *Systematics and techniques in research procedures:* There must be some kind of logic in the way the researcher interacts with the empirical mate-rial, and some kind of systematic approach when collecting it.
- *Clarification of the primacy of interpretation:* A reflective researcher acknowledges the primacy of interpretation (that even "raw data" are in-terpretations), which implies that research cannot be disengaged from ei-ther theory or self-reflection.
- *Awareness of the political-ideological character of research:* What is explored, and how it is explored, cannot but support or challenge some

values and interests in the society. The political and ideological aspects of research must therefore be acknowledged.

- *Reflection in relation to the problem of representation and authority:* There are problems of representation and authority connected to any research text, and awareness of rhetoric elements and the relationships between text, author, and world need to be examined.

These four issues have been treated differently by different traditions of research, and a possibility for learning exists in examining these traditions. Consider for instance the concern about systematics and techniques found in Grounded Theory, empirical phenomenology, and other inductive approaches. Similarly hermeneutics has much to offer concerning clarification of the primacy of interpretation, while Critical Theory, feminism, and related metatheories have given valuable inputs concerning the political-ideological character of research and knowledge. Postmodern (text-oriented) approaches, admired by some and held in contempt by others, should have something to offer to all researchers, by sensitizing them to the problems of representation and authority in research texts. Alvesson and Sköldberg (2000) therefore argue that reflexivity in research involves some kind of *search for a balance* between these four perspectives, and that this is necessary to avoid reductionism with focus only upon data, interpretation, critique, or language. The researcher thus must search for some kind of interplay between the four levels, and avoid the totalization of any one of them. These suggestions also have a practical aspect: reflexivity in research means to restrict the time you use for data collection and analysis, to be able to make room for interpretations of interpretations.

I believe Alvesson and Sköldberg's (2000) eclectic approach is relevant for a multifaceted field like music therapy. There are of course epistemological problems connected to pluralism and the integration of perspectives as different as those discussed here. When Alvesson and Sköldberg suggest a balancing of four perspectives, one might state that to be able to balance something you need something to stand on and you need a force of gravitation, and what should that "platform" and "force of gravitation" be in relation to research? This chapter runs short of space for the discussion of questions like these. Instead I will accept Alvesson and Sköldberg's suggestions as a tool for consideration, by elaborating briefly on the four elements of reflexivity outlined above. Examples will be taken from imagined "typical" examples of ethnographically informed clinical research in music therapy, since I in Chapter 10 argued that this approach to research is essential for the development of culture-centered perspectives:

The process of collecting data is in many ways identical with the process of producing material for interpretation. These materials – such as musical recordings, field notes from therapy sessions, and interview transcriptions – will be the result of musical and/or verbal interactions with clients or other agents of the setting. The first task is to produce as rich materials as possible. A high degree of sensitivity of the researcher-as-instrument is thus asked for. It might be necessary to help the participants to develop richer statements, that is, richer texts for interpretation. In this the researcher's role as (co)actor becomes essential. As stated earlier, the *interpretation* starts already with the collection of data, with the construction of a text. Once, for instance, an interview is conducted, the transcription process starts. While Grounded Theory is based on the idea that "data speaks to the researcher," a hermeneutic stance would be to start asking questions, start a dialogue with the text.

A discussion of the *political/critical and rhetoric aspects* of the research is then necessary, and might illuminate problems and possible critique that need to be reflected more upon in a research project. We could start with the rhetoric problems. Already any choice of material to analyze is rhetoric. From the enormous amount of materials usually produced in an ethnographically inspired project, only a selection of samples and sequences are usually chosen for analysis. To choose fragments of materials like this is a little more complicated than to pick flowers when you want to talk about flowers. Reflecting upon the multiple functions of texts and materials, we can see that when selecting materials the researcher has the possibility to – consciously or unconsciously – select those that construct himself in a positive way. Consider, for instance, a music therapy researcher studying his own clinical work, choosing to analyze those improvisations where he sounds good, where he thinks he is emphatic, etc. In clinical research, then, there may be a double need for reflexivity, since researchers may have two roles to defend. They would like to present themselves as empathic and effective therapists and also as credible and reflective researchers (or, if more refined, they could construct their trustworthiness by presenting a human blend of failures and successes).

An integration of the four concerns and orientations outlined above – from concerns about the empirical material to concerns about interpretation and critique – Alvesson and Sköldberg (2000) call "reflexive interpretation." Again, their main message is the need to counteract any one of those orientations to totalize and "take over" the operations in the field. There are several levels of interpretation to deal with, from data-collection and analysis ("low-abstract" interpretations) to critical and self-critical interpretations that focus upon ideology and the selectivity of voices represented in the research text (Alvesson & Sköldberg, 2000, p. 238ff.).

A THIRD CULTURE?

The basic question of this chapter has been: If gaps between cultures of research exist, could they be bridged? If we go back to Snow's 1959 lecture, we may note that four years later he published an essay called "The Two Cultures: A Second Look."[8] Snow then suggested that a *third culture* could emerge and close the communications gap between scientists and literary intellectuals. In Snow's third culture the literary intellectuals would be on speaking terms with the scientists, to the benefit of both groups and society at large. It is an open question if this has been achieved to any significant degree in any society. Certainly the gap has not been closed yet. Some would say that it is increasing, while others would say that some bridges have been built. Some scientists have started to speak of themselves as *the* third culture. In a book with just that title, *The Third Culture,* John Brockman (1995) is arguing that *science* is emerging as the intellectual center of our society: There is no reason for the scientists to bother with the literary intellectuals, as Snow suggested. The scientists can speak directly to the educated public themselves, Brockman proposes. The readable and stimulating chapters of his book indeed proves that they can, but the attempt of totalizing the scientific perspective and silencing other voices may be less encouraging.

The polarized positions concerning qualitative and quantitative research in some milieus of music therapy are understandable if one considers the sociology of knowledge involved. When presenting an alternative to an established and powerful tradition many feel they need to polarize in order to be heard, or even in order to survive. Another question is how fruitful such a polarization is. I am not advocating that qualitative and quantitative research should be conducted after the same principles and judged after the same criteria. I may illuminate by giving a different but related example: The value of poetry is hardly dependent on whether T. S. Eliot in fact produced an empirically probable statement when he wrote "This is the way the world ends/Not with a bang but a whimper." Truth as correspondence is not the main issue in poetry (while it *may* at times play its part). Similarly one may advocate that quantitative and qualitative research are two different ways of getting to learn about the world, and that the criteria for evaluating qualitative research should be different from those used when evaluating quantitative research. As I have tried to show above, to accept this does not imply that one needs to insist on a dichotomy between an empiricist and interpretive perspective.

An alternative would be to accept some division of labor between humanist scholars and scientists, between qualitative and quantitative researchers. In a way we have to acknowledge this division. Qualitative researchers are not going to help us much with the development of new medicines. Quantitative trials of these medicines will reveal little about client experiences. Etc. To "let the others to their own thing" will still not be a satisfactory solution for the two cultures of music therapy researchers. As Nerheim (1995) has demonstrated in a philosophical discussion of the field of medicine and health work in general, there are aspects of this field that need to be explored through nomothetic research and other aspects that are idiographic and cultural. At the same time, there is a general hermeneutic problem in *all* research, with the element of double or multiple hermeneutics added when the subjectivity of the agents involved is of interest. This suggests that the two cultures need to deal with each other. Maybe a third culture can never be achieved fully, but it could still function as a regulative idea. A direction of development is given, however, if scholars of the two cultures start communicating and learning from each other.

To work in the direction of a third culture of music therapy research would mean to be concerned with going beyond the discussion of quantitative versus qualitative perspectives. Both traditions of research have something to offer. Analysis of quantifiable data versus interpretation of meanings is not all there is. What also matters is the role research plays in society in relation to the field of study. One will therefore necessarily need to go beyond the idea of peaceful coexistence, and approach the issue of social critique. While quantitative research may be especially important for convincing employers and policy makers, qualitative research may be especially helpful for contributing to clinical colleagues' understanding of music therapy processes. There is also a third type of audience that researchers should be concerned about: the clients themselves, the users of the music therapy services. Participatory action researchers argue that these people are so important that they should not just be treated as audience for research efforts; they should in fact be co-researchers. While this recommendation is not always applicable, it could serve as a reminder about clinical researchers' obligations concerning the people they study.

Based on personal and convincing clinical experiences, most music therapies argue that the beauty and power of music and the arts is captivating. Nevertheless, music therapy is often neglected by health authorities and funding agencies. No wonder researchers try to better understand the processes of music therapy and to show that music works! Problems of power and oppression exist, though, in the midst of music therapy practices and other supposedly nice activities, and it is hard to defend the suggestion that this should *not* have any influence on our research practices. The issue of research as social critique, or the relationship between research and social change, therefore earns a central position on the agenda when music therapy research is to be discussed. The issue of social critique is inevitably linked to ethics, values, and notions of what constitutes quality of life in decent communities and societies. In conclusion this therefore illuminates the links that exist between clinical work, research, theory, and metatheory. As the researcher interacts with empirical material, multiple interpretive possibilities are dealt with. In choosing among these, a theory is developed through a process where metatheoretical assumptions are taken into consideration. This may lead to problematization of dominant theory and stimulation of alternative views (Alvesson & Sköldberg, 2000, p. 253). A constant interplay between empirical material, interpretive repertoire, and available critical metatheory is therefore an essential strategy for the development of theories of music therapy to a more refined level.

NOTES

[1] This argument is related to the early language philosophy of Ludwig Wittgenstein, discussed in Chapter 2. In *Tractatus,* Wittgenstein (1921/1961) proposed that the meaning of a sentence is its correspondence with the facts of the world. A sentence, to be meaningful, has a logical structure that is in *correspondence* with the logical structure of the actual state of affairs in the world.

[2] A frequently used example to illuminate this point is the following: Consider the statement "All swans are white." This statement could easily be verified by observations in northern countries, where swans generally are white. What difference does it make, though, for the truth-status of this statement, to verify it one thousand times? One single observation of a black swan in Australia could falsify the statement. Sound scientific practice, Popper argued, should search for examples that possibly could falsify statements.

[3] Postpositivist empirical scientists are generally unassuming in stating that they have found the truth; "this is the most solid knowledge available today" would be a more typical statement than "this is the truth."

[4] Saugstad's (1998) argument is not that there is no qualitative or interpretive research in psychology, only that this is a marginal stream compared to the dominating tradition of mainstream psychological research.

[5] The establishment of Nordic music therapy in the 1970s must be seen in this light. An academic climate was developed that did not make an adoption of a quantitative paradigm of research the only or most logical option. When the first Nordic doctoral theses in music therapy were written (Lehtonen, 1986; Ruud, 1987/1990), qualitative and interpretive approaches to research were considered legitimate and not viewed as controversial. This situation differs from that of the American pioneers of qualitative music therapy research in the 1980s, which is a reminder about the relationship between research, society, and culture.

[6] Cf. the discussion of the concept of health in Chapter 7.

[7] While methodological rigor and refinement of tools for analysis are central criteria

for evaluation of quantitative research, this tradition may have something to learn from qualitative researchers' awareness about problems of interpretation, not least in research on humans and health (Nerheim, 1995).

[8] This essay was added to the second publication (in 1963) of Snow's (1959/1998) Rede lecture.

EPILOGUE

The meaning of a cultural form and its place or position in
the cultural field is not inscribed inside its form. Nor is
its position fixed once and forever. This year's radical symbol
or slogan will be neutralized into next year's fashion; the year
after it will be the object of a profound cultural nostalgia.
(Stuart Hall)

I have focused upon the implications for music therapy suggested by a culture-centered perspective. This perspective is not denying the biological, personal, and social aspects of human life, but is focusing upon how these aspects must be understood culturally. Culture is then not considered an epiphenomenon but an integrated part of our personal and social life. The musical, intrapersonal, and interpersonal processes of music therapy are therefore also cultural. As we have seen, outcomes of music therapy not only could relate to the development of individuals and groups, but also to milieus, communities, and societies. Some readers therefore may choose to read this book as an argument for expansion of the territory of music therapy practice and discourse. Although I think the territory of music therapy *will* increase in the years to come, my main intention has not been to provide a legitimization of that. It is rather more important to be sensitive to the fact that the territory not only is growing, it is changing, and it is changing rapidly. A self-critical awareness of the positive and negative roles played by music therapy in and as culture in a society is therefore to be preferred.

DRAPETOMANIA AND OTHER PECULIARITIES

In an 1851 article about "diseases and physical peculiarities of the Negro race," the Louisiana surgeon and American Medical Association member, Dr. Samuel A. Cartwright, suggested a new diagnostic category: "Drapetomania." The mental disease that he had in mind spread at an alarming tempo in the southern states of the United States at that time, and there were serious reasons for concern. The term chosen to denote this contagious disease was created by combining the Greek words *drapeto* (to flee) and *mania* (craze or obsession). Drapetomania thus was the mental disease that induced the Negro slave to run away from service. Cartwright argued that Drapetomania was as much a disease of the mind as any other species of mental alienation, and that it was a curable disease. It was of course essential to recapture run-away slaves so that the condition could be properly treated. Simple procedures, including corporal punishment, were then available for the cure of this disease (Wackerhausen, 1994).[1]

Commentaries of the twentieth and twenty-first centuries tend to give the disease of Drapetomania another name: the longing for freedom. To a contemporary reader the so-called peculiarities of "the Negro race" read more like peculiarities of Cartwright's mind. Cartwright's proposals could hardly be interpreted as idiosyncratic, though, they should rather be read in relation to their historical context. The processes of black emancipation in nineteenth-century America increased the pressure for medical justification of white supremacy (Littlewood & Dein, 2000). The diagnosis-category of Drapetomania is an illustrative example of how knowledge, values, and social power may be linked. In relation to this, Littlewood & Dein (2000) also discuss the input of another American doctor, Benjamin Rush, who proposed that African ancestry in itself was an attenuated disease, the black color being derived from leprosy. While Cartwright probably would have been a forgotten man today, if not for the infamous diagnosis he proposed, Rush is not just anybody in the American history of medicine. As a signer of the Declaration of Independence and dean of the Medical School at the University of Pennsylvania, he is also considered the "Father of American Psychiatry." His portrait adorns the official seal of the American Psychiatric Association.[2]

That Drapetomania was no disease is of course commonly accepted today. What the lesson learned from this example could be, is another question. Some suggest that this and similar cases show that the concepts that characterize psychopathology are social constructions that reflect cultural values, and that health services are services of social and political power.[3] In the light of the suggested cultural relativity of psychopathology, the depathologization of Drapetomania may then be considered an example of moral, rather than scientific, progress. Others argue that psychopathology results from malfunctions that can be described by terminology that is objective and scientific, and that the embarrassment of some previous claims on pathology is due to bad science. We know now that there is no flawed psychological mechanism underlying the desire to escape slavery, and the continuous revision of categories of classification in the history of medicine is no argument for relativism. It simply demonstrates scientific progress, the claim goes (Woolfolk, 1998).

The arguments outlined in this book, from the discussion of phylogeny and cultural history in Chapter 1 to the discussion of a possible third culture of research in Chapter 12, indicate that music therapy should be considered a complex endeavor that includes science and the hermeneutic quest for self-knowledge and understanding. It is not plausible that the problems clients suffer from could be considered either merely as social constructions *or* as objective and context-independent entities. Complex interactions of biological, psychological, social, and cultural processes are involved in the construction, shaping, and maintenance of such problems. While it is far beyond the scope of this epilogue to outline these complex interactions, it is relevant to address the issue of classification of pathology at this point.

It is commonly considered a sign of maturity of a therapeutic discipline if effects and processes may be specified, and future music therapists will to an increasing degree experience that the general public as well as colleagues and health authorities expect them to be able to specify the efficiency and relevance of their approach in relation to client populations. In order to be able to communicate with other professional health workers it may be absolutely necessary, then, to use diagnostic systems. Music therapists working in a cultural perspective or in any other perspective can therefore not overlook the information given in international systems of categorization, such as ICD-10 and DSM-IV. There is a difference between using the diagnoses of these systems as pragmatic tools in professional communication and treating them as transparent names of real world entities, however. I will therefore briefly elaborate on some possible problems inherent in these systems of categorization, through a critical consideration of their relevance and their cultural and social function. I will do this by referring briefly to some recent debates in the field of psychiatry as examples.

A starting point could be Thomas Szasz's discussion of the *Myth of Mental Illness* (Szasz, 1961/1974). He advocated that mental illness or disease is a metaphor only. While the word *disease* denotes a demonstrable biological process that affects the bodies of living organisms, the terms *mental illness* or *mental disease* refer to the undesirable thoughts, feelings, and behaviors of *responsible persons*. Szasz argued that to classify thoughts, feelings, and behaviors as diseases is a logical and semantic error, like classifying the whale as a fish. Partly in line with Szasz's arguments, the 1960s and 1970s fostered a strong antipsychiatry movement, with inputs from radical authors such as David Cooper and Ronnie Laing. The arguments of Szasz and allies, while important in raising awareness about the problem of medicalization of everyday social problems, may suffer from the Western tendency of separating mind and body. Contemporary theorists argue that this dualism limits our understanding of human life, and that the definition of pathology as social and cultural deviancy is as much reductionism as any categorization that biomedicine has ever been capable of producing. It is obvious, then, that some of the most radical suggestions of the 1960s and 1970s were, if not too radical, too one-sided.

A clear case in point is the debate on the etiology of schizophrenia. An exclusively cultural and political understanding of schizophrenia, as advocated by Gregory Bateson and the British antipsychiatrists of the 1960s, seems hard to maintain today. Taking the existing body of knowledge into consideration, biological vulnerability and predisposition is impossible to ignore even for the most culturally inclined clinician (Littlewood & Dein, 2000). While most scholars today accept the biological component in, for instance, schizophrenia, this does not reduce the problem of culture, politics and values in relation to diagnoses. It is important to note that "more biology" does not necessarily mean "less culture" in the description of factors that may lead to a disorder and/or personal distress. On the contrary; there will often be a logical connection between biological vulnerability and vulnerability for malevolent social and cultural factors.

In the two most common classification systems internationally today, ICD-10 and DSM-IV, the term "mental disease" is not used, but the more open term "mental disorder." "Disorder" is not an exact term, but both classification systems, with some differences in wording, utilize it to imply the existence of a set of symptoms or behaviors that are associated with personal distress and/or disability, disability then defined as impairment in one or more important areas of *functioning*. In ICD-10 (p. 5) it is underlined that social deviance or conflict alone, without personal dysfunction, should not be considered a mental disorder. In DSM-IV (p. xxi) it is stressed that the syndrome or pattern should not be merely an expectable and culturally sanctioned response to a particular event, for example, the death of a loved one.[4]

Disorders, then, are feelings, thoughts, and behaviors that are not culturally sanctioned. They are thus not absolute, but relative to the culture and community of the person, which makes ethnic and cultural considerations necessary. DSM-IV deals with this by providing an outline for cultural formulation in the diagnostic process and by offering a glossary of culture-bound syndromes, with amok and koro as two of the more famous examples.[5] In ICD-10 (p. 16) it is argued that the need for a separate category for such disorders has been expressed less often in recent years, and that the literature on these disorders suggests that they may be regarded as local variants of anxiety, depression, somatoform disorder, or adjustment disorder. Thinking it over, we see that things may be a little bit more complex than what is suggested in the ICD-10 text. How could we understand suffering and dysfunction without a context? The only possibility would be to "naturalize" and reify disorders and treat them like independent entities, which makes them look very much like diseases. This is one of the reasons why critics of ICD-10 and DSM-IV suggest that these systems of classifications support a biomedical perspective on psychiatry, although they are supposed to be "theory free."

Are Western health workers disposed to think of diagnostic categories as culture- and value-free, because they themselves are "fish in the water" where the diagnostic systems were developed?[6] Why is anorexia nervosa, which is mainly found in the Occidental world, not defined as a culture-bound disorder, while koro in ICD-10 is defined as a local variant of neurotic disorders? When ICD-10 claims to give us the main categories of mental disorders, as universal categories of which local variants can be subsumed, is this just a new example of "the west against the rest" (Littlewood & Dein, 2000)?[7] A radical criticism might suggest that all categories of disorder should be locally defined, and that all disorders are culture-bound. Since humans share a common phylogeny, it is more plausible to suggest that shared biological vulnerabilities exist worldwide. There are reasons to believe that some disorders do exist worldwide, albeit in several variants depending on culture and context. The problem with any international system of categorization would then be that one of these variants is constituted as the "real" or primary version.

The above relates to the suggestions made in Part IV of this book, where the relevance of an ethnographic approach to music therapy research is advocated. This is not to say that more conventional quantitative research looking for tendencies at group levels is not relevant and important. In evaluating a clinical case one needs information from different sources; from the idiographic study of this particular client in context, from what can be learned of possible preceding analogous cases, and from probabilities suggested by quantitative and nomothetic research. One of the main challenges for the future development of music therapy theory will be to integrate such sources of knowledge.

CULTURAL SENSITIVITY

In this text I have argued that "humans are cultural beings," and that they are so to a degree that makes the phrase a pleonasm; to say "humans" should suffice. This premise provides us with metatheoretical assumptions with implications for music therapy practice, theory, and research[8].

The argument I have developed is by no means meant to be a comprehensive presentation of a cultural perspective to music therapy. Theoretical problems and implications *not* dealt with in the previous chapters are legion. For instance, population-specific implications have hardly been touched upon, except in the previous paragraphs of this Epilogue. In this respect, the text has been more concerned with metatheoretical problems and discipline-specific theory than with specific clinical theory. The caveats given above concerning the existing systems of diagnoses imply a critical examination of these systems, but we also need to move beyond assumptive polarities such as "all clients are the same" or "all clients are different." In some respects we are all the same, in others we are all different, but there are also patterns of problems and possibilities shared by groups of people. The fact that the definition of clinical populations may not be made in any culture- or value-free language should not stop music therapists from trying to grapple with such patterns. It is, for instance, quite possible that the factors of the music therapy process discussed in Chapter 8 will have to be specified differently with different populations. This is one of the reasons why a multi-disciplinary perspective on music therapy is so important. Music therapists may learn from – preferably also contribute to – the discussions and developments in related disciplines as to which populations need which approaches to therapy.

It is more than probable that the benefits of music therapy lie in part in the components that different forms of psychotherapy share: an emotionally charged interpersonal relationship, a healing setting, a rationale, and a ritual that requires active participation by both client and therapist (Frank, 1989). These components are probably present in most areas of music therapy, not only in those that are usually categorized as psychotherapeutic. This is no sufficient legitimization of music therapy, however. If it was, why should any health authority or funding agency bother with engaging music therapists? They generally make more noise and need more equipment than other therapists. If music therapists deserve their salary there must also be some factors that are *specific* for music therapy. Are these extra factors specific for music therapy but general for all populations, or are they also specific to some populations? To what degree could these specific questions be answered generally, or must they be answered relative to specific contexts? To what degree are these factors specific to specific approaches of music therapy? To what degree are they linked to the personality and qualifications of the therapist?

What I am trying to communicate is not only that there is a long way to go for music therapy clinical theory, but also that the field of study is so complex that cultural isolationism on behalf of music therapy is not warranted. As Thor of Norse mythology drank with a horn connected to the ocean, the theoretical and clinical problems of music therapy are connected to a multidisciplinary pool of problems, questions, and answers. The culture-specific and culture-centered challenges outlined in Chapter 1 and elaborated upon throughout the text are therefore also shared with other disciplines, even though some aspects may be specific for music therapy, for instance in the ways human protomusicality and the cultural history of musics merge in acts of musicking.

A culture-specific perspective sensitizes the music therapist to the cultural context of music therapy practice, which will bring an increased *pluralism in practice*. Future developments hopefully will present us with descriptions of this in urban as well as rural settings; northern, southern, eastern and western countries; traditional, modern, and postmodern cultures, etc.[9] The examples I have given have mostly been from my own cultural context. The ambition has not been to give these examples any authoritative or normative status, rather to illustrate how the theoretical ideas developed in this text may relate to the everyday reality of clinical practice. *Culture-centered music therapy* was in Chapter 1 described as awareness about music therapy *in* and *as* culture. I therefore stated that culture-centered music therapy is necessarily also culture-specific, and that what comes in addition is the willingness to rethink music therapy at a basic level, taking a notion of culture in relation to humankind into serious consideration. The notion developed in Chapter 1, which links culture to human nature, suggests plurality in practice but also represents a modest quest for *integrative theory*, linking biological, psychological, social, and cultural aspects of human life.

Implications have been outlined throughout this book, starting with discussions of metatheoretical perspectives on meaning as situated use and music as situated practice based on a shared human protomusicality. In Part III some theoretical implications were specifically discussed, such as proposals for culture-sensitive definitions of music therapy and a context-inclusive model of the music therapy process. Some shared themes were suggested, such as a relational concept of health, a focus upon learning in relationship, an understanding of music therapy as a ritual authorized by society, and an understanding of the mutuality between the immediacy of the experience of communitas and the mediating quality of cultural contexts. The metaphor of music therapy as "giving voice" and the notion of reflexivity both relate to this, by integrating the personal and the sociocultural level of experience. To be human must then be considered a continuous project of *becoming* human, through interpersonal communication and cultural learning. "He not busy being born is busy dying."

Consequences of taking a culture-centered perspective do exist not only in relation to discipline, clinical population, and cultural context. They also exist on a *personal level*. Music therapists do not work with populations, but with persons, albeit sometimes in a group or community perspective. While as persons we cannot but be cultural, the question is to what degree the therapist has developed *cultural sensitivity,* which I think is characterized by openness to the possibility that things may always be different. Or maybe it could be put this way: Cultural sensitivity is willingness to accept that what is taken for granted may be questioned. In order to acknowledge what is different one needs an understanding of what is similar. In Chapter 9 culturally informed empathy was discussed in relation to ethics, and I underlined that empathy may have different forms of expression in different cultures. If it is at all meaningful to talk about empathy across cultures there must be some shared human capacity for empathy, though, and the integrative aspect of the argument is again illuminated.

At times the therapist's ability to "go local" is very important, that is, the ability to relate competently to the client's culture. To be like the client is not necessarily necessary, however, as the concept of *polyphonic dialogue* outlined in Chapter 2 illuminates. Neither the therapist nor the client relate only to the local community they happen to live in. To an increasing degree individuals link their identities to aesthetic communities, that is, to virtual or real communities that share values, practices, and interests more than physical location. In this way culture is much more than a blueprint determining the values and customs of groups of people living in the same place, it is also webs of meaning in which persons position themselves. Cultural sensitivity therefore includes but goes beyond an individual level of empathy. What is requested is a flexible set of tools for communication and for interpretation of interpersonal relationships. This obviously requires emotional and cognitive flexibility at a personal level, and could be enhanced and developed in theoretically informed cultures of music therapy supported by inclusive cultures of research.

NOTES

[1] Most of the discussions of Drapetomania that I have seen "credit" Dr. Cartwright for having coined the term, but Littlewood & Dein (2000, p. 25) refer to an 1832 article by A. Brigham on the "influence of mental cultivation upon health."

[2] See for instance (Szasz, 1970/1997, pp. 137-159).

[3] The problems of power and misuse of science were especially clearly demonstrated in Soviet psychiatry under Stalin, where the label "schizophrenia" was convenient to use in order to have political dissidents locked away. The social and political function of health services of contemporary Western countries could hardly be compared to this. It is possible, though, to argue that health services in these countries are part of the authorities' strategy for disciplining the public, although the mechanisms are more sophisticated and harder to detect than those of Soviet psychiatry. The American psychiatrist Thomas Szasz (1970/1997, p. 138) argues for instance that the field of psychiatry has been ahistoric in its conceptions, especially in ignoring the history of its own traditions and errors, and that the discipline today represents a serious problem in society by endorsing medicalization of everyday problems.

[4] In DSM-IV other caveats are also taken. The term "mental disorder" is admitted to be "a reductionistic anachronism," since it implies a distinction between "mental" and "physical" disorders, while there is much "physical" in "mental" disorders and

vice versa.

[5] Amok is an acute, murderous frenzy, by some considered a culture-specific syndrome particular of certain Malaysian groups. Koro is a culture-specific disorder found among Southeast Asian males, the primary symptom being a fear that the penis will retract into the abdomen and cause death.

[6] The panel that created ICD-10 had international representatives from all continents, so the legitimacy of this question is based upon an argued dominance of Western values in contemporary science.

[7] The geographical specifications given above are of course not absolute, but used to illuminate the argument. One may find women with anorexia nervosa in Nairobi and men with koro in San Francisco, to give two alternative examples (since anorexia nervosa seems to be linked to modern ways of living found in countries all over the world and since Southeast Asian cultural groups are well established in San Fransisco and other Western cities).

[8] In closing I again want to draw attention to the value of sensitizing concepts (see Chapter 1). While specific definitions are important for scholarly discourse, in everyday life and in clinical practice the specifics of definitions guide our actions only to a limited degree. Sensitizing concepts may at times be more important, by suggesting *ways to look* rather than describing in detail what to see. In many respects culture may work as a sensitizing concept, and as such promote the development of new practices and sensitive adjustments of established practices. In this way a mutual influence of theory, research, and practice may be established, and the canon of music therapy models would continuously be challenged. Culture as a sensitizing concept may guide practicing music therapists and help them see in new directions and listen in new ways, and thus to develop new practices. One example, linking to the opening of this book could be: When Knut asked "May we too play in the brass band?" Even Ruud's sociologically inspired definition of music therapy sensitized the music therapists to the importance of this question, and thus helped us to keep searching for an answer, while *not* giving the specific answer. That answer had to be found locally.

[9] An avenue for these kinds of dialogue within the broad field of music therapy was established in 2001 with the free, international electronic journal *Voices: A World Forum for Music Therapy,* www.voices.no.

GLOSSARY

A glossary in a book like this is not simply a collection of definitions; to some degree it is a statement of perspective. It must also be noted that some of the terms listed below belong to traditions within the humanities that treat concepts as sensitizing rather than categorical, so that they could *not* be given very specific or short definitions. In these cases I will briefly illuminate aspects of the origin of the term and also my use of it in this text.

A few references to literature have been included for some terms, so that readers may follow up on differences that do exist in interpretations and uses of the term. Cross-references within the glossary are marked with < in front of the term referred to.

Acculturation: This term is used somewhat differently in different contexts, but it usually describes *lessening of cultural distance.* Often the term refers to the process where a person or group adopts the cultural traits and social rules of another group, but the process may also be more reciprocal. Acculturation may take several routes and be related to processes such as immigration, where the immigrants may acculturate to their new contexts, or emulation, where one (usually dominated) group takes on features from another group. These processes may mix and interact in many complex ways, especially in modern multicultural societies where persons may belong to several different groups. See <enculturation.

Action: In some contexts this term is used synonymously with behavior, while in the context of cultural theory it more often refers to acts that one consciously wills, usually to pursue goals and to realize values. In this perspective the term action is closely linked to terms such as intention and reflection.

Action research: Sometimes used very broadly, to denote all kinds of research aimed at informing or improving practice. Another usage of the term, relevant to a culture-centered perspective, focuses upon the researcher's social responsibility in relation to the participants of a particular community or context. Three dimensions are then usually in focus: a) action research is more than research on practice, it is research *for* social change, b) *participatory* influence is a key value, and c) *empowerment* of the participants is a major goal of the research process. To distinguish from the broader usage, the term *participatory action research* is sometimes used to denote situated research advocating the primacy of the voices and goals of the participants themselves.

Activity theory: A theory based on the pioneering <cultural-historical psychology of Vygotsky and other Russian psychologists of the early twentieth century. Contemporary Activity Theory is concerned with cultural and contextual foundations of

human development, focusing upon the interplay and reciprocal influence between individual <actions and culturally organized activities. The entity of study is the individual in context, but the individual is not seen as a product of context. Instead the focus is upon the transactional character of the relationship between the individual and the milieu.

Adaptation: A term in evolutionary theory denoting a biological trait that in the phylogeny of a species promoted survival or reproduction in a particular way. Two main mechanisms have been proposed: natural selection and sexual selection. There is no agreement yet as to whether music is an adaptation or not. Focusing upon natural selection Pinker (1997) suggests that music is not; focusing upon sexual selection Miller (2001) suggests that music in fact meets the criteria set by evolutionary theory for defining an adaptation.

Aesthetics: In philosophy often treated as a branch of axiology; the field of value theory (ethics being another important branch). Aesthetics developed as a philosophic subdivision since the eighteenth century, and traditionally deals with issues related to art; such as beauty and value, structure and texture, narrative and meaning, and may also include the study of the "nature," the perception, and the judgment of these issues. The archaic meaning of the Greek word *aisthetikos* is "of sense perception," and some contemporary theories underline the importance of bodily experience, sensation, and perception in relation to aesthetics. Culturally oriented critics have commented

upon the tendency within aesthetic theory to essentialize the nature of art (to treat it as <universal, timeless, etc.), and suggest that this is a construction of <ideology and that aesthetic discourses always are historical and situated, cf. the arguments developed in Chapter 2 related to Wittgenstein's (1953/1967) philosophy. Other contemporary contributions include the argument that perception and judgment of art has a biological, and therefore <universal, basis (Dissanayake, 1992/1995, 2000b). As art and aesthetic experience and judgment are multifaceted phenomena these perspectives are, by this author, not considered as incompatible.

Affordance: In the ecological psychology of James J. Gibson (1979/ 1986) affordance refers to the "invitational" quality of a milieu, percept, or event. Affordance is relative to the properties of a milieu, object, or event *and* to the individual in question. The notion therefore describes a relationship, not an essence. After Gibson launched the notion in relation to visual perception it has been given a broader usage in the psychology and sociology of experience, and it is in this book applied for description of the relational character of the basic components of the music therapy process.

Agency: In the context of social and cultural theory, agency refers to the capacity of human individuals and groups to influence history; that is, to act and to promote changes in their lives and the conditions of their lives. Cultural psychologists advocate that human agency is constituted through internalization and creative use of cultural artifacts in social contexts, and often enhanced through conjunction.

Anthropology: The systematic study of human beings. The discipline is commonly divided into several subfields, such as archeology, biological anthropology, and social and cultural anthropology. Linguistics is also sometimes subsumed under (cultural) anthropology. The study of human beings may focus upon human evolution and the homogeneity of human nature, or upon human cultures and as such upon human diversity. Integrative attempts do exist, and have increased in strength.

Artifact: An important concept in cultural psychology. Artifacts are the products of cultural processes, and both physical objects and meaning systems such as languages and musics are understood as artifacts. Artifacts are passed down from generation to generation, often with novel enhancements made to them. Modifications are made, individually or collaboratively. Over time therefore artifacts evolve in complexity, form and/or functionality. Children grow up in the midst of culturally constituted artifacts and traditions, and may use these as tools for their own development. The child benefits from the accumulated knowledge of the group.

Communitas: A term proposed in the 1970s by social anthropologist Victor Turner, to denote interpersonal relationships that are direct, non-differentiated, and existential. The word is Latin (for community, friendship), and the term is inspired by Martin Buber's (1923/1992) concept of I-Thou. According to Turner, communitas characterizes the middle (liminal) and most important phase of rites de passage. Even Ruud (1992, 1995, 1998) has proposed that improvisation in music therapy may produce liminal experiences, and that communitas is an important concept for the understanding of human relationships in music therapy.

Community: Traditionally conceived of as a social group whose members live in a specific locality. In social and cultural theory communities have often been considered vital for human well-being, as they represent opportunities for direct and directly responsible relationships. The value of community has then been seen in relation to society at large. Modern societies, for instance, have sometimes been understood as characterized by individualism and fragmentized relationships. Communities have then been understood as vehicles for human agency in relation to authorities and centers of power. In a less political vein the value of community has been seen in relation to human biological need for coexistence, for "being-with." As societies change, possibilities for community change. In contemporary information societies, for instance, virtual communities build up through the use of the Internet. These communities represent no shared locality, less mutuality, and usually very little of the direct and directly responsible relationships referred to above, and it is therefore disputable to what degree these communities are comparable to traditional communities. Such communities – breaching with a specific locality – are of high relevance, however, for contemporary cultural theory, as they open up for diversity within one locality, and for integration of the local and the global.

Community music therapy: Music therapy practices that are linked to the local communities in which clients live and therapists work, and/or to communities of interest. Basically two main notions of community music therapy exist: a) music therapy *in* a community <context, and b) music therapy *for change in* a community. Both notions require that the therapist be sensitive to social and cultural contexts, but the latter notion to a more radical degree departs from conventional modern notions of therapy in that goals and interventions relate directly to the community in question. Music therapy, then, may be considered cultural and social engagement and may function as community action; the community is not only a context for work but also a context to be worked with. Both variants of community music therapy suggest the relevance of project-oriented approaches in which sometimes the therapy process of several groups or individuals may belong to the same community music project. Projectoriented approaches usually require untraditional therapist roles and tasks (including project coordination, interdisciplinary consultation, and local political information and action). Community music therapy requires a broad spectrum of interdisciplinary theory in order to be well founded, and relevant models of research include <ethnography and <participatory action research (the latter being especially relevant for the

more radical definition of community music therapy). Community music therapy is necessarily <ecological, since individuals, groups, and communities function in and as systems.

Consultation-collaboration music therapy: A proposed approach to music therapy, mentioned in Chapters 4 and 5 and discussed briefly in Chapter 8 in relation to the role of the music therapist. Consultation-collaboration music therapy would be concerned with the overall functioning of a care system supporting a client. A care system, as used here, could include didactic, medical, and psychotherapeutic components as well as nonprofessional resources such as family, neighborhood, and cultural activities in a community. The music therapist could have the role as coordinator and consultant, or could contribute as a node in a system coordinated by other professionals.

Context: While being a major concept in theories about <culture and meaning, the meaning of the term context often remains rather vague. Different traditions of use may be identified. As Cole (1996) illuminates, context is often conceived of as the situation or structure *surrounding* (in time and/or space) an event, phenomenon, or text, but it may also be understood as the link *connecting* events, phenomena, or texts (this latter meaning is essential for the hypertext discussion in Chapter 6). The relationships between events/phenomena/texts and contexts are also conceived in different ways; sometimes the context is understood as given and "static" (coloring the

events, phenomena, and texts), other times the relationships are conceived of as more reciprocal constitutive.

Critical Theory: The term critical theory sometimes refers to German nineteenth-century idealism based on Kant's three critiques, other times to all kinds of nonconformist contemporary theory, but often – and in this text – the term is used to denote the approach to social thought developed by the so-called Frankfurt School since the late 1920s, with pioneers such as Max Horkheimer, Walter Benjamin, and Theodor W. Adorno, and with Jürgen Habermas as the most important contemporary figure. Critical Theory may be seen as a revision and criticism of Marxism, with important influences from humanist thinking and psychoanalysis. Critical Theorists emphasize the interplay between social conditions and individual <agency, and the social responsibility of scholars is stressed. The advocates of Critical Theory suggest that theory should go beyond being descriptive and explanatory; it should also be normative, practical, and self-reflexive. Emancipation and empowerment of individuals and groups in social contexts is a main objective. Knowledge is considered linked to power and to social and material conditions. It is consequently advocated that the social researcher needs to take an active political stand.

Cultural psychology: The contemporary field of cultural psychology is concerned with the biological, psychological, and social foundations of cultural communities as well as with the cultural foundations of mind.

Cultural psychology therefore is concerned with how culture and mind make up each other, over the history of groups, <communities, and societies, and over the life course of the individual. See <cultural-historical psychology.

Cultural-historical psychology: a) The school of Russian pioneers of cultural psychology, among whom Lev Vygotsky usually is considered to be the most prominent scholar, b) A subfield of contemporary cultural psychology. Inspired by Marxist social theory, cultural-historical psychology is especially concerned with the historicity of human societies and the importance this has for the psychological development of individuals. See <cultural psychology.

Culture: A term of almost endless application, usually referring to processes and products that are initiated by groups of human beings, as opposed to processes and products of <nature. While this distinction may work in everyday discourse, it is not unproblematic. The term "nature" is in itself cultural and informed by specific worldviews, humans are themselves part of nature, and various interactions between nature and culture occur. Problems in delineation increase in view of the fact that the term culture also is used in a variety of ways. The argument in this book is that despite the conceptual difficulties outlined above, culture is an indispensable term in research, theory, and practice on human interaction. Problems of definition may be countered by acknowledging the value of <sensitizing concepts and by providing more precise definitions when rele-

vant in specific contexts. The definition given in the context of this book on culture-centered music therapy is: "Culture is the accumulation of <customs and technologies enabling and regulating human coexistence."

Custom: Established pattern of behavior and belief. See <culture.

Ecology: The notion of ecology has an etymology that goes back to a Greek word, namely *oikos*, which means household. As a scientific concept, ecological analyses were originally developed in biological science, as a tool for description of relationships between organisms and environments. The term has been extended for usage within psychology, both due to the pioneering work of Kurt Lewin who discussed the factors that contributed to a person's life space, and due to a general increase in interest for sociosystemic perspectives.

Ecological Music Therapy: As used by Bruscia (1998a), the term denotes music therapy practices based on the notion that individuals, groups, and communities function in and as systems. Ecological music therapy implies that goals and interventions are focused upon more than one system; they are centered on the fostering of health-promoting relationships between systems.

Emic and etic: These terms distinguish between the understanding of culture as experienced by a native (emic perspective) and an outside observer (etic perspective). The terms were coined by Kenneth Pike in the 1950s, by an analogy with the linguistic terms "phonemic" and "phonetic" (an analogy which is not obvious or clear, according to some critics). While the value of outsider (etic) description was taken for granted by the pioneers of anthropology, and usually not considered problematic, several twentieth-century critics advocated that the terms "objective" and "Western" had been confused. In many research milieus, then, emic description became the ideal to pursuit. If one accepts that pre-understanding is a prerequisite for understanding, see <hermeneutics, this ideal must be considered rather illusory, even when the researcher actively tries to experience another belief system as potentially valid. An alternative strategy that has gained strength is to engage in some kind of emic-etic dialectics in a dialogical search for understanding and meaning. A research requirement is then <reflexivity in attempts of achieving clarity of voice in how emic and etic perspectives are presented in the research report.

Enculturation: Usually understood as the process of learning the rules, customs, and values of one's own culture. As such it may be seen as corresponding, at the level of culture, to the process of <socialization. See also <acculturation.

Ethnography: Ethnography is a tradition of social research, and may be understood as a scholarly approach to the study and learning about the culture of a person or – more frequently – a group of people.

Ethology: (also called behavioral biology). A branch of evolutionary biology focusing upon the study of behavior in animals (including humans). Ethology is based upon the assumption that behavior, like anatomy and physiology, has evolved in phylogeny as adaptations to the habitat. See <evolutionary psychology, and <sociobiology.

Etic: See <emic and etic.

Evolution (biological): Descent with cumulative genetic adaptation of organisms or species to environmental conditions. The main mechanisms in operation, the so-called evolutionary forces, include the production or introduction of new genetic material (mutation and migration), the selection of types best adapted to the environment (natural selection and sexual selection), and various more accidental effects, such as genetic drift (random fluctuation of the frequencies of genes in a population).

Evolutionary psychology: An approach to psychology focusing upon the biological origins of cognitive psychological mechanisms. Evolutionary psychology may be considered a development of and a criticism of <sociobiology. A key tenet in evolutionary psychology is that the mind is not a general-purpose "computer," as has been assumed by some cognitive psychologists, but rather an intricate network of "functionally specialized computers." These interconnected "computers," often called *modules*, have evolved as <adaptations in the evolution of the human species, and are assumed to impose structure on human mental organiza-

tion as well as on culture. See <ethology.

Family resemblance: A term used by Ludwig Wittgenstein in his later philosophical work (1953/1967). He argued that there is no essence, no one thing common, to all the phenomena that we call language. Language is a set of games (see <language game) that are too various to be given one common definition. There are common features between *groups* of games, but no common features of all games, he argued. Wittgenstein's arguments have proved to be helpful in distinguishing between classical categories, in which there are clear criteria for membership, and family resemblance categories in which members have no shared single trait, but where subgroups share traits. In addition to games, tools (such as instruments) and furniture may be considered typical examples of this. See also <vagueness. Music may be a family resemblance category; there may be no or very little essence shared by all musics. If this is so, music (and music therapy) could be seen as a set of games with common features between groups of games but with few essential features. This then should suggest skepticism toward general theories of music therapy and stimulate the acknowledgement of <local knowledge.

Gene-culture co-evolution: The term refers to the hypothesis that there was a co-evolution of culture and genes in the phylogeny of the human species. Brains increased to make learning of culture possible. This enabled development of more complex culture, which created selective pressure for larger brains. In the next "round" this enabled learning of even more complex culture, with subsequent selection pressures, and so on.

Hermeneutics: Originally the art and science of interpreting texts, especially connected to the disciplines of theology and law. In the nineteenth century Dilthey and others developed hermeneutics as a research method for the humanities (in comparison to and partly in opposition to the methods of natural science). In the literature on research methodology hermeneutics is therefore sometimes treated as one of several interpretative research methods. The perspective on hermeneutics used in this book is closer to the more radical tradition of philosophical hermeneutics developed by Heidegger and Gadamer (1969/1999) in the twentieth century, in which hermeneutics is seen as the process of understanding the existential conditions of other human beings. Understood in this way hermeneutics is a basic discipline to all research on human culture and on health-care services such as music therapy.

Hypertextuality: The original Greek meaning of the word *text* is "web," but conventional texts to a large degree have been characterized by a predefined linearity (by having a beginning, middle, and end, by demanding a unidirectional way of reading, etc.) In this respect *hypertexts* – as series of text chunks or nodes that are connected by links – may represent an explicit alternative by offering possibilities for interactivity and multidirectional reading.

The idea of producing nonlinear texts is not new, but has become increasingly important, as computer technology has opened up new possibilities for realizing such an idea. In this book hypertextuality is used as a metaphor for the multimedia multidimensional character of meaning-making in music therapy, seen in relation to a proposed inescapability of narrative and discourse in human interaction and experience. The metaphor, as used here, is therefore informed by literary theory and inspired by Bakhtinian notions such as intertextuality, dialogic imagination, and polyvocal text.

Ideology: In some contexts the term may denote the body of myth, symbol, or doctrine of a group or class of people. In <Critical Theory (the Frankfurt School) the notion is developed from Marxian thinking and refers to *repressive trains of thought* that makes it possible for subordinates to accept their social position as "natural" or "inevitable." Ideology is produced as people in dominating roles and positions communicate that things are the way they are because that is necessary and normal. Ideology thus conceals the power relations involved. The ideas of the ruling people become the ruling ideas for most people.

Language game: A term used by Wittgenstein (1953/1967) to illustrate that meaning is not a function of some necessary logic but of social use. According to Wittgenstein meaning in language is dependent on actions and interactions in specific contexts and forms of life. Meaning is thus not given, but created through social use. I suggest that this is a relevant perspective for the study of the meaning of music in music therapy. Instead of developing general theories on the meaning of music in music therapy, music therapists could develop their skills of interpreting meaning in concrete contexts.

Local knowledge: In anthropology the term was brought to light by Clifford Geertz (1983), who advocated that ethnography is a craft of place, working by the light of local knowledge. Used in this way the term local knowledge highlights the <situatedness of human activities; they are located in a specific cultural context of space and time. The term local knowledge has gained relevance in relation to so-called postmodern sensitivities, in which <reflexivity and the confrontation of "grand narratives" by "local knowledge" are central characteristics.

Mediated Learning Experience (MLE): A term advocated by Reuven Feuerstein, and later appropriated by Pnina Klein and others. The notion is based on the social perspective on learning proposed by cultural psychologists (Vygotsky and others), and MLE has been defined as "a quality of interaction between the organism and its environment. This quality is ensured by the interposition of an initiated, intentional human being who mediates the stimuli impinging on the organism" (Feuerstein & Feuerstein, 1991). Feuerstein argues that mediated learning experiences can be described by twelve different parameters, four of them being critical and necessary (Klein, 1989): 1) Focusing (communicating inten-

tionality and reciprocity, 2) Affecting (mediating meaning), 3) Expanding (transcending or going beyond the immediate goals of the interaction), 4) Rewarding (mediating feelings of competence in the child).

Metatheory: Often defined merely as theory about <theory, or theory about theorizing. To understand how theory and metatheory interact it may be helpful to delineate three interrelated but distinguishable usages of the term: a) basic conscious and unconscious assumptions about humankind, knowledge, health, music, etc., b) broad and general theories, such as (post)positivism, critical theory, and feminism, that inform discipline specific theories, and c) specific theories from other disciplines that in certain contexts, historically and culturally, gain heuristic or corrective importance for discipline specific theories.

Musicality: At least three different usages of this term may be identified: a) In traditional music psychology (such as in Seashore's work) musicality has been defined as a special ability or talent for music which some people have and some have not, b) In contrast to the above, some anthropologist (such as Blacking) have defined musicality as a general human capacity for musical expression and experience, c) Partly inspired by the second meaning above, some researchers and scholars working with early mother-child interaction (such as Trevarthen and Dissanayake) have developed notions of respectively communicative musicality and protomusicality that refer to a biologically evolved human capacity for communication through sound.

Nature: May be considered as the material world as it exists independently of human activities. Nature is commonly considered, then, to be "everything that is not culture." As culture is a relative notion, the notion of nature may then also be considered as such. See <culture.

Ontogeny: A term from biology, denoting the development – or often the course of development – of an individual organism. According to the perspective taken in this book (informed by <cultural psychology) ontological development for humans depends on biological as well as environmental and cultural factors. Biological factors are shaped by shared human traits evolved in <phylogeny as well as by the specific genetic inheritance of the individual in question. Environmental and cultural factors include physical and social conditions, the cultural history of the group or community the individual belongs to, as well as the personal history (biography) of the individual.

Participatory action research: See <action research.

Phylogeny: A term from biology, denoting the <evolution of a species. Phylogeny is a biological process based on the continuous biological adaptation of a species to its environment. For the human species, a <gene-culture co-evolution hypothesis has been proposed by some researchers.

Polyphony: A term proposed by the Russian writer on literature and culture, Michael Bakhtin (1895-1975), referring to the value of open-ended and polysemic texts. Bakhtin borrowed the term from music theory, and also used it in combinations such as "polyphonic dialogues" and "polyvocal texts." Readings and interpretations of the novels of Dostoevsky were particularly important in Bakhtin's (1929/1984) development of the notion. In discussing the poetics of this prominent Russian author Bakhtin suggested that in order to value his novels one needs to understand their polyphonic character. From the viewpoint of the traditional monologic canon of the European novel, Dostoevsky's world may seem chaotic. His novels are not characterized by unity and completion, rather the construction of his novels could be seen as some sort of conglomerate of disparate materials with incompatible principles for shaping them. Dostoevsky's material is heterogeneous and multistyled and his world is a multivoiced world, Bakhtin advocated. The characters of Dostoevsky's novels are allowed to voice their own worldviews without being reduced to the unity of a single world and a single consciousness. This may be considered a philosophical and psychological characterization, but polyphony clearly also affected Dostoevsky's artistic style, which precedes what has later been termed "impure art," art that combines esoteric and banal, sublime and vulgar, tragic and trivial elements. Bakhtin's thesis is that *the affirmation of someone else's consciousness* is the major principle behind Dostoevsky's work. The voices of the characters create an open-ended polyphonic structure; all voices are important, even though they might be moving in different directions. In this book I propose that the notion of polyphony is of direct relevance for an understanding of aesthetics and interpersonal relationships in music therapy, in that affirmation of someone else's consciousness certainly should be compatible with the values underlying culture-centered music therapy.

Postcolonialism: A critical orientation to the sociology of knowledge, focusing upon the study of the <ideological and cultural impact of Western colonialism and its aftermaths (neocolonialism, globalization, etc.). The interest for postcolonial thinking was fueled by Edward Said's (1978/1995) seminal book *Orientalism*, which demonstrated how Western attitudes toward the East have been important in Western identity-building, through an active construction of the Orient as "the Others." That the values and perspectives of a person or group are colored by their own cultural context is of course inevitable and in itself not problematic. Problems arise when this is linked to political power and becomes integrated as ideology in oppressive practices. Postcolonialism represents a (multi)cultural critique of power that uses knowledge in order to advance itself. Constructive counterstrategies include the acknowledgement of hybridity and exploration of its potentials. Postcolonialism represents a challenge for all modern disciplines based on Western science and scholarship, and is specifically relevant for contemporary music

therapy as practices now are developing in all six continents.

Private language argument: An argument developed by Wittgenstein (1953/1967) in *Philosophical Investigations* to show that meaning systems *cannot* be private. There cannot be a completely private language, for instance. This is not to say that there is nothing like personal meaning, but since meaning in language is use of signs that have received their "life" from so-called <language games (situations of interactions with other people), even personal meaning in language is always related to culture and context. In the private language argument, Wittgenstein illuminates the idea that our grasp of our inner life is dependent on the existence of outer criteria. This suggests that our psychological reality is dialogical.

Reflexivity: The ability to think of oneself in relation to others, which for humans is enhanced greatly by the operation of signs belonging to cultural systems. Some social theorists (see for instance Beck, Giddens & Lash, 1994) have proposed that reflexivity is an increasingly important human capacity in late modernity. Reflexivity is a complex term that also has gained importance in the discussion of qualitative research methodology. Reflexivity, then, describes the relationship between the knower and the field or phenomenon studied. It is proposed that what is known about a phenomenon, person, or culture is greatly influenced by the circumstances in which this is known, including the subject-position of the researcher. If the researcher is part of the context that is studied, this of course influences the results produced. This takes on the character of a hermeneutic circle, since the results – or more precisely, the researcher's understanding of them – also influence how the investigator acts and reacts in the field. A reflexive methodology (Alvesson & Sköldberg, 2000) takes these processes into consideration, and goes beyond the investigator's scrutiny of personal context and preunderstanding to include scrutiny of the *techniques of collecting data* as well as of the *interpretive, critical,* and *rhetoric* aspects of the research process, from the first planning through the fieldwork to the final reporting of the research.

Ritual: Structured and formalized patterns or modes of behavior, regulating the interaction of a group or community. Rituals were first studied (mainly by anthropologists) in magic and religious contexts, but almost any group has its rituals regulating the roles and behaviors of its members. In studying the rituals of health practices such as music therapy one may learn about the values, narratives, and rationales shared and cultivated by the group. Members of a group rarely are in equal power to preserve or change a ritual.

Sensitizing concepts: See <vagueness.

Situatedness: A term used in some scholarly discourses to denote that human activities (thinking, learning, communicating, musicking, etc.) could not be described in abstract or general; they are located in space and time, that is, in a specific cultural-historical context. Scholars using the term usually have a cultural psychology conception of the relationships between agent, activity, and world (viewing them more or less as mutually constitutive) and therefore also suggest that meanings of the activity are negotiated and relational to context.

Socialization: The process that enables a person (especially a child, although a life span perspective is also relevant) to understand and relate to the values and social norms of a group, community, or society. Socialization may be seen in relation to <enculturation, and is essential for an individual's sense of self and identity. Social institutions – such as schools, health clinics, and mass media – play an active role in the process of socialization, but the individual is usually not reduced to a passive recipient. Various forms of <agency and resistance do come into operation.

Sociobiology: A term coined by Edward O. Wilson (1975/2000) to denote the study of the biological foundations of social behavior. See <ethology, and <evolutionary psychology.

Species: The major subdivision of a genus and a basic category of biological classification. A species is a class of related individuals that resemble each other and are able to mate with each other and produce fertile offspring. Humans comprise a single species.

Systems theory: A system is a complex whole of interdependent variables in dynamic interaction. The term *systems theory* is sometimes used to designate one specific theory, sometimes to any theory about systems. In sociology, for instance, system theory was considered one of the dominating paradigms in the 1950s and 1960s, and often used to designate the theory of Talcott Parsons (1902-1979). Parsons's theory is sometimes called functionalism (function is what keeps a system together). More generally systems theories have developed as a cross-disciplinary focus upon the interconnectedness of systems. See <ecology.

Theory: In a multifaceted discipline like music therapy, at least two conceptions of theory are of relevance: a) In the sciences theory is usually considered a body of consistent statements in correspondence with the facts of the world, that is, a body of propositions conveying relatively stable and certain knowledge (see <universal); b) In contrast to this, theory about cultural and historical phenomena must be conceived as <situated, it develops out of particular personal and sociohistorical <contexts and reflects the norms, assumptions, and values of these contexts. This illuminates how theory is related to <metatheory. See also <reflexivity.

Thick description: A style of ethnographic writing in which there is a close integration of description and interpretation. This is achieved through careful attention to *detail and context*. The term was made popular by social anthropologist Clifford Geertz in the 1970s. The example he used when introducing the concept was taken from Gilbert Ryle: "Consider ... two boys rapidly contracting the eyelids of their right eyes. In one, this is an involuntary twitch; in the other, a conspirational signal to a friend" (Geertz, 1973/1993, p. 6ff.). The example illuminates that attention to detail is not enough when meaning is the focus of study. It is not sufficient to gather data through descriptions of what is seen or heard by the researcher; contexts and possible meanings must also be captured. In the example given above an endless series of complexities is possible: A boy could be contracting his eyelids as a parody of one of the other boys. Before doing this he could be contracting his eyelids as a rehearsal to the parody, etc. To give a thick description, then, is to try to capture as many as possible and relevant of these possible meanings, as a basis for the process of guessing meanings and assessing the guesses. For music therapists this may suggest that analysis and interpretation of music as heard is insufficient. The meaning of music cannot be understood if isolated from the <context or <language game it is a part of.

Universal: Capacities and traits typical of human beings across times and cultures. Universality suggests that the capacity or trait in question belongs to human nature, and as such is evolutionary rather than cultural in origin. Several complexities have been involved in developing theories about universal capacities and traits, for instance due to the possibility that dominating cultures may advocate predominant phenomena in their own culture as expressions of universal traits. See <culture, <nature, and <postcolonialism.

Vagueness: The meaning of a term is considered vague when the range of applicability is unclear or changing over time. Everyday words denoting concrete phenomena may be vague, such as the term "baldness" (how much hair must be missing before the term applies?). Science has traditionally dealt with the problem of vagueness through operational definition; through specifying quantifiable or observable conditions for the application of a term. This strategy is not always helpful for an understanding of cultural phenomena, such as music and language, as these terms are necessarily vague due to their <situatedness in a diversity of social and historical contexts.

Zone of Proximal Development (ZPD): A term coined by Russian cultural psychologist Lev Vygotsky, who distinguished between a child's actual developmental level (mental functions established as a result of already completed developmental cycles), and the potential developmental level (his ability to perform under the guidance of an adult). Vygotsky defined ZPD as the distance between the actual development level as determined by independent problem solving and the level of potential development as determined through problem solving under adult guidance or in collaboration with more capable peers (Vygotsky, 1978, p. 88). This notion may be generalized to any process of learning (not only children's learning); the learner learns in interaction with more mature or experienced learners. See also <Mediated Learning Experience (MLE).

REFERENCES

A note to the reader: Some Scandinavian names include the letters Æ/æ, Ø/ø, or Å/å. In the list these vowels are placed in accordance with the Norwegian alphabet, that is, after the letter Z/z. Aa/aa is treated as double a, and not as Å/å.

Aasgaard, Trygve (1999). "Music Therapy as a Milieu in the Hospice and Pediatric Oncology Ward." In: Aldridge, David: *Music Therapy in Palliative Care. New Voices.* London: Jessica Kingsley Publishers.

Aasgaard, Trygve (2000). " 'A Suspiciously Cheerful Lady.' A Study of a Song's Life in the Paediatric Oncology Ward, and Beyond...." *British Journal of Music Therapy,* Vol. 14, No. 2, 70-82.

Abbott, Andrew (1988). *The System of Professions. An Essay on the Division of Expert Labor.* Chicago: University of Chicago Press.

Adelman, Clem (1997). "Action Research: The Problem of Participation." In: McTaggart, Robin (ed.) *Participatory Action Research. International Contexts and Consequences.* Albany: State University of New York Press.

Adelman, Howard S. (1995). "Clinical Psychology: Beyond Psychopathology and Clinical Interventions." *Clinical Psychology,* Vol. 2, nr. 1.

Aigen, Kenneth (1995a). "An Aesthetic Foundation of Clinical Theory: An Underlying Basis of Creative Music Therapy." In: Kenny, Carolyn (ed). *Listening, Playing, Creating: Essays on the Power of Sound.* Albany: State University of New York Press.

Aigen, Kenneth (1995b). "Principles of Qualitative Research." In: Wheeler, Barbara (ed.). *Music Therapy Research. Quantitative and Qualitative Perspectives.* Phoenixville, PA: Barcelona Publishers.

Akombo, David Otieno (2000). "Reporting on Music Therapy in Kenya." *Nordic Journal of Music Therapy,* 9(1).

Aldridge, David (1996). *Music Therapy Research and Practice in Medicine. From Out of the Silence.* London: Jessica Kingsley Publishers.

Aldridge, David (1998). *Suicide. The Tragedy of Hopelessness.* London: Jessica Kingsley Publishers.

Aldridge, David (2000). *Spirituality, Healing and Medicine. Return to the Silence.* London: Jessica Kingsley Publishers.

Altrichter, Herbert & Peter Gstettner (1997). "Action Research: A Closed Chapter in the History of German Social Science?" In: McTaggart, Robin (ed.). *Participatory Action Research. International Contexts and Consequences.* Albany: State University of New York Press.

Alvesson, Mats & Kaj Sköldberg (1994). *Tolkning och reflektion. Vetenskapsfilosofi och kvalitativ metod* [Interpretation and Reflection. Philosophy of Science and Qualitative Methods]. Lund, Sweden: Studentlitteratur.

Alvesson, Mats & Kaj Sköldberg (2000). *Reflexive Methodology: New Vistas for Qualitative Research.* London: Sage Publications.

American Psychiatric Association (1995). *Diagnostical and Statistic Manual of Mental Disorders.* Fourth edition (DSM-IV). International Version with ICD-10 Codes. APA, Washington DC.

Amir, Dorit (1992). Awakening and Expanding the Self: Meaningful Moments in Music Therapy Process as Experienced and Described by Music Therapists and Music Therapy Clients. New York: Unpublished Doctoral Dissertation, New York University.

Amir, Dorit (1993). "Research in Music Therapy: Quantitative or Qualitative." *Nordic Journal of Music Therapy,* 2(2).

Amir, Dorit (2001). "Layers of Meaning." Dorit Amir interviewed by Brynjulf Stige. *Nordic Journal of Music Therapy,* 10(2).

Ansdell, Gary (1995). *Music for Life. Aspects of Creative Music Therapy with Adult Clients.* London: Jessica Kingsley Publishers.

Ansdell, Gary (1997). "Musical Elaborations. What has the New Musicology to Say to Music Therapy?" *British Journal of Music Therapy,* 11(2): 36-44.

Ansdell, Gary (1999). Music Therapy as Discourse & Discipline. A Study of 'Music Therapist's Dilemma.' London: Doctoral thesis, City University, Department of Music.

Ansdell, Gary (2001). "Musicology: Misunderstood Guest at the Music Therapy Feast?" In: Aldridge, David, Gianluigi DiFranco, Even Ruud & Tony Wigram. *Music Therapy in Europe.* Rome: Ismez.

Ansdell, Gary (2002). Community Music Therapy and the Winds of Change – A Discussion Paper. In: Kenny, Carolyn B. & Brynjulf Stige (eds.) (2002). *Contemporary* Voices *of Music Therapy: Communication, Culture, and Community.* Oslo: Unipub forlag.

Antonovsky, Aaron (1987/1991). *Hälsans Mysterium* [Unraveling the Mystery of Health: How People Manage Stress and Stay Well]. San Francisco: Jossey-Bass Publishers.

Austern, Linda Phyllis (2000). " 'No Pill's Gonna Cure my Ill': Gender, Erotic Melancholy and Traditions of Musical Healing in the Modern West." In: Gouk, Penelope (ed.). *Musical Healing in Cultural Contexts.* Aldershot, UK: Ashgate Publishing Company.

Bakhtin, Mikhail (1929/1984). *Problems of Dostoevsky's Poetics.* Minneapolis: University of Minnesota Press.

Bakhtin, Mikhail (1996). *Speech Genres & Other Late Essays.* Austin: University of Texas Press.

Barker, Andrew (1984). *Greek Musical Writings: I. The Musician and His Art.* Cambridge, UK: Cambridge University Press.

Barkow, Jerome H., Leda Cosmides & John Tooby (1992). *The Adapted Mind. Evolutionary Psychology and the Generation of Culture.* New York: Oxford University Press.

Baron-Cohen, Simon (1995). *Mindblindness. An Essay on Autism and Theory of Mind.* Cambridge, MA: A Bradford Book, The MIT Press.

Bateson, Gregory (1972). *Steps to an Ecology of Mind.* Chicago: Chicago University Press.

Bateson, Gregory (1980). *Mind and Nature: A Necessary Unity.* Toronto: Bantam Books.

Beck, Ulrich, Anthony Giddens & Scott Lash (1994). *Reflexive Modernization. Politics, Tradition and Aesthetics in the Modern Social Order.* Cambridge, UK: Polity Press.

Bender, Michael, Paulette Bauckham & Andrew Norris (1997). *The Therapeutic Purposes of Reminiscence.* Thousand Oaks, CA: Sage Publications.

Benestad, Finn (1976). *Musikk og tanke. Hovedretninger i musikkestetikkens historie fra antikken til vår egen tid* [Music and Thought. The Main Traditions in the History of Music Aesthetics since Antiquity.] Oslo: Aschehoug.

Berger, Peter & Thomas Luckman (1966). *The Social Construction of Reality. A Treatise in the Sociology of Knowledge.* London: Penguin Books.

Berkaak, Odd Are (1993). *Erfaringer fra risikosonen: opplevelse og stilutvikling i rock* [Experiences from the Zone of Risks: Experience and Development of Style in Rock]. Oslo: Universitetsforlaget.

Bernstein, Richard J. (1983). *Beyond Objectivism and Relativism. Science, Hermeneutics, and Praxis.* Philadelphia: University of Pennsylvania Press.

Blacking, John (1973). *How Musical Is Man?* Seattle: University of Washington Press.

Blacking, John (1990). "Music in Childrens's Cognitive and Affective Development: Problems Posed by Ethnomusicological Research." In: Wilson, Frank R. & Frantz K. Roehmann (eds.). *Music and Child Development.* St. Louis, MO: Magna-Music Baton.

Bonde, Lars Ole (1999). "Metaphor and Metaphoric Imagery in Music Therapy Theory: A Discussion of a Basic Theoretical Problem – with Clinical Material from GIM Sessions." *Paper at the 9th World Congress of Music Therapy.* Washington, DC.

Boyce-Tillman, June (2000). *Constructing Musical Healing. The Wounds that Sing.* London: Jessica Kingsley Publishers.

Bright, Ruth (1993). "Cultural Aspects of Music in Therapy." In: Heal, Margaret & Tony Wigram (eds.): *Music Therapy in Health and Education.* London: Jessica Kingsley Publishers.

Brockman, John (1995). *The Third Culture.* New York: Touchstone.

Bronfenbrenner, Urie (1979). *The Ecology of Human Development. Experiments by Nature and Design.* Cambridge, MA: Harvard University Press.

Brown, Julie (2001). "Towards a Culturally Centered Music Therapy Practice." *Canadian Journal of Music Therapy,* Vol VIII, no.1 (Fall 2001), pp. 11-24.

Brown, Steven, Björn Merker & Nils L. Wallin (2000). "An Introduction to Evolutionary Musicology." In: Wallin, Nils L., Björn Merker & Steven Brown (eds.). *The Origins of Music.* Cambridge, MA: The MIT Press.

Bruner, Jerome (1990). *Acts of Meaning.* Cambridge, MA: Harvard University Press.

Bruscia, Kenneth (1987). *Improvisational Models of Music Therapy.* Springfield, IL: Charles C. Thomas Publisher.

Bruscia, Kenneth (1989). *Defining Music Therapy.* Spring City, PA: Spring House Books.

Bruscia, Kenneth (1995a). "The Boundaries of Music Therapy Research." In: Wheeler, Barbara L. (ed.). *Music Therapy Research. Quantitative and Qualitative Perspectives.* Gilsum, NH: Barcelona Publishers.

Bruscia, Kenneth (1995b). "Topics. Phenomena, and Purposes in Qualitative Research." In: Wheeler, Barbara L. (ed.). *Music Therapy Research. Quantitative and Qualitative Perspectives.* Gilsum, NH: Barcelona Publishers.

Bruscia, Kenneth (1995c). "The Process of Doing Qualitative Research: Part I: Introduction." In: Wheeler, Barbara L. (ed.). *Music Therapy Research. Quantitative and Qualitative Perspectives.* Gilsum, NH: Barcelona Publishers.

Bruscia, Kenneth (1995d). "The Process of Doing Qualitative Research: Part II: Procedural Steps." In: Wheeler, Barbara L. (ed.). *Music Therapy Research. Quantitative and Qualitative Perspectives.* Gilsum, NH: Barcelona Publishers.

Bruscia, Kenneth (1995e). "The Process of Doing Qualitative Research: Part III: The Human Side." In: Wheeler, Barbara L. (ed.). *Music Therapy Research. Quantitative and Qualitative Perspectives.* Gilsum, NH: Barcelona Publishers.

Bruscia, Kenneth (1996). "Authenticity Issues in Qualitative Music Therapy Research." In: Langenberg, Mechtild, Kenneth Aigen & Jörg Frommer (eds.). *Qualitative Research in Music Therapy. Beginning Dialogues.* Gilsum, NH: Barcelona Publishers.

Bruscia, Kenneth (1998a). *Defining Music Therapy,* second edition. Gilsum, NH: Barcelona Publishers.

Bruscia, Kenneth (1998b). "Techniques for Uncovering and Working with Countertransference." In: Bruscia, Kenneth (ed.). *The Dynamics of Music Psychotherapy.* Gilsum, NH: Barcelona Publishers.

Bruscia, Kenneth (1998c). "Standards of Integrity for Qualitative Music Therapy Research." *Journal of Music Therapy,* XXXV (3), 176-200.

Bruscia, Kenneth (2000). "The Nature of Meaning in Music Therapy." Kenneth Bruscia interviewed by Brynjulf Stige. *Nordic Journal of music Therapy,* 9(2).

Buber, Martin (1923/1992). *Jeg og du* [I and Thou]. Oslo: Cappelen.

Bunt, Leslie (1994). *Music Therapy. An Art Beyond Words.* London: Routledge.

Byrkjedal, Ingunn (1992). "Musikkterapi ved klassemiljøutvikling [Music Therapy for Classroom Climate Development]." *Nordic Journal of Music Therapy,* 1(1).

Bø, Inge (1989). *Nettverk som pedagogisk ressurs* [Social Networks as Pedagogical Resource]. Oslo: Tano.

Cartwright, Samuel (1851). "Diseases and Peculiarities of the Negro Race." [online] Made accessible by *Africans in America.* Available from: www.pbs.org/wgbh/aia/part4/4h3106.html [accessed, 3 February 2001].

Cattaneo, Mariagnese (1994). "Addressing Culture and Values in the Training of Art Therapists." *Art Therapy. Journal of the American Art Therapy Association,* Vol. 11, No. 3.

Cavalli-Sforza, Luigi Luca (2001). *Genes, Peoples and Languages.* London: Penguin Books.

Christensen, Erik (2000). "Music Precedes Language. Comment on Grinde's Article." *Nordic Journal of Music Therapy,* 9(2).

Clamp, Alan (2001). *Evolutionary Psychology.* London: Hodder & Stoughton.

Clifford, James (1986). "Introduction: Partial Truths." In: Clifford, James & George E. Marcus. *Writing Culture. The Poetics and Politics of Ethnography.* Berkeley: University of California Press.

Clifford, James & George E. Marcus (1986). *Writing Culture. The Poetics and Politics of Ethnography.* Berkeley: University of California Press.

Cole, Michael (1996). *Cultural Psychology. A Once and Future Discipline.* Cambridge, MA: The Belknap Press of Harvard University Press.

Cole, Michael, Yrjö Engeström & Olga Vasquez (eds.) (1997). *Mind, Culture, and Activity. Seminal Papers from the Laboratory of Comparative Human Cognition.* Cambridge, MA: Cambridge University Press.

Collini, Stefan (1998). "Introduction". In: Snow, Charles P. (1959/1998). *The Two Cultures.* Cambridge, UK: Cambridge University Press.

Csikszentmihalyi, Mihaly (1990). *Flow. The Psychology of Optimal Experience.* New York: Harper Perennial.

Dalgard, Odd Steffen & Tom Sørensen (eds.) (1988). *Sosialt nettverk og psykisk helse* [Social Networks and Psychological Health]. Oslo: Tano.

Davis, William B., Kate E. Gfeller & Michael H. Thaut (1999). *An Introduction to Music Therapy. Theory and Practice* (second edition). Dubuque, IA: WCB/McGraw-Hill.

Darwin, Charles (1859/1962). *The Origin of Species.* New York: Collier Books.

Darwin, Charles (1871/1998). *The Descent of Man.* Amherst, NY: Prometheus Books.

Dawkins, Richard (1976). *The Selfish Gene.* Oxford: Oxford University Press.

DeNora, Tia (2000). *Music in Everyday Life.* Cambridge, UK: Cambridge University Press.

Denzin, Norman K. (1997). *Interpretive Etnography. Ethnographic Practices for the 21st Century.* Thousand Oaks, CA: Sage Publications.

Denzin, Norman K. & Yvonna S. Lincoln (eds.) (1998). *The Landscape of Qualitative Research. Theories and Issues.* Thousand Oaks, CA: Sage Publications.

Dewey, John (1934/1980). *Art as Experience.* New York: Perigee Books.

Diamond, Jared (1997/1998). *Guns, Germs and Steel. A Short History of Everybody for the Last 13000 years.* London: Vintage, Random House.

Dileo, Cheryl (2000). *Ethical Thinking in Music Therapy.* Cherry Hill, NJ: Jeffrey Books.

Dissanayake, Ellen (1992/1995). *Homo Aestheticus. Where Art Comes From and Why.* Seattle: University of Washington Press.

Dissanayake, Ellen (2000a). "Antecedents of the Temporal Arts in Early Mother-Infant Interaction." In: Wallin, Nils L., Björn Merker & Steven Brown (eds.). *The Origins of Music.* Cambridge, MA: The MIT Press.

Dissanayake, Ellen (2000b). *Art and Intimacy: How the Arts Began.* Seattle: University of Washington Press.

Dissanayake, Ellen (2001). "An Ethological View of Music and its Relevance to Music Therapy." *Nordic Journal of Music Therapy,* 10(2), pp. 159-175.

Dreier, Ole (1994). "Sundhedsbegreber i psykososial praksis [Concepts of Health in Psychosocial Practice]." In: Jensen, Uffe Juul & Peter Fuur Andersen (eds.). *Sundhedsbegreper i filosofi og praksis.* Århus, DK: Philosophia.

Dyndahl, Petter (1998). "IT-relatert musikkundervisning mellom moderne utopi og postmoderne ironi [IT-related Music Education Between Modern Utopia and Post-modern Irony]." In: Dyndahl, Petter (ed.): *IT og musikk.* Hamar, Norway: Høgskolen i Hedmark, Allmennlærerutdanningen, Rapport nr. 2, 1998.

Elliott, David J, (1995). *Music Matters. A New Philosophy of Music Education.* New York: Oxford University Press.

Eriksen, Thomas Hylland (1995). *Small Places, Large Issues. An Introduction to Social and Cultural Anthropology.* London: Pluto Press.

Estrella, Karen (2001). "Multicultural Approaches to Music Therapy Supervision." In: Forinash, Michele (ed.). *Music Therapy Supervision.* Gilsum, NH: Barcelona Publishers.

Feld, Steven (1994a). "Aesthetics as Iconicity of Style (uptown title); or, (downtown title) 'Lift-up-over Sounding': Getting into the Kaluli Groove." In: Keil, Charles and Steven Feld: *Music Grooves.* Chicago: The University of Chicago Press,

Feld, Steven (1994b). "From Schizophonia to Schismogenesis: On the Discourses and Commodification Practices of 'World Music' and 'World Beat.' " In: Keil, Charles & Steven Feld: *Music Grooves.* Chicago: The University of Chicago Press.

Feld, Steven (1996). "Pygmy POP. A Genealogy of Schizophonic Genesis." *Yearbook for Traditional Music,* Vol. XXVIII.

Feuerstein, Reuven & S. Feuerstein (1991). "Mediated Learning Experience: A Theoretical Review." In: Feuerstein, Reuven, Pnina Klein & Abraham Tannenbaum (eds.). *Mediated Learning Experience (MLE): Theoretical, Psychological and Learning Implications.* London: Freund Publishing House Ltd.

Fjelland, Ragnar & Eva Gjengedal (1990). *Sykepleie som vitenskap* [Nursing as Science]. Oslo: Gyldendal Norsk Forlag.

Forinash, Michele (2000). "I have to wait for the moment that I'm doing the music to figure out what the meaning is." Michele Forinash interviewed by Brynjulf Stige. *Nordic Journal of Music Therapy,* 9(1), pp. 74-82.

Fornäs, Johan (1995). *Cultural Theory & Late Modernity.* London: Sage Publications.

Forrest, Lucy C. (2000/2001). "Addressing Issues of Ethnicity and Identity in Palliative Care Through Music Therapy Practice." The *Australian Journal of Music Therapy,* Vol. 11. Republished [online] in *Voices: A World Forum for Music Therapy.* Available from: www.voices.no/mainissues/Voices1(2)Forrest. html [accessed, 1 March 2002].

Frank, Jerome D. (1982). "Therapeutic Components Shared by all Psychotherapies." In: Harvey, J. H. & M. M. Parks (eds.). The Master Lecture Series, Vol. I, *Psychotherapy Research and Behavior change* (pp. 5-37) Washington, DC: American Psychological Association.

Frank, Jerome D. (1989). "Non-specific aspects of treatment: the view of a psycho-therapist." In: Shepherd, M. & N. Sartorius (eds.). *Non-specific Aspects of Treatment*. Toronto, Canada: Hans Huber Publishers.

Frank, Jerome D. & Julia B. Frank (1991). *Persuasion & Healing. A Comparative Study of Psychotherapy*. Baltimore: The Johns Hopkins University Press.

Frayer, David W. & Chris Nicolay (2000). "Fossil Evidence for the Origin of Speech Sounds." In: Wallin, Nils L., Björn Merker & Steven Brown (eds.). *The Origins of Music*. Cambridge, MA: The MIT Press.

Frazer, James (1922/1996). *The Golden Bough. A Study in Magic and Religion* (abridged edition). London: Penguin Books.

Fredriksson, Gunnar (1993). *Wittgenstein*. Stockholm: Albert Bonniers Förlag.

Frith, Simon (1996). "Music and Identity." In: Hall, Stuart & Paul de Gay (eds). *Question of Cultural Identity*. London: Sage Publications.

Frohne-Hagemann, Isabelle (1998). "The 'Musical Life Panorama' (MLP). A Facilitating Method in the Field of Clinical and Sociocultural Music Therapy." *Nordic Journal of Music Therapy*, 7(2).

Frohne-Hagemann, Isabelle (2001). *Fenster zur Musiktherapie. Musik-therapie-theorie 1976-2001*. Wiesbaden, Germany: Reichert Verlag.

Gadamer, Hans-Georg (1960/1999). *Truth and Method*. New York: Continuum.

Gadamer, Hans-Georg (1993/1996). *The Enigma of Health. The Art of Healing in a Scientific Age*. Cambridge, UK: Polity Press.

Garred, Rudy (1996). "Musikkterapeutisk improvisasjon som 'møte' [Improvisational Music Therapy as 'Encounter']." *Nordic Journal of Music Therapy*, 5(2).

Garred, Rudy (2001). "The Ontology of Music in Music Therapy. – A Dialogical View" [online] *Voices, Vol.1* no.3. Available from: www.voices.no/ mainissues/mainissue1.html [accessed, 18 January 2002].

Gaston, E. Thayer (ed.) (1968). *Music in Therapy*. New York: Macmillan Publishing.

Gaston, E. Thayer (1968/1995). "Man and Music." In: Gaston, E. Thayer (ed.). *Music in Therapy*. New York: Macmillan Publishing. [Reprinted in *Nordic Journal of Music Therapy*, 4(2)]

Geertz, Clifford (1973/1993). *The Interpretation of Cultures*. London: Fontana Press.

Geertz, Clifford (1983). *Local Knowledge. Further Essays in Interpretive Anthropology*. New York: Basic Books.

Geertz, Clifford (1988/1997). *Works and Lives. The Anthropologist as Author*. Stanford, CA: Stanford University Press.

Gennep, Arnold van (1909/1999). *Rites de Passage. Overgangsriter*. Oslo, Norway: Pax.

Gibson, James J. (1979/1986). *The Ecological Approach to Visual Perception*. Hillsdale, NJ: Lawrence Erlbaum Associates, Publishers.

Giddens, Anthony (1986/1989). *The Constitution of Society: Outline of the Theory of Structuration*. Cambridge, UK: Cambridge University Press.

Giddens, Anthony (1991). *Modernity and Self-Identity: Self and Society in the Late Modern Age.* Cambridge, UK: Polity Press.

Giddens, Anthony (2001). *Sociology.* Oxford: Blackwell Publishers.

Gilhus, Ingvild Sælid (1999). "Forord [Foreword (to the Norwegian translation of van Gennep's *Rites de Passage*)]." Oslo: Pax Forlag.

Gouk, Penelope (ed.) (2000). *Musical Healing in Cultural Contexts.* Aldershot, UK: Ashgate Publishing Company.

Gourlay, Kenneth A. (1984). "The Non-Universality of Music and the Universality of Non-Music." *The World of Music,* 26(2): 25-39.

Greenwood, Davydd J. & Morten Levin (1998). *Introduction to Action Research. Social Research for Social Change.* Thousand Oaks, CA: Sage Publications.

Grimen, Harald (1992). "On Text and Human Action." In: Gilje, Nils (ed.). *Modernitet: differensiering og rasjonalisering* [Modernity: Differentiation and Rationalization]. Bergen, Norway: Ariadne Forlag.

Grinde, Bjørn (2000). "A Biological Perspective on Musical Appreciation." *Nordic Journal of Music Therapy,* 9(2).

Haaland, Øyvind (1991). "Om terapivirksomhet [On Therapy as Activity.]" In: Broch, Hedvig et al. (eds.). *Virksomhetsteorien. En innføring – og eksempler* [Activity Theory. An introduction – With Examples.] Oslo: Falken forlag.

Habermas, Jürgen (1968/1971). *Knowledge and Human Interests.* Boston: Beacon Press.

Habermas, Jürgen (1981/1987). *The Theory of Communicative Action.* Boston: Beacon Press.

Hagberg, Garry L. (1994). *Meaning and Interpretation: Wittgenstein, Henry James, and Literary Knowledge.* Ithaca, NY: Cornell University Press,

Hagberg, Garry L. (1995). *Art as Language. Wittgenstein, Meaning and Aesthetic Theory.* Ithaca, NY: Cornell University Press,

Hammer, Espen (1995). "Innledning [Introduction]." In: Kant, Immanuel (1790/1995). *Kritikk av dømmekraften.* Oslo: Pax Forlag.

Hammersley, Martyn & Paul Atkinson (1983/1987). *Feltmetodikk. Grunnlaget for feltarbeid og feltforsking* [Ethnography]. Oslo: Universitetsforlaget.

Hammersley, Martyn & Paul Atkinson (1983/1995). *Ethnography. Principles in Practice.* London: Routledge.

Handelman, Don (1982). "Reflexivity in Festival and Other Cultural Events." In: Douglas, Mary (ed.). *Essays on the Sociology of Perception.* London: Routledge and Kegan Paul.

Hastrup, Kirsten (1999). *Viljen til Viden. En humanistisk grundbog* [The Will for Knowledge. A Humanist Basic Text]. Copenhagen: Gyldendal.

Heidegger, Martin (1927/1962). *Being and Time.* San Francisco: Harper.

Hjort, Peter F. (1989). "Tanker om et forskingsprogram om forebyggende helsearbeid i Norge. En rapport til NAVF [Thoughts About a Research Program on Preventive Health Work in Norway]." Oslo: Statens institutt for folkehelse.

Horden, Peregrin (ed.) (2000). *Music as Medicine: The History of Music Therapy since Antiquity.* Aldershot, UK: Ashgate Publishing Limited.

Janzen, John M. (2000). "Theories of Music in African Ngoma Healing." In: Gouk, Penelope (ed.). *Musical Healing in Cultural Contexts*. Aldershot, UK: Ashgate.

Jennings, Sue (ed.) (1992). *Dramatherapy. Theory and Practice 2*. London: Routledge.

Jennings, Sue (ed.) (1997). *Dramatherapy. Theory and Practice 3*. London: Routledge.

Jensen, Uffe Juul (1994). "Sundhed, liv og filosofi [Health, Life, and Philosophy]." In: Jensen, Uffe Juul & Peter Fuur Andersen (eds.) *Sundhedsbegreber. Filosofi og praksis*. Århus, Denmark: Philosophia.

Jensen, Uffe Juul & Peter Fuur Andersen (eds.) (1994). *Sundhedsbegreber. Filosofi og praksis* [Concepts of Health. Philosophy and Practice]. Århus, Denmark: Philosophia.

Johannesen, Kjell S. (1994). "Philosophy, Art and Intransitive Understanding." In: Johannesen, Kjell S., Reidar Larsen & Knut Olav Åmås. *Wittgenstein and Norway*. Oslo: Solum forlag.

Jónsdóttir, Valgerður (2002). Musicking in Early Intervention. [online] *Voices: A World Forum for Music Therapy,* Vol.2(2) 2002. Available at: www.voices.no/mainissues/Voices2(2)jonsdottir.html [Accessed 25. Jun. 2002.]

Jungaberle, Henrik, Rolf Verres & Fletcher DuBois (2001). "New Steps in Musical Meaning – The Metaphoric Process as an Organizing Principle." *Nordic Journal of Music Therapy,* 10(1).

Kant, Immanuel (1790/1951). *The Critique of Judgment*. New York: Hafner.

Keil, Charles (1994a). "Motion and Feeling through Music." In: Keil, Charles & Steven Feld. *Music Grooves*. Chicago: The University of Chicago Press.

Keil, Charles (1994b). "Participatory Discrepancies and the Power of Music." In: Keil, Charles & Steven Feld. *Music Grooves*. Chicago: The University of Chicago Press.

Keil, Charles & Steven Feld (1994). *Music Grooves*. Chicago: The University of Chicago Press.

Kennair, Leif Edward Ottesen (1998). Evolutionary Psychology: An Emerging Integrative Perspective within the Science and Practice of Psychology. Bergen, Norway: Unpublished thesis (Hovedoppgave), Department of psychology.

Kennair, Leif Edward Ottesen (2000). "Developing Minds for Pathology and Musicality: The Role of Theory of Development of Personality and Pathology in Clinical Thinking Illustrated by the Effect of Taking an Evolutionary Perspective." *Nordic Journal of Music Therapy,* 9(1).

Kennair, Leif Edward Ottesen (2001). "Origins – Investigations into Biological Human Musical Nature." *Nordic Journal of Music Therapy,* 10(1).

Kenny, Carolyn B. (1982). *The Mythic Artery. The Magic of Music Therapy*. Atascadero, CA: Ridgeview Publishing Company.

Kenny, Carolyn B. (1985). "Music: A Whole Systems Approach." *Music Therapy,* 5(1), 3-11.

Kenny, Carolyn B. (1989). *The Field of Play. A Guide for the Theory and Practice of Music Therapy*. Atascadero, CA: Ridgeview Publishing Company.

Kenny, Carolyn B. (2002). "Keeping the World in Balance – Music Therapy in a Ritual Context." In: Kenny, Carolyn B. & Brynjulf Stige (eds.) (2002). *Contemporary* Voices *of Music Therapy: Communication, Culture, and Community.* Oslo: Unipub forlag.

Kenny, Carolyn B. & Brynjulf Stige (eds.) (2002). *Contemporary* Voices *of Music Therapy: Communication, Culture, and Community.* Oslo: Unipub forlag.

Kincheloe, Joe L. & Peter L. McLaren (1998). "Rethinking Critical Theory and Qualitative Research." In: Denzin, Norman K. & Yvonne S. Lincoln. *The Landscape of Qualitative Research. Theories and Issues.* Thousand Oaks, CA: Sage Publications.

Klausen, Arne Martin (1970). *Kultur – variasjon og sammenheng* [Culture – Variation and Continuity.] Oslo: Gyldendal Norsk Forlag.

Klein, Pnina (1989). *Formidlet læring* [Mediated Learning Experience]. Oslo: Universitetsforlaget.

Klein, Pnina (ed.) (2001). *Seeds of Hope. Twelve Years of Early Intervention in Africa.* Oslo: Unipub forlag.

Kleive, Mette and Brynjulf Stige (1988). *Med lengting, liv og song* [With Longing, Life, and Song.] Oslo: Samlaget.

Kristeva, Julia (1980). *Desire in Language. A Semiotic Approach to Literature and Art.* New York: Columbia University Press.

Kuhn, Thomas S. (1970). *The Structure of Scientific Revolutions* (second edition). Chicago: University of Chicago Press.

Kümmel, Werner Friedrich (1977). *Musik und Medizine: Ihre Wechselbeziehungen in Theorie und Praxis von 800 bis 1800* [Music and Medicine: Their Reciprocal Effect in Theory and Practice from 800 to 1800]. Freiburg and Münich: Karl Aber.

Kunej, Drago & Ivan Turk (2000). "New Perspectives on the Beginnings of Music: Archeological and Musicological Analysis of a Middle Paleolithic Bone 'Flute.' " In: Wallin, Nils L., Björn Merker & Steven Brown (eds.). *The Origins of Music.* Cambridge, MA: The MIT Press.

Kvale, Steinar (1996). *InterViews.* London: Sage Publications.

Langenberg, Mechtild, Kenneth Aigen & Jörg Frommer (eds.) (1996). *Qualitative Music Therapy Research. Beginning Dialogues.* Gilsum, NH: Barcelona Publishers.

Langer, Susanne K. (1948). *Philosophy in a New Key.* New York: Mentor Books.

Langer, Susanne K. (1953). *Feeling and Form. A Theory of Art.* New York: Charles Scribner's Sons.

Lave, Jean & Etienne Wenger (1991). *Situated Learning. Legitimate Peripheral Participation.* Cambridge, UK: Cambridge University Press.

Leakey, Richard (1994). *The Origin of Humankind.* New York: Basic Books.

Leakey, Richard & Roger Lewin (1993). *Origins Reconsidered. In Search of What Makes Us Human.* New York: Anchor Books.

Lecourt, Edith (1998). "The Role of Aesthetics in Countertransference: A Comparison of Active Versus Receptive Music Therapy." In: Bruscia, Kenneth E. (ed.): *The Dynamics of Music Psychotherapy.* Gilsum, NH: Barcelona Publishers.

Lee, Colin (1996). *Music at the Edge. The Music Therapy Experiences of a Musician with AIDS.* London: Routledge.

Lee, Colin (2000). "A Method of Analysing Improvisations in Music Therapy." *Journal of Music Therapy,* 37(2): 147-167.

Lehtonen, Kimmo (1996). Musiikki psyykkisen työskentelyn edistäjänä. (Doctoral Thesis). Turku, Finland: Annales Universitatis Turkuensis C:56.

Leontjew, Alexejev N. (1979). *Tätigkeit – Bewusstsein – Persönlichkeit.* Volk und Berlin: Wissen Volkseigener Verlag.

Lerner, Richard M. (1998). "Theories of Human Development: Contemporary Perspectives." In: Damon W. & R.M. Lerner (eds.). *Handbook of Child Psychology. Volume 1.* New York: John Wiley & Sons.

Lewin, Kurt (1946/1948). "Action Research and Minority Problems." In: Lewin, Kurt. *Resolving Social Conflicts. Selected papers on Group Dynamics.* New York: Harper & Brothers Publishers.

Lewith, George T. & David Aldridge (eds.) (1993). *Clinical Research Methodology for Complementary Therapies.* London: Hodder & Stoughton.

Lippe, Anna Louise von der (1988). "Perspektivbetraktninger på klinisk psykologisk forskning [Perspectives on Clinical Psychological Research]." *Tidsskrift for Norsk Psykologforening* [Journal of the Norwegian Psychological Association], Vol. 25, pp. 21-38.

Littlewood, Roland & Simon Dein (eds.) (2000). *Cultural Psychiatry & Medical Anthropology. An Introduction and Reader.* London: The Athlone Press.

Maranto, Cheryl Dileo (ed.) (1993). *Music Therapy. International Perspectives.* Pipersville, PA: Jeffrey Books.

May, Elizabeth (1983). *Musics of Many Cultures.* Berkeley: California University Press.

McLeod, John (1997). *Narrative and Psychotherapy.* London: Sage Publications.

McTaggart, Robin (ed.) (1997). *Participatory Action Research. International Contexts and Consequences.* Albany: State University of New York Press.

Merker, Björn (2000). "A New Theory of Music Origins. Comment on Grinde's Article." *Nordic Journal of Music Therapy,* 9(2).

Merriam, Alan P. (1964). *The Anthropology of Music.* Evanston, IL: Northwestern University Press.

Meyer, Leonard B. (1956). *Emotion and Meaning in Music.* Chicago: The University of Chicago Press.

Miller, Geoffrey (2000). "Evolution of Human Music through Sexual Selection." In: Wallin, Nils L., Björn Merker & Steven Brown (eds.). *The Origins of Music.* Cambridge, MA: The MIT Press.

Miller, Geoffrey (2001). *The Mating Mind. How Sexual Choice Shaped the Evolution of Human Nature.* London: Vintage, Random House.

Molino, Jean (2000). "Toward an Evolutionary Theory of Music and Language." In: Wallin, Nils L., Björn Merker & Steven Brown (eds.): *The Origins of Music.* Cambridge, MA: The MIT Press.

Monsen, Nina Karin (1987). Det elskende menneske. Om person og etikk [The Loving Human Being. About Personhood and Ethics]. Oslo: Cappelen.

Moreno, Joseph (1988). "The Music Therapist: Creative Arts Therapist and Contemporary Shaman." *The Arts in Psychotherapy,* 15(4), pp. 271-280.

Moreno, Joseph (1995). "Candomblé: Afro-Brazilian Ritual as Therapy." In: Kenny, Carolyn B. (ed.). *Listening, Playing Creating. Essays on the Power of Sound.* Albany: State University of New York Press.

Morris, Pam (1994). *The Bakhtin Reader. Selected Writings of Bakhtin, Medvevev, Voloshinov.* London: Arnold.

Morton-Cooper, Alison (2000). *Action Research in Health Care.* Oxford: Blackwell Science.

Mørstad, Erik (1998). "Jung og Picasso – Henderson og Pollock. Jungianismen som billedanalytisk verktøy [Jung and Picasso – Henderson and Pollock: Jungian Thought as Tool for the Analysis of Art]." *Kunst og Kultur,* Årg. 81, nr. 1

National Institutes of Health (1997/2001). "Minutes of the National Advisory Environmental Health Sciences Council, Feb 12-13, 2001/NIH Director's Panel on Clinical Research 1997 Report" [online]. *Department of Health and Human Services.* Available from: www.niehs.nih.gov/dert/council/2001/ feb2001.htm [accessed, March 27 2002].

Nerheim, Hjördis (1995). *Vitenskap og kommunikasjon. Paradigmer, modeller og kommunikative strategier i helsefagenes vitenskapsteori* [Science and Communication. Paradigms, Models and Strategies of Communication in the Health Disciplines' Theory of Science.] Oslo: Universitetsforlaget.

Nettl, Bruno (1983). "Ethnomusicology: Definitions, Directions, and Problems." In: May, Elizabeth (ed.). *Musics of Many Cultures.* Berkeley: California University Press.

Nettl, Bruno (2000). "An Ethnomusicologist Contemplates Universals in Musical Sound and Musical Culture." In: Wallin, Nils L., Björn Merker & Steven Brown (eds.). *The Origins of Music.* Cambridge, MA: The MIT Press.

Nielsen, Henrik Kaare (1996). *Æstetik, kultur & politik* [Aesthetics, Culture & Politics]. Århus, Denmark: Aarhus Universitetsforlag.

Nketia, J. H. Kwabena (1974). *The Music of Africa.* New York: Norton Company.

Nordoff, Paul & Clive Robbins (1971/1983). *Music Therapy in Special Education.* Saint Louis, MO: Magna-Music Baton.

Nordoff, Paul & Clive Robbins (1977). *Creative Music Therapy.* New York: John Day.

Orchard, Andy (1997). *Dictionary of Norse myth and Legend.* London: Cassell.

Pavlicevic, Mercédès (1997). *Music Therapy in Context.* London: Jessica Kingsley Publishers.

Pavlicevic, Mercédès (2001). "Music Therapy in South Africa: Compromise or Synthesis?" [online] *Voices: A World Forum for Music Therapy.* Available from: www.voices.no [accessed, 19 June 2001].

Pepper, Stephen C. (1942). *World Hypotheses.* Berkeley: University of California Press.

Pinker, Steven (1997). *How the Mind Works. The New Science of Language and Mind.* London: Penguin.

Popper, Karl R. (1959/1992). *The Logic of Scientific Discovery.* London: Routledge.

Priestley, Mary (1975/1985). *Music Therapy in Action.* St. Louis, MO: MagnaMusic Baton.

Ricoeur, Paul (1983/1984). *Time and Narrative, Volume I.* Chicago: Chicago University Press.

Ricoeur, Paul (1984/1985). *Time and Narrative, Volume II.* Chicago: Chicago University Press.

Ricoeur, Paul (1985/1988). *Time and Narrative, Volume III.* Chicago: Chicago University Press.

Ricoeur, Paul (1986/1991). *From Text to Action. Essays in Hermeneutics, II.* Evanston, Il: Northwestern University press.

Robbins, Clive (1998). "- It's so universal!" Clive Robbins interviewed by Brynjulf Stige. *Nordic Journal of Music Therapy,* 7(1).

Robbins, Clive & Carol Robbins (eds.) (1998). *Healing Heritage: Paul Nordoff Exploring the Tonal Language of Music.* Gilsum, NH: Barcelona Publishers.

Rolvsjord, Randi (1998). "Another Story about Edward." *Nordic Journal of Music Therapy,* 7(2).

Rolvsjord, Randi (2002). *Når musikken blir språk. Musikalsk kommunikasjon i musikkterapi – et dialektisk perspektiv* [When Music Becomes Language. Musical Communication in Music Therapy – A Dialectical Perspective]. Oslo: Unipub forlag.

Rustøen, Tone (1991). *Livskvalitet. En sykepleieutfordring.* Oslo: Gyldendal Norsk Forlag.

Ruud, Even (1981). *Hva er musikkterapi?* [What is Music Therapy?] Oslo: Gyldendal.

Ruud, Even (1987/1990). *Musikk som kommunikasjon og samhandling. Teoretiske perspektiv på musikkterapien.* [Music as Communication and Interaction. Theoretical Perspectives on Music Therapy.] Oslo: Solum.

Ruud, Even (1992). "Improvisasjon som liminal erfaring – om jazz og musikkterapi som overgangsritualer [Improvisation as Liminal Experience – On Jazz and Music Therapy as Rites de Passage]." In: Berkaak, Odd Are & Even Ruud. *Den påbegynte virkelighet. Studier i samtidskultur.* Oslo: Universitetsforlaget.

Ruud, Even (1995). "Jazz and Music Therapy as Modern 'Rites de Passage.' " In: Kenny, Carolyn (ed.). *Listening, Playing, Creating. Essays on the Power of Sound.* Albany: State University of New York Press.

Ruud, Even (1996). "Interpretation and Epistemology in Music Therapy: Dealing with Competing Claims of Knowledge." In: Langenberg, Mechtild, Kenneth Aigen & Jörg Frommer (eds.). *Qualitative Music Therapy Research. Beginning Dialogues.* Gilsum, NH: Barcelona Publishers.

Ruud, Even (1997). *Musikk og identitet* [Music and identity]. Oslo: Universitetsforlaget.

Ruud, Even (1998). *Music Therapy: Improvisation, Communication and Culture.* Gilsum, NH: Barcelona Publishers.

Ruud, Even (2000). " 'New Musicology', Music Education and Music Therapy" [online]. *Paper at the 13ᵗʰ Nordic Congress of Musicology, Århus, Denmark.* Available from: www.njmt.no [accessed, March 31 2002].

Ruud Nilsen, Venja (1996). "Musikk i fengsel og frihet [Music in Prison and Freedom]." *Nordic Journal of Music Therapy,* 5(2).

Rye, Henning (1993). *Tidlig hjelp til bedre samspill* [Early Intervention for Better Social Interaction.] Oslo: Universitetsforlaget.

Said, Edward (1978/1995). *Orientalism. Western Conceptions of the Orient.* London: Penguin Books.

Saugstad, Per (1998). Psykologiens historie – en innføring i moderne psykologi. [The History of Psychology – Introduction to Modern Psychology.] Oslo: Ad-Notam Gyldendal.

Schafer, Roy (1980). "Narration in the psychoanalytic dialogue." *Critical Inquiry.* Vol. 7, pp. 29-53.

Schjødt, Borrik & Thor Aage Egeland (1989). *Fra systemteori til familieterapi* [From Systems Theory to Family Therapy.] Oslo: Tano.

Schullian, Dorothy & Max Schoen (eds.) (1948). *Music and Medicine.* New York: Henry Schuman.

Scott, Derek B. (ed.). (2000). *Music, Culture, and Society. A Reader.* Oxford: Oxford University Press.

Sears, William (1968/1996). "Processes in Music Therapy." In: Gaston, E. Thayer (ed.): *Music in Therapy.* New York: Macmillan Publishing. [Reprinted in *Nordic Journal of Music Therapy,* 5(1), with an Introduction by Carolyn Kenny].

Sekeles, Chava (1996). "Music in the traditional healing rituals of Morocco." *Paper at the 8th World Congress of Music Therapy,* Hamburg, July 1996.

Skjervheim, Hans (1959/2000): *Objektivismen – og studiet av mennesket* [Objectivism and the Study of Man.] Oslo: Gyldendal Akademisk.

Skårderud, Finn (1984). *Farvel til institusjonen* [Taking Farewell with the Institutions.] Oslo: Gyldendal.

Small, Christopher (1987). *Music of the Common Tongue. Survival and Celebration in African American Music.* Hanover, NH: Wesleyan University Press.

Small, Christopher (1998). *Musicking. The Meanings of Performing and Listening.* Hanover, NH: Wesleyan University Press.

Smeijsters, Henk (1997). *Multiple Perspectives. A Guide to Qualitative Research in Music Therapy.* Gilsum, NH: Barcelona Publishers.

Smeijsters, Henk (1998). "Developing Concepts for a General Theory of Music Therapy. Music as Representation, Replicas, Semi-representation, Symbol, Metaphor, Semi-symbol, Iso-morphé, and Analogy." Paper at the 4th European Music Therapy Congress, Leuwen, Belgium. In: Aldridge (ed.). (1999). *Music Therapy Info, Vol. II, CD-Rom.*

Snow, Charles P. (1959/1998). *The Two Cultures.* Cambridge, UK: Cambridge University Press.

Sokal, Alan D. (1996a). "Transgressing the Boundaries: Toward a Transformative Hermeneutics of Quantum Gravity." [online] *Social Text #46/47* (spring/ summer 1996): 217-252. Available from: www.physics. nyu.edu/faculty/sokal/ transgress_v2/ transgress_v2_singlefile.html [accessed, February 6 2002].

Sokal, Alan D. (1996b). "A Physicist Experiments with Cultural Studies." [online] *Lingua Franca,* 6(4): 62-64. Available from: www.physics.nyu.edu/ faculty/sokal/lingua_franca_v4/lingua_franca_v4.html [accessed, 6 February 2002].

Spence, Donald P. (1982). "Narrative Truth and Theoretical Truth." P*sychoanalytic Quarterly.* LI.

Steier, Frederick (ed.) (1991). *Research and Reflexivity.* London: Sage Publications.

Stern, Daniel (1985/1998). *The Interpersonal World of the Infant, A View from Psychoanalysis and Development Psychology.* London: Karnac.

Stern, Daniel (1995). *The Motherhood Constellation. A Unified View of Parent-Infant Psychotherapy.* New York: Basic Books.

Stige, Brynjulf (1983). Ngoma, musirør og anna rør [Ngoma, Music, and Movement]. Unpublished thesis. Oslo: Østlandets musikkonservatorium.

Stige, Brynjulf (1992). "Prosjekt 'Aktiv musikk for alle' [The Project 'Music Activities for Everybody.']" *Musikkterapi,* no. 3-4/92.

Stige, Brynjulf (1993/1999). "Music Therapy as Cultural Engagement. Or: How to Change the World, if Only a Bit." In: Aldridge, David (ed). (1999). *Music Therapy Info, Vol. II,* CD-Rom.

Stige, Brynjulf (1995). *Samspel og relasjon. Perspektiv på ein inkluderande musikkpedagogikk* [Interaction and Relationship. Perspectives on Inclusive Music Education.] Oslo: Samlaget.

Stige, Brynjulf (1996). "Music, Music Therapy, and Health Promotion." In: *Report. International UNESCO-conference, Oslo, September 1995.* Oslo: The Norwegian National Commission for UNESCO.

Stige, Brynjulf (1998). "Qualitative Research Interviews as a Part of the Music Therapy Process." *Musiikkiterapia* (Finnish Journal of Music Therapy), 1998 (2).

Stige, Brynjulf (1999). "The Meaning of Music – From the Client's Perspective." In: Wigram, Tony & Jos DeBacker (eds.). *Clinical Applications of Music Therapy in Psychiatry.* London: Jessica Kingsley Publishers.

Stige, Brynjulf (2001). "The Fostering of Not-knowing Barefoot Supervisors." In: Forinash, Michele (ed.). *Music Therapy Supervision.* Gilsum, NH: Barcelona Publishers.

Stortingsmelding nr. 52 (1973-74). Ny kulturpolitikk [New Policy of Culture, White Paper to the Norwegian Parliament.].

Streeter, Elaine (1999). "Finding a Balance between Psychological Thinking and Musical Awareness in Music Therapy Theory – A Psychoanalytic Perspective." *British Journal of Music Therapy,* 13, 5-20.

Summer, Lisa & Joseph Summer (1996). *Music: The New Age Elixir.* Amherst, NY: Prometheus Books.

Szasz, Thomas (1961/1974). *The Myth of Mental Illness. Foundations of a Theory of Personal Conduct.* Revised Edition. New York: Harper & Row, Publishers.

Szasz, Thomas (1970/1997). *The Manufacture of Madness. A Comparative Study of the Inquisition & the Mental Health Movement.* Syracuse, NY: Syracuse University Press.

Taylor, Charles (1985). "Language and human nature." In: Taylor, Charles. *Human Agency and Language. Philosophical Papers 1.* Cambridge, UK: Cambridge University Press.

Tomasello, Michael (1999). *The Cultural Origins of Human Cognition.* Cambridge, MA: Harvard University Press.

Tooby, John & Leda Cosmides (1992). "The Psychological Foundations of Culture." In: Barkow, Jerome H., Leda Cosmides & John Tooby (eds.). *The Adapted Mind. Evolutionary Psychology and the Generation of Culture.* New York: Oxford University Press.

Trehub, Sandra (2000). "Human Processing Predispositions and Musical Universals." In: Wallin, Nils L., Björn Merker & Steven Brown (eds.). *The Origins of Music.* Cambridge, MA: The MIT Press.

Trevarthen, Colwyn (1988). "Infants Trying to Talk: How a Child Invites Communication from the Human World." In: Söderbergh, Ragnhild (ed.). *Children's Creative Communication.* Lund, Sweden: Lund University Press.

Trevarthen, Colwyn (1995). "The Child's Need to Learn a Culture." *Children and Society,* 9(1), pp. 5-19.

Trevarthen, Colwyn (1997). "Music and Infant Interaction." Colwyn Trevarthen interviewed by Brynjulf Stige. *Nordic Journal of Music Therapy,* 6(1).

Trevarthen, Colwyn & Stephen Malloch (2000). "The Dance of Wellbeing: Defining the Musical Therapeutic Effect." *Nordic Journal of Music Therapy,* 9(2).

Troppozada, Manal R. (1995). "Multicultural Training for Music Therapists: An Examination of Current Issues Based on a National Survey of Professional Music Therapists." *Journal of Music Therapy,* 32(2), pp. 65-90.

Turkle, Sherry (1995/1997). *Life on the Screen. Identity in the Age of the Internet.* New York: Touchstone.

Turner, Victor W. (1967a). "Betwixt and Between. The Liminal Period in Rites de Passage." In: *The Forest of Symbols: Aspects of Ndembu Ritual.* Ithaca, NY: Cornell University Press.

Turner, Victor W. (1967b). "A Ndembu Doctor in Practice." In: *The Forest of Symbols: Aspects of Ndembu Ritual.* Ithaca, NY: Cornell University Press.

Turner, Victor W. (1969). *The Ritual Process: Structure and Anti-Structure.* Chicago: Aldine.

Turry, Alan (1998). "Transference and Countertransference in Nordoff-Robbins Music Therapy." In: Bruscia, Kenneth (ed.): *The Dynamics of Music Psychotherapy.* Gilsum, NH: Barcelona Publishers.

Tylor, Edward Burnett (1871/1958). *The Origins of Culture* (Part I of *Primitive Culture.*) New York: Harper & Row, Publishers.

Vetlesen, Arne Johan (1994). *Perception, Empathy, and Judgment. An Inquiry into the Preconditions of Mortal Performance.* University Park, PA: The Pennsylvania State University Press.

Vico, Giambattista (1744/1976). *The New Science.* Ithaca, NY: Cornell University Press.

Vink, Annemiek (2001). "Music and Emotion. Living apart together: A Relationship between Music Psychology and Music Therapy." *Nordic Journal of Music Therapy,* 10(2), pp. 144-158.

Voestermans, Paul & Cor Baerveldt (2000). "Cultural Psychology Meets Evolutionary Psychology: Toward a New Role of Biology in the Study of Culture and Experience." [online] *Paper presented the NCPG on the 8th conference of the International Society for Theoretical Psychology,* April 25-28, 2000, Sydney. Available from: www.socsci.kun.nl/psy/cultuur/voestermans_baerveldt. html [accessed, January 1 2001].

Vygotsky, Lev (1978). *Mind in Society. The Development of Higher Psychological Processes.* Cambridge, MA: Harvard University Press.

Wackerhausen, Steen (1994). "Et åbent sundhedsbegreb – mellem fundamentalisme og relativisme [An open Concept of Health – Between Fundamentalism and Relativism.]" In: Jensen, Uffe Juul & Peter Fuur Andersen (eds.) (1994). *Sundhedsbegreber. Filosofi og praksis.* [Concepts of Health. Philosophy and Practice.] Aarhus, Denmark: Philosophia.

Wallin, Nils L. (1991). *Biomusicology. Neurophysiological, Neurospychological and Evolutionary Perspectives on the Origins and Purposes of Music.* Stuyvesant, NY: Pendragon press.

Wallin, Nils L., Björn Merker & Steven Brown (eds.) (2000). *The Origins of Music.* Cambridge, MA: The MIT Press.

Walker, Scott (ed.) (1993). *Changing Community.* Saint Paul, MN: Graywolf Press.

Weisethaunet, Hans (1999). "Critical Remarks on the Nature of Improvisation." *Nordic Journal of Music Therapy,* 8(2).

Wheeler, Barbara (ed.) (1995a). *Music Therapy Research. Quantitative and Qualitative Perspectives.* Phoenixville, PA: Barcelona Publishers.

Wheeler, Barbara (1995b). "Introduction: Overview of Music Therapy Research." In: Wheeler, Barbara (ed.). *Music Therapy Research. Quantitative and Qualitative Perspectives.* Phoenixville, PA: Barcelona Publishers.

White, Michael & David Epston (1990). *Narrative Means to Therapeutic Ends.* New York: W.W. Norton.

Wilson, Edward O. (1975/2000). *Sociobiology: The New Synthesis.* (25th Anniversary Edition). Cambridge, MA: Belknap Press of Harvard University Press.

Willis, Paul (1990). *Common Culture.* Buckingham, UK: Open University Press.

Wing, Lorna (1981). "Asperger's Syndrome: A Clinical Account." *Psychological Medicine,* 11, 115-129.

Wittgenstein, Ludwig (1921/1961). *Tractatus Logico-Philosophicus.* London: Routledge.

Wittgenstein, Ludwig (1953/1967). *Philosophical Investigations.* Oxford: Blackwell.

Wittgenstein, Ludwig (1958/1969): *The Blue and Brown Books.* Oxford: Blackwell.

Wittgenstein, Ludwig (1978). *Lectures and Conversations on Aesthetics, Psychology and Religious Belief.* Edited by C. Barrett. Oxford: Blackwell.

Wittgenstein, Ludwig (1980). *Culture and Value.* Edited by G.H. von Wright. Chicago: University of Chicago Press.

Woolfolk, Robert L. (1998). "Malfunction and Mental Illness." [online] Piscataway, NJ: *Rutgers Center for Cognitive Science.* Available from: http://ruccs.rutgers. edu/ArchiveFolder/sassstich/WoolfolkMMI.html [accessed, January 7 2002].

World Health Organization (1946). Official Records of World Health Organization, No.2. New York: WHO/UN.

Østerberg, Dag (1997): *Fortolkende sosiologi II. Kultursosiologiske emner.* [Interpretive Sociology II. Aspects of the Sociology of Culture.] Oslo: Universitetsforlaget.

AUTHOR INDEX

Aasgaard, Trygve;6; 249; 289; 339
Abbott, Andrew;197; 339
Adelman, Clem;295; 339
Adelman, Howard S.;137; 149; 339
Aigen, Kenneth;58; 68; 69; 71; 76;
   263; 264; 299; 339; 342; 348; 351
Akombo, David;246; 258; 339
Aldridge, David;6; 75; 114; 177; 188;
   189; 255; 258; 339; 340; 349; 352;
   353
Altrichter, Herbert;279; 286; 339
Alvesson, Mats;256; 269; 274; 284;
   285; 293; 295; 303; 307; 308; 309;
   310; 313; 336; 339
American Psychiatric
   Association;143; 316; 340
Amir, Dorit;48; 76; 299; 340
Andersen, Peter Fuur;185; 344; 347;
   355
Ansdell, Gary;xiii; 6; 17; 67; 75; 76;
   100; 107; 177; 249; 340
Antonovsky, Aron;188; 189; 340
Atkinson, Paul;127; 259; 260; 262;
   263; 270; 274; 275; 346
Austern, Linda Phyllis;72; 340

Baerveldt, Cor;34; 35; 355
Bakhtin, Mikhail;15; 45; 69; 74; 75;
   155; 166; 177; 227; 270; 332; 334;
   340; 350
Barker, Andrew;80; 340
Barkow, Jerome H.;44; 340; 354
Baron-Cohen, Simon;45; 340
Bateson, Gregory;100; 135; 151; 251;
   318; 340; 341
Bauckham, Paulette;36; 341
Beck, Ulrich;335; 341
Bender, Michael;36; 341
Benestad, Finn;80; 81; 241; 341
Berger, Peter;304; 341
Berkaak, Odd Are;223; 224; 341; 351
Bernstein, Richard J.;53; 306; 341

Blacking, John;85; 87; 88; 98; 333;
   341
Bonde, Lars Ole;48; 75; 177; 341
Boyce-Tillman, June;195; 341
Bright, Ruth;6; 341
Brockman, John;311; 341
Bronfenbrenner, Urie;129; 130; 131;
   135; 137; 138; 151; 152; 234; 279;
   341
Brown, Julie;6; 42; 248; 341
Brown, Steven;21; 84; 85; 86; 87;
   341; 343; 345; 348; 349; 350; 354;
   355
Bruner, Jerome;6; 25; 30; 32; 35; 45;
   47; 56; 194; 305; 341
Bruscia, Kenneth;xiii; 5; 12; 75; 115;
   121; 131; 132; 141; 149; 151; 153;
   177; 188; 189; 196; 199; 229; 231;
   232; 233; 263; 264; 265; 274; 275;
   341; 342
Buber, Martin;223; 327; 342
Bunt, Leslie;6; 131; 194; 219; 229;
   342
Byrkjedal, Ingunn;xiii; 2; 119; 249;
   342
Bø, Inge;116; 117; 342

Cartwright, Samuel;315; 316; 322;
   342
Cattaneo, Mariagnese;6; 342
Cavalli-Sforza, Luigi L.;21; 26; 342
Christensen, Erik;107; 342
Clamp, Alan;44; 343
Clifford, James;257; 268; 269; 270;
   273; 343
Cole, Michael;6; 23; 27; 28; 29; 30;
   32; 35; 44; 45; 96; 239; 296; 328;
   343
Collini, Stefan;297; 298; 343
Cosmides, Leda;20; 34; 44; 340; 354
Csikszentmihalyi, Mihaly;224; 343